INTERNATIONAL RELATIONS:
A TRANSNATIONAL APPROACH

INTERNATIONAL RELATIONS: A TRANSNATIONAL APPROACH

Werner J. Feld
UNIVERSITY OF NEW ORLEANS

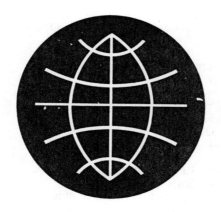

Alfred Publishing Co., Inc.

Library of Congress Cataloging in Publication Data

Feld, Werner J.
    International relations.

    Includes index.
    1. International relations 2. International
relations—Research. I. Title.
JX1395.F42   327'.07'2   77-25959
ISBN 0-88284-058-4

    Alfred Publishing Co., Inc.
    15335 Morrison Street
    Sherman Oaks, California 91404

Current printing last digit:
10 9 8 7 6 5 4 3 2 1

CONTENTS

PREFACE   xi

A LIST OF ACRONYMS USED IN THIS BOOK   xiii

PART I: THE STUDY AND BACKGROUND OF INTERNATIONAL RELATIONS   1

Chapter One: **International Relations and You   2**
Approaches to the Study of International
   Relations   5
The Approach of This Book   13
Suggested Readings   18

Chapter Two: **The Setting of International Politics   19**
The Actors   19
Relations Between Actors   24
The Physical Environment   25
The Dynamics   27
Summary   28
Suggested Readings   30

Chapter Three: **The Determinants of National Power:**
   Objective Factors   31
Geography   32
Population   41
Economic Development   48
Science and Technology   55
Summary   58
Suggested Readings   60

Chapter Four: **The Determinants of National Power: Variable Factors** **61**
Tradition and Social Psychology 61
Government and Administration 66
Military Organization 70
Summary 75
Suggested Readings 76

Part II: INTERNATIONAL ACTIONS AND REACTIONS **77**

Chapter Five: **The Formulation of Foreign Policies** **78**
The National Interests 79
Three Perspectives of Foreign Policy Making 82
The Notion of Image in Foreign Policy Decision Making 87
Intelligence and Foreign Policy Making 90
Summary 95
Suggested Readings 98

Chapter Six: **Foreign Policy and Domestic Politics** **99**
The Influence of Powerful Groups on Foreign Policy 99
Domestic Structure and Foreign Policy Making 111
Foreign Policy Effects on Domestic Politics 119
The Use of Foreign Policy for Domestic Political Purposes 122
Summary 124
Suggested Readings 128

Chapter Seven: **Instruments for Policy Implementation** **129**
Diplomacy 130
Economic Measures 137
Psychological Warfare and Propaganda 145
Political Warfare 150
War 153
Summary 161
Suggested Readings 164

Chapter Eight: **Collaborative International Relations** **165**
Alliances 166
Economic Cooperation Arrangements 171
Summary 178
Suggested Readings 180

Chapter Nine: **Conflict in International Behavior** **181**
The Balance of Power and Interstate
Conflict 181
Causes and Effects of War 197
International Law 203
Summary 210
Suggested Readings 214

PART III: THE DYNAMICS OF TRANSNATIONAL NETWORKS **215**

Chapter Ten: **Intergovernmental Organizations** **216**
Nature 216
A Brief Historical Review 218
The League of Nations 220
The United Nations 224
Regional IGOs 240
Summary 251
Suggested Readings 254

Chapter Eleven: **Nongovernmental Organizations** **255**
Growth and Distribution 257
Organizational Effectiveness and Financial
Revenues 259
Contacts and Coalitions 262
Effects of IGOs 265
The Consequences for the International
System 267
Summary 268
Suggested Readings 270

Chapter Twelve: **Regional Integration and Transnational
Coalitions** **271**
Economic Integration 272
Social Integration 272
Political Integration 273
Stimulants for the Integration Process 274
Functionalism 276

Neofunctionalism   277
The European Community   278
Developments in the 1970s and Prospects for
    the Future   289
The Latin American Free Trade
    Association   297
The East African Community   303
Summary   307
Suggested Readings   312

PART IV: NEW FORCES IN INTERNATIONAL RELATIONS   **313**

Chapter Thirteen: **The Multinational Enterprise as an
                            International Actor   314**
                        What is the MNE?   315
                        The Pattern of Growth   316
                        Foreign Investments   323
                        The Transfer of Knowledge   328
                        Lobbying and Exertion of Influence   329
                        Summary   333
                        Suggested Readings   336

Chapter Fourteen: **The Impact of Multinational Enterprises on
                            International Relations   337**
                        Benefits of MNE Initiatives   337
                        Drawbacks and Problems for Governmental
                            Actors   341
                        Labor's Responses to MNE
                            Challenges   349
                        Consequences for the International
                            System   354
                        Conclusions   358
                        Summary   361
                        Suggested Readings   365

Chapter Fifteen: **The Changing Physical Global
                            Environment   366**
                        Nuclear Energy and Electric Power   367
                        The Resources of the Sea   373
                        Population Explosion and World
                            Hunger   377
                        The Use of Outer Space for Communications
                            and Meteorology   379

Ecological Concerns and World
    Politics   384
Economic Growth or Zero Growth?   389
Summary   392
Suggested Readings   394

PART V: CONCLUSIONS   **395**

Chapter Sixteen: **World Without Walls**   **396**
    Suggested Reading   405

Glossary: 407

Index: 413

PREFACE

Over the past two decades the concerns of international relations scholars have undergone gradual change. While issues of war and peace remain crucial for the territorial integrity of nation states and for the protection of their citizens, the physical environment of the globe and the growing influence of nongovernmental forces have had an increasing impact on world affairs.

I wrote this book with these changes in mind. I have attempted to provide the students with an introduction to the broader spectrum of international issues on a more balanced basis than has been done previously. The need for such an approach is obvious when we consider the effects of the international oil crisis on national economies and on prevailing lifestyles, the exhaustion of natural resources, the impact of environmental concerns in many parts of the world on the production of energy, the appearance of advanced technologies, and the immense economic and political power of multinational corporations on international and national politics.

I have attempted to obtain the latest available data for the tables and figures throughout this book. In some cases, however, the latest available data were not as recent as in others. This should cause no concern since the purpose of these tables is to enhance the pedagogic value of the text, and the trends and comparisons indicated are of more value than the figures themselves.

Since I have attempted to develop a text that would be especially appealing to students who are novices in the field of international relations, I would like to express my gratitude to my own students who have helped me to obtain the proper perspective for this task. I also would like to thank Professor Alan Leonhard of my own department who read the first draft of the manuscript, and Professors Carol E. Baumann of the University of Wisconsin, Milwaukee, and Robert Pfaltzgraff of Tufts University who read later versions of the manuscript. All provided me with valuable criticism and suggestions, many of which I accepted. My very deep gratitude goes to Janet Davis for her very thoughtful and worthwhile editorial comments and her tireless efforts and superior expertise in typing and retyping many drafts of the manuscript. Last, but certainly not least I would like to thank John Stout, my editor, for restraining this impatient author and for providing very valuable suggestions that were accepted with alacrity, to Sherri Butterfield for an excellent copyediting job, and to Bob Tinnon for turning the manuscript into a handsome book.

Werner J. Feld
New Orleans, Louisiana

A LIST OF ACRONYMS USED IN THIS BOOK

ABM Anti-Ballistic Missile
AGITPROP Department of Agitation and Propaganda in the Soviet Union
ANZUS Australia–New Zealand–United States Council
ASPAC Asian and Pacific Council
CACM Central American Common Market
CAP Common Agricultural Policy
CENTO Central Treaty Organization
CIEC Conference on International Economic Cooperation
COMSAT Communications Satellite
EAC East African Community
EAGGF European Agricultural Guidance and Guarantee Fund
ECA Economic Commission for Africa (United Nations)
ECAFE Economic Commission for Asia and the Far East (United Nations)
ECLA Economic Commission for Latin America (United Nations)
ECOSOC Economic and Social Council
EDF European Development Fund
EEC European Economic Community
ECSC European Coal and Steel Community
EFTA European Free Trade Association
EURATOM European Atomic Energy Community
FAO Food and Agricultural Organization

GATT General Agreements of Tariffs and Trade
GNP Gross National Product
IAEA International Atomic Energy Agency
ICA International Communication Agency (U.S.)
ICBM Intercontinental Ballistic Missile
ICFTU International Confederation of Free Trade Unions
IGO Intergovernmental Organization
IMCO Intergovernmental Maritime Consultative Organization
IMF International Monetary Fund
IOC International Oceanographic Commission
LAFTA Latin American Free Trade Association
MNE Multinational Enterprise
MPLA Marxist Popular Movement for the Liberation of Angola
NASA National Aeronautics and Space Agency
NATO North American Treaty Organization
NGO Nongovernmental Organization
NPT Nonproliferation Treaty
NSF National Science Foundation
OAS Organization of American States
OAU Organization of African Unity
OECD Organization for Economic Cooperation and Development
OPEC Organization of Petroleum Exporting Countries
ONUC United Nations Organization for the Congo
PFLP Popular Front for the Liberation of Palestine
SALT Strategic Arms Limitations Talks
SEATO South East Asia Treaty Organization
SLBM Submarine Launched Ballistic Missile
UAW United Auto Workers Union
UNCTAD United Nations Conference on Trade and Development
UNEF United Nations Emergency Force
UNIEFICYP United Nations Forces in Cyprus
UNESOC United Nations Educational, Scientific, and Cultural Organization
USIA United States Information Agency
USW United Steel Workers Union
WCL World Confederation of Labor
WMO World Meteorological Organization

PART I
The Study
and Background of
International Relations

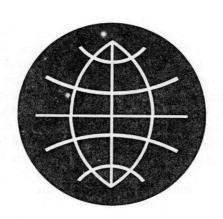

CHAPTER ONE
INTERNATIONAL RELATIONS AND YOU

With few exceptions, American newspapers and magazines have traditionally given less space to international news items than to national and local affairs. Of course, major international events have made headlines and appeared on front pages; but generally, newspaper coverage of them has lacked details and full analysis. Television network programs emphasize the international scene more than do the other media, but when taken together with local station news programs, the balance in overall television news coverage may not be much different from that found in print. It should not be surprising, therefore, that you, as a typical student in an American college or university, are more interested in national or local politics than in activities on the international scene. You may well argue that international activities hardly affect your life or your future career. What seems to be important is to have a full understanding of your social, economic, and political environment at home and, more generally, in the United States; and you feel this kind of knowledge will be of greater value in the occupation you are considering.

But are your assumptions justified? Is concern with international relations and politics, while perhaps interesting, a luxury you really cannot afford when deciding which college courses to take to complete your degree requirements? The following observation may help you answer these questions.

Our world has been shrinking as a result of high-speed communications and globe-circling jet transportation, and the countries on our planet have become increasingly interdependent. These changes not only affect relations between the national governments, but have a direct impact on your personal life. But even before these changes, certain events in faraway places affected your parents, and similar ones may influence the course of your life, either directly or indirectly. Here are some examples.

War and Military Draft   During this century the United States has fought in four major wars: World Wars I and II, the Korean conflict, and the Vietnam War. Americans were either motivated to volunteer for military service or were drafted. All lost considerable time from their civilian pursuits, and some came home maimed. The social and political impact on the United States and its citizens, especially during and following the Vietnam War, was severe. Future international tensions and hostilities will directly affect you despite the fact the American military forces are now recruited on a volunteer basis. Without doubt, a new war will see the reinstitution of the draft.

Raw Materials, Life-style, and Jobs   We all remember the oil embargo imposed by the Arab petroleum-producing countries following the Israeli-Arab War in October 1973 and the very rapid rise of gasoline prices in the wake of the embargo. Most of us have not forgotten the long lines of automobiles seeking to buy five or ten gallons of gasoline at practically any price. Because service station operators had little gas to sell, they shortened their business hours and laid off many of their employees. But more important, the sharp rise in oil prices that the Organization of Petroleum Exporting Countries (OPEC) forced on the consumer countries in all parts of the world, including the United States and Western Europe, contributed materially to the double-digit inflation we suffered in 1975 and to the severe recession, with its high percentage of unemployment, from which we recovered only very slowly. The resulting chain reaction has altered the life-style of many Americans: smaller cars are becoming a necessity, vacation travel by automobile has had to be curtailed, highway speed has had to be cut down, and air conditioning and heating habits have had to be adjusted. Most serious, however, was the reduction in job opportunities, which continues to plague graduating seniors.

OPEC is likely to continue its influence on oil prices in the future. Other producers of raw materials, such as copper and bauxite (to manufacture aluminum), may seek to emulate OPEC and create organizations to assure a high price for their raw materials. They may have an impact on future job opportunities and life-styles if their pricing policies encourage inflationary spirals or force changes in manufacturing methods.

Changing International Trade Patterns and Job Markets   The OPEC-engineered extraordinary increase in fuel cost has necessitated a large outflow of dollars to pay for the import of petroleum. Although the United States did not have to curtail the import of other goods, some countries were forced to do so. Italy temporarily restricted the importation of consumer products because she did not earn sufficient foreign currency through exports of Italian-made goods to pay the huge bill for imported oil. If the United States were forced to follow a similar course, you would probably have to pay more for some goods, because many items can be produced less expensively abroad than in America. On the other hand, import restrictions might increase job opportunities in the United States.

Another international trade factor that may affect the availability of jobs is the activity of American multinational corporations. If these corporations feel that they can produce goods more cheaply in foreign countries, such as Mexico or Taiwan, where labor costs are lower, American exports may suffer and jobs be eliminated. An example is the production of radios in Taiwan by subsidiaries of American companies, which cuts into the potential exports of such products from the United States. Indeed, the Taiwan-made radios are likely to be imported into the United States and to thus reduce the market for American-produced goods.

A furthur reason for a decision by a multinational corporation to produce abroad is the existence of high customs duties in a particular country which make it difficult to import American-made goods into that country. American labor unions have criticized the "exportation of jobs" by these corporations; but regardless of the justification for this criticism, the international actions described above are likely to affect your own chances for a career, at least indirectly.

International Relations, Domestic Politics, and You   During the past few years and particularly during the 1972 and 1976 presidential elections, the interdependency of and linkage between international relations and domestic politics has become more and more evident. In these elections, candidates not only expressed their views on domestic issues, but also sought to use their international activities and knowledge of foreign affairs to project an image of expertise in these areas. Former President Nixon and the men around him skillfully manipulated international politics to present him as an expert in international relations whose knowledge would be beneficial to the American people. His trips to China and other parts of the world were carefully timed so that the extensive news media coverage of them would influence the election outcome. President Ford also used his image in foreign affairs for the same purpose, although the staging was less elaborate. In fact, many presidents, including President Carter, have used foreign policy matters to enhance their image at home.

Similar image-building efforts have been undertaken at times by U.S. senators and congressmen who have particular knowledge in international relations or are involved in, or advocate, certain foreign policy positions. For example, Senator J. William Fulbright was recognized as an expert in international politics, and Senator Henry "Scoop" Jackson made a name for himself by insisting on American foreign policy measures toward the Soviet Union that would help the emigration of Soviet Jews to Israel. Congressman John Brademas of Indiana became the leader of the pro-Greek forces during the severe crisis between Greece and Turkey over Cyprus. Projecting an image of having profound knowledge concerning the origins of the crisis that led to an invasion of the troubled island by Turkish forces, he persuaded Congress to halt military aid to Turkey, an important NATO ally of the United States. Activities of this type by a senator or a congressman may not be in the best interest of most Americans, but this silent majority often finds itself ill-equipped to make a sound judgment about their domestic and international implications and consequences.

The examples cited suggest that knowledge about international relations is an important asset to any college student. It helps you understand forces that cross national boundaries in many, often complex, ways and can have varying impacts on cherished life-styles, the pursuit of careers, and your voting behavior in national elections. It may enable you to anticipate economic and political trends, thereby enhancing your predictive capability and personal decision making.

APPROACHES TO THE STUDY
OF INTERNATIONAL RELATIONS

The next question is how to study the obviously vast subject matter of international relations. There are a number of approaches to this study, which we will review briefly before discussing the plan of this book.

The Historical-Descriptive Approach

During the early 1900s, the most common approach to the study of international relations was historical-descriptive. Significant events in relations between states were described, and emphasis was placed on discovering recurring patterns in different time periods. Diplomatic historians searched for causes or origins of major conflicts.[1] Political, economic, demographic, and strategic factors were described to discover why certain patterns occurred in international relations.[2] Attention was also paid to international law, especially the frequent discrepancy between the formal obligations of states and their actual behavior in pursuit of objectives they perceived as vital.

The Realist Approach

A theoretically more sophisticated approach to international relations study is the approach of the realists who make *power* the central concept to explain the behavior of states in international relations. The best-known exponent of the realist approach is Hans J. Morgenthau, who contends that statesmen think and act in terms of interest defined as power and that historical data prove this contention.[3] States seek to either keep power, increase power, or demonstrate power to protect their physical, political, and cultural identity against encroachments by other states. Survival is always the paramount goal of states, and only when it is assured are they free to pursue lesser goals.[4] The power of states is measured not only in terms of military forces, but also by geographic factors, natural resources, patterns of population, levels of technology, forms of government, political leadership, and ideology. We should note that power must be seen in terms of a relationship between two or more units, wherein the unit having greater power can impose its will on other units, thereby making them do something they do not want to do or *not* do something they would like to do.

Morgenthau states: "universal moral principles cannot be applied to the actions of states in their abstract, universal formulations, but that they must be filtered through the concrete circumstances of time and place."[5] Because the statesman's primary responsibility is the survival of his nation-state, his obligation to his citizenry takes on a morality of its own, which is quite different from that of an individual.[6]

Economic Determinism

As you most likely have gathered from the first few pages of this chapter, economic factors can have pervasive effects across national boundaries. Indeed, during recent years international economics have assumed an increasingly important role in international relations. Economic interdependence among the countries of the world has grown markedly, and economic power has often had more influence on the behavior of states than military might. It should therefore not surprise you that one approach to the study of international relations is based on economic factors.

In inquiries into the causes of international conflict, economic factors have long been considered important. Some observers of the international scene have predicted that rising standards of living and national economic growth will contribute to peace among nations. Free trade will create a division of labor based on specialization in the international economy in which countries will become so interdependent that war will be seen as highly disruptive to the pursuit of the good life. Moreover, the rise of individual and national prosperity will divert public attention and governmental leaders from military adventures.

Another school of thought, however, views economics as the principal cause of conflict, and it bases its arguments mainly on the theories of social conflict developed by Marx and Lenin. Indeed, a number of Western students of international relations have accepted and continue to espouse the Marxist analysis of the causes of international conflict and war.

This is not the place to involve ourselves with the various philosophical, societal, and economic theories and concepts that have flown from the fertile mind of Karl Marx. Suffice it to say that, according to Marx, history was directed by changes that occurred in the forces of production, each of which required a particular set of social relations to be operative, that is, ownership or nonownership of the means of production. In a broad sense, economic factors determined the course of human events.*

Marx anticipated that the antagonism between the capitalist class (the bourgeoisie, as Marx often called it) and the workers (the

---

* Feudal farming arrangements, for example, were the result of a specific set of social relations, inasmuch as land was cultivated by nonowners for the owners in return for personal and economic security. Small-scale manufacturers required another set of relations, namely, the individually owned factory and workers subject to the orders of their employers.

proletariat) would culminate in a revolutionary overthrow of the capitalist system, the abolition of private property, and eventually, the establishment of a classless society. Lenin converted the Marxian theory into an operational code for revolution and in Russia in 1917 succeeded in overthrowing the tsarist regime and replacing it with a communist dictatorship. In Western Europe and America, workers banded together into labor unions and were gradually able to improve wages and working conditions in the 20th century.

Before the turn of the century, however, the growth of an impoverished proletariat, anticipated by Marx, brought capitalist societies face to face with the dilemma of overproduction and underconsumption. A solution to this dilemma was to reinvest capital surplus accumulated in profit-making ventures abroad either to extract raw materials or to market products that could not be sold or used at home. According to Marxist-Leninist theory, the result was the complex phenomenon of *imperialism* through which capitalist states, such as Great Britain, France, or the United States, expanded their control over the people and governments of other countries, regardless of whether they were colonies or not. You should note, however, that, contrary to the theory, this expansion of control was motivated not only by economic factors, but by strategic and political considerations as well.

Lenin saw imperialism as a special, advanced stage of capitalism during which competition would eventually be replaced by capitalist monopolies.[7] Indeed, Marxist-Leninist theory sees the affluence of Western society stemming to a large degree from the exploitation by European and American capitalism of the peoples of Asia, Africa, and Latin America.

The Marxist-Leninist approach to international relations is based on economic determinism. Economic factors and developments as viewed through Marxist theory determine events and trends in international relations. A contemporary writer suggests that the history of international society is identical with the development of modern capitalism and that worldwide anticapitalist movements have been provoked by the existence of capitalism.[8] Others see the spreading global network of giant American multinational corporations, such as Exxon and General Motors, or the Philips Company headquartered in the Netherlands, as manifestations of imperialism.[9]

The Systems Approach

Perhaps the most widely used approach in the contemporary international relations literature is system theory. A *system* consists of interdependent parts that function together as a whole. The method that seeks to discover how a system functions and why changes in a system occur has been called general *system theory*. Examples of systems are an automobile motor, a business organization, and the human body.

Every system may have subsystems that exist and function within the larger system. For example, a regional system, such as the European Common Market, which consists of nine member states, is a subsystem of the global international system. The totality of interactions of states can be identified as the global international system. Interactions of states within particular regions of the world, for example Europe or Africa, are regarded as subsystems.

Every system has boundaries that distinguish it from its environment and from other systems. Your body, as a biological system, is a good example. Moreover, every system is, in a certain sense, a communications net with information flowing from one part to another. Looking at yourself, your brain sends messages to your hands to hold this book in such a way that you can read it. At the same time, if you drop this book on your toes, pain signals are sent to your brain. Every system has inputs from the inside and outside and corresponding outputs. Sometimes the outputs of one system become the input to another. If somebody hits you, you experience the output from another person or human system and it creates an input in your system in the form of pain. In turn, it will also evoke another system boundary-crossing output if you try to hit the person who hurt you in the first place.

Systems may be in equilibrium, may be disturbed and lose their equilibrium temporarily but later return to it, may be permanently transformed, or may die. Healthy human beings may be regarded as having their biological systems in equilibrium. The same can be said of the international system.

In the study of international relations, system theory identifies, examines, and measures interaction within a system and its subsystems, comprised mainly of states and international organizations whose members are also mostly states. It provides for the examination of recurrent sequences of behavior of these entities (or the individual acting on their behalf), as well as of behavior originating in one system and reacted to in another. If such sequences can be isolated and categorized, it may be possible to gain theoretical insights into the nature of the interdependence among global and regional international systems and national systems as well.[10]

Inputs into international systems may come from states, organizations of states, or the environment. They may cause disturbances in a particular system, such as shortages of raw materials, or even cause a war. Disturbances may also be produced when alliances between states are formed or disintegrated. Outputs of international systems may be the formation of price-fixing cartels for the maintenance of high prices for raw materials or the boycott initiated by consumer countries if such cartels drive prices too high. Regional systems may form counteralliances for defensive purposes if they perceive that a new military alliance poses a threat.

System theorists assume that disturbing input activates a regulating mechanism seeking to adapt the system to the disturbance and, if possible, to return it to some kind of equilibrium, although in the process the nature of the particular system may be modified or transformed into another system, or may disintegrate completely.[11] An example is the Southeast Asia Treaty Organization (SEATO), to which a number of states, including the United States, belonged and which was designed as a defensive alliance to contain the threat of communist expansion. Following the debacle of the Vietnam War, SEATO, already plagued by recurring lack of cooperation by the alliance partners, was dissolved in 1976.

By studying past and present international systems, system theory attempts to discover patterns on which to base projections about the future of international relations and politics. Because international society and every intranational system change constantly, these patterns can be studied comparatively; and doing so may enable us to construct an "ideal" system that would increase our understanding of relations among states and could become the basis for foreign policy strategies of governmental decision makers.

The Decision-Making Approach

In the systems approach, we take a somewhat detached look at the global international system and its subsystems, as if we were viewing it from a distance. We notice patterns of movements, but we really do not know how the behavior of the entities in the system has been initiated and what have been the motivations for this behavior. The decision-making approach focuses not on the international system as a whole, but on a relatively limited and well-defined decisional unit. International relations specialists looking at the overall system often personify nation-states as if they were the basic actors on the international scene.[12] For example, they speak of consultation between the United States and France, or about Egypt's going to war with Israel. The decision-making approach, however, does not divert attention to states as a legal person or to their "governments," but seeks to analyze the motivations, actions, and behavior of the human decision makers who shape and implement governmental policies. In other words, this decision-making approach is an exercise in micro analysis, whereas the systems approach deals with macro analysis.

What do we mean by decision making? Fundamentally, we talk about the act of choosing among available alternatives about which a certain amount of uncertainty exists.[13] But this simple statement conceals the difficulty of analysis. Problems abound and include the sufficiency of information available to decision makers, uncertainty about alternatives and their consequences, and the manifold pressures exerted on policy makers to accommodate special interests of domestic groups and foreign governments. These problems make it very difficult to reach a *rational decision*, one directed toward the attainment of a clearly defined goal reflecting the highest preference of the decision makers, with the assumptions that, for the choice of alternatives, comprehensive, relevant information was available *and* used; that the consequences of all alternative courses were fully established; and that the selected alternative has the highest utility in reaching the goal desired. Social scientists must assume, nevertheless, that in all human relations, rational elements predominate over the irrational.[14] These elements must be discovered rather than taken for granted, and their discovery requires an assessment of the various influences bearing on every decision made. They include the social and economic backgrounds of the decision makers; their personal goals, interests, and aspirations; their prior commitments, and specific motivations that may stem from the bureaucratic position they hold.

Despite the many factors that affect the making of governmental decisions in the field of international relations and the recognition that action in this area involves not a single decision to be analyzed but a continuum of interrelated decisions, the decision-making approach provides significant insights into the dynamics of international relations and the politics used to obtain objectives in the international arena. Indeed, movement in the international arena flows from hundreds of decisions made in the governmental and nongovernmental institutions and enterprises around the world. It is on the basis of the analysis of these decisions that some predictions for the future can be made, although there are, of course, hazards that goals may change as the policy-making process progresses, decision makers may not be aware of discrepancies between anticipated and actual consequences of alternatives, and new information may become available.

A specialized and somewhat controversial form of the decision-making approach to the study of international relations is *game theory*. It is a special method of studying decision making in conflict situations and obviously can be applied to international relations, for example, to conflicts between the United States and the Soviet Union, or between Israel and Egypt.

Game theory assumes that participants in a conflict situation try to win, or to accomplish a desired objective, which another party seeks to deny them. In other words, each opponent seeks to outwit the other.

Every game is characterized by the following elements: (1) two or more participants (players) each seek to get the best of the other so that one wins what the other loses (zero-sum game), or they work to find a solution that provides some payoffs for each (non-zero-sum game); (2) the information available to them, including information about the choices made by the other player, conditions the quality and quantity of knowledge each player has; and (3) their competing moves interact, that is, a choice by one may prompt the other to modify subsequent choices.[15]

As already pointed out, game theory appears to be particularly applicable to conflict situations between two countries. For example, during the past few years, the United States and the Soviet Union have attempted to negotiate a limitation of nuclear weapons, but at the same time the Soviet Union has installed new intercontinental missiles and equipped them with more powerful and versatile nuclear warheads. The United States has not stood idly by, but has instead developed new and more sophisticated weapons to counter the Soviet threat. Thus we can observe a continuing effort on the part of each country to gain some advantage over the other while the weapons limitation negotiations are going on. But the U.S.-Soviet conflict—which is, of course, much more complex than the term *game* implies—is only one of many in international relations. Indeed, an almost infinite variety of games and subgames characterizes international politics. Moreover, game theory may also provide insights into the continuing bargaining between governments that is the hallmark of diplomatic intercourse all over the world.

The Normative Approach

The approaches examined so far have focused on research, ordering, and analysis of factual data in order to better understand and explain the vast number of interactions in the international arena and perhaps make some predictions for future behavior in international relations. However, while it is extremely important to determine with accuracy the nature and relevance of international relations phenomena, as well as their connections to other phenomena on the international and national levels, statesmen must make choices of alternative courses of action, and these choices often reflect their personal values, moral standards, and views of what is best for their countries in particular and mankind in general. These values and views of decision makers involved in international relations may be shaped not only by ideologies and moral considerations, but also by pressures emanating from advances in technology and environmental concerns, especially as far as they affect political institutions.

Normative theory revolves around the question of what *ought* to be done rather than what *is*. The answer depends on the value judgments of decision makers, as well as of scholars who, after examining and analyzing particular international situations or foreign policy problems, may suggest solutions. A normative approach will be most helpful when decision-making analysis is the chosen conceptual tool for understanding and explaining international relations. Indeed, even when game theory is the chosen analytical instrument, cost-benefit calculations may hinge on normative considerations.[16]

THE APPROACH OF THIS BOOK

Because this book is designed to *introduce* large numbers of students to international relations, it would be unrealistic to assume you already possess vast knowledge about past and current international events; therefore, this book relies on the historical-descriptive approach to furnish you with a firm foundation for understanding recurrent patterns in world politics. To be able to form valid judgments for the future, however, you must learn to apply some conceptual tools to the bewildering array of information about international activities. You must categorize, analyze, compare, and evaluate these activities in an orderly fashion. For this reason, we shall draw on the concept of power as developed by the realists whenever this notion helps explain the behavior of states and other entities on the international stage. Because the concept of power may not always be sufficient to give you a full insight into the motivation and causes of international action, we shall also take advantage of the knowledge we might gain from the decision-making approach.

The traditional assumption has been that foreign policy formulation and implementation by the governments of the world's many countries have been the major impetus for movement and change on the international stage; however, domestic policies of states may also have intended or unintended border-crossing effects. For example, U.S. acreage control to reduce wheat production and curb recurring surpluses in the United States affected worldwide grain prices and production as other countries were prompted to grow more wheat. Changes in fiscal laws and policies may induce large corporations in a particular country to reduce production in their plants abroad and increase their exports to external markets from manufacturing facilities at home. Therefore, the decision-making approach must focus on all public policy formulation and implementation that has transnational effects, regardless of whether that policy originates in the foreign ministry of a country (the State Department in the United States) or in a ministry concerned primarily with domestic issues, such as the U.S. Department of Agriculture. Thus, when we resort to the decision-making approach as a useful instrument for the study of international relations, the spotlight is on the analysis of *transnational* public policy.

Public policy analysis has been used increasingly in American politics to explain policy formulation, implementation, and impact. Thomas Dye, who has been a leader in this approach, has defined public policy in a very broad sense and considered it "whatever governments choose to do or not to do."[17] This broad definition of public policy is very suitable for transnational policy analysis. Moreover, any public policy may not only address itself to the governments of other states, but may also seek to induce desired behavior on the part of nongovernmental actors.

When we use transnational policy analysis for the understanding, explanation, and prediction of events in the international arena, we must realize that there are certain differences in the formulation and implementation of purely domestic and border-crossing policies. The latter are much more complex because participants in several countries may contribute to shaping transnational policies. Border crossing coordination is therefore essential for the formulation of effective transnational policies, and the difficulty of this process is directly proportional to the number of states and nongovernmental organizations involved. For example, the formulation of policies for NATO, which has a membership of fifteen states, is much more difficult than it would be if only the United States or Great Britain were involved.[18]

In the implementation of transnational policies, the level of complexity also exceeds that in the exclusively domestic policy field. To carry out a transnational policy, the number of governmental agencies in different countries that can make authoritative decisions is increased. Coordination of actions through diplomacy or bilateral or multilateral agreements may be required. Lines of authority are often discontinuous and difficult to trace.

In the analysis of public policy, we can distinguish between *inputs* into policy formulation and implementation; the *output* of these processes, which is the particular policy evolved; and the *outcome*, which refers to the consequences and impact of a particular policy. These outcomes may conform to the expressed purposes, but do not necessarily do so. Unintended outcomes and effects are not uncommon in domestic and transnational policy efforts and actions. At times, states fail in their efforts to shape certain conditions or to control events through public policies.

In the analysis of the input into policy formulation, particular attention must be paid to the societal problems and demands for governmental action by various domestic groups, the domestic and external linkages involved, and the authority and responsibilities of governmental institutions. Forces and conditions in the external environment also shape the policy input. They include the availability of natural resources in different parts of the world, wealth and poverty, urbanization, class structures, cultural patterns, and racial composition.

The governmental institutions producing transnational policies are not only foreign ministries, but also ministries or specialized agencies dealing with domestic affairs (especially economic matters), working individually or jointly. National and international bureaucracies often interact with each other across national boundaries. In some countries political party organizations may play significant roles in shaping or legitimizing policy decisions. This is not only true in one-party systems, such as the Soviet Union, where the leadership of the Communist party approves all major transnational policy formulations, but also in certain parliamentary democracies, such as Great Britain, where the party in power takes a stand on major policy problems. Major interest groups and various economic and political elites may also be consulted and their advice and interests taken into consideration before final policy decisions are made by governmental institutions.

Transnational policy and its implementation are the output of the complex process described so far. Such policy may deal with issues covering every aspect of societal needs and demands, including security, economic welfare, social concerns, fiscal matters, and education. As already suggested, the intended purpose of the policy and the actual consequences of its implementation (the outcome) may be at considerable variance; therefore, the distinction between output and outcome is significant when explaining the pattern of interaction among actors in the international arena. Moreover, whatever the outcome of a particular transnational policy, it is likely to have a feedback effect on the policy initiating forces and environmental conditions, which may result in policy modifications, new policy demands, or enhanced support of existing policies. The policy

Figure 1.1: The Environment of Transnational Policy Making

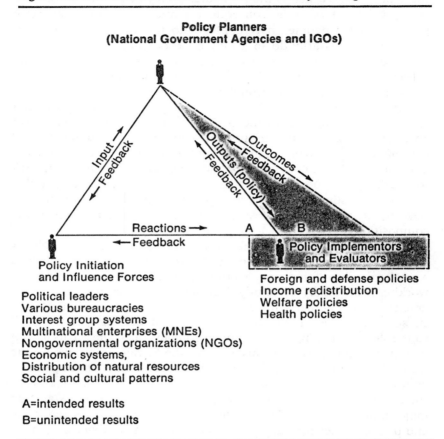

**Policy Planners
(National Government Agencies and IGOs)**

Input → / Feedback ←

Outputs (policy) / Feedback

Outcomes → / Feedback ←

Reactions →
← Feedback

A   B

Policy Implementors and Evaluators

Policy Initiation
and Influence Forces

Political leaders
Various bureaucracies
Interest group systems
Multinational enterprises (MNEs)
Nongovernmental organizations (NGOs)
Economic systems,
Distribution of natural resources
Social and cultural patterns

Foreign and defense policies
Income redistribution
Welfare policies
Health policies

A=intended results
B=unintended results

outcomes are also likely to have a feedback effect on the governmental institutions involved in the policy-making process, which may change these processes and the behavior of bureaucratic and nongovernmental participants in the process. Figure 1.1 is a schematic representation of transnational policy making.

It is important to stress that the problems associated with identifying cause-effect relationships in public policy analysis at the national or subnational level are compounded on the international scene. One reason is that most changes in the global arena are brought about by multiple causes. Another is that, even if one were able to isolate monocausal-effect relationships in particular instances, some of the effects might not have been intended. There are many examples of unintended effects of particular policy. During the 1950s the United States foreign policy toward the Southern Hemisphere attempted to oust dictatorships wherever possible and substitute democratic governments. This policy led the United States to aid in ousting the right-wing dictatorship of Batista in Cuba, but United States policy makers did not foresee and certainly did not intend that the succeeding government of Fidel Castro would become a communist dictatorship. The economic policies of President Nixon—devaluing the dollar in December 1971 and February 1973—were primarily designed to lower the prices and encourage purchase of American exports while keeping prices stable inside the United States; however, the extraordinary increase in exports of agricultural commodities, especially to the Soviet Union, and the food shortages caused by expanding world population and drought in Africa brought higher food prices in the United States and encouraged the inflationary spiral of food prices worldwide. As a result, farm incomes increased throughout the world, producing higher demands for goods and food in both developed and developing countries. This increased demand, in turn, created shortages, and these shortages were responsible for yet higher prices for food.

It may be puzzling to some of you that transnational policies of one country toward another may undergo extensive changes and, at times, complete reversals. Take, for example, U.S. policy toward Germany. During World War II, the Germans were our most bitter enemies; ten years after the end of the war, they were becoming our friends; and in the 1970s, the Federal Republic of Germany became one of the United States' closest allies. The application of transnational policy analysis can explain this change for you, but before we involve ourselves further in the details of this approach, we must learn more about the main actors on the international stage and how they interact with each other. They are the subject of the next chapter.

NOTES

1. For example, Sidney B. Fay, *The Origins of the World War*, 2nd ed. (New York: Macmillan, 1930).

2. See, for example, Raymond L. Buell, *International Relations* (New York: Holt, 1929) and Frederick L. Schuman, *International Politics* (New York: McGraw-Hill, 1933).

3. Hans J. Morgenthau, *Politics Among Nations*, 5th ed. (New York: Knopf, 1973).

4. Ibid., pp. 5–36.

5. Ibid., pp. 11–14

6. See in this respect also Reinhold Niebuhr, *Moral Man and Immoral Society* (New York: Charles Scribner's Sons, 1947).

7. V. I. Lenin, *Imperialism: The Highest Stage of Capitalism* (New York: International Publishers, 1939), pp. 16–30.

8. D. Senghaas, "Conflict Formation in Contemporary International Society," *Journal of Peace Research*, no. 3 (1973), pp. 163–184.

9. Harry Magdoff, *The Age of Imperialism* (New York: Monthly Review Press, 1969).

10. See Charles A. McClelland, *Theory and the International System* (New York: Macmillan, 1966); Richard N. Rosecrance, *Action and Reaction in World Politics* (Boston: Little, Brown, 1963); and Morton A. Kaplan, *System and Process in International Politics* (New York: Wiley and Sons, 1962). All are adherents of system theory.

11. See Rosecrance, op. cit., pp. 220–221.

12. See Richard A Snyder, H. W. Bruck, and Burton Sapin, "Decision-Making as an Approach to the Study of International Politics," in their *Foreign Policy Decision Making* (New York: Free Press, 1963), pp. 14–185; and Joseph Frankel, *The Making of Foreign Policy: An Analysis of Decision Making* (New York: Oxford University Press, 1967).

13. See James E. Dougherty and Robert L. Pfaltzgraff, Jr., *Contending Theories of International Relations* (Philadelphia: Lippincott, 1971), p. 312.

14. Ibid., pp. 316–317.

15. See ibid., pp. 349–358, for additional details.

16. For additional details see Dougherty and Pfaltzgraff, Jr., op. cit., pp. 396–398.

17. Thomas R. Dye, *Understanding Public Policy* (Englewood Cliffs, N.J.: Prentice-Hall, 1971), p. 1.

18. Much of this discussion follows the concepts of William D. Coplin and Michael K. O'Leary as expressed in their paper, "A Policy Analysis Framework for Research, Education and Policy-Making in International Relations," delivered to the 1974 International Studies Association Convention, St. Louis, Missouri.

SUGGESTED READINGS

KNORR, K., AND J. N. ROSENAU, eds. *Contending Approaches to International Politics.* Princeton, N.J.: Princeton University Press, 1969.

LaBARR, D. F., AND J. D. SINGER. *The Study of International Politics.* Santa Barbara, Calif.: Clio Press, 1976.

TANTER, R., AND R. W. ULLMAN, eds. *Theory and Policy in International Relations.* Princeton, N.J.: Princeton University Press, 1972.

YOUNG, O. R. *Systems of Political Science.* Englewood Cliffs, N.J.: Prentice-Hall, 1968.

ZAWODNY, I. K. *Guide to the Study of International Relations.* New York: Chandler, 1966.

CHAPTER TWO
THE SETTING OF INTERNATIONAL POLITICS

THE ACTORS

The units interacting with each other in a significant way on the international stage have changed over time. Some have exerted their impact since the beginning of recorded history, while others have only recently been recognized as influencing international society.

Nation-States

Until the end of World War II, international relations specialists centered their attention on large and small nation-states,* such as the United States, France, or Costa Rica, and regarded them as the dominant actors on the international stage. While the term *state* is abstract, inasmuch as you cannot see or feel a state, the component parts of the state, its citizens and a particular territory, are very concrete indeed. Acting for the state is the *government*, which possesses the means, coercive if necessary, to control its citizens. At the same time, it is not subject to a higher will or outside legal

---

* The terms *nation-state* and *state* are used synonymously in this book.

authority, which makes it a *sovereign* entity under international law. In the global arena the approximately 155 states of the contemporary world interact with one another in various ways: some collaborate with each other; others are engaged in various conflicts, some of which reach the severity of either a cold or hot war; and still others attempt to remain aloof and to go their own way.

Nation-states as we know them now are normally considered as dating from 1648, the end of the Thirty Years' War, which brought to a conclusion the era of feudalism. This war represented struggles of several dimensions: shifts in the European balance of power; the struggle by France against encirclement by the Hapsburg powers, namely Austria and Spain; the determination of the Netherlands to preserve independence from Spain; the rivalry between Sweden and Denmark for control of the Baltic; and conflict between German princes and the Holy Roman Emperor based on religious differences (Protestantism versus Catholicism) and centralization versus decentralization (emperor versus princes). The Treaty of Westphalia ending this war settled the affairs of Europe, reduced the very large number of German ministates, and resulted in an uneasy balance between the major European countries; but it also left the German economy in very bad shape.

While states did exist before 1648—for example, the very small Greek city-states, the empire of Alexander the Great, and the Roman Empire—the emergence of the modern nation-state was based on the development of the doctrine of sovereignty and the concept of nationalism. The notion of sovereignty was elaborated by political philosophers in the 16th century; the Frenchman, Jean Bodin, was perhaps the first and best-known exponent of this doctrine.[1] *Sovereignty* was defined as that power in a state whose actions are not subject to the control of any other human will. This power might be centered in an individual (the king or, in the more general terms, a monarch) or in a group (such as the people in a republic). The power of the state, while unchallengeable within its own territory, was limited by its frontiers as other states also possess the same type of sovereignty within their own territories. As a consequence, externally every sovereign state is *legally* the equal of all other sovereign states. *In theory* it is free to decide on any action it wants to undertake in relationship to the other states of the world; *in practice*, however, the military, political, and economic strengths of other states may impose limitations on this freedom, and the consequences of such actions may not always be what they were intended to be.

The cohesive element of the nation-state has been *nationalism*, a very complex phenomenon that can be defined as strong identification with and loyalty to a particular state by the people of that state.

This loyalty has its main sources and finds continuing strength in the common values, traditions, and historical experiences of the people of a state; it is bolstered when the people speak the same language, or perhaps belong to the same ethnic group. Before the emergence of nationalism as a unifying force, loyalty had a much more personal character: one person gave allegiance to another person, usually a king or noble. This relationship between ruler and ruled characterized the period of feudalism, which stretched from the disintegration of the Roman Empire to the emergence of the modern state system after the Thirty Years' War.

Intergovernmental Organizations

Beginning with the 20th century, the nation-states were joined on the international stage by intergovernmental organizations (IGOs), often simply referred to as international organizations. Examples of these entities are the League of Nations,* the United Nations, the Organization of American States, the North Atlantic Treaty Organization (NATO), and the European Common Market. These IGOs are either global or regional in character. The United Nations falls into the first category, while NATO falls into the second. Although the legal competence of an IGO is carefully circumscribed by the governments of the states that are its members, IGOs are now recognized as actors on the international stage.

Nongovernmental Forces

Since World War II new forces have emerged on the international scene to challenge the dominance of the old ones.

We have already mentioned the energy crisis of the 1970s. The large multinational oil companies, such as Exxon, Gulf, and Texaco, were deeply involved in this crisis; in fact, some observers suspected during the early part of 1974 that the executive suites of the multinational oil companies worked closely with the governments of the Arab oil-producing countries in establishing the embargo and increasing oil prices.[2] Regardless of the truth of this allegation, the grave global problem of petroleum availability and cost cannot be

---

* The League of Nations, formed at Versailles in 1919, had lost almost all of its prestige and influence by the time World War II began in 1939 and was replaced by the United Nations in 1945.

solved through state interaction alone but will require a mixture of governmental and nongovernmental action. A second example involves the activities of Arab guerrillas, essentially also a nongovernmental group despite their often close relationships to Arab governments. Governments of states whose airplanes were hijacked by Arab terrorists had to deal directly with members of the Arab terrorist organizations to counteract international lawlessness and to protect their citizens. The government of Lebanon, where many of the Arab groups were headquartered, did not have the power to control their actions. Golda Meir, the former Prime Minister of Israel, the country singled out as a prime target of guerrilla attacks, declared in the summer of 1973 that the state of Israel was engaged in a secret international war against Arab guerrillas. She said, "The state of Israel is practically fighting a battle all over the world."[3]

To appreciate the power of some nongovernmental forces, let us compare multinational enterprises (MNEs) with nation-states. MNEs, approximately 4000 in number, half of which are headquartered in the United States and the remainder mainly in Western Europe, are business establishments that have factories, research institutions, and sales facilities in many countries of the world. In 1975, the largest MNE, General Motors, produced $36 billion worth of goods and services. If we compare this figure with the gross national product (GNP) of Switzerland, we find that the Swiss GNP is $40 billion, only $4 billion more than the output of General Motors.* The next country below GM is Denmark, whose GNP is nearly $10 billion less than the General Motors figure. If we add to this that more than 400 American and European MNEs have an output of over $1 billion each and that more than half of the approximately 155 states of the world have a GNP below $1 billion, we can see that economic giants have been created whose power cannot help but make an impact on the international stage.

This impression is strengthened if we look at some additional data. General Motors employs more than 700,000 people all over the world. This figure is larger than the total of all civil servants (national and local) of New Zealand. Moreover, the production of multinational corporations has been growing twice as fast as that of national companies. In 1968 it amounted to $400 billion, of which half came from American MNEs. It is anticipated by some observers that, by 1985, 75 percent of the world's production of goods and

---

* We should point out that GNP includes expenditures for investments and construction, while the GM figure only contains revenues from the sale of manufactured goods and services.

services will be under the control of 300 MNEs that may employ 20 percent of the world's total labor force.[4]

Perhaps the most dramatic illustration of the power of these corporations is the amount of financial muscle they possess. At the end of 1971, MNEs could dispose of over $250 billion in liquid assets, a figure twice as large as the currency reserves of the central banks of all states of the world taken together. This means that, under many circumstances, private organizations can utilize enormous financial means without any governmental control; and it is this financial power that contributed significantly to the serious monetary crises of the early 1970s.

From the foregoing it can be seen that the MNEs constitute a very potent force in the global arena. But the MNE is not the only nongovernmental actor on the international stage. Powerful labor unions have responded to the challenge of MNEs when the latter moved some of their operations into countries with lower labor costs. They have attempted to organize workers in the countries where new production facilities have been established and have thus engaged in transnational activities themselves. They have been joined by international trade union federations operating in many countries of the world and seeking to promote the interests of their members.

In addition, a host of other nongovernmental organizations (NGOs) promoting a variety of interests have sprung up and become internationally active. Although their power cannot be compared with that of MNEs, they have begun to intrude into the spheres of international activity traditionally reserved to the nation-states. Within this category are the very extensive organizations of the different religious denominations, welfare and scientific organizations, and cultural and charitable foundations. Finally, there are transnational political parties. At first regional in scope, they have later sought to operate globally.

In view of their growing influence in the world arena, at least the more powerful nongovernmental entities are now being accorded actor status on the international stage. The underlying reason for these entities to qualify as international actors may well be, as E. Raymond Platig argues, that despite claims to the contrary, few governments if any have total control over the people residing in their territories. To the extent that their control is less than total, individual groups within states can and do enter into independent border-crossing relations and activities, thus becoming direct actors in the international system.[5] Arnold Wolfers traces international actor status of nongovernmental entities to the fact that men identify themselves and their interests with corporate bodies other than the nation-states.[6] While considering Platig's argument as the more potent one, it should be pointed out that national governments at times encourage and support, financially and otherwise, the transnational activities of national and international nongovernmental entities, especially if such activities tend to buttress governmental objectives. As Platig himself states, the practices of governments vary greatly as to when and to what degree they attempt to encourage, monitor, restrict, manage, or control the international transactions resulting from initiatives other than their own.

RELATIONS BETWEEN ACTORS

Although international actor status is now accorded powerful NGOs, we must note a basic distinction in the quality of the status between these forces and nation-states. Only states have the legitimate governmental authority to make decisions for their citizens by either providing benefits for, or imposing restrictions on, them. They also are the only units to apply coercive means against their citizens on a legitimate basis. On the other hand, some nongovernmental entities, through their extraordinary economic power, can influence states to utilize the means at their disposal for a variety of international actions, including perhaps engaging in war. Moreover, while the state does have the legal authority to do many things for or against its citizens (and a multinational corporation may also be a "citizen" of a particular state), it may not be able to exercise this authority because of economic and political considerations occasioned by the existence and activities of a particular nongovernmental entity. Yet while nongovernmental forces are often powerful and influential instigators of change in the global arena, their actor status ranks below that of nation-states and their influence is exercised, in many instances, indirectly through the governments of nation-states.

Nongovernmental actors are difficult to fit into our transnational policy analysis scheme: for example, when an MNE makes an investment in another country and thereby produces a variety of possible cross-national effects through the construction of new factories, the rise in wages, and perhaps added inflationary pressures in that country, it appears that these effects occur independently of governmental policy or decisions. Or when the treasurer of an MNE decides to convert large amounts of dollars into German marks in anticipation of making a handsome profit when the dollar loses on the international money market and he in fact thereby contributes to the devaluation of the dollar, it seems that his action is exclusively nongovernmental. However, nation-state policies and decisions could have prevented these effects; therefore, for actions such as these to occur, we must assume that governments have given either their explicit or their tacit approval, or at least their assurance of noninterference.

MNEs especially, but also some other nongovernmental actors, have special capabilities to influence effectively the formulation and implementation of transnational public policy because they can coordinate their action across many states and extend their influence to the subnational levels of those states. Sophistication in lobbying and coalitions with various groups in society that share their interests have made the influence on public policy coming from MNEs particularly effective. Our analytical framework is capable of capturing these intricacies and, therefore, of helping us understand the interactions of both government and nongovernmental actors on the international stage.

In examining these interactions and the great variety of relationships that exist, it might be useful to distinguish three types of relationships: (1) the traditional interactions and relations between the governments of states and IGOs, which we will label as *international relations;* (2) interactions and relations between nongovernmental actors, as well as between these actors and the governments of states or IGOs, for which we will use the term *transnational relations;* and (3) relations among nongovernmental actors as well as between these actors and governments within a particular country that will be termed *intranational relations.* Figure 2.1 provides a graphic illustration of these types of relationships.

THE PHYSICAL ENVIRONMENT

Interaction among the international actors does not take place in a vacuum. Rather, the physical environment of the world, made up of the geographical distribution of natural resources, differences in topography and climate, and such man-made features as urbanization, transportation nets, and canals connecting international bodies of water (the Panama and Suez canals, for example), influences significantly these interactions. Again the energy crisis following the embargo by the Arab oil-producing countries and the increase in oil prices is a good case in point. And the possible exhaustion of other raw materials, such as copper, will have important effects on the behavior of international actors.

The effects of environmental factors may be modified by advances in technology or concerns with pollution. To return to the

Figure 2.1: The Variety of International Relations

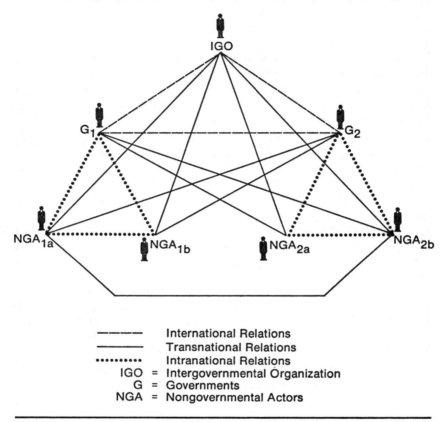

⎯ ⎯ ⎯ ⎯	International Relations
⎯⎯⎯⎯⎯	Transnational Relations
••••••••••	Intranational Relations
IGO =	Intergovernmental Organization
G =	Governments
NGA =	Nongovernmental Actors

SOURCE: Adapted from J. S. Nye and Robert D. Keohane, "Transnational Relations and World Politics: An Introduction," *International Organization*, vol. 25, no. 3 (Summer 1971), pp. 351–352.

problem of the exhaustion of oil resources, nuclear and solar energy could become significant substitutes for oil if, especially with respect to solar sources, the necessary technical progress can be made. Thus technological advances could lessen our dependence on petroleum and lower the effects this particular environmental factor would have on interactions among international actors. Pollution concerns, on the other hand, could sharpen these effects. Not only in the United States, but also in many other countries that have installed nuclear power plants and are planning to increase further their use of nuclear energy, fear of pollution and contamination expressed by influential groups has slowed down or halted construction of nuclear power plants. Such actions are apt to have a bearing on the goals and behavior of national governments, IGOs, and nongovernmental actors affected by dwindling oil reserves.

THE DYNAMICS

The pattern of interactions among individual nation-states and between states and nongovernmental units on the international stage depends on the objectives pursued by the actors. Perceived needs and aspirations of states and their people lead to the articulation of demands and goals, such as security and economic well-being, to be realized through the formulation and implementation of pertinent transnational policies. They provide the major initiatives and dynamics for the interactions within the international society. The pursuit of these often converging or conflicting policies is also at the base of the manifold, multilevel interactions taking place in the international arena and helps to explain moves and countermoves among the actors.

The differential distribution of needs, aspirations, and capabilities of states, their people, and other international actors is also the basis for global and regional economic and political interdependence. Coplin and O'Leary define *interdependence* as

the existence of conditions in which the perceived needs of some individual groups in one state are satisfied by resources or capabilities that exist in at least one other state. Thus patterns of transnational interdependence are a product of the interface between needs and capabilities across national boundaries.[7]

Interdependence is manifested by flows of people, civilian and military goods and services, capital, and information across national boundaries in response to needs in one or more countries and in accordance with the capabilities of others. These flows are often referred to as *transactional flows* and can be quantitatively measured. Depending on their particular interests, IGOs, MNEs, and a variety of governmental groups and nongovernmental organizations, such as particular bureaucracies or economic pressure groups, may be involved in these flows. The existence of similar needs may lead to formal and informal coalitions among states, states and IGOs, and governmental and nongovernmental actors. Complementary capabilities may also produce alliances. On the other hand, the unequal distribution of capabilities may conjur up perceptions of dependence by less favored states, creating apprehension and envy and possibly leading to friction and conflict. Similar capabilities coupled with unequal resources may sharpen economic competition in international trade and in the search for sources of raw materials. The competition between the United States and Japan is one example; that between the United States and the European Common Market is another.

From the foregoing discussion it is evident that the different capabilities of governmental and nongovernmental actors play a crucial role not only for present and future interdependence relationships in regional and global contexts, but also for the successful pursuit of the satisfaction of needs and aspirations of individual actors. Such capabilities as military forces, economic and financial means, and industrial and technological proficiency can be translated into international power and influence, while their absence may signal serious vulnerability. Hence, small states usually must be more modest in their policy aspirations than the big powers because of more limited resources, although the skillful exploitation of a larger country's weaknesses may compensate for the limitations in resources. If the hostilities in Vietnam have proved anything, it is that even the largest power on earth, the United States, does not possess unlimited resources and means to achieve anything she wants in the face of internal dissension and increasing domestic political pressures against an unpopular, protracted war. Few observers and statesmen realized this when the United States began to engage in open hostilities in Vietnam; however, one foreign policy expert, Hans Morgenthau, warned the nation that the complexities of a war in Vietnam would eventually lead to an exhaustion of the resources of the United States, considering that these resources would not only consist of conventional military men and weapons difficult to employ in jungle warfare and against guerrilla tactics, but also of the sustained support of the American people, which eroded steadily during the war.[8]

SUMMARY

The actors on the international stage include nation-states, intergovernmental organizations (IGOs), and nongovernmental organizations (NGOs).

Modern **nation-states** date from 1648 when the Treaty of Westphalia ended the Thirty Years' War and feudalism as well. Because such states are not subject to a higher will or outside legal authority, they are said to be **sovereign.** The cohesive element of the nation-state is **nationalism,** the strong identification with and loyalty to a particular state.

Intergovernmental organizations (IGOs) are organizations in which different state governments are members. They may be global or regional in character. Examples are the United Nations, the Organization of American States, and the European Common Market.

Since World War II, **nongovernmental organizations (NGOs)** have been accorded actor status on the international stage. NGOs include multinational corporations, powerful labor unions, religious denominations, welfare and scientific organizations, cultural and charitable foundations, transnational political parties, and terrorist bands. Interactions between governments of states and IGOs fall into three broad categories: (1) **international relations,** (2) **transnational relations,** and (3) **intranational relations.** While the status of NGOs is below that of nation-states, their power and influence are growing. Some observers predict that, by 1985, 75 percent of the world's production will be under the control of 300 **multinational enterprises (MNEs)** that may be employing 20 percent of the world's labor force.

Interaction among international actors is influenced significantly by the world's physical environment, including the distribution of natural resources, differences in topography and climate, and such man-made features as urban development and transportation nets. The effects of these environmental factors may be modified by technological advances or concerns about pollution.

The pattern of interactions among actors on the international stage depends upon their needs and objectives. The differential distribution of needs, aspirations, and capabilities is the basis for **interdependence,** manifested in **transactional flows.** These flows can be quantitatively measured.

Certain capabilities and resources can be translated into international power and influence. Because the aspirations of international actors are limited by real or perceived strengths and weaknesses, we need to learn what determines these strengths and weaknesses to understand the dynamics of international relations; therefore, the determinants of national power are the subject of the next chapter.

NOTES

1. *Six Books on the State,* translated by William Ebenstein, 1576.
2. See M. A. Adelman, "The Changing Structure of Big International Oil," in Frank N. Trager, ed., *Oil, Divestiture, and National Security* (New York: Crane, Russak, 1977), pp. 1–10, especially p. 4.
3. *Atlanta Journal,* July 30, 1973, p. 9a.
4. See also Raymond Vernon, "Economic Sovereignty at Bay," *Foreign Affairs,* vol. 47, no. 1 (October 1968), p. 114; and Sidney E. Rolfe, "The International Corporation in Perspective," in Rolfe and Damm, eds., *The Multinational Corporation in the World Economy* (New York: Praeger, 1970), pp. 6–7.
5. E. Raymond Platig, "International Relations as a Field of Inquiry," in James N. Rosenau, ed., *International Politics and Foreign Policy* (New York: Free Press, 1969), pp. 6–19, especially pp. 16–17.
6. Arnold Wolfers, *Discord and Collaboration* (Baltimore: Johns Hopkins Press, 1962), p. 23.
7. William D. Coplin and Michael K. O'Leary, "A Policy Analysis Framework for Research, Education and Policy-Making in International Relations," delivered to the 1974 International Studies Association Convention, St. Louis, Missouri.
8. *New York Times,* April 18, 1965, Magazine Section, pp. 24–25 and 85–87.

SUGGESTED READINGS

HAAS, ERNST B., AND ALLEN S. WHITING. *Dynamics of International Relations.* New York: McGraw-Hill, 1956.
KEOHANE, R. O., AND J. S. NYE, eds. *Transnational Relations and World Politics.* Cambridge, Mass.: Harvard University Press, 1972.
MANSBACH, R. W., Y. H. FERGUSON, AND D. E. LAMPERT. *The Web of World Politics: Non-State Actors in the Global System.* Englewood Cliffs, N.J.: Prentice-Hall, 1976.
ROSECRANCE, RICHARD. *Action and Reaction in World Politics.* Boston: Little, Brown, 1969.

CHAPTER THREE
THE DETERMINANTS
OF NATIONAL POWER:
OBJECTIVE FACTORS

The differential between the strengths and weaknesses of two or more countries is the basis for understanding the term *power* in international relations, inasmuch as it refers to the ability of a country to influence the behavior of other countries in accordance with its own goals.[1] Clearly, the relative strengths and weaknesses of a country play a significant role in determining this ability, although other factors, such as diplomatic skill or superior management of meager resources, may also be important. For example, Finland has successfully withstood Soviet encroachment since World War II, despite the fact that, in general terms, the Soviet Union is much more powerful than tiny Finland. While skillful use or manipulation of resources may indeed increase a nation's power, a careful analysis of the elements of power is an essential input into the transnational policy-making process.

The basic elements that determine the actual and potential power of a state can be grouped into seven categories:

1. Geography, including natural resources
2. Population
3. Economic development
4. Science and technology
5. Traditions and social psychology
6. Government and administration
7. Military organization

The first four determinants consist primarily of objective factors, susceptible in general to quantitative measurement and analysis. These will be examined in this chapter. The fifth determinant is mostly subjective in nature, while the last two are characterized by a mixture of objective and subjective aspects. Their assessment often requires qualitative evaluation although hard data, including surveys of public attitudes, are also available. The last three determinants will be discussed in the next chapter.

GEOGRAPHY

Size

In any discussion of possible vulnerabilities of states, the size and shape of the territories and the locations of these states relative to other countries are significant. Large size is a clear advantage. It was the ability of Russia to give up space for time to organize its military defense that proved to be decisive in 1812 and 1941. Moreover, the difficulty of occupying captured territory is directly proportional to its size. Today, when invasion forces are often airborne, space is a much less significant factor in countering attacks; its value may lie, instead, in making possible the dispersion of vital industries to avoid complete nuclear destruction. Although the United States has sufficient space, the Soviet Union has achieved a much higher degree of dispersal of industrial capacity. The vast expanses of the People's Republic of China's territory offer many opportunities for dispersal.

It is noteworthy that, while small countries have never achieved great power status, middle-sized countries, such as Great Britain and France, were able to attain this status in the 19th and early 20th centuries as the result of early industrial development, a strong military establishment, and colonial conquest. In a sense, these conquests added to their size, suggesting again the importance of this geographic factor. On the other hand, size remains only one of many elements determining the total power of a country. Many of the states possessing vast territories (see Table 3.1) are not popularly identified as powerful.

Geopolitics

The relative location of countries has been the basis for many theories of geopolitics. One of these, propounded in 1904 by Sir Halford Mackinder in London, has as its central concept that the

Table 3.1: Twenty Largest Countries by Area (in square miles)

Country	Area
Soviet Union	8,649,489
Canada	3,851,787
People's Republic of China	3,691,502
United States	3,540,939
Brazil	3,286,470
Australia	2,967,877
India	1,261,502
Argentina	1,072,157
Sudan	967,494
Algeria	919,590
Congo (Kenshasa)	905,562
Saudi Arabia	829,995
Mexico	761,600
Libya	679,358
Iran	636,293
Mongolian People's Republic	604,247
Indonesia	575,893
Peru	496,222
Chad	495,752
Niger	489,189

SOURCE: *The New Information Please Almanac, 1972,* pp. 725–726.

pivotal region for international power is Euro-Asia, a region stretching from the Volga River in Russia to the Yangtse River in China, and from the Himalayas to the Arctic Ocean. This, according to Mackinder, was the "heartland" of the world, which was surrounded by an inner crescent (running from Germany, Turkey, and India to China) and an outer crescent (comprised of Britain, South Africa, Antarctica, Japan, the United States, and Canada). Europe, Asia, and Africa were regarded as the "world-island" and the principal conclusion was: "Who rules East Europe commands the Heartland; who rules the Heartland commands the World-Island; who rules the World-Island commands the world."[2]

This theory was picked up by General Karl Haushofer, a German geopolitician in the 1920s, and later became a potent idea in the shaping of Nazi foreign policy. It rationalized the conquest of Eastern Europe by German armed forces as being necessary to make Germany the dominant power on earth. Combined with the need for more "living space" for the burgeoning German population, geopolitics in Germany became a powerful mystique for the German destiny in the East and an ideological force for military attacks on the Soviet Union.

Today the "science" of geopolitics is discredited because it sought to make an element of geography into an absolute law by which the power of states could be determined. While the relative location of states does influence their power status, it is only one factor among many. For example, Austria's being close to the Soviet Union has caused her to defer to her big neighbor on strategic and economic matters. On the other hand, the vulnerability of relative location can be overcome by countervailing forces: Gibraltar's proximity to Spain has not led to Spanish control because of British power and political skill.

Topography

Other salient aspects of geography, such as the topographic nature of a country's frontiers (mountainous or flat, protected by rivers or the seashore), also have lost their defensive significance as the result of the technological advances in the instruments of warfare. Topographic barriers do not hamper air or space attacks, although they may impede invasion by ground forces.

Climate

Climate is another geographic feature influencing the power of a state. It affects the size of population, because climatic extremes may render vast areas practically uninhabitable. It may also limit agricultural production: little grows in the extremely cold climate of the Arctic and the deserts of Africa. Climatic variation is evident in the length of the growing season and in the simultaneous existence of drought and flood. Drought has caused a severe famine in West Africa in recent years.

In terms of human activity, the temperate zone areas between 20 and 60 degrees north and south have been most favorable; and it may be no accident that, in modern times, the great powers of the world have been located in these areas. Because the land masses in the Northern Hemisphere are much more extensive than those in the Southern Hemisphere, it is not surprising that the great powers are concentrated in the north.

Technical advances have mitigated the significance of climate as a determinant of power. While the process of industrialization spread initially in the temperate zones and avoided areas in which extended periods of very hot weather depressed worker productivity, air conditioning has now overcome this impediment. As a consequence, industry in many parts of the Northern Hemisphere has moved southward, lured by lower labor costs and the availability of year-round recreation. Modern irrigation methods have made arable many areas that climate formerly rendered agriculturally unproductive.

Natural Resources

An aspect of geography important in determining the strength of a country is the availability of natural resources within its borders. These resources consist of minerals (fuels and metals) and of the products of the soil. Without these resources, modern economies cannot operate, the construction of a viable military force is impossible, and large populations cannot be fed. When vital resources are not available within a country, they must be imported. For many developing countries, the export of natural resources and agricultural products is essential for their economic survival and political stability.

It is important to understand that both the needs for natural resources and their availability change for particular countries over time. Altered economic conditions and technological advances bring about different needs in different countries, accelerating or slowing down the consumption of existing resources and requiring greater imports or the discovery of substitutes. At the same time, the availability of resources is expanded when new reserves of minerals are found or new methods for expanding or speeding up crop growth are discovered.

Coal and iron were once considered to be the minerals whose availability was most indicative of international power because they were needed to manufacture steel and to produce military weapons. In the 19th century, Great Britain was self-sufficient in these two minerals, a factor undoubtedly contributing to her great-power status at that time. It enabled her to build a large navy to protect the merchant vessels bringing to Britain other needed minerals and foodstuffs.

The two largest powers in the world, the Soviet Union and the United States, have not only been self-sufficient in coal and iron ore, but also in many other minerals. During the past decade or two, however, the United States has been compelled to import iron from Venezuela, Canada, and other places, because domestic sources of high-grade ores were being exhausted. Many other materials needed to keep the American industrial machinery running must also be imported, as indicated in Table 3.2. Some of these materials, such as chromite and industrial diamonds, come from potential enemies, such as the Soviet Union. Western Europe and Japan are

Table 3.2: Major Vital Minerals Imported into the United States

Mineral	Percent Imported	Mineral	Percent Imported
Columbium	100	Mercury	65
Manganese	98	Zinc	59
Cobalt	98	Tungsten	59
Platinum	92	Titanium	53
Chromium	89	Vanadium	31
Aluminum	87	Iron	21
Tin	85	Lead	15
Flourine	79	Copper	15
Nickel	71		

SOURCE: *International Economic Report of the President,* January 1977 (Washington, D.C., U.S. Government Printing Office), p. 32.

in an even worse predicament regarding such minerals as copper, iron ore, and tungsten.[3] Table 3.3 illustrates the importance of imported raw materials to American industry by indicating the amount of each needed to manufacture jet engines.

Stockpiling   Stockpiling can be used to overcome deficiencies in materials that must be imported and may be essential in times of war. The United States has made use of this system, but it is feasible only if stockpiled materials do not deteriorate. The search for and discovery of domestic substitutes is another means of overcoming the problem of possible shortages of needed materials. Sometimes the production of substitutes develops into a major industrial pursuit, and the resulting products serve not only the purposes for which they were originally intended, but completely different purposes as well. The plastics industry is an example.

Petroleum Products   The increasing need for petroleum products has become the Achilles heel of industrially advanced countries (see Table 3.4). The United States, which for many years was almost entirely self-sufficient in its petroleum needs, must import continuously increasing amounts from other countries, including the tremendously oil-rich Arab states of the Middle East and North Africa. Although new reserves may be found in the United States or along its shores and are beginning to be exploited in the North Sea near Great Britain, Norway, and the Netherlands, the United States and other highly industrialized nations of the Free World will probably remain dependent for adequate oil supplies on the Arab World. Table 3.4 illustrates the predicament for 1976 and shows the substantial excess of demand over supply to which es-

Table 3.3: Critical Materials Used for Jet Engines

Mineral	Pounds Used in Jet Engine	Imports as Percent of Consumption	Where Material is Produced (Percent)
Tungsten	80 to 100	24	United States (30) South Korea (19) Canada (12) Australia (8) Bolivia (8) Portugal (7)
Columbium	10 to 12	100	Brazil (54) Canada (21) Mozambique (18)
Nickel	1300 to 1600	75	Canada (71) New Caledonia (20)
Chromium	2500 to 2800	100	South Africa (31) Turkey (19) S. Rhodesia (19) Philippines (18)
Molybdenum	90 to 100	0	United States (79) Canada (10)
Cobalt	30 to 40	100	Zaire (60) Morocco (13) Canada (12) Zambia (11)

SOURCE: Harry Magdoff, *The Age of Imperialism* (New York: Monthly Review Press, 1969), p. 52, Table XI.

pecially Western Europe, but also the United States, Australia, and New Zealand, are exposed. That this situation is expected to take a sharp turn for the worse beginning in 1985 can be seen from Figure 3.1. Petroleum shortfall may squeeze especially the United States, Europe, and Japan. While the very large oil reserves of many Arab states are by themselves a factor of considerable strength, this dependence reinforces their power considerably, and any threat by the Arab states to withhold oil from certain countries or to reduce the permissible output of the wells owned by the international oil companies is not taken lightly. It is, therefore, not surprising that this threat was used again and again by the Arab countries in the Israeli-Arab conflict to put pressure on the governments of the industrially advanced countries to make their policies more favorable to the Arab cause.

To overcome these difficulties, the industrialized states may turn to coal, whose use as an energy source had declined in the face

Table 3.4: World Petroleum Demand and Supply by Regions, 1976 (in thousands of barrels per day)

Region	Domestic Demand (consumption)	Domestic Supply			Excess Supply over Demand	Excess Demand over Supply	Percent of World	
		Crude Oil	NGL	Total			Domestic Demand	Domestic Supply
United States	17,180	8,119	1,642	9,761	--	7,419	29.0	16.13
Canada	1,799	1,255	322	1,577	--	222	3.0	2.62
Latin America	3,832	4,345	227	4,572	740	--	6.5	7.6
Western Europe	14,410	774	89	863	--	13,547	24.3	1.43
East Europe and Soviet Union	9,528	10,835	272	11,107	1,579	--	16.1	18.3
Africa	1,119	5,927	121	6,048	4,929	--	1.9	10.0
Middle East	1,443	21,949	289	22,238	20,795	--	2.4	36.8
Japan	5,203	12	--	12	--	5,191	8.8	0.02
Australia and New Zealand	763	421	56	477	--	286	1.3	0.8
China	1,492	1,700	N.A.	1,700	208	--	2.5	2.8
Other, Asia, and Oceania	2,475	2,083	37	2,120	--	355	4.2	3.5
World Total	59,244	57,420	3,055	60,475	1,231[a]	--	100.0	100.0

[a]Increase in stocks (crude en route, in storage, etc.)

SOURCE: *World Oil* (August 15, 1977), p. 48.

Figure 3.1: Free World Petroleum Demand by Area

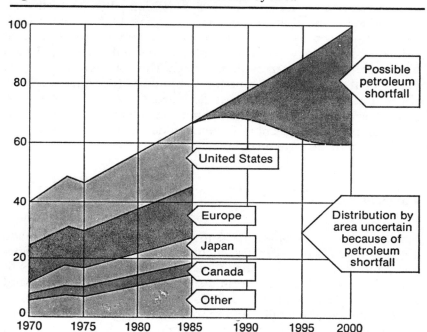

SOURCE: *Oil and Gas Journal,* vol. 75, no. 35 (August 1977), p. 59.

of wider utilization of oil and natural gas. Gasoline may well be produced synthetically from coal if the present technology costs for the conversion process can be lowered. The demand for coal, which is available in very large quantities in Western countries, has already risen as it is being utilized increasingly to supply fuel for electric generating plants. This demand may go up steeply when conversion to gasoline becomes economically feasible. Other long-range substitutes for energy derived from petroleum may be nuclear and solar power.

In Developing Countries   Many of the raw materials of the world, including of course oil, are found in developing countries, some of which only recently became independent. In most instances, the minerals are the only major assets these countries have, and exploitation of these resources by large Western business corporations has fostered growing resentment and strong demands for indigenous control of producing wells and mines.

Food Production   Self-sufficiency in food production has also been a frequent concern of countries wishing either to feed their population in time of war or to assure adequate farm incomes. Deficiency of homegrown food has been a permanent weakness of Great Britain and Germany, while the United States and the Soviet Union have usually produced more than enough. The Common Agricultural Policy of the European Economic Community (Common Market), which Britain joined in 1973, is designed to attain regional self-sufficiency in farm products, eliminating most deficiencies of Community-grown agricultural commodities and at the same time assuring adequate farm incomes.

Physical Features

Finally, a few observations need to be made about the man-made physical features of a country, such as cities, roads, railways, pipelines, and airports. Well-planned and well-built cities are factors of strength, inasmuch as they form a sound basis for a physically and mentally healthy population and for a viable economy; however, large slums sap the vitality and morale of the population. We have already mentioned that dispersion of industrial plants represents a factor of strength in view of the threat of nuclear war. We should add that concentration of population, as found in Belgium or the northeast United States, constitutes a factor of weakness.

Transportation nets are also important in determining the strength or weakness of a state. The number and location of airports must be such that there are sufficient alternate landing places for planes in the event first-choice facilities are destroyed or rendered inoperable by a major catastrophe. The denser and more integrated the transportation net of roads, railroads, canals, and pipelines and the more alternate means there are by which to travel or ship goods to the same spot, the higher is the possibility that vital governmental and economic functions can be continued in the event of air or nuclear attack. If these conditions do not exist and the transportation net is poor and inflexible, it may be damaged to such an extent that the country is immobilized by the attack and unable to mount a counterstrike.

In summary, various elements of geography affect the strength and weakness of a particular state; but geography is only one of many factors determining the power status of a country, and its influence changes over time. Another determinant is population.

POPULATION

Our analysis of population to determine how it affects the strengths and weaknesses of a country focuses on its size, structure, quality, and composition.

Size

A large population does not confer great power status upon a country, as Table 3.5 indicates; but on the other hand, a very small population precludes such a status, inasmuch as high economic development requires a good-sized labor force, an adequate number of consumers, and an extensive manpower pool to establish credible military capabilities. In general, the size of population must exceed 35 million if a state aspires to great or even medium power status, but there are exceptions. Canada, with only 21.5 million inhabitants, has much greater economic and military strength than has Indonesia with a population of 121 million.

The vast majority of the world's 155 states have less than 35 million inhabitants. Some states, such as Monaco and San Marino, have tiny populations. Many states have between 5 and 15 million people. Twenty-two states each have a population of 15 to 35 million people, but only seventeen countries exceed the power status threshold of 35 million inhabitants.

Structure

The structure of the population is also an important factor in measuring the strength of a state because knowing the percentages of the population in certain age brackets permits inferences as to a country's economic and military potential. Members of the population between 15 and 44 years of age are most capable of maximizing these potentials; therefore, a high percentage in this bracket is an indication of national strength. On the other hand, large percentages in the category above 44 years suggest a declining national effort and an increasing burden on the productive middle bracket because most senior citizens (65 and up) require social security support from the state. A large percentage of the population *under* the age of 15 may augur well for future strength. The significance of these age brackets may vary, of course, depending whether the society in a

Table 3.5: Largest Countries by Population

Country	Population
China	787,180,000
India	547,367,926
Soviet Union	241,720,124
United States	208,232,000
Indonesia	124,890,000
Japan	103,720,060
Brazil	100,100,000
Bangladesh	75,000,001
Pakistan	64,890,000
West Germany	61,670,000
Nigeria	56,510,000
United Kingdom	55,525,205
Italy	54,080,000
France	51,260,000
Mexico	48,381,547
Philippines	36,684,486
Turkey	36,160,000
Thailand	34,152,000
Spain	34,130,000
United Arab Republic	33,329,000
Poland	32,589,209
Korea, South	31,469,132
East Germany	17,040,926

SOURCE: *Information Please Almanac Atlas and Yearbook,* 1973, pp. 308–309.

particular state falls into the preindustrial (developing) or postindustrial (developed) category.

Table 3.6 provides population data for selected states. As shown in the table, France, West Germany, the United Kingdom, and the United States have large percentages of their populations in the older categories; while Brazil, Honduras, India, Indonesia, and Zambia have a very large proportion of their population in the youngest category. For the United States and the Soviet Union, the figures for the youngest and middle brackets are comparable, but the United States has a larger percentage in the oldest group.

Perhaps more important than the current structure of the population is the projected future pattern, because foreign-policy makers must plan for events that are yet 5, 10, and 25 years away. Their plans must take into consideration the relative size of the population at these intervals in any countries with which they plan either to collaborate or to compete. The importance of comparative projections of population can be illustrated by a historical example involv-

Table 3.6: Manpower of Selected Nations

Nation	Age Distribution		
	0-14	**15-44**	**Over 45**
Brazil	29,931,481	30,249,531	9,938,059
France	11,790,960	20,655,544	17,208,052
Germany, East	3,834,726	5,997,508	6,108,235
Germany, West	11,898,190	22,168,189	19,911,039
Honduras	900,739	752,909	231,117
India	180,018,660	188,888,204	69,867,865
Indonesia	40,544,678	42,458,049	13,316,102
Japan	25,166,182	50,001,677	23,107,102
Soviet Union	74,710,000	104,880,000	62,130,000
United Kingdom	12,355,703	20,857 063	19,516,168
United States	57,909,564	83,421,410	61,834,725
Zambia	1,554,063	1,609,394	329,231

SOURCE: *UN Demographic Yearbook, 1970.*

ing France and Germany between 1870 and 1940. During that period, the population of France increased by 4 million, while Germany's population grew by 27 million. Consecutive French governments viewed with alarm the much more rapid population growth rate of their neighbors to the east. Their apprehension was clearly justified: by 1940 Germany had at her disposal about 15 million men fit for military service, whereas France had only 5 million.[4]

Growth Rate   We have noted earlier that Brazil, Honduras, and a number of other less developed countries had a very large percentage of their population in the youngest bracket. Indeed, as the projections in Table 3.7 indicate, the growth rate of the population in the areas where most of the less developed countries are located (Asia, excluding the Soviet Union; Africa; and Latin America) is much higher than in the areas of the economically advanced countries. As a consequence, by the year 2000 nearly 80 percent of the world's population will be found in Asia, Africa, and South America, whereas this percentage in 1920 was only 67 percent.

What are the reasons for the population explosion in the less developed areas, the so-called Third World?* Two basic factors account for this development: higher birthrates than in the economically advanced countries and falling death rates during the past 35 years. Table 3.8 shows that the birthrates in the less developed countries are generally higher than in the developed states, although in

---

* The Free World and Communist countries constitute the first two "worlds."

Table 3.7: Estimated Populations for 1920, 1940, 1960, 1980, and 2000
(in millions)

Major Area	1920	1940	1960	1980	2000
World Total	1860	2295	2991	4318	6112
More developed areas	604	729	854	1042	1266
Europe	325	379	425	479	527
North America	116	144	199	262	354
Soviet Union	155	195	214	278	353
Oceania	8	11	16	23	32
Less developed areas	1256	1566	2137	3276	4846
East Asia	553	634	794	1041	1287
South Asia	470	610	858	1408	2153
Latin America	90	130	212	378	638
Africa	143	192	273	449	768
Other developed areas	673	821	976	1194	1441
Other less developed areas	1187	1474	2015	3125	4671

SOURCE: United Nations, *Growth of the World's Urban and Rural Population, 1920–2000* (New York, 1969), p. 59, Table 32.

some of the Third World countries they begin to register a decline between 1964 and 1970. On the other hand, the death rates in the Third World which, because of high infant mortality and a relatively short span of life, were very high in 1938, dropped dramatically by 1970. This drop was the result of two main factors: (1) more and better food plus improved facilities for transporting and storing food, and (2) better sanitary conditions and health care made possible by the introduction of pesticides and antibiotics in many formerly backward areas.[5]

These conditions have produced annual population growth rates that have exceeded 3 percent in some Asian and Latin American countries (for example, Malaysia and Costa Rica), a rate that would double the population every 23 years or less. If these trends were to persist, the consequences for the less developed countries would be insufficiency of food for their people and widespread unemployment, imposing severe burdens on governments already struggling with difficult economic and political problems.

We must realize, of course, that long-range projections of population growth are hazardous. Inventions, such as birth control pills, and specific governmental policies either providing tax incentives for large families or propagandizing birth control measures have an impact on population growth rates, although the effect of the latter in less developed countries with high rates of illiteracy is often

Table 3.8: Crude Birth and Death Rates for Selected Countries, 1938–1970 (per thousand)

Country	Birthrate				Death Rate			
	1938	1953	1964	1970	1938	1953	1964	1970
North America								
Canada	20.7	28.1	23.4	17.6	9.7	8.6	7.5	7.3
Costa Rica	45.0	49.2	43.0	33.9	17.7	11.7	8.5	7.5
El Salvador	43.7	47.9	47.1	39.9	19.1	14.7	10.4	9.9
Mexico	43.5	44.7	44.8	41.3	22.9	. 15.8	9.9	9.2
Nicaragua	40.8	42.3	42.8	43.8	14.5	10.2	7.3	8.0
Panama	45.5	37.9	33.9	36.2	14.2	9.2	7.3	7.3
Puerto Rico	38.6	35.3	30.6	25.7	18.7	8.2	7.2	5.9
United States	17.6	24.7	21.0	18.2	10.6	9.6	9.4	9.4
South America								
Chile	36.1	34.6	34.1	26.6	23.1	12.4	11.1	9.0
Peru	--	36.0	38.9	31.9	16.2	12.2	10.1	7.6
Venezuela	33.7	46.1	43.4	43.6	18.3	9.9	7.1	6.7
Europe								
Austria	13.9	14.8	18.5	15.1	14.0	12.0	12.3	13.2
Belgium	16.0	16.6	17.2	14.7	13.2	12.1	11.7	12.7
Bulgaria	22.8	20.9	16.1	16.9	13.7	9.3	8.2	9.5
Czechoslovakia	16.7	21.2	17.2	15.8	13.2	10.5	9.6	11.4
Denmark	18.1	17.9	17.7	16.8	10.3	9.0	9.9	9.8
Finland	21.0	21.9	17.6	13.7	12.8	9.6	9.3	9.5
France	15.0	18.9	18.2	16.7	15.8	13.1	10.8	10.6
Germany, West	19.7	15.8	18.5	13.3	11.4	11.2	10.8	11.6
Hungary	19.9	21.5	13.1	14.7	14.3	11.7	10.0	11.6
Ireland	19.4	21.2	22.4	21.8	13.6	11.7	11.4	11.5
Italy	23.8	17.7	19.9	16.8	14.1	10.0	9.6	9.7
Luxembourg	14.9	15.2	16.0	13.0	12.7	12.5	11.8	12.2
Netherlands	20.5	21.7	20.7	18.4	8.5	7.7	7.7	8.4
Norway	15.4	18.7	17.7	16.2	9.9	8.5	9.5	9.8
Portugal	26.6	23.4	23.8	18.1	15.4	11.3	10.6	9.7
Romania	29.5	23.8	15.2	21.1	19.1	11.6	8.1	9.6
Spain	20.1	20.6	22.2	19.8	19.3	9.7	8.7	8.6
Sweden	14.9	15.4	16.0	13.6	11.5	9.7	10.0	9.9
Switzerland	15.2	17.0	19.2	15.9	11.6	10.2	9.1	9.0
United Kingdom	15.5	15.9	18.8	16.2	11.8	11.4	11.3	11.9
Asia								
Ceylon	35.8	38.7	33.2	31.8	21.0	10.7	8.8	7.9
India	33.3	24.8	--	--	23.7	14.5	--	10.3
Israel	26.3	32.1	25.7	27.0	8.1	6.7	6.3	7.0
Japan	27.1	21.5	17.8	18.9	17.7	8.9	6.9	6.9
Other								
Australia	17.4	22.9	20.6	20.5	39.6	9.1	9.0	9.0
New Zealand	19.3	25.4	24.2	22.1	10.5	9.0	8.8	8.8
South Africa	25.0	25.2	23.7	23.6	9.5	8.6	7.7	7.3

SOURCE: *Information Please Almanac Atlas and Yearbook,* 1971 ed. pp. 665–673.

relatively small. Especially in Latin America, doctrines of the Catholic church opposing birth control severely hamper attempts to curb the population explosion. Nevertheless, there are signs that at least in the industrially advanced countries the rate of population growth has been slowed; in fact, the United States may experience stability or even a slight loss during the next decade. There are also indications that the population growth in the Third World is beginning to slow down, especially in India and China. Hence, the much feared doubling of the world's population from 4 billion to 8 billion by the year 2000 is now far from certain.

Quality

Although large populations provide labor and military manpower, the quality of that manpower, in terms of education and health, is a crucial matter in assessing its contribution to the strength of a nation.

Education   A high percentage of illiteracy and low levels of education in the labor force preclude the establishment of advanced industrial plants, although extensive training programs and automated production lines may overcome these deficiencies in certain instances. Some less developed countries, such as Taiwan, Singapore, and Mauritius, with a relatively well-educated labor force have been able to attract investments for assembly plants for sophisticated electronic equipment while, because of the lack of appropriate and sufficient educational facilities, the bulk of the labor force in some of the African countries so far has been usable only for traditional farming chores and primitive manufacturing jobs. A variety of skills and varied consumption needs are the ingredients necessary for the development of a prosperous and varied economy.

Although a large manpower pool is required for a powerful military establishment, literacy plus an adequate education are needed to employ sophisticated weapon systems and to maintain tanks, missile launchers, supersonic jet planes, and electronic gear in operating condition. However, as the Israeli-Arab War of October 1973 demonstrated, intensive training programs by Russian advisers have been able to overcome some of the educational deficiencies that plagued Egyptian military manpower during the 1950s and 1960s.

Health   Good health is also important if the population is to represent a factor of strength in a country. Good health assures stamina in the execution of economic and military tasks; hence higher productivity rates can be achieved and the military can obtain a better type of soldier. A healthy population is also a strong morale factor. Although conditions vary from country to country and from region to region within a country, the quality of health in most economically advanced countries, whether capitalist or communist, is relatively good, and hospital facilities are satisfactory. But in many countries of the Third World, this has not been so. In fact, most less developed countries have been characterized by a high degree of disease and often poor medical facilities with the small number of available medical personnel seriously overtaxed. In the Third World, one physician must serve 4,300 people; whereas, in developed countries, the figure drops to 800. Unfortunately, the improvement of these deplorable conditions has been very slow.

Composition

Racial Differences Finally, a few observations need to be made about the composition of a population. A racially divided population constitutes a vulnerability that can be exploited by outside forces. This does not mean that two or more races cannot live together successfully and congenially within a state; but as every American recognizes, it requires a special effort to erase racial prejudices and to bring about a large degree of integration on the basis of full equality. Great Britain, which during the past decade has seen an influx of Blacks and East Indians, has grappled with the problem of integrating the races, but so far a fully satisfactory solution has been elusive. One solution is expulsion of the racial minority, and this has been the approach of President Idi Amin of Uganda, who expelled the East Indians living in his country.

Ethnic Diversity Ethnic diversity poses problems similar to those created by racial division, but is less a source of vulnerability. Despite adhering to many of their own traditions, habits, and sometimes language, ethnic groups in the United States have largely been able to live successfully together and, therefore, are not a liability to be reckoned against the country's strength. The same can also be said of Switzerland. The Soviet Union, another example of ethnic and racial diversity, has so far successfully managed this problem through insistence upon ideological uniformity, the pervasive nature of the Communist party apparatus, and centralized planning of the economy. On the other hand, the split between the Flemish and Walloons in Belgium is a distinct weakening factor and has made government in that country a cumbersome and often inefficient affair. Regional minorities, such as the Bretons in France, the Welsh in Great Britain, or the Siebenbuergen Germans in Romania, are but minor weakening elements, but individual cases need to be judged separately for specific periods of time.

Religious Differences   Religious differences can constitute serious vulnerabilities in some countries, as events in Northern Ireland and the history of Pakistan demonstrate; but in many other states, such as the Federal Republic of Germany and the United States, these differences have only very minor significance in terms of national power.

In summary, population is one factor that determines the strength or weakness of a country. Such aspects of population as size, structure, quality, and composition must be assessed before a balanced judgment can be made. Comprehensive, accurate calculations and projections are often difficult, and other factors such as economic development have a bearing on demographic assessments.

ECONOMIC DEVELOPMENT

One of the most decisive elements of a country's strength is its economic development. In many respects this element may have a greater bearing on its political power position than its military strength because, without a strong economic posture, it is difficult to build a powerful military establishment. Economic activities have a direct impact on the implementation of foreign policy: a government's ability to press its demands on other states, to have appeal as an ally, and to exert viable pressure on foes is dependent upon a high level of economic development. In today's world of enormous economic interchange and giant economic entities such as MNEs, the line between economic and political activities is often blurred, and the name of the game is "ecopolitics."

How Is It Measured?

Gross National Product   How can we measure the economic development of a country? The most common way is by comparing the national output of goods and services known as the Gross National Product (GNP). GNP is computed in money paid for goods and services. Table 3.9 shows the GNP of selected top-ranking countries, as well as figures for selected other states, including some in the Third World. This table suggests that the United States and the

Table 3.9: Indicators of the Economic Element of Power of Selected Countries

Country	GNP Millions of Dollars	GNP per Capita	GNP Growth Rate	National Income	National Income per Capita	Rank per Capita
United States	$1,151,800	$5,515	6.4%	$875,379[a]	$4,274[a]	1
Soviet Union	570,000[c]	2,325[c]	5.6[f]	410,400[c]	1,673[c]	14
Japan	341,035	3,218	9.2	171,385[b]	1,658[b]	15
West Germany	292,045	4,736	2.9	166,112[b]	2,698[b]	6
France	220,800	4,269	5.5	132,344[b]	2,606[b]	8
United Kingdom	152,340	2,731	3.5	111,010[b]	1,993[b]	11
China	125,000[c]	156[c]	4.0[c]	--	--	--
Italy	118,440	2,179	3.1	85,197[b]	1,587[b]	16
Canada	103,000	4,714	5.5	68,812[b]	3,214[b]	3
India	52,920[b]	96[b]	3.5[e]	46,219[a]	86[a]	25
Australia	52,740	4,069	2.0	32,999[b]	2,629[b]	7
Spain	50,725	1,471	7.5	29,928[b]	889[b]	20
Netherlands	50,000	3,751	4.0	28,075[b]	2,156[b]	10
Poland	48,600[c]	1,480[c]	5.1[c]	37,070[b]	1,123[b]	17
Sweden	44,350	5,462	2.4	29,704[b]	3,695[b]	2
East Germany	40,000[c]	2,300[c]	4.5[e]	--	--	--
Brazil	34,600[b]	364[b]	4.8[d]	32,482[b]	341[b]	22
Czechoslovakia	34,000[c]	2,360[c]	4.1[c]	26,231[b]	1,809[b]	12
Mexico	33,180[b]	1,300[c]	9.9[b]	--	--	--

[a] Figures from 1969
[b] Figures from 1970
[c] Figures from 1971
[d] Figures from 1960–69
[e] Figures from 1960–70
[f] Figures from 1966–70

SOURCE: *The United Nations Statistical Yearbook 1971; The United Nations Statistical Yearbook 1972; Overseas Business Reports,* U.S. Department of Commerce; "Market Profiles for Eastern Europe, U.S.S.R. and People's Republic of China," March 1973; "Basic Data on the Economy of the People's Republic of China," September 1972; *The 1973 World Almanac and Book of Facts;* News Release, Bureau of Public Affairs, Department of State, August 1973.

Soviet Union are the top producers of goods and services. It is interesting to see, for example, that an enormous disparity exists between the GNP of the United States (accounting for more than $1 trillion) and that of Sweden.

GNP per Capita   It is often useful to relate GNP to the population of a country, which gives us the so-called GNP per capita. When we do so, we see that Sweden ranks much higher and the Soviet Union drops down. However, GNP per capita figures do not accurately indicate the economic benefits derived by individual citizens. For example, a country such as Kuwait with its tremendous production of oil may have a very high GNP per capita, but the benefits stemming from the high GNP flow only to a very small portion of the population.

Per Capita Income   A more refined way of looking at the strength of a nation in terms of economic development is to look at statistics for per capita incomes. Table 3.9 reveals that on this basis the United States was the leader in 1970, but that the Soviet Union ranked relatively low. Sweden and Switzerland were able to surpass the United States in 1975 by a small amount, and their citizens now enjoy the highest per capita income.

Per capita income in the Third World has remained desperately low. Less developed countries normally are those whose population have average annual incomes of $150 per person or less, with the *very* poor countries struggling to attain $50 per person. More than two-thirds of the world's people fall into the underdeveloped category; and despite large-scale foreign aid from the industrially advanced countries in the Free and Communist worlds, only a few countries have been able to improve their economic position materially.* Most of these countries are characterized not only by low incomes, but by a low level of education and high degree of disease as well. Their populations are often engaged in traditional agriculture, and their societal structures reflect long-standing traditions and tribal loyalties.

Industrialization   One of the greatest ambitions of the less developed countries has been industrialization. The leaders of the Third World have looked toward industrialization as the key to solving their economic problems. Whether industrialization is always the appropriate long-term solution is doubtful because many of these countries have only very limited markets for their goods. A better way to upgrade their economies may be diversification in agricul-

---

* Because of the disparity of incomes among the developing countries—Brazil, Mexico, Taiwan have done quite well while Chad and the Central African Republic are examples of the very poor countries—some scholars now divide the developing countries into Third, Fourth, and Fifth worlds with the latter being comprised of the poorest countries.

Table 3.10: Countries Most Industrialized on the Basis of the Percentage
of Nonagricultural Activities in Total Civilian Employment

Country	Percentage of Nonagricultural Activities in Total Civilian Employment
United Kingdom	97.07
United States	95.37
Belgium	94.81
Canada	92.47
Netherlands	92.40
Switzerland	92.16
Sweden	91.23
West Germany	90.38
Luxembourg	88.39
Denmark	88.14
Japan	86.02
Norway	85.33
France	84.93
Iceland	82.21

SOURCE: *Labor Force Statistics 1958–1969* (Paris: Organization for
Economic Co-operation and Development, 1971).

tural crops. Whatever the solution, there is no doubt that the degree
of industrialization of a country is a meaningful element in determining its economic strength. An indicator of industrialization is the
proportion of the working population engaged in nonagricultural
pursuits. Table 3.10 lists most industrialized nations of the world,
and it is apparent that some of the most powerful countries are
ranking members of this group. Significantly, the Soviet Union is
not among the top-ranking members because it continues to employ
large numbers of its population in agriculture.

Production and Consumption of Electric Energy   An important measure of a country's strength is its production of electric
energy and the per capita consumption of energy produced by all
sources, including petroleum, natural gas, and coal. Tables 3.11 and
3.12 indicate that the United States and the Soviet Union are the
leading producers of electric energy, followed by Japan, West Germany, and Canada; but in the per capita consumption of energy,
Canada, Australia, Germany, and the United Kingdom surpass the
Soviet Union. We want to reemphasize that all of the economically
advanced countries with the exception of the Soviet Union depend
on the Third World, especially the Middle East and South America,
for their supplies of oil, a major source of energy production.

Table 3.11: Electric Energy Production, 1974 (in billions of KWH)

Country	Billions of Kilowatt Hours
United States	1967.3
Soviet Union	975.8
Japan	460.7
United Kingdom	273.3
West Germany	311.6
Canada	278.9
France	180.4
Italy	147.1
East Germany	80.3
Poland	91.6

SOURCE: *UN Statistical Yearbook*, 1975 (New York: United Nations Publishing Service).

Production of Goods and Services   Another means of measuring the economic development of a country is to make a careful analysis of the goods and services it produces. Some economic systems are oriented predominantly toward the welfare of their people and thereby attain a relatively high standard of living for their citizens. These systems normally emphasize production of consumer goods. Other systems are geared to increase as quickly as possible the country's productive capacity, which means that the output of factories is focused on capital goods. Finally, some countries, such as the Soviet Union, have sought to maximize their military capabilities; and if one makes a comparative analysis of the GNP of the Soviet Union and the United States, especially during the 1950s and 1960s, one can see that a large portion of the Soviet GNP stems from the production of military items and capital goods.

Other Analyses of GNP

Another way of analyzing GNP is to determine its allocation into goods and services for (1) personal consumption, (2) domestic investment, (3) government expenditures, and (4) foreign investment.

Personal Consumption   We have already suggested that personal consumption varies considerably from country to country. In some countries it reaches as high as 80 percent, but on the other hand it rarely drops below 50 percent. There is a tendency in all countries for personal consumption to absorb an increasing share of the nation's production of goods and services.

Table 3.12: Per Capita Consumption of Energy in Selected Countries, 1974 (in kilograms)

Country	Kilograms per Capita
United States	11,485
Canada	9,816
Australia	5,997
West Germany	5,689
United Kingdom	5,464
Soviet Union	5,252
France	4,330
Japan	3,830
Italy	3,227
Mexico	1,269
Brazil	646
Colombia	636
China	632
Turkey	629
India	201
Pakistan	188
Ghana	184
Paraguay	173
Indonesia	158
Nigeria	94

SOURCE: *UN Statistical Yearbook, 1975* (New York: United Nations Publishing Service).

Domestic Investment   Savings play an important role in economic growth as they may be the major source for the accumulation of capital, which in turn provides a major source for investment; therefore, domestic investment is a factor in a country's economic strength in that the higher the rate of investment, the higher the rate of increase in the nation's GNP. In the marginal economies of the Third World, expenditures on goods and services may reduce savings to an extent that economic growth is impossible.

Government Expenditures   Another category of allocation that has increased continually over the past two or three decades is the percentage of GNP allocated to government. Normally, this percentage is greater in communist countries than in capitalistic countries because the bureaucracy plays a much larger role in every aspect of society, including the provision of goods and services, in communist countries.

The proportion flowing into the military establishment can also be seen from the percentage of the GNP allocated to the country's

Table 3.13: Comparisons of Defense Expenditures, 1977

Country	Millions of Dollars	Dollars per Capita	Percent of Government Expenditure	Percent of GNP (1976)
NATO Countries				
Belgium	2,476	253	10.4	3.0
Britain	11,214	201	11.4	5.1
Canada	3,348	144	N.A.	1.9
Denmark	1,103	217	6.8	2.8
France	13,740	256	20.4	3.7
Germany, West	16,602	263	22.9	3.6
Greece	1,100	120	N.A.	5.5
Italy	4,416	78	8.3	2.6
Luxembourg	28	80	2.9	1.2
Netherlands	3,357	241	9.7	3.4
Norway	1,194	295	9.9	3.1
Portugal	508	52	19.2	3.9
Turkey	2,653	64	21.1	5.6
United States	113,000	523	24.4	6.0
Warsaw Pact Countries				
Bulgaria	538	61	7.3	2.6
Czechoslovakia	1,805	108	6.2	3.5
Germany, East	2,889	167	7.8	6.0
Hungary	590	56	3.6	2.6
Poland	2,438	70	N.A.	3.6
Romania	824	38	N.A.	1.8
Soviet Union	127,000 (est.)	N.A.	N.A.	12.0 (est.)

SOURCE: *The Military Balance, 1977–78* (London: International Institute for Strategic Studies), p. 82.

military effort. Table 3.13 indicates that as of 1977 the United States devoted 6 percent of its GNP to defense expenditures, the largest allocation of any of the NATO countries. Among the communist countries, the Soviet Union spends the largest percent of its GNP on defense (about 12 percent), and Romania spends the least (1.8 percent). In terms of net figures, the Soviet Union expended $127 billion on defense in 1977, while the United States spent only $113 billion. We should stress that statistics regarding allocation of the GNP to the military establishment can be taken only as information about the level and intensity of a country's military effort: they say nothing about its quality and specific characteristics.

Foreign Investment   Finally, the share of the GNP going to foreign investment is important, particularly if it is linked to balance-of-payments data. The ratio of imports and exports to GNP provides some insights into the strength or vulnerability of a country. The higher this ratio, the more a country is dependent for its economic posture on external factors and often on the goodwill of other countries. A low ratio suggests relative independence from external factors and conditions. An example is the United States, whose economic well-being is assured primarily by the tremendous business generated within its boundaries and whose exports amount to only 7 percent of GNP. As indicated earlier, however, despite her high degree of self-sufficiency in raw materials, the United States must import certain essential items from abroad, and this constitutes a definite vulnerability. Indeed, the U.S. balance-of-payments deficit reached record dimension in 1977 as a result of the continually growing oil imports (about $30 billion).

There are other means for determining a country's economic strength, but detailed discussion of them would exceed the scope of this book. Suffice it to reiterate that a strong industrial economy is a very important element in the power status of a country. Not only does it produce the weapons and supplies required for modern warfare, but it also provides important international rewards that flow from the use of consumer goods and capital equipment for border-crossing trade and aid. At the same time, a strong economy offers markets for the goods of other countries. These factors help a country build a strong position of power in the global arena and, at the same time, assure a high standard of living at home with favorable implications for governmental and political stability.

SCIENCE AND TECHNOLOGY

Perhaps the most pervasive determinants of a country's strength are its capabilities in scientific research and advanced technology. These determinants can modify the impact of all other elements of power, but their direct effect is most noticeable on economic development, communications, and the offensive and defensive capabilities of the military establishment.

Economic Development

In the field of economic development, science and technology play a dramatic role in modifying the traditional factors. Many manufacturing processes have been revolutionized through the application of computer technology. Push-button manufacturing techniques may make it less essential to have a well-educated labor force, a condition that could make it possible to use uneducated laborers in less developed countries to produce sophisticated goods. Science and technology have also produced substitutes for scarce materials. In some instances, these substitute materials, such as industrial fibers and plastics, have become attractive products in their own right, serving new markets.

Transportation and Communication

Radical technological advances have been made in transportation and communications. Regardless of their impact on the environment, supersonic planes are here to stay and will be used increasingly. Trains that will move at speeds of 300 miles per hour or more are on the drawing boards. Hydrofoils and hovercrafts offer rapid transportation across waterways and, perhaps, oceans.

The transmission of communications has also benefited from new technology. Pictures can be transmitted by electronic means in a matter of minutes, and space satellites offer instant and very reliable communications across vast distances.

Technological advances have improved the collection of information for intelligence purposes and have already revolutionized the traditional means of diplomacy. Sophisticated bugging devices, miniature tape recorders, and miniature cameras have given intelligence collection agencies new tools for their trade. Observation by space satellites and immediate transmission of these observations have made it very difficult for individual countries to hide military preparations.

The Military

In the military field, science and technology have influenced the mobility and fire power of the armed forces. During World War I, the development of mines, torpedoes, and submarines provided new and effective weapons against the enemy's merchant marine and navies. A long sequence of inventions multiplied the per capita fire power of military forces. Aircraft, although still in their infancy, gave promise of the ability to overcome topographic barriers and strongly fortified frontiers.

While during World War II the defensive advantages of geographic space still constituted a viable defensive cushion against military attack, excepting perhaps aerial bombardment, no country in Western Europe was large enough to absorb the shock of modern mobile warfare. Although the Soviet Union could still trade space against time and move factories to the comparative security of inner Asia, Western Europe did not possess this capability. The Blitzkrieg was made possible by the invention of rapidly moving tanks and other mechanized equipment. Radio and later radar made it feasible to control military operations far from their bases.

Since World War II, science and technology have further increased military capabilities. Missiles with extraordinary destructive power can reach virtually every part of the world. Nuclear power is used to fuel ships which carry nuclear missiles over long distances. Chemical and bacteriological weapons have been invented but, fortunately, little used. At the same time antiballistic missiles, if they can be refined further, may bolster the defensive capabilities of countries. At present, the full military potential of space satellites and space stations cannot be foreseen.

To appreciate the international significance of the revolution in science and technology, we must keep in mind the tendency of scientific discoveries and their engineering applications to be cumulative, to accelerate quickly, and to diffuse rapidly from the country of origin. The discovery of nuclear energy and its application to the generation of electricity are examples. Thus, most of the important discoveries and inventions of the past 300 years are links in a chain of interrelated events. Engineering advances are made faster than individuals and governments can adjust to them. In other words, mankind may well be faced with a "runaway technology."[6] Finally, knowledge of scientific discoveries, new theories, and technological advances can be spread from country to country despite governmental efforts to prevent such movements. The reason is that much of the recently gained knowledge can be communicated in the universal language of mathematics, which can easily overcome linguistic barriers.

Research and Development

Countries not possessing advanced technologies may well become technologically dependent on other countries, which may impair their political independence and constitute a serious element of weakness. In turn, scientific and technological advances have become a symbol of national prestige and an indicator of status and rank in international political systems. Much depends on governmental attitude toward supporting research and development activities and the financial capability of individual governments to extend such support. Of course, the private sector can also be a potent source of funds for research and development; subsidiaries of multinational corporations may offer smaller and weaker countries a chance to improve their research and development potential.

SUMMARY

The differential between the strengths and weaknesses of two or more countries is the basis for understanding the term **power.** The basic elements that determine the actual and potential power of a state are the geography (including natural resources), population, economic development, science and technology, traditions and social psychology, government and administration, and military organization.

In terms of **geography,** large **size** is a clear advantage. Small countries have never achieved great power status, although such middle-sized ones as Great Britain and France were able to do so in the 19th and early 20th centuries. In a large country, people and industrial plants can be dispersed, rendering the total population less vulnerable to nuclear attack, and vast territories are more difficult for an occupation force to control.

Technological advances have made **topography** a less important consideration than it once was in that topographic barriers that impeded ground forces do not hamper air and space attacks.

Climate is another geographic feature influencing the power of a state. In terms of human activity, the temperate zone areas between 20 and 60 degrees north and south have been most favorable; and in modern times, the great powers of the world have been located in these areas. Technological advances are now being used to temper climatic extremes and make other zones more attractive.

Natural resources, consisting of both minerals and the ability to produce foodstuffs, are another determinant of self-sufficiency and national strength. Nations must import essential resources they do not have, and the need to import renders them more vulnerable. For example, petroleum shortfall may squeeze the United States, Europe, and Japan by 1985.

Man-made **physical features,** including transportation and communication nets, also play an important role in determining national strength.

When assessing **population** as a determinant of power, we must look at its size, structure, quality (in terms of both health and education), and racial, ethnic, and religious composition. One important consideration is the proportion of the population in the most productive age bracket, that is, between the ages of 15 and 44 years. Another is the growth rate.

Economic development is often measured in terms of Gross National Product (GNP), or per capita income. The United States and the Soviet Union are top producers of goods and services, while the citizens of Sweden and Switzerland enjoy the highest per capita income.

Economic development can also be assessed in terms of production and consumption of energy and of the type of goods and services produced. Some countries concentrate on producing **consumer goods** while others focus on the production of military items or **capital goods** to increase their productive capacity.

The degree of **industrialization** of a country is also a meaningful element in determining its strength. An indicator of industrialization is the proportion of the working population engaged in nonagricultural pursuits.

Perhaps the most pervasive determinants of a country's strength are its capabilities in **scientific research** and **advanced technology.** Science and technology have produced substitutes for raw materials, improved transportation and communication, made more sophisticated the collection of intelligence information, and revolutionized the traditional means of diplomacy. Countries not possessing advanced technologies may well become technologically dependent on other countries, which may impair their political independence and constitute a serious element of weakness.

NOTES

1. A. F. K. Organski, *World Politics* (New York: Knopf, 1967), p. 96.

2. Sir Halford J. Mackinder, *Democratic Ideals and Reality* (New York: Holt, 1919), p. 150. An American Admiral, Alfred T. Mahan, considered sea power to be the most important determinant for national power strategy. Cf. his book *The Influence of Sea Power Upon History* (Boston: Little, Brown, 1890).

3. See David H. Blake and Robert S. Walters, *The Politics of Global Economic Relations* (Englewood Cliffs, N.J.: Prentice Hall, 1976), p. 176.

4. Hans J. Morgenthau, *Politics Among Nations*, 5th ed. (New York: Knopf, 1973), p. 126.

5. For more details on the demographic transition from preindustrial agrarian economies to advanced industrial societies, see Harold and Margaret Sprout, *Foundations of International Politics* (Princeton, N.J.: Van Nostrand, 1962), pp. 399–405.

6. Sprout and Sprout, op. cit., p. 216.

SUGGESTED READINGS

Baldwin, Robert E. *Nontariff Distortions of International Trade.* Washington, D.C.: The Brookings Institution, 1970

Bhagwati, J. N., ed. *Economics and World Order.* New York: Macmillan, 1972.

Borrie, W. D. *The Growth and Control of World Population.* London: Weidenfeld and Nicolson, 1970.

Ehrlich, Paul R., and Anne H. Ehrlich. *Population, Resources, Environment: Issues in Human Ecology.* 2nd ed. San Francisco: W. H. Freeman, 1972.

Fox, Annette B. *The Power of Small States: Diplomacy in World War II.* Chicago: University of Chicago Press, 1959.

Kindleberger, Charles P. *Power and Money: The Economics of International Politics and the Politics of International Economics.* New York: Basic Books, 1970.

Morgenthau, Hans J. *Politics Among Nations.* 4th ed. New York: Knopf, 1968.

Organski, Katherine, and A. F. K. Organski. *Population and World Power.* New York: Knopf, 1961.

Robbins, Lionel. *The Economic Causes of War.* New York: H. Fertig, 1968. .

CHAPTER FOUR
THE DETERMINANTS
OF NATIONAL POWER:
VARIABLE FACTORS

Up to now we have discussed elements of a state's strength or weakness that lend themselves to generally quantitative evaluations, or whose effects can be measured quantitatively. We will turn now to more subjective factors, whose evaluation depends more on subjective judgments than on statistical or mathematical analyses and later in this chapter to factors with both objective and subjective elements.

TRADITION AND SOCIAL PSYCHOLOGY

Common historical experiences of a people leave a definite imprint and are apt to create traditions bearing on their persistence in the pursuit of national objectives and on their morale. If these experiences have been favorable, they are likely to bolster the resolve of citizens of a country to persevere even in the face of serious obstacles. If the reverse is true, quick demoralization may set in. Thus the dead hand of the past continues to influence the present and becomes a factor of either strength or weakness.

Historical experiences and evolved traditions also affect what is often called the "national character" of a people. They influence values and belief systems held by the people in a particular state, contribute to their images of themselves and of other people in the world, and affect their social behavior in general.

National Stereotypes and Character

All of us generalize from time to time about our national character and that of other people. Figure 4.1 shows some of the stereotyped attitudes displayed by nationals of various countries toward Americans, Russians, and the British. Clearly the images of citizens of these three nations held, for example, by Germans differ drastically —some are favorable and others, unfavorable—but we should also note that the British and French views of the Americans are at considerable variance as well.

The aspects of national character as they affect the strength of a country go far beyond the stereotypes in Figure 4.1. They include attitudes toward authority, obedience, loyalty, service to the state, and toward those who serve the state, as well as what roles should be played by particular members of the national community. These attitudes affect the conception of national purpose and destiny and create an image of a state as a desirable ally or a foe. All these aspects of national character are likely to have a significant bearing on how well the people of a country stand up under stress and react to adversity and overwhelming disaster such as a nuclear attack. National character is also likely to be important in deciding whether a people will fight an aggressor, either by open warfare or guerrilla tactics, or quickly accept defeat and acquiesce to occupation.* In 1938 and again in 1968, the Czechs chose the latter against the German and Soviet armies, respectively. The Yugoslavs employed effective guerrilla tactics against their German occupiers during World War II, and few doubt that the British would have battled to the finish if Hitler had initiated an invasion of Great Britain.

Nationalism

We stated earlier that national character affects attitudes toward authority and loyalty and colors images of a country's own people as well as those of other peoples. These attitudes are also ingredients

---

* Other factors may be the topography of a country, which also may influence national character. For example, mountains have had an impact on the national character of the Swiss.

Figure 4.1: Popular Stereotypes of Other Nationalities

Popular Stereotypes of Other Nationalities

The six adjectives most frequently used to describe three nations
in descending order of percentage
(braces indicate a tie in percentage)

Description of Americans (U.S.) by:

Australians	British	French	Germans
progressive	progressive	practical	progressive
practical	⎰conceited	progressive	generous
intelligent	⎱generous	domineering	practical
conceited	peace-loving	⎰hardworking	intelligent
peace-loving	⎰intelligent	⎱intelligent	peace-loving
generous	⎱practical	⎰generous	hardworking
		⎱self-controlled	

Italians	Dutch	Norwegians
generous	practical	hardworking
practical	progressive	practical
hardworking	hardworking	progressive
intelligent	⎰generous	generous
progressive	⎱peace-loving	peace-loving
peace-loving	intelligent	intelligent

Description of Russians by:

Australians	British	French	Germans
domineering	hardworking	backward	cruel
hardworking	domineering	hardworking	backward
cruel	cruel	domineering	⎰hardworking
backward	backward	brave	⎱domineering
brave	brave	cruel	brave
progressive	⎰practical	progressive	practical
	⎱progressive		

Italians	Dutch	Norwegians	Americans (U.S.)
backward	cruel	hardworking	cruel
cruel	domineering	domineering	⎰hardworking
domineering	backward	backward	⎱domineering
⎰hardworking	hardworking	brave	backward
⎱brave	brave	cruel	⎰conceited
⎰intelligent	progressive	practical	⎱brave
⎱progressive			

Description of British by:

Germans	Dutch	Americans
intelligent	self-controlled	intelligent
self-controlled	peace-loving	⎰brave
conceited	⎰practical	⎱hardworking
domineering	⎱conceited	peace-loving
practical	hardworking	conceited
progressive	intelligent	self-controlled

SOURCE: Harold Sprout and Margaret Sprout, *Foundations of International Politics* (Princeton, N.J.: D. Van Nostrand, 1962), pp. 494–495.

in the powerful force of *nationalism*,[1] which has played such an important role in world politics. Much has been written about the causes and nature of nationalism, but its base is clearly found in the common experiences, common values, common cultures, and common outlook of a distinct group of people who constitute a nation or aspire to become a nation. The highest value is placed on loyalty to the nation: when conflicts of loyalty arise between the nation or other groups, they must be resolved in favor of the former. A common language, or religion, or color may assist in the growth of nationalism, but such shared characteristics are not essential, as is demonstrated by Switzerland, the Soviet Union, and the United States. Territorial contiguity may not be necessary for the force of nationalism to operate, as East Prussia's separation from the rest of Germany between 1918 and 1939 proved; however, territorially divided Pakistan did not survive when the people of East Pakistan opted overwhelmingly for autonomy, and the state of Bangladesh emerged in December 1971.

Once strongly imbedded in a country, nationalism gains strength and momentum by itself and becomes an ingrained attitude. It is usually reinforced by a variety of symbols, such as flags, national anthems, national shrines, and sacred literature. Powerful slogans have been used to bolster nationalism, as exemplified by "the sun never sets on the British empire," and more than one nation considers itself to be "God's chosen people" or "God's country."

Nationalism arose as a mass movement following the French Revolution when the national feelings of the "common man" became an immensely important factor in the relations between states. From then on, wars were fought by common men who proudly called themselves citizens but no longer felt themselves subjects. The battle flags were deployed in the name of freedom and equality, as well as for the sacred and inalienable rights of nations. Thus, the common man was entering on his new political career, both as a citizen and as a patriot. The French example of genuine mass patriotism infected the whole continent of Europe, and mass nationalism began to spread all the way from Spain to Russia. The idea that man owed his highest allegiance to his nation was taking hold among all European peoples, reinforcing political structures that had previously come into existence.

Although a destructive factor, inasmuch as it has produced international tension and hostility, nationalism has also been a constructive element in that it has provided a cohesive force in the newly independent states in Asia and Africa that have emerged since 1945. It has transformed the political map of the world during the past

200 years and has been gaining in importance as an element in social solidarity as other social ties, such as those of the family, the church, and the local community, have been weakening.

Societal Cleavages

We have already discussed the possible problems of racially, ethnically, or religiously divided countries. Such cleavages may weaken a country politically by reducing its ability to engage in war successfully and may also weaken it economically. In addition, these cleavages may change attitudes toward education and lower academic standards and achievement. As a result, scientific research efforts may be adversely affected and technological advances may be slow in coming. Similar consequences may be the result of hostile attitudes toward intellectuals, whose prestige may be downgraded when they are seen as "eggheads" and "ivory tower dreamers" who have lost all touch with reality. On the other hand, if intellectuals and scientists feel that their accomplishments are appreciated, they are likely to be spurred on in their research efforts.

Another important attitudinal factor is acceptance of change. If a people objects to change and insists on maintaining traditional ways of life, economic, scientific, and industrial development suffers. By definition, science and technology must be innovative. The major question must be: How can something be done better than before? If such aspirations permeate a society, economic development is likely to be helped. The people in some, but by no means all, of the very backward nations have resisted innovations and chosen to cling to the life-style of their forefathers, thereby impairing economic progress.

Ideological Cohesion

Ideologies are systematic complexes of ideas and beliefs that may either be nonpolitical (for example, a religious creed such as that of Islam or Christianity) or political (oriented toward political institutions, forms of action, and goals). Democracy or communism fall into the latter category. Ideologies are assumed to have universal relevance. When efforts are made to spread them, the appeal is to reason and experience. Within our context we are chiefly interested in political ideologies and especially in liberal democracy as developed in the 19th century, Marxism and communism, and militant nationalism.

Although political ideologies have usually been forces for revolutionary change and continue to be employed as such by some of the communist states and the developing countries, ideologies can also serve as a cohesive element in a polity. Strong attachments by the population to a particular ideology tend to unify a country and therefore are signs of strength. Sometimes an ideology may be bolstered by a strong dose of conventional nationalism, as occurred in the Soviet Union during World War II. But the intrusion of new political ideas and beliefs into a country may also slowly erode and subvert existing ideologies and therefore become divisive, if not explosively disruptive. Such conditions could affect a country's morale and other capabilities and constitute a serious weakness.[2]

GOVERNMENT AND ADMINISTRATION

Another element of a country's strength defying precise quantitative analysis and evaluation is governmental and administrative style and performance. One factor influencing governmental style and performance is the form of government. We are not talking here about the influence of ideologies and the difference between democratic and autocratic governments, but about the details of the constitutional framework and actual constitutional practice. We should state from the outset that the form of the constitution itself does not automatically reflect constitutional practice. The Soviet Constitution is cast in democratic form and claims to be a federation, but actual practice follows authoritarian and unitary lines. It is also not important whether we are looking at a monarchy or a republic because most monarchies in the industrially advanced countries really are parliamentary democracies with the monarch playing primarily a ceremonial role. The factors that are important in evaluating the form of government are the rapidity of decision making, frictions between branches of government, and the stability and continuity of governments.

Rapidity of Decision Making

The separation-of-powers principle imbedded in the United States Constitution has been an active ingredient in American constitutional practices during the past 200 years and has often caused considerable delays in decisions bearing on American foreign policy. While in national security affairs the executive branch can act with great speed and decisiveness if the need arises, frequent frictions between Congress and the Executive in foreign economic and political matters have reduced the credibility of the United States in the pursuit of its foreign policy goals. Recent examples are the efforts of the Nixon and Ford administrations to enter into new tariff-cutting negotiations with world trading partners and to extend the "most-favored-nation" clause to the Soviet Union. Delays in Congress from 1972 to 1974 in the enactment of necessary legislation hampered these efforts, but an appropriate trade bill was finally passed and signed by the president. This legislation also made it possible to offer special tariff advantages for imported goods manufactured in the Third World, something the U.S. State Department wanted to initiate as early as 1971.

On the other hand, the close cooperation between legislature and executive in parliamentary democracies often makes it possible to arrive at a policy decision quickly. Such efficiency in governmental decision making as exists in Great Britain usually requires a two-party system and a high degree of party discipline. It means that the executive, which is drawn from the ranks of the majority party, can count on the support of the party in most governmental decisions, including those pertaining to foreign policy. In contrast, multiparty parliamentary democracies, such as the Netherlands and Italy, have much greater difficulty in arriving at decisions promptly because coalition governments must bargain with the leaders of various constituent parties for support of each specific decision.

Instability

Perhaps the greatest weakness of governments is instability. The prime example has been France during the Third and Fourth Republics (1875–1958): toward the end of that period, French governments had an average longevity of about six months. Italy's strength has also been sapped by similar governmental problems. Since World War II we have witnessed a continuous succession of different governments although it should be noted that the same individuals were present in many of these governments but held different ministerial posts.

Attitude of the People

The attitude of the people and of elites toward a particular government in power or toward the governmental system in general affects its performance and may raise the question of the legitimacy of its authority. When the population has confidence in the governmental system and accepts it as the proper decision-making unit, governmental authority is legitimized; however, in the event that large segments of the general public and of certain elites lose this confidence and refuse to accept its authority, the country is seriously weakened.

A very good example of the effect the attitude of the people has on governmental performance is Germany under the Weimar Republic from 1919 to 1933. With a large portion of the German people looking at the governmental structure as having emerged from defeat and treason, and continuing to long for the more authoritarian system that prevailed under the emperors, the governments in Germany at that time had difficulty performing their functions and implementing their policies. When the republic was confronted by strong Communist and right-wing gains in various elections between 1930 and 1933, the legitimacy of the government was almost completely eroded and the way cleared for the takeover by Hitler. Although substantially different, the style of actions revealed in the Watergate hearings, as well as activities of White House employees prior and subsequent to the Watergate break-in, eventually weakened the American government's ability to govern. As Henry Kissinger stated at a news conference following his appointment to the post of secretary of state, Watergate affected adversely American foreign policy all over the world.[3] The credibility of American commitments and the ability to implement policy were seriously called into question, and major efforts were required to restore international confidence in U.S. policy declarations.

Another aspect of attitude toward government is the way the population expects to be treated by its bureaucracy, whether the people expect equal treatment and whether they feel that serious consideration is given their point of view. Table 4.1 suggests that in the United States and the United Kingdom the expectation of equal treatment is very high, whereas in Italy and Mexico it is quite low. In Germany, it is between the two extremes. With respect to expectations that different points of view receive serious consideration, we find the United Kingdom ranks highest, followed by Germany and the United States, while in Italy and Mexico such expectations are very low. It is reasonable to assume that the higher the expectations regarding proper treatment by government authorities, the more solid the basis for a strong government.

Administrative Efficiency

Finally, a few words need to be said about the administrative efficiency of government. The general style and performance of the totality of a civil service in a country plays an important role in

Table 4.1: Popular Expectations Regarding Bureaucratic Behavior

Percent Who Say/Expect	United States		United Kingdom		Germany		Italy		Mexico	
	Bureaucrats	Police	Bureaucrats	Police	Bureaucrats	Police	Bureaucrats	Police	Bureaucrats	Police
Question A										
They expect equal treatment	83	85	83	89	65	72	53	56	42	52
They don't expect equal treatment	9	8	7	6	9	5	13	10	50	57
Depends	4	5	6	4	19	15	17	15	5	5
Other	--	--	--	--	--	--	6	6	--	--
Don't Know	4	2	2	0	7	8	11	13	3	5
Total percent	100	100	98	99	100	100	100	100	100	99
Total number	970	970	963	963	955	955	995	995	1007	1007
Question B										
Serious consideration for point of view	48	56	59	74	53	59	35	35	14	12
A little attention	31	22	22	13	18	11	15	13	48	46
To be ignored	6	11	5	5	5	4	11	12	27	29
Depends	11	9	10	6	15	13	21	20	6	7
Other	0	--	--	--	1	2	6	6	--	1
Don't Know	4	2	2	1	8	11	12	14	3	4
Total percent	100	100	98	99	100	100	100	100	98	99
Total number	970	970	963	963	955	955	995	995	1007	1007

Question A: Suppose there were some question that you had to take to a government office, for example, a tax question or housing regulation. Do you think you would be given equal treatment? I mean, would you be treated as well as anyone else? If you had some trouble with the police—a traffic violation maybe, or being accused of a minor offense—do you think you would be given equal treatment? That is, would you be treated as well as anyone else?

Question B: If you explained your point of view to the officials, what effect do you think it would have? Would they give your point of view serious consideration, would they pay only a little attention, or would they ignore what you had to say? If you explained your point of view to the police, what effect do you think it would have? Would they . . . [same choices as before]?"

Source: Gabriel A. Almond and Sidney Verba, *The Civic Culture: Political Attitudes and Democracy in Five Nations*, (Boston: Little, Brown, 1965) pp. 70–72.

determining the strength of a country. Civil services, known for their corruptibility and inefficiencies, cast serious doubt on responsible government action. Waste of time and frequent moonlighting of civil servants, as in Italy, create unfavorable impressions on the population and reduce the power potential of a country. On the other hand, a well-trained, efficient, neutral bureaucracy with a strong commitment to public service bolsters a country's strength. Great Britain and Germany are outstanding examples of countries where this is true. While we must recognize that bureaucratic aspirations and politics play a role in all civil services, the greater the virtues of a civil service as just described and the more a civil service can reflect the objectives of the political leadership in its activities, the stronger is that country's potential for power.

MILITARY ORGANIZATION

The final element in evaluating the strengths and weaknesses of a state is its military organization. We have already discussed some components of this evaluation: the proportion of the population suitable and available for the military services, a high level of economic and industrial development to furnish military materiel and provide financial support, a relatively large-sized allocation of the national output to the military effort, and last, but certainly not least, a high capability in scientific research and technology. What remains to be assessed in the evaluation of the military organization is the size and quality of the armed forces and the quantity, composition, and quality of military equipment.

Size

Table 4.2 provides a quantitative breakdown of military forces for 1975 and certain equipment for a number of countries in 1972. It shows that the size of population of a country does not correlate with the size of its armed forces. Despite the very large populations of China and India, the United States and the Soviet Union have more men under arms than do these two countries. On the other hand, tiny Israel has military personnel of nearly 160,000 men and women and when fully mobilized, can put nearly 300,000 men in the field, almost as many as France's peacetime forces, although the population of France is twenty times as large as that of Israel.

Table 4.2: Quantitative Breakdown of Military Forces and Equipment

| Country | Military Personnel, 1976 (in thousands) | | | | Ships, 1972 | | | | | Planes, 1972 |
	Total Number of Personnel	Army	Navy	Air Force	Submarines[a] FBMS	N	C	Destroyer/ Frigates	Carriers	Combat Planes[b] (Air Force)
United States	2130	785	733	612	41	53	46	208	18	6000
Soviet Union	3525	1825	500	400	30	60	266	103	--	10000
China	3250	2800	230	220	--	--	35	8	--	2800
India	956	826	30	100	--	--	11	20	--	504
China (Taiwan)	494	340	72	80	--	--	--	39	--	290
Germany, West	495	345	39	111	--	--	11	39	--	375
Pakistan	392	365	10	17	3	--	19	46	--	500
Britain	345	175	76	94	4	4	17	64	2	500
Egypt	323	275	18	30	--	--	4	21	2	625
Indonesia	266	200	38	28	--	--	--	15	1	122
Iran	250	175	15	60	--	--	--	28	--	385
Japan	236	155	39	42	--	--	4	7	--	285
Syria	178	155	3	25	--	--	1	8	--	163
Israel	156	135	5	16	--	--	12	7	--	523
Germany, East	143	98	17	28	--	--	3	1	--	374
Jordan	80	75	--	5	--	--	--	--	--	--
South Africa	51	38	4	9	--	--	--	--	--	--

[a]Fleet Ballistic Missile Submarines (FBMS), Nuclear Hunter-Killers (N), Conventional Submarines (C).

[b]Plus additional strategic forces including ICBM (intercontinental), IRBM (intermediate-range), and MRBM (medium-range) ballistic missiles.

SOURCE: *The Military Balance, 1971–72 and 1975–76* (London: Institute for Strategic Studies).

Education and Training

Numbers alone are not the only criterion by which to judge a country's military organization. We have already shown the importance of education as a crucial variable for this judgment. Other significant factors are training and fighting spirit. The best raw material will not make good soldiers, sailors, and airmen without proper, high-quality training. Moreover, a comprehensive school system must exist for all ranks to provide specialized education in technical matters, tactics, and strategy. As officers rise in rank and responsibility, the curriculum in service schools must broaden to include all aspects of strategy, international politics, and relevant economic subjects. To a large extent then, the quality of a country's armed forces depends on the excellence of its military educational system; and it is no accident that militarily powerful countries present and past have outstanding educational facilities for the armed forces. The United States, Soviet Union, Great Britain, France, and Germany are good examples.

Spirit and Commitment

Another significant factor governing the quality of a country's armed forces is fighting spirit and commitment to the cause for which a war is waged. At the beginning of World War II, the fighting spirit of French armed forces was more a matter of rhetoric than substance, and only toward the end of that war did the so-called Free French Forces under General Charles de Gaulle begin to live up to the famed "glory of the French Army." If the Soviet Union were to embark on a military adventure toward Western Europe, it is doubtful that the soldiers of her satellite allies in South-Central Europe, that is, Poland, Czechoslovakia, Hungary, Romania, and others, would show much fighting spirit because their commitment to the cause of the war would be questionable.

The fighting spirit of the armed forces of a country is not only influenced by their own morale, but also by the morale of the population in general. The extraordinary feats of the Soviet Army in Stalingrad and Leningrad in stopping and defeating Hitler's powerful war machine were made possible by the strong fighting spirit and high morale of its soldiers and by the intense patriotism and high morale of all the Soviet people.

Reserves

Many countries maintain large reserves of so-called civilian soldiers for their military establishment. These reserves must be taken into account when assessing the military forces of a country, but their value is often marginal. Perhaps with the exception of Israel and Switzerland, the reserves, when mobilized, often require long periods of training. Considering the highly technical nature and speed of modern warfare, the decisive moment of victory or defeat may pass before reserves can be usefully employed.

Weapons and Materiel

The tools for any successful employment of the armed forces are weapons and the materiel necessary to use these weapons effectively. The proper composition of the arsenal for the power status of a country is at least as important as the quality of materiel. Table 4.2 offers a breakdown of naval ships and combat planes for the countries listed and suggests that not only is the number of submarines significant, but also the type. For example, the Soviet Union has a much larger number of conventional submarines than the United States, but the latter leads in ballistic missile submarines and thus has more flexibility and punch in the delivery of strategic nuclear weapons. On the other hand, the Soviet Union has more land-based intercontinental ballistic missiles (ICBMs) than the United States, which has so far been compensated for by the fact that American missiles were outfitted with so-called multiple independently targeted reentry vehicles (MIRVs), meaning that each ICBM can deliver from three to ten weapons. The Soviet Union, however, has now developed MIRVs and has deployed them on more than 200 ICBMs, a development that requires a new assessment of the balance of nuclear power between the two countries.

Table 4.2 also illustrates the overwhelming capabilities of the two superpowers, the United States and the Soviet Union, within the nuclear club, that is, the six countries that now have nuclear weapons.* We should note that basic technology for building nuclear

---

* The six countries are China, France, Great Britain, India, the Soviet Union, and the United States.

weapons is pretty well known and not too costly. A number of countries (for example, Germany, Sweden, and Israel) could become members of this club if they wanted; however, to reach the sophistication of the weapons attained by the superpowers would involve a tremendous investment of funds, scientific talents, and time, which very few countries may be able to afford. Of course, many countries may, in fact, not need such weapons, because types of armament depend on who is considered a potential enemy and what kind of war will probably be fought.

Serious questions have been raised in recent years about the validity of numbers given with respect to ICBMs equipped with nuclear weapons and their bearing upon national power. Hans Morgenthau points to two paradoxes flowing from the enormous destructiveness of nuclear weapons:

> ... It is by virtue of that destructiveness that a quantitative increase in nuclear weapons, in contrast to conventional ones, does not of necessity signify a corresponding increase in national power. Once a nation possesses all the nuclear weapons necessary to destroy all the enemy targets it has chosen for destruction, taking all possible contingencies, such as a first strike by the enemy, into consideration, additional nuclear weapons will not increase that nation's power.
>
> The other paradox lies in the inverse relationship between the degree of destructiveness of nuclear weapons and their rational usability. High-yield nuclear weapons are instruments of indiscriminate mass destruction and can therefore not be used for rational military purposes. They can be used to deter a war by threatening total destruction; but they cannot be used to fight a war in a rational manner. A nation armed with nothing but high-yield nuclear weapons could draw very little political power from its military posture; for it would have no military means by which to impose its will upon another nation, aside from threatening it with total destruction.[4]

Morgenthau's comments suggest forcefully that conventional weapons have not lost their significance, and the history of war since 1945 shows the extensive employment of these weapon systems all over the world. Tremendous progress has been made in the development of these weapons, which today fire with incredible speed and over long ranges. Machine guns can fire 1,000 rounds a minute, and rocket launchers can fire over long distances. The payload and range of bombers have increased many times between 1945 and the Vietnam War with the result that the destructive power of bombs and shells dropped by American B-52s and fighter bombers on South

Vietnam during that war was twice as much as that of all the bombs dropped on Germany during World War II.[5]

The employment of any weapons system can only be successful if the necessary logistical means are available. Weapons and troops must be transported to the front and ammunition delivered. Mechanized equipment, such as tanks and personnel carriers, require gasoline and maintenance. Planes need to be serviced regularly and require large quantities of fuel. For these reasons, it is essential that the logistical system of each military establishment be carefully evaluated when a judgment is made about the strength of a country. Small countries, especially in the Third World, often are eager to buy modern weapons. In the developing countries, this eagerness stems at least in part from the fact that the military either control the government or have aspirations for governmental takeover. Some of the industrially advanced countries, including the United States, the Soviet Union, and France, are anxious to sell such equipment; but whether this equipment can be fully employed when needed depends on the quality of the logistic support available in a particular country.

SUMMARY

In this chapter we have examined factors that had both subjective and objective elements. Primarily, the factor of traditions and social psychology has been subjective.

Historical experiences and evolved tradition affect the **national character** of a people and their attitudes. These attitudes, in turn, affect their conception of national purpose and destiny and create an image of a state as a desirable ally or foe. They are also ingredients in the powerful force of **nationalism.**

Societal cleavages may weaken a country politically by reducing its ability to engage in war successfully and may also weaken it economically. **Political ideologies** may be unifying or divisive elements.

Important in assessing **government** and **administration** are the constitutional framework and practice of the government, the speed with which it is able to make decisions, the attitude of the people toward it, and its administrative efficiency. When the population has confidence in the governmental system and accepts it as the proper decision-making unit, governmental authority is legitimized; however, when large segments of the population lose confidence in government and refuse to accept its authority, the government and the country are seriously weakened.

The final element in evaluating the strengths and weaknesses of a state is the nature of its **military organization.** To assess military strength, we must look at the size, education and training, spirit and commitment, and weapons and materiel of the country's active military forces and also evaluate its reserves.

Analyzing the determinants of power gives us an appreciation of the strengths and weaknesses of a country and tells us what that country is capable of doing as an actor on the international stage. How the data obtained in such an analysis are actually used in the policy making process and what other factors are considered are the topics examined in the next chapter.

NOTES

1. A vast literature exists on the subject of nationalism. Outstanding works are Hans Kohn, *The Idea of Nationalism* (New York: Macmillan, 1961), and Karl N. Deutsch, *Nationalism and Its Alternatives* (New York: Knopf, 1969).

2. Cf. Sprout and Sprout, op. cit., pp. 522–536. See also Vernon Van Dyke, *International Policies*, 2nd ed. (New York: Appleton-Century-Crofts, 1966), pp. 180–181.

3. *New York Times*, September 22, 1973.

4. Hans J. Morgenthau, *Politics Among Nations*, 5th ed. (New York: Knopf, 1973), p. 122.

5. *New York Times*, June 22, 1973.

SUGGESTED READINGS

KNORR, KLAUS. *Military Power and Potential.* Lexington, Mass.: D. C. Heath, 1970.

KOHN, H. *Nationalism: Its Meaning and History.* Rev. ed. New York: Van Nostrand, 1955.

PARKIN, F. *Class Inequality and Political Order.* New York: Praeger, 1971.

PREWITT, K., AND A. STONE. *The Ruling Elites.* New York: Harper & Row, 1973.

PYE, L. W., AND S. VERBA, eds. *Political Culture and Political Development.* Princeton, N.J.: Princeton University Press, 1965.

SCHELLING, THOMAS C. *Arms and Influence.* New Haven: Yale University Press, 1966.

PART II
International
Actions and Reactions

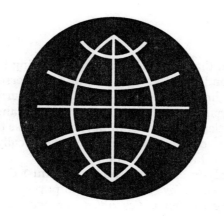

CHAPTER FIVE
THE FORMULATION OF FOREIGN POLICIES

We have stated that transnational policy making is a long and complex process ending in an act of will of a person or a group of persons who choose between two or more alternatives. When we consider transnational policies, the formulation and implementation of foreign policies is especially important because these policies constitute that part of the national policy specifically concerned with the relation of a state to other states.

In the analysis of foreign policy we must distinguish between *long-range foreign policy goals,* usually important national objectives, and *short-range foreign policy objectives and actions.* In many instances, the latter can be regarded as means to achieve long-range foreign policy goals, but it is also possible that there is a means-ends relationship between short-range foreign policy objectives and actions. Because every state must frequently react to current situations and problems, a greater degree of flexibility is inherent in the formulation and application of particular policies than in the establishment of long-range policy goals. Long-range foreign policy goals and short-range policy objectives may be *compatible* or *incompatible.* They are compatible when the attainment of one goal reinforces the attainment of other goals. They are incompatible if one goal or objective can be attained only at the expense of the other.

We know from our previous discussion of the intricacies of decision making that many choices precede the final decision. Particularly in foreign policy making these choices include determining which sources of information about the external environment should be used and how this information should be interpreted and considering what should be the means for carrying out a particular policy and what may be the likely reactions of other states; whether the state has the resources to carry out a particular policy successfully; and what effects different policy alternatives will have on domestic politics.

Constraints limit the final foreign policy decision. One of these constraints is chiefly mechanical and consists of the framework of foreign policy goals and particular transnational policies already existing in an individual country. Unless a definite change is intended, the decision makers must work within this framework to assure that new objectives and policies are compatible with former ones. Three other constraints on foreign policy choices are even more binding. They are: (1) the overriding, paramount security and economic needs and political aspirations of the people of a country that may find expression in part or wholly in the national interest of this country; (2) the extent of the capabilities and vulnerabilities of a country, mainly in the military, economic, financial, and political fields determining the limits of support for a specific policy or goal, and (3) the extent of capabilities and vulnerabilities of other countries permitting the latter to obviate, interpose, or perhaps support the desired policy depending on the foreign policy goals of individual countries affected by that policy.

THE NATIONAL INTERESTS

Winston Churchill said in 1939, "I cannot forecast to you the action of Russia. It is a riddle wrapped in a mystery inside an enigma; but perhaps there is a key. That key is Russian national interest."[1]

While at first glance the notion of national interest seems indeed to provide an objective guide to foreign policy making, the term is elusive and has been understood by political scientists and statesmen in various ways. One way to define *national interest* is to consider it as an ideal set of purposes a nation *should* seek to realize in the conduct of its foreign relations. This concept of national interest is termed *normative:* national interest is defined in terms of what *ought* to be done. National interest is often viewed in this way when citizens and politicians deliberate on the general goals for their nations.

A second definition focuses on what policies a state, through its leadership, has pursued over a period of time. This kind of definition deals with a historic description of facts, but does not necessarily offer prescriptions for the future.

Finally, some observers look at national interest as a kaleidoscopic process by which forces in a society seek to express certain political and economic aspirations in world politics, usually through the highest organs of the state. To understand fully the configuration of national interest under this notion requires becoming familiar with the values and beliefs held by the people, inquiring into their concrete interests, and assessing the ideologies they may espouse. Again, we see in this definition primarily a description of what exists at present in terms of the national interest and a functional view as to the motivations for the continuance of or change of the way that interest is defined.[2]

If we can learn one lesson from the three concepts delineated, it is that perceptions of national interest differ not only among individual decision makers but also among individual citizens. Your own view of the national interest may vary appreciably from that of your neighbor. Moreover, the national interest may change over time as domestic and external circumstances change. Such a change is illustrated by the Monroe Doctrine, a policy regarded as a cornerstone in protecting U.S. national interests in the Western Hemisphere during the 19th century. This policy not only sought to prevent outside interference in the Western Hemisphere, but also suggested that U.S. interests were mainly limited to North and South America. Today such a restricted view of American relationships with international society would be considered by most Americans as incompatible with the world leadership role assumed by the United States.

Another example is the national interest of Great Britain which, until the 1950s, included as a major part the maintenance of the empire and later the British Commonwealth. Today the word *British* has been dropped, and Britain's relation with some of the commonwealth member states (for example, Grenada in the Caribbean) is seen more as a burden than a benefit and therefore no longer significant in terms of national interest. And perhaps the most burdensome of all commonwealth relationships exists between Pakistan and Uganda under its volatile and unpredictable President Idi Amin.

In view of the differing interpretations that may be attributed by different decision makers to the national interest and the difficulty of giving operational meaning to this concept, a number of international relations specialists have cast doubt on the reliability of using national interest as an objective guide to making or understanding the foreign policy of a country;[3] nevertheless, by using the term in the plural and equating it to the vital interests of a state, a number of national interests applicable to all countries can be identified.[4] They are the protection of the integrity of a state's territory, the achievement of maximum security, the preservation of national self-determination, and the attainment and maintenance of optimum economic well-being.

The very breadth of these universal national interests makes them useful only as broad guides for foreign policy making. It is yet necessary to determine more specific goals. For this determination, it is necessary to undertake a careful analysis of a country's determinants of power—that is, its geography, economy, technological capability, population, social makeup, and political system—to discover not only elements of strength but also specific vulnerabilities, for which protection must be a matter of priority. For example, a country that is very narrow, such as Chile, would have to defend a very long coastline in a war and could be cut easily into several parts by an aggressor. On the other hand, a large country may be able to use its extensive territory to good defense advantage by having its armed forces fall back slowly and exhaust the aggressor, as the Soviet Union did in 1941 when Hitler invaded her land and as Imperial Russia did in the face of Napoleon's invasion about 130 years earlier.

An ethnically and racially divided population represents a clear vulnerability. The fact that Israel has in its midst a large number of Palestinians needs to be considered in Israeli foreign policy.

Another example is economic dependence. Countries that do not have necessary raw materials or agricultural commodities within their own boundaries must make sure that they will not be cut off from sources of supply. Japan's lack of sufficient coal resources and her deficiencies in soybeans and other agricultural commodities are serious economic and strategic weakness. Finally, small and militarily weak countries have a need for alliances to counterbalance their military and political vulnerabilities. From all these vulnerabilities spring certain interests whose promotion must be translated by foreign policy makers into specific goals to be attained through carefully chosen policies supported by resources available in the country.

For the foreign policy maker it is not only important to define the chief interests of his country, but also to learn about the interests of the other states as evidenced by statements made by the governments of the these states or revealed through a careful analysis of their strengths and weaknesses. If the interests of two or more countries are common or at least compatible, friendships or alliances among them may be mutually beneficial. It has been said that there are no real enduring friendships among nations but only enduring interests. To this should be added that the commonality of interests may at times outweigh conflict of ideologies, such as between Marxism and democracy, something that has been clearly demonstrated by the conclusion of the Non-Proliferation Treaty regarding nuclear weapons of 1970 promoted strongly by the United States and the Soviet Union, and by the dramatic changes in United States–Chinese relations after 1972. Of course, as we have already pointed out, interests of states change, and such changes affect the relationships among states. In the 19th century the traditional foe of the United States was Great Britain. In the 20th century, Great Britain became a close American ally in two wars and a partner in the North Atlantic Treaty Organization (NATO). During the major part of the first half of the 20th century, the interests of Germany and the United States clashed; but during the past twenty years, a growing commonality of interests has developed between the United States and Germany, and today they are not only allied in NATO, but have generally become close friends.

Analyzing strengths and weaknesses of one's own country and those of other countries with which relations exist or are desired is crucial not only as a basis for the elaboration of goals and policies, but also for determining whether or not proper resources are available to assure the successful pursuit of these policies. These resources, such as well-trained and well-organized military forces, a powerful economy, adequate financial means, and extensive technological capabilities, must be measured not only in absolute terms, but also in relation to the capabilities of the states toward which a specific policy is being developed. Furthermore, in determining policy goals and capabilities of one's own country with respect to a particular area, it is necessary to evaluate the capabilities of other states with interests in the same area. The pursuit of these interests may compete with or perhaps reinforce the implementation of goals sought by one's own country.

THREE PERSPECTIVES OF FOREIGN POLICY MAKING

With inputs into foreign policy making coming from a bewildering variety of sources, students of foreign policy have attempted to explain the foreign policy making process by constructing a number of models.[5] For our purposes the three models developed by Graham T. Allison appear to be most useful to offer three possible perspectives of this process.[6] Although drawn from the American experiences with policy making, they have general application—of course, *mutatis mutandis*—to most other countries as well, with the only exception being very small countries. The three models are:

1. The *rational policy model*, which is based on the assumption that the making of foreign policy is done through a rational intellectual process.
2. The *organizational process model*, which is based on the concept that foreign policy is the output stemming from the interplay among major governmental organizations participating in the formulation and implementation of foreign policy goals and actions.
3. The *bureaucratic politics model*, which is based on the notion that foreign policy making is the result of overlapping bargaining activities among officials in various governmental ministries and agencies.

Rational Policy Model

According to the rational policy model, the policy-making process consists of purposive acts of a rational, unitary decision maker, namely the national government. The national government is, therefore, seen as having one set of major goals, one set of perceived objectives and alternatives, and a uniform estimate of the existing situation, as well as of the consequences that may follow from each alternative. Choices are made on the basis of the maximization of a value, such as a desired goal or a highly regarded objective. For example, to ensure maximum security against Soviet attack, United States policy has consistently supported the strength of the Atlantic Alliance. As we have noted earlier, to make such a choice requires consideration by the decision maker of: (1) the alternate potential goals in relation to his value standard (perhaps the preservation of a "Free World"); (2) the alternate courses of action open to reach these goals; and (3) the probable significant effects of each of the possible alternate courses of action.

While the goal-selection process may seem clear-cut at first, we are aware of many pitfalls. The selection of goals depends very much on the value standards of the individual policy maker, and these values may be coherent or contradicting. Rational decision making may also be impaired by incomplete thought or information. There is often a tendency to make decisions intuitively or impulsively with regard more to personal experience than to actual knowledge of the situation obtained by outside agencies. There may also be the habit of conforming with tradition, or what is conceived of as tradition. To return to our example, the United States has followed support of the Atlantic Alliance so long that other alternatives, such as defending America exclusively from American soil, tend to face an intuitive adverse bias regardless of the fact that the defense of Western Europe may indeed be a crucial factor for the U.S. national security.

Organizational Process Model

The second perspective, the organizational process model, recognizes that the government of a state does not really operate in a unitary fashion because it consists of a conglomerate of "semi-feudal, loosely allied organizations, each with a substantial life of its own."[7] While government leaders have formal control over the various ministries and agencies, they can only understand and solve problems and arrive at solutions through these organizations. The organizations involved are the Foreign Ministry, the Ministry of Defense, and in almost all cases, the Ministry of Finance. But these may not be all the organizations participating in policy-making processes: the ministries of Economics, Agriculture, Labor, Science and Technology may also share to varying degrees in seeking to produce foreign policy decisions. With so many agencies participating in the foreign policy process, coordination becomes one of the major tasks of governmental leaders. Coordination, however, implies so-called standard operating procedures (SOP) in the various ministries and agencies; and from this point of view alone, coordination becomes difficult because individual ministries and agencies have differing SOPs. Each of the organizations often is more concerned with its own goals and objectives than with a generally agreed-upon program of policy, and these goals and objectives at times may not be compatible with rational conceptions of national goals. These organizations are concerned not only with the continued existence of their own institutions but also with expansion of their activities. They are frequently influenced by outside pressures from citizens and special interest groups and by bargaining among their own officials. As a consequence of this interplay among organizational goals, values, and interests, the final output in terms of foreign policy may not really be what the governmental leaders had in mind originally. Yet the organizational constraints that exist in the different participating ministries and agencies are likely to make it impossible to modify greatly the final decision. These problems occur not only in the United States, but in almost all countries of the world, regardless of whether they have a democratic or dictatorial government. The tug-of-war between the State Department and the Department of Defense regarding the United States's negotiating stance in the Strategic Arms Limitation Talks (SALT) with the Soviet Union is an interesting example.

Bureaucratic Politics Model

The third perspective of foreign policy making focuses on the internal politics of the bureaucracy of the government and the bargaining that usually takes place between officials participating in the policy-making process. The essence of this model lies in the fact that civil servants, as human beings, look at the promotion of their own personal interests, including the expansion of their position of power and prestige, as important guides and motivations for their actions and decisions, and this colors their images of the public interest. Of course, civil servants will not openly admit to this situation, but it is a problem found in all governments of the world. It produces bureacratic attitudes and behavior which tend to reduce the influence of the wishes of governmental and political leaders. Max Weber, a German sociologist living in the early part of this century, stressed in his study of bureaucracy that large, long-established state bureaucracies are capable of considerable independence and insulation from the political leadership and are far from being passive tools of those who wield political power in a state.[8] Barbara Castle, who held several ministerial posts in Harold Wilson's Labor Government in Great Britain during the 1960s, declared in an address to a seminar of senior civil servants

> . . . I have no doubt that the civil service is a State within a state. . . . The Civil Service is also highly aware of its own excellence. It is extremely status-conscious. In fact if any government in this country really tried to undermine that status we should certainly see a thing or two. . . . So I think there is a crying need for the Civil Service to be trained and retrained and re-retrained in two things. The first is in accepting the supremacy of the political function in a democracy over the administrative function. And the second is in getting into the mind of a Minister.
> What the Civil Service has not taken on board, and what politicians do not take on board until they become Ministers, is the extent to which, from the moment a Minister walks out of that Cabinet room at No. 10 Downing Street, having been asked by the Prime Minister to take on such a job, the Civil Service takes over his life.
> . . . How instantly the forces of the Civil Service move in! It isn't only

the "bureaucratic embrace," . . . it is the companionable embrace. From that moment, the Minister is cut off from every source of political activity that has given [his or] her life meaning and expression. Political activity continues only to the extent that it is authorised by the management of the Minister's life.[9]

Former Secretary of State Henry Kissinger had experiences similar to those of Mrs. Castle. Recognizing that even on the highest level it is impossible to implement an order easily, he made the following comments:

> When I first started advising at high levels of the government in the early days of the Kennedy Administration, I had the illusion that all I had to do was walk into the President's office, convince him I was right, and he would then naturally do what I had recommended. There were a number of things wrong with this view. . . . [E]ven if by chance I persuaded him that his whole bureaucracy was wrong and I was right, he would then have the next problem of going about implementing what had been suggested. And that is not a negligible issue. There is only so much that even a President can do against the wishes of the bureaucracy, not because the bureaucracy would deliberately sabotage him, but because every difficult issue is a closed one. The easy decisions are made at subordinate levels. A closed issue is characterized by the fact that the pros and cons seem fairly evenly divided and/or because the execution really depends on certain nuances of application. Unless you can get the willing support of your subordinates, simply giving an order does not get very far.[10]

Positions of power of individual civil servants, their prestige, their reputation for effectiveness, and their skill in using bargaining advantages are important variables for the results of bureaucratic bargaining with respect to a particular foreign policy decision. In many instances, coalitions are formed among individuals and departments to assure that the final outcome is that which they view as significant not only for national public policy, but also for their own personal advancement. This does not mean that the interests of the nation are sacrificed for primarily personal gains. The officials want to enhance these interests, and most of them share common basic values and traditions with respect to the ways of life within their nation and to the national purposes. But the specific outcome on a particular foreign policy decision may well be conceived as flowing, according to Allison, from

> . . . intricate and subtle, simultaneous, overlapping games among . . . [civil servants] located in positions, the hierarchical arrangement of

which constitutes that government. These games proceed neither at random nor at leisure. Regular channels structure the game. Deadlines force issues to the attention of busy . . . [civil servants]. The moves in the chess game are thus to be explained in terms of the bargaining among . . . [civil servants] with separate and unequal power over particular pieces and with separable objectives in distinguishable subgames.[11]

It is difficult to judge which perspective or model is closest to reality for understanding the foreign policy making process. Conceivably, this process contains elements of all three models, with more weight given to the organizational and bureaucratic models. Moreover, the external situation has a distinct bearing on the policy-making process because frequently policies are made in response to what happens beyond national boundaries. This means that the promotion of the public interest according to the foreign policy direction of the top political leadership in a state is heavily dependent on the perceptions of domestic and external conditions, belief systems, and personal aspirations of major participating bureaucrats, and that the impact of these factors is in turn circumscribed by the interests, objectives, and procedure of the organizations in which these officials are employed. The end product then is the result of much skillful bargaining among the major participants in a particular foreign policy decision. As Kissinger observes, these "decisions emerge from a compromise of conflicting pressures in which accidents of personality or persuasiveness play a crucial role."[12] Bargaining may dominate over substance, and the quality of the decision may suffer.

As a result of these factors and limitations, William D. Coplin's observations are appropriate:

> Foreign policy decision makers tend to avoid new interpretations of the environment, to select and act upon traditional goals, to limit the search for alternatives to a small number of moderate ones, and finally to take risks which involved low costs if they prove unsuccessful.[13]

THE NOTION OF IMAGE IN FOREIGN POLICY DECISION MAKING

Closely related to the foreign policy making process as discussed in the preceding pages is the notion of the image that foreign policy makers hold of the external environment of their country and of its strengths and weaknesses. These images shape the input into the policy-making process. During the last few years psychologists and political scientists have studied more and more the problem of the image, and it is now fairly well known that past experiences, current attitudes, value commitments and beliefs, as well as the development of the individual's personality, bear on the manner in which an official or a political leader perceives the outside world. Because these factors vary from individual to individual, different decision makers look at the external and internal environment differently, and foreign policy decisions are significantly influenced by the perceptional components of their internal image of the world and special situations they face.

Open versus Closed Images

Images are regarded as either *open* or *closed*. An individual who has an open image accepts new information and adjusts his image to this information. Such information may come from a variety of sources, such as advisors, supervisors, colleagues, intelligence agencies, or the press. On the other hand, an individual with a closed image does not adjust to any information. He rejects new conditions for a variety of reasons and thereby may move away from the reality of his country's environment and of the world.

It would be an error to assume that an individual falls entirely into the category of open image or of closed image. There are many gradations between these two extremes; and there are circumstances, such as a very radical change of the international environment, that compel even an official with a very closed image to adjust to a new situation. One example is the change in British governmental leaders during the late 1930s when Hitler attacked Poland and subsequently invaded the Soviet Union in 1941. Prior to the attack on Poland, many British leaders felt that they could do business with Hitler and that somehow Nazism would go away.

The Conservative Nature of Images

The conservative nature of images developed at a certain time can be illustrated by some of the foreign policies in which the Kennedy administration engaged. Although it appeared at first that the liberal nature of John F. Kennedy, as portrayed in many of his speeches, would lead to an innovative foreign policy, the old image of "evil communism" continued to persist, and the Cold War mentality initiated right after World War II continued to control not only the president, but also his special assistant for national security affairs, McGeorge Bundy. As David Halberstam observed in his best-selling book, *The Best and the Brightest,* the men around Kennedy reflected the post-Munich, post-McCarthy pragmatism of the age. He goes on to say,

> One had to stop totalitarianism, and since the only thing the totalitarians understood was force, one had to be willing to use force. They justified each decision to use power by their own conviction that the Communists were worse which justified our dirty tricks, our toughness.[14]

The result was that Vietnam became a reflection and a consequence of the containment policy initiated by President Harry S Truman in 1947. If the images of the decision makers around Kennedy had been more open and they had been more willing to accept some of the new information that became available during the early 1960s, perhaps a different policy would have been followed.

One of the problems in changing a decision maker's image is the clarity with which he receives new information. Communication scientists call this the clarity of the signal received by the decision maker, and the more the clarity of the signal is impaired, the greater is the probability that the meaning of that signal will be obscured. Spurious signals or static that interferes with signal reception is called noise, and the clarity of the signal is often expressed in terms of a signal-to-noise ratio. The higher this ratio is, the stronger is the signal, and the more likely is a change in the image of the decision maker.

Public versus Private Image

We should stress that the notion of image must be understood in psychological terms. It refers to what the individual decision maker perceives the world to be. However, today we frequently talk about the image the decision maker has as it appears to the world. Sometimes a decision maker would like to make his image public in order to defend his policies. Once he has done so, it is very difficult for him to change the impression he has created in his constituency or in other people of his country. Under such conditions new information may be seen as a threat that may destroy the integrity of his own image and undermine the political support he has built for himself and his policies. On the other hand, foreign policy decision makers may have two images of a particular situation, one for their own use and one for public consumption.[15] This may well have been true of President Kennedy and his associates. Many people considered him as wishing to take fresh approaches to foreign policy, but he remained a prisoner of the foreign policy images built up during the 1940s and 1950s. When, during the Republican presidential primaries in 1976, Ronald Reagan challenged President Ford's foreign policies toward the Soviet Union as not being tough enough, the latter attempted to change the image projected by dropping the word *détente* from his foreign policy description.

INTELLIGENCE AND FOREIGN POLICY MAKING

Accurate, relevant information available to participants in the policy making process provides an important base for the formulation of effective policies. However, considering the vast range of subjects discussed in the preceeding chapters with respect to the elements of power that may be significant for policy making, it is clear that simply to have masses of raw information would not be very helpful. What is needed is careful, selective collection and collation of information, followed by systematic analysis, interpretation, and evaluation. The end product of this sequence of steps is *intelligence;* when it pertains to foreign countries and the international environment in general, it is called *foreign intelligence*. Obviously, this latter type of intelligence is usually of the greatest interest to foreign policy makers, although *domestic intelligence* may also have to be taken into account in the foreign policy formulation process. The sources of foreign intelligence information are mostly found abroad, but some information is also collected from within the country through counterintelligence activities and debriefing of travelers who have been in foreign countries.

Intelligence Collection

The information may be collected by secret agents, diplomats assigned to the country's embassies in various capitals of the world, research officials in the intelligence agency headquarters, or by mechanical means and electronic devices. Spy-in-the-sky satellites take pictures of weapons installations, and governments monitor the coded international cable traffic of other governments. We should note that the bulk of pertinent information is gathered by researchers who scan every bit of printed material emanating from foreign countries, especially newspapers, scientific articles, and other publications available to the public-at-large and not classified as secret or confidential. On the other hand, the least information comes usually from secret agents, although from time to time their input may be most crucial. In this connection we must draw attention to an important asymmetry in the collection of information encountered by intelligence agencies in (closed) totalitarian and (open) democratic countries. In the latter many more open sources are available. For example, one can read about U.S. defense matters in American periodicals, such as *Aviation Week and Space Technology* or even the *New York Times*. In totalitarian societies such as the Soviet Union, all publications are carefully censored to prevent disclosure of items useful to foreign intelligence organizations.

By the United States In the United States the Central Intelligence Agency (CIA) is the leading producer of foreign intelligence; in addition, it has the mission of coordinating the intelligence activities of the other agencies making up the so-called intelligence community. One of these agencies is the Defense Intelligence Agency (DIA) which ties together and seeks to strengthen the intelligence-producing efforts of the Army, Navy, and Air Force. Other important members are the National Security Agency (NSA), concerned primarily with monitoring international electronic communications and cryptographic work (the breaking of secret codes of foreign governments); the Bureau of Intelligence and Research of the Department of State, dealing mainly with political and economic intelligence; the Department of Energy, focusing on developments in the nuclear field; and the FBI, whose function in the field of foreign affairs is primarily the production of counterintelligence. Other executive departments, such as the Department of Commerce, also have sections concerned with the production of specialized intelligence. Finally, during recent years nongovernmental research organizations have also been drawn into the intelligence-producing efforts. Some examples are the Air Force–supported Rand Corporation and the Lincoln Laboratories of the Massachusetts Institute of Technology (MIT).

By the Soviet Union In the Soviet Union no basic distinction is made between internal and external intelligence activities; however, the Political Intelligence Service, the foreign branch of the State Security Committee (KGB), has been primarily responsible for foreign nonmilitary intelligence, while foreign military intelligence is handled by the main intelligence directorate (GRU) of the Soviet Army. The officials of the Political Intelligence Service have diplomatic rank and therefore enjoy diplomatic immunity. They work with selected members of the embassy to which they are assigned, and the latter become "associate members" on a part-time basis while retaining their full status as diplomats. In addition, code clerks, messengers, drivers, and other technical personnel are attached to the Political Intelligence Service, but they do not enjoy diplomatic immunity. The military intelligence officers report directly to the GRU and operate through the offices of the military attaché. Security officers in the Soviet embassies are officials of the so-called Tenth Department of the Ministry of Foreign Affairs, which in fact is the KGB section in that ministry.[16] The Soviet intelligence apparatus, operating through the Soviet embassies in different countries, is supported also by intelligence personnel of the East European satellites, organized along the same lines as found in the Soviet governmental structure. Obviously the final result is a huge number of Soviet agents that may exceed 10,000 operating throughout the world.

By Great Britain   The intelligence services in Western Europe are much smaller than the CIA and the Soviet agencies. In Great Britain the counterpart of the Central Intelligence Agency as far as coordination of intelligence activities is concerned is the Joint Intelligence Committee, which is attached to the Ministry of Defense. This committee's functions differ somewhat from those of the CIA because it is primarily concerned with providing broad intelligence estimates and encyclopedic intelligence. The counterpart of the State Department's Bureau of Intelligence and Research is the Research Department of the Foreign Office. Set up along geographic lines, its foremost task is a study of historical backgrounds of current foreign policy problems for the use of the political departments in the Foreign Office. The popular fame British intelligence has accumulated over the past decades stems mainly from its military intelligence organization (MI), with the MI5, MI6, and MI11 bureaus having the responsibility for espionage and counterespionage.

By West Germany   In West Germany the foreign intelligence activities are primarily carried out by the Federal Information Service (*Bundesnachrichtendienst,* BND), which is subordinate and directly responsible to the Office of the Chancellor of the Federal Republic. Some intelligence is also produced by the armed forces through the *Militärische Abschirmdienst* (MAD), which is set up in the Ministry of Defense. Within the Foreign Ministry special units have been formed to provide the specialized intelligence necessary for the formulation and implementation of policies. Another organization that has received considerable publicity during the past few years is the agency of General Gehlen, which has primarily engaged in clandestine operations; however, the publicity has not always been favorable, and there have been reports of corruption. Rivalries have marked the work of all these agencies, and since 1975 a high official in the Office of the Chancellor exercises supervisory control over all intelligence activities. All requests for intelligence gathering must now be cleared through that office. Furthermore, the agencies are now required to share information and to cooperate with each other.

By France   In France the most famous intelligence organ is the Deuxième Bureau which has been the setting for many spy thrillers. Other French intelligence services are scattered throughout the Ministry of Foreign Affairs. Institutes of higher learning are also utilized outside the governmental framework.

Types of Information Needed

As a background or basis for decision making, a foreign policy official may need encyclopedic knowledge about a foreign country; knowledge of military, economic, or technological vulnerabilities; knowledge about what kind of action one or several foreign states may be able to take in the world arena; or immediate spot knowledge about a current event. The first type of knowledge can be gleaned from so-called national intelligence surveys, which deal individually with most countries of the world and cover a broad range of topics, including geography and national resources; transportation and telecommunication capabilities; every aspect of economic intelligence; full sociological data about the population, education, and morale of the people; scientific and technological intelligence; an evaluation of the political structure and processes; and finally military resources and capabilities. Before World War II the British were the most capable and comprehensive producers of this type of intelligence, and the United States was forced to use British surveys during that war because the American government did not have such comprehensive materials available for military and foreign policy decisions. Now, however, these surveys are made in the United States through a coordinated effort of the members of the intelligence community who prepare different parts of the surveys in accordance with their special knowledge and skills, with the CIA being responsible for final approval and editing. These surveys are periodically revised and updated to keep pace with changes in each country.

Knowledge about a foreign country's capabilities, vulnerabilities, and probable courses of action can be gleaned from national intelligence estimates. Such knowledge is important because foreign policy goals are not attained in a vacuum, but in interaction with other states. Those who would pursue them must take into consideration the foreign policy aspirations of other countries, their pressures to have these aspirations recognized, and their capabilities of implementing their own policies. As a consequence, most major countries prepare intelligence estimates on foreign foes and friends alike. In Washington's language of abbreviation these estimates are called NIEs (National Intelligence Estimates), and in the United States they represent the intelligence community's agreed evaluation of pertinent facts and likely future developments. These estimates may be the result of periodic intelligence reviews, or may be requested as part of a reassessment of foreign policy toward a particular country or area. In some instances, these estimates may not focus on an entire foreign country, but on a particular question of current concern. For example, the West German and other foreign governments probably requested an intelligence estimate on the impact of Watergate on the courses of action the United States policy makers might take with respect to Western Europe and the Communist World. In view of recent nuclear tests by the People's Republic of China, U.S. foreign policy officials may have sought an estimate on future Chinese nuclear missile developments and their impact on probable Chinese foreign policy actions. Requirements for spot intelligence are usually met by summaries prepared within a matter of hours or by longer estimates which can be worked up if necessary in two to four days.

Acceptance of Intelligence Information

Although the production of foreign intelligence is a very extensive and expensive activity in many countries, the acceptance of the knowledge received from the intelligence agencies as a basis for decisions is often uncertain. If the intelligence received confirms the image held by an official participating in the foreign policy making process, it is likely to be considered accurate and to be accepted; however, if it conflicts with the image, it may be rejected. As you might suppose, officials having closed images are more likely to reject intelligence information than are those with open images. There are a number of specific reasons for these rejections. In some instances, doubt is cast on the quality of the intelligence produced. In others long-standing perceptions of the foreign policy maker regarding the reliability of his own knowledge (partly based on his own experience), coupled with a low regard for the performance of intelligence producers, leads to the partial or complete rejection of intelligence.[17] Finally, intelligence estimates of different U.S. agencies may be conflicting, as was true of estimates concerning Soviet capabilities during the middle-1970s, prompting policy makers to rely on their own judgments and perceptions.

Throughout history there have been instances of top-ranking governmental leaders or military commanders choosing to disregard the products of their own intelligence services, sometimes with unfortunate results. Their images were closed and could not be cracked. One such example is Joseph Stalin. In the spring of 1941, he refused to accept the very explicit warning of his secret intelligence apparatus in Switzerland that Hitler planned to attack the Soviet Union in June of that year. Another example is the intelligence provided, according to some observers, by the Office of U.S. Naval Intelligence in December of 1944 that the Japanese divisions stationed in Manchuria were skeleton units with very low troop strength and that the emperor himself had decided to explore the prospects of surrender. Had this intelligence been coordinated with similar information available in various intelligence offices in the Army, it might not have been disregarded in favor of the much more somber estimate of the situation by General George C. Marshall, then chief of the Joint Chiefs of Staff. If the intelligence developed from naval sources had been given greater credibility, and efforts been made to confirm it by other sources, it might have greatly strengthened the U.S. position at the Yalta Conference in February of that year during which President Roosevelt requested, in accordance with his image of a persistently strong Japan, that the Soviet Union enter the war against Japan in return for American concessions.[18]

SUMMARY

Transnational policy making is a long and complex process ending in an act of will of a person or a group of persons who choose between two or more alternatives. When we consider transnational policies, the **formulation and implementation of foreign policies** is especially important because these policies constitute that part of national policy specifically concerned with the relation of a state to other states.

In the analysis of foreign policy, we distinguish between **long-range goals** and **short-range objectives and actions.** These goals and objectives may be **compatible** or **incompatible.** They are incompatible if one goal or objective can be attained only at the expense of the other.

Many choices precede and many constraints limit a final foreign policy decision. Among these constraints are national interest, and the capabilities and vulnerabilities of a country and of the countries with which it interacts or plans to interact.

National interest can be defined in terms of what **ought** to be done (the **normative** view), as a series of policies that have been pursued in the past, or as a kaleidoscopic process by which forces in a society seek to express certain political and economic aspirations. Perceptions of national interest differ among decision makers and among individual citizens and change over time, but all countries desire to protect the integrity of their own territory, to achieve maximum security, to preserve national self-determination, and to attain and maintain optimum economic well-being.

The breadth of these universal national interests makes them useful only as broad guides for foreign policy making. It is necessary to determine more specific goals by analyzing a country's strengths and weaknesses. From vulnerabilities spring certain interests whose promotion must be translated by foreign policy makers into specific goals to be attained through carefully chosen policies supported by resources available in the country.

If the interests of two or more countries are common or at least compatible, friendships or alliances among them may be mutually beneficial. In fact, commonality of interests may outweigh conflict of ideologies.

A number of models have been constructed to explain the foreign policy making process. The three models developed by Graham T. Allison are the **rational policy model,** the **organizational process model,** and the **bureaucratic politics model.**

The foreign policy making process is influenced by the **image** each foreign policy maker holds of the external environment of his country and of its strengths and weaknesses. Such images usually fall somewhere on a continuum between **open** and **closed,** depending upon how receptive the person holding them is to new information and consequent change. The foreign policy making process is also affected by the image each decision maker has of himself and the image he creates for the public.

Accurate, relevant information provides an important basis for the formulation of effective policies. Information that has been analyzed, interpreted, and evaluated becomes **intelligence** and may be either **foreign** or **domestic.** It is collected by secret agents, diplomats, mechanical means, and electronic devices; but the bulk of it is gathered by researchers who scan every bit of printed matter emanating from foreign countries. Their resulting analyses range in size from spot summaries to comprehensive surveys.

NOTES

1. Statement in London, October 1, 1939.

2. For a more comprehensive discussion of the notion of national interest, see James N. Rosenau, *The Scientific Study of Foreign Policy* (New York: The Free Press, 1971), pp. 239–249; and Hans J. Morgenthau, *In Defense of the National Interest: A Critical Examination of American Foreign Policy* (New York: Knopf, 1951).

3. See Morton A. Kaplan, *System and Process in International Politics* (New York: Wiley, 1964), pp. 151–165; and Stanley Hoffmann, *Contemporary Theory in International Relations* (Englewood Cliffs, N.J.: Prentice-Hall, 1960), p. 33.

4. Frederick H. Hartmann, *The Relations of Nations* (New York: Macmillan, 1973), pp. 6–12.

5. See, for example, Joseph Frankel, *The Making of Foreign Policy: An Analysis of Decision-Making* (New York: Oxford University Press, 1963); and Richard C. Snyder, H. W. Bruck, and Burton Sapin, eds., *Foreign Policy Decision-Making* (New York: Free Press of Glencoe, 1963).

6. The following discussion follows closely the concepts developed by Graham T. Allison, "Conceptual Models and the Cuban Missile Crisis," in Morton H. Halperin and Arnold Kanter, eds., *Readings in American Foreign Policy: A Bureaucratic Perspective* (Boston: Little, Brown, 1973), pp. 45–83.

7. Ibid., p. 55.

8. Max Weber, from *Max Weber: Essays in Sociology*, translated and edited by H. H. Gerth and P. W. Mills (New York: Oxford University Press, 1958), pp. 228–235.

9. *Sunday Times* (London), June 10, 1973, pp. 17 and 19.

10. Henry A. Kissinger, "Bureaucracy and Policymaking: The Effects of Insiders and Outsiders on the Policy Process," in Halperin and Kanter, op. cit., pp. 84–97, on p. 86.

11. Graham T. Allison, op. cit., p. 71. For a detailed case study of the Cuban missile crisis decision in 1962 see ibid.

12. Kissinger, op. cit., p. 33. For critical comments regarding the bureaucratic politics model and other concepts, see Stephen B. Krasner, "Are Bureaucracies Important? or Allison Wonderland," *Foreign Policy*, no. 7 (1972), pp. 159–179; Robert Art, "Bureaucratic Politics and American Foreign Policy," *Policy Sciences* (December 1973); Linda P. Brady, *Bureaucratic Politics and Situational Constraints*, papers delivered at the 1974 Annual Meeting of the APSA, Chicago, Ill., August 27–September 1974; and Howard Bliss and M. Glen Johnson, *Beyond the Water's Edge: America's Foreign Policy* (Philadelphia: Lippincott, 1975), pp. 127–180.

13. William D. Coplin, *Introduction to International Politics: A Theoretical Overview* (Chicago: Markham, 1971), p. 56.

14. David Halberstam, *The Best and the Brightest* (New York: Random House, 1972), p. 22.

15. In this connection see also K. J. Holsti, "National Role Conception in the Study of Foreign Policy," *International Studies Quarterly*, vol. 14, no. 3 (September 1970), pp. 233–309.

16. For more details see Jan F. Triska and David D. Finley, *Soviet Foreign Policy* (New York: Macmillan, 1968), pp. 289–291.

17. See, for example, Patrick J. McGarvey, "DIA: Intelligence to Please," *The Washington Monthly*, vol. 2, no. 5 (July 1970), pp. 68–75.

18. Ladislas Farago, *War of Wits: The Anatomy of Espionage and Intelligence* (New York: Funk & Wagnalls, 1954), pp. 25–27; and Ellis M. Zacharias, *Secret Missions* (New York: G. P. Putnam's Sons, 1946), p. 335, and *Behind Closed Doors* (New York: G. P. Putnam's Sons, 1950), p. 57.

SUGGESTED READINGS

HALPERIN, M. H., et al. *Bureaucratic Politics and Foreign Policy.* Washington, D.C.: The Brookings Institution, 1974.

KISSINGER, H. A. *American Foreign Policy: Three Essays.* New York: Norton, 1969.

MACRIDIS, R. C., ed. *Foreign Policy in World Politics.* 5th ed. Englewood Cliffs, N.J.: Prentice-Hall, 1976.

ROSENAU, J. N., ed. *Comparing Foreign Policies: Theories, Findings, and Methods.* New York: Halsted Press, 1974.

SAPIN, B. *The Making of United States Foreign Policy.* New York: Praeger, 1967.

CHAPTER SIX
FOREIGN POLICY AND DOMESTIC POLITICS

We mentioned earlier that there is a considerable amount of interaction between foreign policy formulation and implementation and domestic politics. Indeed, every kind of transnational policy formulation must be analyzed within the context of domestic political considerations. Four aspects of this interrelationship are especially significant and deserve closer examination:

1. The influence of powerful groups on a state to shape foreign policies in accordance with their beliefs, values, and aspirations.
2. The influence of the domestic structure of a state upon the making of foreign policy.
3. The domestic political reactions evoked by particular foreign policy goals and actions.
4. The use of foreign policy by governmental leaders to influence outcomes in domestic politics and to gain political advantage.

THE INFLUENCE OF POWERFUL GROUPS
ON FOREIGN POLICY

In his seminal work, *The American People and Foreign Policy*, Gabriel Almond[1] has identified four categories of influential domestic groups who seek to have their goals and values reflected in the formulation of foreign policy. They are:

1. The *administrative or bureaucratic elites* which include the professional corps of the executive establishment who enjoy special powers by virtue of their interest in and familiarity and immediate contact with particular policy problems.
2. The *interest elites* which include the representatives of the vast number of private, policy-oriented associations, ranging from huge nation-wide aggregations to local formations and organized around aims and objectives which in their variety reflect the economic, ethnic, religious, and ideological complexity of the American population.
3. The *political elites* which include the publicly elected, high appointive, as well as the party leaders.
4. Finally, there are the *communications elites*, the most obvious representatives of which are the owners, controllers, and active participants of the mass media—radio, [television], press, and movies. . . .[2]

Almond's categories apply not only to the United States, but to all countries in the democratic political systems. We will examine the administrative and bureaucratic elites first because some aspects have already been discussed. This will be followed by observations on the interest, political, and communications elites.

Administrative and Bureaucratic Elites

In view of our previous discussion of the input into foreign policy by the civil servants who participate directly in the making of foreign policy decisions, our comments regarding administrative elites can be relatively brief. First, we must admit that it is difficult at times to draw a sharp distinction between those officials who participate directly in the decision-making process and those who can influence decisions only indirectly. Obviously, the direct participants need large amounts of information and must coordinate decision proposals with many offices in a ministry or in fact with officials in other ministries. This provides a definite channel for the indirect participants to express views and present their own arguments. Thus, for example, bureaucrats in the Ministry of Economics or Agriculture may have opportunities to modify the decision-making process in the Foreign Ministry in accordance with what they perceive as the most significant organizational and personal goals, even if the essence of the decision touches their assigned competence only very peripherally.

Other possibilities for civil servants to influence foreign policy making stem from personal relationships and coalitions with the other three elites, that is, elected politicians, interest groups, or the controllers of mass communications. Civil servants in a particular ministry may also seek interest in and support for their positions by appealing to the administration and political leadership of their own organizations, who in turn may attempt to exert influence laterally on the highest level of government. Finally, if bureaucratic elites are unable to influence the formulation of policy, they may have direct or indirect opportunities to sabotage its implementation by interpreting and applying directives in a way different from that intended by the policy formulators.

Bureaucratic elites can exercise influence on foreign policy making not only in democratic systems of government, but also in dictatorial and autocratic systems as found in communist countries. In fact, the role of bureaucracies is so central to communist forms of government that high-ranking Soviet civil servants, especially those with close affiliation to the KGB, can be very effective in influencing foreign policy making if they have the proper contacts in the Soviet foreign ministry and with pertinent members of the top leadership of the Communist party.[3]

Interest Elites

Interest groups whose leading echelons may want to have a hand in shaping foreign policy are found in all segments of the society; but without doubt, the most important groups in democratic countries are in the economic field. Business associations (and some individual large corporations), farmers' organizations, and labor union federations often have a major stake in a specific kind of policy and possess the staff and financial resources to engage in extensive lobbying. Examples of this type of influence abound. The Federation of German Industry has always insisted on close ties of West Germany with the West, and especially the United States, and has been successful in seeing that this policy is maintained. The French farmers' organizations wanted certain objectives pursued in France's foreign policy toward and inside the European Common Market, and the French government fully agreed to their set of goals. The British Confederation of Industry wanted Great Britain to enter the Common Market despite the widespread popular opposition, and its viewpoint ultimately won out. The American chemical industry opposed the elimination of certain nontariff barriers against foreign imports of tar products (the so-called American Selling Price Clause) which were contained in the international agreements ending the multilateral Kennedy Round negotiations on the reduction of trade barriers between the United States and her major trading partners in the world. Although the agreement bore the signature of the duly authorized American negotiator, Congress gave in to pressure by the chemical industry and refused to approve legislation for the elimination of this clause, which adversely affected the American administration's credibility for future trade negotiations.[4]

Despite the success stories alluded to in the above examples, we must guard against overestimating the influence of economic interest groups in shaping foreign policy. Certainly, in the formulation of national security policy and the strictly political aspects of foreign policy, their influence is often likely to be minimal. But even in the field of economic foreign policy, where, according to one of the myths about American politics, economic interest groups are assumed to be especially successful, this claim may at times be exaggerated. There can be little doubt that congressmen are apt to take economic group pressures more seriously when it comes to the definition of economic foreign policy than national security policy, but on many occasions conflicting interests may mitigate the pressures and encourage a measure of responsibility that looks beyond the economic interests immediately affected and takes into account long-range national goals.[5]

Similar considerations, though varying from country to country, seem to apply also to Western Europe. Professor Jean Meynaud, a very knowledgeable student of French interest group activities, states that "it is impossible to accept without serious reservations the theses which attribute to business a decisive influence upon [foreign] policy."[6] However, he concedes that economic interest groups may be moderately effective in influencing economic foreign policies. Even in communist dictatorships such as the Soviet Union we find limited influence exerted on the foreign policy making process by economic managers and technicians, although channeling appropriate demands to the highest councils of the Communist party and Soviet government requires a certain skill.[7]

The question of how much influence economic groups in developing countries have on foreign policy cannot be answered in clear-cut terms. With respect to India, Richard L. Parks[8] states:

> For the most part, interest groups do not have much influence in shaping India's foreign policy. Tradition excludes them from indirect involvement as informal advisers, and the law bars them from direct pressures. Such groups do, of course, have spokesmen in Parliament; they publish

their views; they influence individuals. But groups such as the trade unions, professional societies, commercial, financial, and industrial organizations, and caste lobbies have a most limited scope of influence.[9]

Similar conditions may exist in many newly independent countries in Asia and Africa, where businessmen are often held in low esteem because of their close connections with the colonial powers.

Lack of success of economic interest groups in influencing security policy does not mean that efforts to modify such policies are not made. A recent example is the attempt of two large American oil companies (Standard Oil Company of California and Mobil) to force the United States to toughen its stand toward Israel to gain assurances from the oil-producing states of the Persian Gulf of the continued flow of petroleum to America and, implicitly, a benevolent attitude toward the American petroleum industry.[10]

In this connection the so-called military-industrial complex needs to be mentioned because it is often assumed that the leaders of industries producing weapons systems and war materiel have a vested interest in seeing that their country pursues policies requiring large financial outlays for armaments, either for the conduct of hostilities or to be prepared for them. There can be little question that, when large manufacturing concerns such as Krupp in Germany, Dassault in France, or Colt Industries in America are dependent on the national government for a substantial part of their business, they are likely to prefer national situations and policies that keep orders coming into their plants. In the United States defense spending generates employment for 7 to 8 million persons directly, or over 10 percent of the total work force. There is also little doubt that the 2,000 high-ranking retired officers hired by large American corporations with military hardware for sale[11] can be utilized not only for the procurement of orders but also indirectly for influencing national policies through close personal ties and social contacts with their former brother officers still on active duty.

Whether the military-industrial complex, if in fact it exists as such, has been a major influence in formulating American security policy or may ultimately be able to prevent peace is questionable. While obviously, with so many civilian jobs at stake, tremendous pressures can be exerted directly and indirectly on national policy makers in the executive branch and Congress to continue and perhaps increase the budget of the Pentagon for the acquisition of military hardware, there is no evidence that decisions to enter the Korean War or concerning Vietnam were initiated by the military-industrial complex per se. Some of the top executives of affected corporations may have been pleased initially and the military leadership encouraged these decisions, but their influence was very minor as far as the grand design was concerned.[12] In this connection, it may also be significant in terms of the expectations of many defense contractors that companies heavily dependent on Pentagon contracts have in recent years attempted to diversify their product line into nonmilitary goods. Profits on defense contracts have dwindled, and the investment community has become disenchanted with those companies relying too much on government work.

In addition to economic organizations, some other interest groups have also been concerned with influencing foreign policy decisions. In the United States and France, veterans organizations fall into this category, and in Germany veterans' groups were active in the foreign policy field between World War I and II. Some church organizations have shown a special interest in foreign policy. For example, the National Council of Churches in the United States opposed the Vietnam War, and groups affiliated with the Catholic church in Italy and Spain have tried to influence the foreign policies of their countries in accordance with the views held by the church hierarchy. Ethnic groups have also attempted to involve themselves in foreign policy: Jewish organizations have played an important role in influencing American policy toward Israel, and Polish and Hungarian groups have often wanted the United States to pursue a strongly anticommunist policy toward the Communist People's Democracies of Eastern Europe.*

Scientists have also formed groups to influence foreign policy. They have claimed that scientific achievement gives them special insights into world politics to make decisions on arms and arms control. The Association of Atomic Scientists has been particularly active and has opposed as much as possible any use of nuclear weapons. Their publication, *The Bulletin of Atomic Scientists*, has obtained a readership going far beyond the circle of specialists it was originally designed to serve.

Finally, we must mention the League of Women Voters (LWV) and the World Affairs Councils (or Foreign Policy Associations) in various cities, which have shown great concern with the formulation of American foreign policy. The LWV undertakes periodic reviews of particular foreign policy issues and takes definite positions on these issues. For example, during 1976–77 the American stand on the United Nations was discussed and re-evaluated by all units in the United States, and considering the extensive membership, LWV

---

* They are the German Democratic Republic (often referred to as DDR, the Deutsche Demokratische Republik), Poland, Czechoslovakia, Hungary, Romania, and Bulgaria.

positions adopted nationally have a measure of influence on American policy makers.

We should note that domestic interest groups sometimes also seek to promote foreign policy goals of foreign countries. They may do this either by open identification with the foreign policy objectives of foreign countries or by employing subtle means without revealing their identification. An example of the former is the support given by Jewish groups to the foreign policies of Israel and their attempt to solicit favorable policies from American decision makers. An example of the latter is a three-day closed conference of American and French top-level industrial leaders which was organized to induce the French component of this meeting to put pressure directly or through their interest groups on the French government to adopt favorable attitudes toward the successful conclusion of the Kennedy Round of tariff-cutting negotiations, a high-priority goal of the U.S. government.

In dictatorships such as the Soviet Union or the People's Republic of China, interest groups as known in the United States and other democracies do not exist. Nevertheless, certain groups of people and enterprises do have common interests and seek to promote them. For example, although managers of various factories are civil servants in the Soviet Union, they may have certain common interests in general or with respect to their special industrial branches. Thus it is not inconceivable that factory managers in a particular industry may make common cause to advocate a particular economic foreign policy for the Soviet Union that is beneficial to them.

The Political Elites

The members of the political elite who, in a democracy, often have a major interest in influencing foreign policy making are national legislators and political party leadership groups. As we have seen, national legislators are often at the receiving end of demands by interest groups and must manifest some degree of responsiveness when groups or members of groups happen to belong to their constituency. Especially when interest groups have succeeded in selling the virtue of their interests to other groups and the public and have been able to generate some kind of consensus that their interests and the public good coincide, legislators may not be able to resist supporting the demands of these groups.*

---

* Chief executives also lobby at times in legislatures. Indeed, in the United States the most powerful lobbyist in Congress is the president.

The leadership of political parties can be influential in foreign policy affairs because parties are the only important links between the policy makers and individual and local interests. In West Germany the constitution specifically recognizes the significant role of the parties in the formulation of national policy. In the past, political parties were mainly concerned with domestic issues, but today foreign policy questions are attracting more and more attention. Moreover, nowadays, most national parties aggregate a variety of interests; even those parties that formerly were primarily ideology-oriented, such as the socialist parties, do not limit themselves to representing only the demands of the working man. As George Modelski observes:

> The bigger the parties, and the fewer parties there are, the more interests they represent, and the greater the difficulties they face in the task of reconciling and coordinating such a variety of interests. Representing clusters of interests, parties can adopt authoritative and consistent attitudes on the whole range of foreign-policy problems confronting the state. But that same breadth of outlook required of them on the large issues makes them liable to lose touch with the multitude of particular interests on whose satisfaction their vitality depends.[13]

Parties become transmission belts for interest group demands in foreign policy matters; but at the same time, they are in a position to reject, reduce, or modify these demands in order to reconcile them with conflicting demands from other groups. Of course, the ability of parties to elicit favorable foreign policy decisions from the government varies from country to country. It is high in Denmark, but was very low in the France of de Gaulle, where party officials, including those of the Gaullist party, admitted that their influence upon government policy making was small at that time. It did not improve much under former President Pompidou, but has been better under Valéry Giscard d'Estaing, the president of France since 1974. Nevertheless, even under de Gaulle, French interest groups wanted to keep open the channels of communication to the party organization and to maintain party contacts in the event the political situation in France changed and parties once again became influential.

It is important to stress that, although the leadership of a party may have decided to stand behind the demands of a particular interest group, its representatives in the legislature may not support it if the issue comes to a vote. In both two-party and multiparty systems, factionalism is not unusual; and unless party discipline is strong, as it is in Great Britain, the votes of the party representatives may be scattered. Moreover, the initiative for foreign policy decisions is normally in the hands of the executive, which further reduces the potential of parties to make a major impact, especially on those decisions dealing with national security matters.[14] In nonsecurity affairs, however, the influence of party elites is normally greater, particularly since the executive in democracies requires continuous support and consent by party leaders, and it is with respect to non-security issues that concessions to party wishes can be made more easily.

In dictatorships, such as the Soviet Union and its East European satellites, normally only a single party exists. Although factional interests are often expressed within the party, they are not permitted to become public; the party's public image is one of unity and har-mony. Nevertheless, debates over foreign policy issues do take place, and when good arguments reach the highest level of the party organi-zation, they may influence impending foreign policy decisions.[15]

The Communication Elites

The communication elites include not only newspapermen and per-sonnel in the radio, television, and movie industries, but also teach-ers, clergymen, publicists, and civic club and fraternal order leaders. The communication leaders who can be most influential in foreign policy affairs are those of the press, radio, and television. Although it is difficult to determine *how much* the public accepts of what it reads and hears, the correspondents and editorialists of the media are in a position to determine *what* the public will read and hear, and consequently can influence what it may remember. They have the power to emphasize certain news items or to play them down; they can conceal or expose, support or attack particular courses of action in a country's foreign policy. Despite governmental warn-ings of media excesses in reporting, they can embarrass individual officials and others in prominent places by making them look ridicu-lous, by publishing alleged wrongdoing, and by revising and distort-ing inconvenient incidents from the past. In all these ways, leaders of the press, radio, and television tend to influence foreign policy decisions by acting as mediators between the interested sectors of broad public opinion and the various elites that participate in the decision-making process of foreign policy formulation and execu-tion. At the same time, leaders of the press, radio, and television present and interpret elite views and actions to their readers and listeners, and, conversely, they are in a position to exert influence over members of the elites in the name of the public they claim to represent.[16]

In the United States the press has become an integral factor in foreign policy making, but it does not function as a pressure group per se. Rather, it seeks to link widely scattered parts and splice them with political and intellectual criticism. Major wire services are mostly only factual conveyors of foreign policy news.

In many respects the press functions are similar to those of intelligence organizations—the collection, evaluation, and dissemination of information. Roger Hilsman describes this function well in his book *The Politics of Policy Making in Defense and Foreign Affairs:*

> . . . An American correspondent in a foreign capital must, of course, rely on public announcements by the local government for much of his information and on briefings by the staff of the American embassy for a lot more. As a result much of what he reports is not new to Washington officials. But foreign correspondents are able to gather information on their own, and what they do gather is useful. So also is their independent judgment and interpretation of events. Wise Washington officials will always welcome the opportunity to hear an independent opinion to compare with the opinion forwarded by the embassy, even though they may not agree with it. Throughout the Vietnam struggle, for example, the views of the reporters who were critical of the Saigon regime and the American effort in Vietnam were valued by at least some of the officials in Washington as an antidote to the sometimes excessive optimism coming through official channels. In these circumstances the press constitutes a *competing* source of judgment and interpretation.[17]

Individual newspapers have the unusual power to place issues they want to emphasize on the front page and report on these issues more heavily than on others. By doing so, they focus attention on a particular issue and may bring enormous pressure to bear on government officials to take action. At the same time, this power to focus attention on an issue gives newspapers the power to kill a planned move by the government by merely publicizing it. An example is the Bay of Pigs fiasco. The *New York Times,* aware of the planned invasion of the Cuban Special Forces group under the sponsorship of the CIA, intended to reveal the plan and thus to put a stop to it. President Kennedy telephoned the publisher of the *New York Times* and asked him not to print the story. In this instance, the *New York Times* acquiesced. As a practical matter the news media are normally very careful before publishing information of this kind. Had the *Times* gone ahead with its plans to publish, it might have gotten credit not for preventing a disaster, but for wrecking a victory.

One of the most important reasons for the power of the press and television in influencing foreign policy is that they are a principal source of the interpretation of events to the public at large. This interpretation is not always clearly labeled as such, as in the writings of the syndicated columnists such as James Reston and Joseph Kraft. Interpretation in a particular sense may also take place when news is ostensibly presented in a straightforward manner on television. The news is "interpreted" not only in editorials, or in the "instant analysis" after a particular speech, but also when Walter Cronkite or John Chancellor determines the sequence of news items to be presented in his nightly news programs. Similarly significant is the location of a story on the pages of a newspaper.

For the Department of State and the Foreign Ministries in other countries, support of official policy by the news media has become an important aspect of foreign policy making. Because disclosures about impending policy actions can be very embarrassing, high officials often seek to establish very good and personal relations with important news writers and TV news commentators.

There has been considerable argument about the impact of the communications media on public opinion and the importance of public opinion in foreign policy making. Gabriel Almond has divided the public into a mass or general public and the so-called attentive public as far as foreign policy is concerned.[18] Almond and many other observers hold that the mass and general public, consisting of 75 to 90 percent of the adult population, is uninformed about specific foreign policy issues or foreign affairs in general. It is without initiative, pays little attention to what goes on, and has no structured opinion. Whatever response it has is mainly emotional and highly fluctuating. It often moves rapidly from pessimism to optimism and vice versa regarding a particular foreign policy issue. Vietnam is an excellent case in point.

The attentive public is small, about 10 percent of the adult population, and may be increasing because of the growing attention paid by the news media to foreign policy problems. Members of the attentive public are interested businessmen, educators on all levels, professional men and women, and increasingly, women's organizations such as the League of Women Voters. These individuals are often members of foreign policy associations and read a number of publications, such as *Time* and *Newsweek*, thereby becoming better informed on foreign policy matters. They are interested in participating in opinion making and are doing so by expressing their views in a variety of public forums, including letters to the editor. In general, these people have higher incomes and are better educated, and their opinions are often more differentiated than those held by the mass public. They constitute the primary and often critical audience for foreign policy discussions among the elites. There has been much argument of how useful it is to mobilize public opinion in support of a particular stand on foreign policy issues. Despite the fact that in a democracy public opinion appears to have a central role, and despite the fact that the people can express their displeasure with policies in political elections, experience has shown that in the field of foreign policy the voice of the public at large plays a distinctly minor role. Again, there are exceptions and the changes of American policy in Vietnam may well be one of these.

What is the influence of public opinion in dictatorships such as the Soviet Union or Nazi Germany during the 1930s? One aspect of these regimes has been the use of modern mass communication media by the foreign policy decision makers to assure support for the decisions made. In other words, the decision makers in these regimes make a concentrated effort to build a favorable climate of opinion for their foreign policies. However, it is a mistake to assume that the approval of the public for these policies is automatic. In Germany prior to World War II, critical opinions were expressed in private, but of course did not find their way into the news media. In the Soviet Union some diversity of opinion is likely to exist as we have pointed out when discussing party factionalism. This disparity of opinion may well come to the attention of foreign policy decision makers; and if they should perceive that there is major and persistent opposition by the public, it may well influence their policies. However, because the mass media are closely controlled, and freedom of expression is severely limited if not completely non-existent, governmental leaders in dictatorships are much better able to manipulate public opinion than in democratic societies, or to ignore it completely. As William Coplin points out, even if the Soviet public were well aware of the issues and all the facts and had given substantial thought to foreign policy issues, it still would not have the capacity to provide clear direction for the foreign policy makers because of the political controls exercised in the Soviet Union.[19] The propaganda and agitation section of the Communist party (AGIT-PROP) has the task of attuning the mass mind to the policies of the Soviet leadership and of stopping at its source any public criticism of actions taken by the government. The virtually complete isolation of communist news media from Western news and views, the secretiveness of communist policies, and the brainwashing process of channeling and controlling thought along party lines prevent citizens in communist-ruled societies from acquiring an objective or informed view.

DOMESTIC STRUCTURE AND
FOREIGN POLICY MAKING

The question of how the domestic structure or forms of government of a country affect the kind of foreign policy it develops has been debated for many years. Do dictatorial governments develop their resources more efficiently and make better use of them than democracies, enabling the former to formulate and implement stronger policies? What is the influence of ideologies espoused by communist governments upon the formulation of policy? What is the influence of different leadership structures on decision making? Do democracies pursue more peace-loving policies than dictatorships?

In the 20th century dictatorships have used a large share of their national efforts to build up the necessary individual and military resources that could support strong foreign policies. Tight control over the economy, regimentation of the population, and disregard of consumer demands have made this possible. The result has been a tremendous increase in their power inventory, even at the cost of millions of human lives. Yet, most democracies have been able to create more prosperous economies than those created by the dictatorships, and their economic success has constituted a significant counterbalance to the military force and enforced regimentation of the latter. Moreover, in wartime, many democracies have instituted centralized control mechanisms of their own, which, coupled with self-discipline and usually superior national resources, have enabled them to create an effective military machine that was more than a match for the armed forces of the dictatorships.

Whether the fact that democracy rests basically on the consent and voluntary support of the governed while dictatorship requires coercion as a source of strength has not been fully established. The Nazi regime in Germany enjoyed the support of most Germans prior to 1941, and modern dictatorships have developed a very effective means of indoctrination through the use of mass media, education, and party organizations. Youth movements were utilized in the Soviet Union, Communist China, Nazi Germany, and Fascist Italy to produce citizens who could not conceive of any alternative to supporting the autocratic regime. The achievement of a broad basis of consensus was thus considered critical, and it is noteworthy that both the Soviet Union and Communist China have found it opportune to use the trappings of democracy to conceal their dictatorial regimes. The constitution of the Soviet Union with its "representative" legislative assemblies projects the image of democracy, and the communist satellite countries of East Europe call themselves

People's Democracies. These facts suggest strongly that democracy has an appeal and a mystique from which dictatorships and autocracies want to benefit, but do not answer the question of what effect the form of government has on the type of foreign policies formulated.

The Influence of Ideologies

An intriguing question is whether decision makers in dictatorships permeated by powerful ideologies are influenced by these ideologies when formulating their foreign policies. As far as the Soviet Union is concerned, a number of theories have attempted to identify the mainsprings of her foreign policies, and one of these theories does indeed consider Marxist-Leninist political doctrine as the most important force motivating the content of Soviet foreign policies.[20] According to this theory, Soviet policy must be seen as part of the strategy of communist world revolution. As early as August 23, 1915, Lenin wrote that after the victory of socialism in a few or even in one single country

> ... the victorious proletariat of that country ... would confront the rest of the capitalist world, attract to itself the oppressed classes of other countries, raise revolts among them against the capitalists, and in the event of necessity, come out even with armed force against the exploiting classes and their states.[21]

Of considerable significance also is Stalin's Report on the Work of the Central Committee to the Seventeenth Congress of the Communist Party of the Soviet Union on January 26, 1934,[22] in which he stated:

> The working class of the U.S.S.R. is part of the world proletariat, its vanguard, and our republic is the cherished child of the world proletariat.

Thus, the Soviet Union is seen as an organic part of an international alliance, which has the task of overthrowing capitalism in both developed and underdeveloped countries of the world and instituting socialism in its place. In order to achieve the ultimate goal of world revolution, the Soviet Union may employ any tactics it considers opportune.[23] At the same time, it must constantly prepare against capitalist attacks, which have been said to be inevitable during most years since 1917. The ultimate inevitability of war between the socialist and capitalist camp was suggested in one of Stalin's favorite quotations from Lenin:

> We live . . . not only in a state but in a system of states, and the existence of the Soviet Republic side by side with the imperialist states for a long time is unthinkable. In the end either we or the other will conquer.[24]

There is no evidence that the statements of Lenin and Stalin quoted earlier are no longer influential bases of Soviet policy. On the contrary, the importance of mastering Marxist theory as amended by Lenin is constantly stressed in the Soviet Union. Many articles on party education open with references to a statement of Lenin that "without revolutionary theory there can be no revolutionary movement."[25] Stalin said that "the attempt of practical workers to brush theory aside runs counter to the whole spirit of Leninism and is fraught with serious dangers to the cause,"[26] a comment that has been repeated and reproduced many times. Articles on theory and communist theoretical writings are frequent features of the communist press. Significant works by Lenin are re-edited and republished periodically. Marxism of the Leninist brand is taught daily as one of the compulsory subjects in all Soviet schools, from the elementary level to postgraduate university training. The various youth, labor, party, farm, and professional organizations and groups, as well as the Soviet Army, discuss and teach Marxism and Leninism.[27]

The question arises as to the extent to which Soviet leaders actually follow theory in the formulation of policy. The Soviet leaders are integral parts of their system. Ideology is both a set of conscious assumptions and purposes and part of the total historical, social, and personal background of the Soviet leaders. First, ideology defines the ultimate purposes to which policy must aspire. Second, it makes it possible for the Soviet leaders to understand and evaluate the various historical phases that underlie policy formulation as means for the realization of the final goal.[28] Consequently, an outsider can understand Soviet attitudes only when he views facts through Soviet eyes and within the framework of Marxist-Leninist ideology.[29]

While the influence of ideology on Soviet foreign policy makers cannot be denied, traditional Russian national interests are a very important input. Indeed, Soviet ideology, aiming at eventual world supremacy of communism, permits great flexibility. The Kremlin is under no ideological compulsion to accomplish its purpose in a hurry. Like the church, it is dealing in ideological concepts that are thought to be of long-term validity, and it can afford to be patient. It does not dare to risk the existing achievements of the revolution.

The teachings of Lenin require great caution, flexibility, and deception in the pursuit of communist purposes. The Soviet leaders have no compunction about retreating in the face of superior force. They endeavor to obtain the fruits of war without resorting to war. Their political actions are like a stream that moves constantly, wherever it is permitted to move, toward a given goal. The primary purpose of the movement is to maintain persistent and if possible increasing pressure toward the desired objective.[30]

The emphasis on flexibility in the pursuit of long-range policy goals is significant inasmuch as it allows the emergence of short-range policies that frequently have a highly opportunistic flavor. Statements of Stalin[31] and Lenin,[32] reflecting the concept that right is what serves the cause of communism, stress the importance of opportunistic tactical policies. Such policies are, at times, excellent instruments to counter effectively hostile power politics, and they may also be used to achieve long-range goals of Soviet policy at less cost to the Soviet Union than armed conflict.[33]

The peace campaigns of the Soviet Union and the quest for peaceful coexistence can also be considered as temporary tactics designed to further the fulfillment of long-range Soviet foreign policy goals based on ideology and traditional Russian national interests, which of course include self-preservation. A period of "peaceful coexistence" was announced by Stalin as early as 1925, when he contended that the revolutionary movement was ebbing and capitalism was achieving a temporary stabilization. The context of Stalin's contention makes it clear that he expected peaceful coexistence to be as temporary as the capitalist stabilization. It was a convenient tactic, which did not preclude a simultaneous call to the international Communist parties to prepare for attack.[34] In the same vein, during the early 1960s, Khrushchev repeatedly advocated "harmonious relations," but the policies he pursued all over the world never lost any of their aggressiveness.[35]

Even the current efforts at détente pursued by the Soviet Union under the leadership of Leonid Brezhnev, as well as the urging for and participation in the European Security Conference, can be understood within the motivational framework discussed so far. The present needs of the Soviet Union to produce a higher level of consumer goods than heretofore to satisfy some of the aspirations of her population have forced the government to advocate a policy of economic and technological cooperation with the countries of the noncommunist world. These needs also are likely to have induced the Soviet Union to support a greater interchange of people and contacts between East and West. The endeavors to reach a mutual and balanced reduction of forces between NATO and the

Warsaw Pact can be understood as tactical means to bring about a reduction of American forces in Europe and at the same time somewhat reduce the burdens of armaments carried by the Soviet Union and its satellites.[36]

Whether in the future Soviet policy will continue to show the congenial face of détente is a highly uncertain question. Stating that Marxist ideology may well constitute a significant input into Soviet foreign policy does not imply that other motivations, such as national security and the desire for continuation in power by a small leadership clique, should be disregarded. As in other countries, inputs into policy making in the Soviet Union come from a variety of sources; but in view of the strong emphasis that the state places on ideology, it seems only reasonable to assume that ideology is important in the formulation and implementation of Soviet foreign policy.

After discussing at such great length the likely impact of Marxist ideology upon Soviet foreign policy, some comments must also be made with respect to democracy as an ideology. After all, the United States fought World War I and, to a lesser extent, World War II to "make the world safe for democracy." Despite this use of the term *democracy* to generate popular support for two difficult wars, democracy does not possess the cohesive and compelling force of Marxist ideology. Democratic ideology today is no longer expansionist, as it was at the time of the French Revolution. Its dynamism, which swept away the legal privileges of the aristrocracy, has today become primarily a doctrine of equality before the law, majority rule, and the principle of the right of disagreement on substantive goals and on the national purpose. At the current time, democracy lacks the fanaticism and uniformity normally associated with the coherence and drive of an ideology; however, commitment to specific ideals, such as human rights, voiced so forcefully by President Carter in 1977 may inject a strong moral tone into the formulation of foreign policy and its implementation as well.

Domestic Structure and Leadership Patterns

The domestic structure of government also affects significantly the nature of foreign policy leadership patterns. Henry Kissinger, in an essay on "Democratic Structure and Foreign Policy,"[37] distinguishes three contemporary types of leadership groups based on their experiences during their rise to eminence, the structure in which they must operate, and the values of their society. These three types are (1) the bureaucratic-pragmatic type, (2) the ideological type, and (3) the revolutionary-charismatic type.

Bureaucratic-Pragmatic Leadership   The main examples of bureaucratic-pragmatic leadership are the American and British elites, though the leadership groups of other Western countries increasingly adopt the same pattern. Shaped by a society without fundamental social schisms (at least until the race problem became visible) and the product of an environment in which most recognized problems have proved solvable, its approach to policy is ad hoc, pragmatic, and somewhat mechanical.

Because pragmatism is based on the conviction that the context of events produces a solution, there is a tendency to await developments. The belief is prevalent that every problem will be solvable if attacked with sufficient energy. It is inconceivable, therefore, that delay might result in irretrievable disaster; at worst it is thought to require a redoubled effort later on.

This tendency is reinforced by the special qualities of the professions—law and business—that furnish the core of the leadership groups in America. Lawyers, at least in the Anglo-Saxon tradition, prefer to deal with actual rather than hypothetical cases; they have little confidence in the possibility of stating a future issue abstractly. In the business world, the executive is rewarded for his ability to manipulate the known, in itself a conciliatory procedure. The special skill of the executive is thought to consist in coordinating well-defined functions rather than in challenging them. The procedure is relatively effective in the business world, where the executive can often substitute decisiveness, long experience, and a wide range of personal acquaintances for reflectiveness. In international affairs, however—especially in a revolutionary situation—the strong will, which is one of the business executive's notable traits, may produce essentially arbitrary choices.

All this gives American policy its particular cast. Problems are dealt with as they arise. Agreement on what constitutes a problem generally depends on an emerging crisis which settles the previously inconclusive disputes about priorities. When a problem is recognized, it is dealt with by a mobilization of all resources to overcome the immediate symptoms. This often involves the risk of slighting longer-term issues which may not yet have assumed crisis proportions. Administrative decisions often reflect compromise under the maxim that "if two parties disagree the truth is usually somewhere in between." Unfortunately the pedantic application of such truisms cause the various contenders to exaggerate their positions for bargaining purposes or to construct fictitious extremes to make their position appear moderate, with the result that the substantive quality of the decision suffers.

Ideological Leadership   As has been discussed above, whatever the ideological commitment of individual leaders, a lifetime spent in the Communist hierarchy must influence their basic categories of thought, especially since Communist ideology continues to perform important functions. In a system where there is no legitimate succession, a great deal of energy is absorbed in internal maneuvering. Leaders rise to the top by eliminating—often physically, always bureaucratically—all possible opponents. Anyone succeeding in Communist leadership struggles must be single-minded, unemotional, dedicated, and above all, motivated by an enormous desire for power. Nothing in the personal experiences of Soviet leaders would lead them to accept protestations of goodwill at face value. Suspiciousness is inherent in their domestic position. It is unlikely that their attitude toward the outside world is more benign than that toward their own colleagues, or that they would expect more consideration from it.

Charismatic-Revolutionary Leadership   The contemporary international order is heavily influenced by yet another leadership type: the charismatic-revolutionary leader. These leaders are found mainly in the new nations of Africa and Asia, whose political systems, in many instances, follow basically autocratic and socialistic principles, although these features may be concealed by some trappings of democracy. For many of these leaders, the bureaucratic-pragmatic approach of the West is irrelevant because they are more interested in the future they wish to construct than in the manipulation of the environment, which dominates the thinking of the pragmatists. And ideology is not satisfactory because doctrine supplies rigid categories that overshadow the personal experiences that have provided the impetus for so many of the leaders of the new nations in their struggle to improve the lot of their people.

As Kissinger observed,

> The type of individual who leads a struggle for independence has been sustained in the risks and suffering of such a course primarily by a commitment to a vision which enabled him to override conditions which had seemed overwhelmingly hostile. Revolutionaries are rarely motivated primarily by material considerations—though the illusion that they are persists in the West. Material incentives do not cause a man to risk his existence and to launch himself into the uncertainties of a revolutionary struggle. If Castro or Sukarno had been principally interested in economics, their talents would have guaranteed them a brilliant career in the societies they overthrew. What made their sacrifices worthwhile

to them was a vision of the future—or a quest for political power. To revolutionaries the significant reality is the world which they are striving to bring about, not the world they are fighting to overcome. . . .

. . . [T]o the charismatic heads of many of the new nations economic progress, while not unwelcome, offers too limited a scope for their ambitions. It can be achieved only by slow, painful, highly technical measures which contrast with the heroic exertions of the struggle for independence. Results are long-delayed; credit for them cannot be clearly established.[38]

As a result of the characteristics of the charismatic-revolutionary type of leadership, there is a great tendency to institute and expand authoritarian rule. At the same time, leadership groups often look at foreign policy as a means of bringing about domestic cohesion.

The Structure of Government and Peace

Finally, a few comments need to be made about the question of whether democracies pursue more peaceful policies than dictatorships. Again, the record is inconclusive. Clearly the policies of Nazi Germany, and to a lesser degree Mussolini's Italy, manifested a penchant for expansion and military aggression; but the policies of the Soviet Union and Communist China, while seeking to expand their external spheres of influence, have generally avoided overt aggression since World War II, except for the Soviet invasion of Czechoslovakia in 1968 and China's limited marches into India in 1959 and 1962. The action in Czechoslovakia can be seen as a protective activity for Soviet security rather than aggressive war, although it clearly violated the sovereignty and integrity of an independent state. However, the justification of this act of war under the so-called Brezhnev theory of limited sovereignty for the Soviet Union's East European allies has met with little enthusiasm in these countries. Communist China's military actions in India were mainly border clashes and were settled rather quickly. But Communist North Korea's attack on South Korea unleashed a major war in 1950. Beyond open aggression, we must note that the Soviet Union and other communist countries have engaged in intensive subversive activities in many parts of the world, including Latin America and Africa.

As far as the democracies are concerned, clearly the United States has conducted more extensive military actions since 1945 than any other country. The expressed purpose of these actions was the containment of communist expansionist designs. In Korea this explanation had validity inasmuch as South Korea, allied to the United States, was invaded by Communist North Korean forces in June of 1950. The situation in Vietnam was less clear-cut because the military actions by the Viet Cong and the North Vietnamese seemed to have more the character of a "war of liberation" than conventional aggression against the state of South Vietnam, America's ally. Subversive activities against different countries have also been carried out by the United States. The actions of the CIA against the Allende government of Chile are a recent example.

FOREIGN POLICY EFFECTS ON DOMESTIC POLITICS

In the interface between foreign policy making and domestic politics, cause-effect relationships do not always flow from domestic interests toward foreign policy making, but also in the opposite direction. The formulation and implementation of particular policies can evoke strong adverse reactions on the part of political elites and the public at large, resulting ultimately in the loss of political support for government leaders and even in their overthrow. An obvious case in point is the reaction of the people in the United States toward America's policy in Vietnam. It may be useful to review the sequence of events briefly.[39]

The Vietnam War

The military commitment of the United States in Vietnam increased slowly but steadily. Before World War II, Vietnam, along with Cambodia and Laos, had been part of a colonial empire known as French Indochina. Lead by a Communist, Ho Chi Minh, Vietnam proclaimed her independence in 1945. A nine-year civil war ended in 1954 with a French military defeat and a series of agreements reached in Geneva. These agreements divided Vietnam temporarily into a northern sector under the leadership of Ho and a southern one supported by the French and Americans. The agreements also stipulated that elections would be held in 1956 in both parts of the country to bring about unification under a single government; however, for a variety of reasons, these elections were not held.

In 1955 an American military assistance group was activated under the 1954 SEATO Treaty, with the justification that North Vietnam was supplying insurgent rebels in the south with weapons.

During the 1960s civil strife intensified in South Vietnam, and the assistance group grew to 23,000 men by 1964.

In August of 1964, President Lyndon Johnson reported (perhaps erroneously) that two American destroyers in the international waters off the coast of North Vietnam had been fired upon without provocation. At his initiative, Congress passed the so-called Gulf of Tonkin Resolution, which authorized the president to take necessary action for the defense of American armed forces in and around Vietnam or to prevent aggression. The next year, after the presidential elections, Johnson ordered the bombing of North Vietnam and sent American forces into combat.

In 1964 an increasingly stormy debate began, especially on the campuses of the United States, about the merits of American foreign policy with respect to Vietnam. A slow but inexorable movement against the Vietnam War began to spread over the nation. This debate reached a crescendo in 1968 when over 543,000 American troops had been sent to Vietnam and more than 33,000 had been killed.

Despite the many optimistic statements made by the American commander in chief in Vietnam, General William C. Westmoreland, that victory was in sight in the future, early in 1968 the general requested an additional 206,000 troops to see the war to a successful end. This request prompted a number of very crucial conferences in the White House to reappraise American foreign policy in Indochina. At the same time, Senator Eugene McCarthy, a leading opponent of the war, scored a stunning upset in the Democratic primary on March 1.

Against this background, influential members of the administration attempted to convince President Johnson to halt the bombing and to get negotiations started. Eventually he seemed to become convinced of the need for a bombing cutback. When the Wisconsin primary approached and the political signs were not favorable for his chances in the contest, President Johnson, considering both external and internal factors, made two startling announcements in a speech on March 31, 1968: he halted the bombing north of the 20th Parallel, and announced that he would not be a candidate in the forthcoming presidential elections.

The president's announcement did not halt the surge of public opinion against the Vietnam War. In the face of this strong public opinion trend, President Richard Nixon, after taking office in 1969, authorized the gradual removal of American ground combat troops and launched a "Vietnamization" program designed to turn most of the fighting over to the Vietnamese.

In the fall of 1972 the negotiations for peace in Vietnam seemed close to success; however, difficulties cropped up, and in December of that year President Nixon ordered renewed and very severe bombing attacks against North Vietnam, while the American Navy was ordered to mine North Vietnamese ports. Finally, in February 1973, a peace accord was concluded that was hailed by the President as an achievement of historic dimension.

While the peace agreements resulted eventually in an uneasy cease fire in Vietnam and Laos, pressure by communist forces in Cambodia prompted the Nixon Administration to continue full-scale bombing in that country to prevent the existing government from falling. However, public opinion increasingly opposed the continued military activities in Cambodia, and finally Congress voted overwhelmingly to stop the war in Cambodia by cutting off funds for military operations. It is interesting to note that the congressional vote had widespread public support and that a Gallup poll published on August 15, 1973,[40] the deadline for the bombing, revealed that 65 percent of the responders were opposed to any extension of this deadline. This expression of opinion paralleled the results of a similar Gallup poll in April, which slowed Americans opposed by a two-to-one margin to the bombing of Cambodia and Laos.

In summary then, Vietnam is an outstanding example of how adverse reactions evoked by a particular foreign policy of a government not only can force a change in policy, but can also reduce general support for the governmental leadership.

The Suez Crisis

Another example of adverse popular reaction to foreign policy action can be found in the attempted capture of the Suez Canal and invasion of Egypt by Great Britain and France in the fall of 1956. The Suez crisis was precipitated in the summer of 1956 when President Gamal Abdel Nasser of Egypt nationalized the Suez Canal Company, which operated that waterway, and thereby abrogated the International Convention of Constantinople of 1888 assuring full freedom of navigation through the canal in time of war as in time of peace without distinction of flag. For Britain, freedom of the canal symbolized her status as an empire and as a world power. It was an emotional reaction to the seemingly insolent and irresistible nationalism represented by the Egyptian movement.

To counter Nasser's move, Britain and France prepared for military action which was to be carried out in close cooperation with Israel, long harassed by Arab-initiated border clashes and made increasingly apprehensive by the Egyptian leader's pronouncement to "drive Israel into the sea." While Israel's armed forces rapidly advanced toward the Suez Canal, the British and French bungled their military missions. Their failures were the result not only of poorly executed military operations but also of the combined opposition of the United States and the Soviet Union and of increasingly hostile opposition at home. Confounded by United Nations resolutions charging Britain with aggression and dismayed by the action of the United States, Prime Minister Sir Anthony Eden had to terminate this military venture. Public opinion in Great Britain was divided almost from the outset about the merits of Eden's policy. As the bungling nature of the military operations became more and more visible, public opinion grew increasingly hostile. The upshot was that Prime Minister Eden had to resign and had to be replaced by another Conservative leader. This was a very unusual situation because under the British political system prime ministers normally retain their office until new elections are held.*

THE USE OF FOREIGN POLICY FOR DOMESTIC POLITICAL PURPOSES

The tendency of a political leader to maintain and improve his political position within his own state has definite consequences for the formulation of foreign policy goals. His aim must be achievement in the foreign policy field and avoidance of failures and reverses. It may produce an attitude that what is good for him politically may also be good for his country.

The area of national security in the broadest sense has best served the ambitions of most political leaders. Although emphasis on national security has generated long debates with domestic political opponents over what the "true" national interest of a country is or should be, the alleged needed counteraction to threats to a country's security has often resulted in bigger budgets and thereby the ability to fulfill more political promises. Able to claim superior knowledge of existing conditions, governmental leaders can criticize opponents with relative ease and contend in the face of dissent that disagreement with the proposed policy will endanger the chances of the state to assure its security. This applies to most countries,

---

* Another example of foreign policy influence on a British prime minister was the Munich Agreement among Prime Minister Neville Chamberlain, the French government, and Hitler over Czechoslovakia. When less than a year later Hitler invaded Poland, Chamberlain had to resign and was replaced by Sir Winston Churchill.

regardless of whether they are democracies or autocracies, economically developed or underdeveloped.

Perceptions of national security, détente, and peace were closely intertwined when President Nixon made his trips to China and the Soviet Union in the winter and spring of 1972 to open a new era of relations with the two communist giants. These visits covered most extensively by television made him a hero and contributed mightily to his impressive victory in the presidential election in November of that year. President Nixon's initiation of the new relationship with the Soviet Union and China was not without some political risks because conservative Republicans were likely to look with disfavor upon these new policies; however, the gamble paid off handsomely, although the long-range effect on U.S.–Soviet relations is not clear as yet.

During the 1976 presidential election campaign, President Gerald R. Ford presented his experience in foreign policy as a strong reason the American people should choose him rather than Carter. Other U.S. presidents have also intermingled foreign policy with domestic politics; Halperin and Kanter[41] cite several main concerns guiding these efforts:

1. The most important concern is getting and keeping office. For this reason presidents easily adopt the belief that their re-election is in the national interest and that their ability to be re-elected should not be adversely affected by a controversial foreign policy decision. An example is President Dwight D. Eisenhower's decision not to support the British-French-Israeli efforts in the Suez crisis of 1956 to oust Egyptian President Nasser to ensure the international nature of the Suez Canal. Alternatively a president may also see a particular foreign policy decision as an effective appeal to a particular group of potential supporters, such as Jewish voters or a group of manufacturers whose economic well-being may depend on a particular trade policy.

2. Presidents must avoid the appearance of failure and therefore are reluctant to undertake policies that have a high likelihood of not succeeding. Each failure tarnishes their reputation for success and creates perceptions in the public mind of reduced probability of success in the future. The fiasco of the Bay of Pigs venture aimed at toppling Fidel Castro could have had this effect upon President Kennedy's reputation.

3. Presidents should avoid rows with Congress, the press, or the public. Even if the president is initially successful in these rows, he may have paid too high a price in terms of generated antagonism, bitterness, and resentment. This was President Kennedy's assessment of his fight with Congress over the B-70 manned bomber.

4. The president must seek to develop a consensus of support

for a particular policy. In seeking this support, he must create the feeling that consistency is maintained. An example is a decision by President Truman to defend Taiwan in 1950 as otherwise he may not have been able to obtain popular support for his defense of Korea.

5. Presidents must be aware at all times that domestic interests and foreign policy interact in the clash over the use of scarce resources. Domestic needs may be so overwhelming as to necessitate economizing in the defense field with the result that aerospace procurement may be reduced or military bases may have to be closed.

We have noted that the tendency of governmental leaders to use foreign policy for their own political purposes is not limited to America or other democracies. It is also practiced by many leaders of the new nations. The importance for them is to escape internal difficulties and to achieve domestic cohesion. As Kissinger points out, the international arena provides frequent opportunities for dramatic measures not available within the domestic scene. Foreign policy can often be cast in an anti-Western mold reflecting the continuing effort in the struggle against imperial or neocolonial rule which has been the principal unifying element for many new nations.[42]

SUMMARY

There is a considerable amount of interaction between foreign policy and domestic politics. The four most significant aspects of this interrelationship are:

- the influence of powerful groups in shaping policies,
- the influence of the domestic structure of a state on its policies,
- the domestic political reactions evoked by foreign policy goals and actions, and
- the use of foreign policy by governmental leaders to influence outcomes in domestic politics.

Gabriel Almond has identified four categories of influential domestic groups. They are **administrative or bureaucratic elites, interest elites, political elites,** and **communication elites.** He holds that 75 to 90 percent of the adult population is uninformed about foreign affairs and has no structured opinion.

Henry Kissinger distinguishes three contemporary types of leaders, based on their experiences during their rise to eminence, the structure in which they must operate, and the values of their society. These three types are the **bureaucratic-pragmatic type,** the **ideolog-**

ical type, and the **revolutionary-charismatic type.** The American and British elites are examples of bureaucratic-pragmatic leadership. Communist leadership is primarily ideological, and revolutionary-charismatic leaders are found mainly in the new nations of Africa and Asia.

Not only do domestic politics affect foreign policy, but foreign policy affects domestic politics as well. Events in the United States during the Vietnam War and in Great Britain during the Suez crisis are examples. Likewise, governmental leaders tend to use foreign policy for their own political purposes.

The secrecy that usually surrounds the foreign policy making process offers myriad opportunities to tilt policy and goals in one direction or another. Cause-effect relationships become blurred when powerful elites employ all of their resources to lobby for the advancement of their interests. Policy effectiveness is likely to suffer because of the plethora of inputs and influences.

The instruments used to implement the policies devised may well determine whether they achieve their intended effects. The next chapter examines the various instruments available to national governments for this purpose.

NOTES

1. (New York: Praeger, 1962).

2. Gabriel Almond, *The American People and Foreign Policy* (New York: Praeger, 1962), pp. 139–140. We have listed these elites in a somewhat different order from that in Almond's book.

3. Cf. Kurt London, *The Making of Foreign Policy* (New York: Lippincott, 1965), pp. 183–194. See also Robert M. Slusser, *The Berlin Crisis of 1961: Soviet-American Relations and the Struggle for Power in the Kremlin* (Baltimore: Johns Hopkins University Press, 1973).

4. For other examples see Werner Feld, *European Common Market and the World* (Englewood Cliffs, N.J.: Prentice-Hall, 1967), esp. pp. 100–107.

5. Raymond A. Bauer, Ithiel de Sola Pool, and Lewis A. Dexter, *American Business and Public Policy* (New York: Atherton, 1963), pp. 396–401. See also Lester W. Milbrath, "Interest Groups and Foreign Policy," in James N. Rosenau, ed., *Domestic Sources of Foreign Policy* (New York: The Free Press, 1967), pp. 161–193.

6. *Nouvelles Etudes sur les groupes de pression en France* (Paris: Librairie Armand Coplin, 1962), p. 391. See also pp. 392–393.

7. Vernon V. Aspaturian, "Soviet Foreign Policy," chapter 5 in Roy C. Macridis, ed., *Foreign Policy in World Politics,* 3rd ed., (Englewood Cliffs, N.J.: Prentice-Hall, 1967), pp. 156–215, esp. pp. 188–198.

8. "India's Foreign Policy," chapter 10 in Macridis, op. cit., pp. 338–358.

9. Ibid., p. 349.

10. For details see *Wall Street Journal*, August 15, 1973, pp. 1 and 19.

11. Patrick M. Morgan, "Politics, Policy, and the Military-Industrial Complex," in Omer L. Carey, *The Military Industrial Complex and U.S. Foreign Policy* (Pullman, Wash.: Washington State University Press, 1969), pp. 55–66.

12. Ibid. A recent example is the cancellation of the construction of the B-1 bomber by President Jimmy Carter, although the last may not have been heard about this weapons system.

13. *A Theory of Foreign Policy* (New York: Praeger, 1962), p. 74.

14. See also the detailed study of James A. Robinson, *Congress and Foreign Policy-Making* (Homewood, Ill.: Dorsey, 1967), pp. 23–71. In the United States the War Powers Act passed by Congress in the aftermath of the Vietnam War has limited the use of armed forces by the president and thereby reduced the foreign policy prerogatives of the executive.

15. See Aspaturian, op. cit., pp. 156–215.

16. For a more comprehensive discussion see Bernard C. Cohen, "Mass Communications and Foreign Policy," in Rosenau, op. cit., pp. 195–212. In a recent poll respondents stated that they have more faith in the TV news services than in the federal executive branch. (See Harris Poll of September 13 and 22, 1973, reported in New Orleans *States-Item*, December 6, 1973.)

17. Roger Hilsman, *The Politics of Policy Making in Defense and Foreign Affairs* (New York: Harper & Row, 1971), p. 110.

18. Almond, op. cit., p. 138.

19. Coplin, op. cit., p. 77.

20. A comprehensive compilation of theories of Soviet foreign policy and a listing of writers supporting the various theories has been made by William A. Glaser, "Theories of Soviet Foreign Policies: A Classification of Literature," *World Affairs Quarterly* (June 1956), pp. 128–152. Other major theories contend that Soviet foreign policy is based upon traditional Russian national expansionism, taking into account historical, geographic, and strategic factors; that its mainspring is self-preservation and national security; or that it is motivated mainly by the quest of a small leadership clique concerned with the perpetuation of its power. For additional insights into Soviet foreign policy, the following books are recommended: David J. Dallin, *Soviet Foreign Policy After Stalin* (Philadelphia: Lippincott, 1961); and Jan F. Triska and David D. Finley, *Soviet Foreign Policy* (New York: Macmillan, 1968), esp. pp. 107–148.

21. V. I. Lenin, *Selected Works*, vol. 5 (New York: International Publishers, 1943), p. 141. See also V. I. Lenin, *Collected Works*, vol. 18 (New York: International Publishers, 1930), p. 395.

22. Joseph Stalin, *Leninism* (New York: International Publishers, 1942), p. 360. See also Stalin, "The Tasks of Business Executives," in ibid., pp. 200–201; and J. Stalin, *Problems of Leninism* (Moscow: Foreign Languages Publishing House, 1940), p. 28, where Lenin is quoted as having said that the task of the victorious revolution is to do the utmost possible in one country for the development, support, and awakening of the revolution in all countries.

23. Historicus, "Stalin on Revolution," *Foreign Affairs*, vol. 27 (January

1949), pp. 205–206. Historicus (his real name is George F. Kennan) points out that Stalin's conception of communist strategy and tactics is highly flexible. It rests on a continual assessment of the status of forces in both the capitalist and socialist systems. According to Stalin, one of the chief conditions to which tactics must be adjusted is the ebb and flow of the forces favoring revolution. "Aggressive tactics should be taken with a rising tide; tactics of defense, . . . and even retreat go with an ebbing tide" (Stalin, *Problems of Leninism*, pp. 81–95).

24. Quoted in Historicus, op. cit., p. 204.

25. J. Stalin, *Problems of Leninism*, op. cit., p. 26.

26. Ibid.

27. Jan F. Triska, "Model Study of Soviet Foreign Policy," *The American Political Science Review* (March 1958), pp. 64–83, esp. p. 70.

28. For an excellent discussion of the problem see Zbigniew Brzezinski, "Communist Ideology and International Affairs," *Journal of Conflict Resolutions* (September 1960), pp. 266–291; also Aspaturian, op. cit., pp. 137–156.

29. Triska, op. cit., p. 70; see also G. F. Kennan, "The Sources of Soviet Conduct," *Foreign Affairs* (July 1947), pp. 566–582, esp. p. 572.

30. G. F. Kennan, "The Sources of Soviet Conduct," op. cit., pp. 574–575. See also Raymond L. Garthoff, "The Concept of the Balance of Power in Soviet Policy Making," *World Politics* (October 1951), pp. 85–111, esp. p. 105.

31. See quotations cited in note 21.

32. Lenin, *Selected Works*, op. cit., vol. 2, part 2, pp. 482–487. The following quotation of Lenin is also significant: "The task of a truly revolutionary party is not to declare the impossible renunciation of all compromises, but to be able through all compromises, as far as they are unavoidable, to remain true to its principles, to its class, to its revolutionary task . . ." (V. I. Lenin, *Collected Works*, op. cit., vol. 21, book 1, p. 152).

33. See also N. Leites, *The Operational Code of the Politburo* (New York: McGraw-Hill, 1951), chapters 15, 16, 17, 19, and 20; Kennan, op. cit., pp. 20–23; and Robert Strausz-Hupe, *Protracted Conflict* (New York: Harper, 1959), which provides many good examples of Soviet tactics.

34. Historicus, op. cit., pp. 207–208.

35. Philip E. Moseley, "Soviet Foreign Policy: New Goals or New Manners," *Foreign Affairs* (July 1956), p. 533, discussing Khrushchev's foreign policy statements to the Twentieth Communist Party Congress, points out that his "restatements of Soviet goals, enlivened by new and flexible tactics, are, at bottom, an expression of continuity of basic goals in Soviet policy."

36. The negotiations between the Soviet Union and its satellites and the members of NATO on the achievement of détente were carried out in Helsinki, Geneva, and Vienna and began in 1973. For a recent view of Soviet ideology as developed under Brezhnev, see R. Judson Mitchell, "The Brezhnev Doctrine and Communist Ideology," *Review of Politics* (April 1972) and "The Revised Two Camps Doctrine in Soviet Foreign Policy," *Orbis* (Spring 1972).

37. *American Foreign Policy: Three Essays* (New York: Norton, 1969), pp. 11–50. The following discussion follows this essay closely.

38. Ibid., pp. 39 and 40.

39. For general discussion of electoral reaction to foreign policy actions, see Kenneth N. Waltz, "Electoral Punishing and Foreign Policy Crises," in Rosenau, op. cit., pp. 263–293.

40. *The Times Picayune* (New Orleans, La.), August 15, 1973, section 6, p. 3.

41. Morton H. Halperin and Arnold Kanter, eds., *Readings in American Foreign Policy: A Bureaucratic Perspective* (Little, Brown, 1973), pp. 13–14.

42. Kissinger, op. cit., p. 41.

SUGGESTED READINGS

BAUER, RAYMOND A., I. DE SOLA POOL, AND L. DEXTER. *American Business and Public Policy.* New York; Atherton, 1963.

GRABER, DORIS A. *Public Opinion, the President, and Foreign Policy.* New York: Holt, Rinehart & Winston, 1968.

RIESELBACH, L. N. *Congressional Politics.* New York: McGraw-Hill, 1972.

RUSSETT, B. M., AND E. C. HANSON. *Ideology and Interest: The Foreign Policy Beliefs of American Businessmen.* San Francisco: Freeman, 1975.

WILCOX, F. O. *Congress, the Executive and Foreign Policy.* New York: Harper & Row, 1971.

CHAPTER SEVEN
INSTRUMENTS
FOR POLICY
IMPLEMENTATION

The implementation of foreign policy and transnational policies as well is a continuous process and is the major stimulus for interaction in international relations and politics. All international actors—nation-states, IGOs, and nongovernmental organizations—may be involved in the policy implementation process; however, the extent and intensity of their involvement varies, depending on what particular policy is to be implemented and which instrument is chosen for its implementation.

For policy implementation, a government can utilize a number of instruments, either individually or concurrently. The most common of these is *diplomacy*, which is carried out chiefly by foreign service officers working in the foreign ministry at home and assigned to the embassies, legations, and missions of the country in the foreign capitals of the world. Because of the expense involved, a number of the smaller countries are selective about where they establish embassies; however, large and rich countries have representation almost everywhere. Other instruments for policy implementation are the use of various *economic measures*, some friendly and others hostile; *psychological warfare* means, especially propaganda; *political warfare* measures, some clandestine; and as a last resort, *military action*.

In some instances, national governments may employ IGOs as executing agencies for particular policies; the United States' use of NATO is an example. Or an IGO such as the United Nations may seek the help of national governments to implement a particular development policy for the poor countries of the world, perhaps to counter an outbreak of famine in central Africa. Nongovernmental organizations may become tools of transnational policy implementation for both national governments and IGOs, as we shall see in later chapters.

DIPLOMACY

Embassies as we know them now date from the middle of the 15th century and had their origin in northern Italy where in 1455 the Duke of Milan announced his intention to establish the first permanent embassy abroad. The legal bases for modern diplomatic practice, including the rules for the classification of ranks, came into being with the Congress of Vienna in 1815 and were finalized in their present form by the Vienna Convention on Diplomatic Relations in 1961. They provide for three top ranks in the following order:

1. Ambassadors or papal nuncios, who represent their heads of state* and are accredited to the heads of state of the country in which they serve;
2. Ministers, envoys, and internuncios, similarly accredited;
3. Chargés d'affaires, who are the foreign-service officers temporarily in charge of a diplomatic mission in the absence of the ambassador or minister.

Seniority at a capital is determined by the date of accreditation and rank, and the senior ambassador in a particular capital is known as the *doyen* or dean of the diplomatic corps.

Below the three top diplomatic ranks we find a hierarchy of lower grades and titles. In large embassies there may be individuals with the rank of minister below the ambassador; but this is merely a title, and the individual does not represent his head of state as does the ambassador. In most other embassies, legations, or missions, the highest-ranking diplomat usually has the title of councillor.

---

* In parliamentary democracies this may be the monarch or the president of a country, but the prime minister, premier, or chancellor (Germany) is usually not called a "head of state."

The functions of diplomats abroad can be classified as *representation, observation,* and *negotiation.* In general, all functions are designed to promote the attainment of the foreign policy goals of the diplomat's government; however, representation includes a number of tasks, such as the protection of citizens in legal disputes abroad, that cannot be linked directly to the pursuit of specific foreign policy objectives.

Representation

Representational functions include many ceremonial duties, such as the ambassador's or minister's attending in France the annual Fourteenth of July celebration of the birth of the First French Republic. Chiefs of diplomatic missions must participate in a large number of official functions of the host country, such as receptions and state dinners, and at the same time entertain high government officials and other leading personalities in the capital where they are stationed. The manner in which they entertain frequently reflects the prestige of their country. Entertainment serves also as an important means of informal intercourse among diplomats and is a convenient forum for conducting various kinds of business, including the transmission and acquisition of information, observation, and even subtle negotiation. Thus, the lavish cocktail parties diplomats give and attend should not be viewed as evidence of a penchant for luxury, but as performance of duty.

The function of representation also includes formal visits to the foreign ministry of the host country and perhaps even to the prime minister or president to convey information, expressions of concern, and requests of the diplomat's government. Among the information provided may be explanations of new policies initiated by the diplomat's home government. At the same time, diplomats may be called to the foreign ministries or the leaders of the host government to receive complaints or messages for their own top officials. An example is Soviet Ambassador Dobrinyn in Washington, whose assignment to the United States goes back to the Kennedy administration and who has had many occassions to talk not only to the secretary of state, but also to Presidents Kennedy, Johnson, Nixon, Ford, and Carter. Thus diplomatic representatives serve as official mouthpieces and message carriers for their governments. In the performance of these tasks they must use a variety of techniques, such as persuasion, veiled threats, or sympathetic listening, to achieve maximum effectiveness.

Observation

Diplomats function not only as the mouthpieces of their governments, but also as their eyes and ears. Observation is a major task of diplomats, who thereby become important cogs in the information-gathering machinery of their country. To introduce as much as possible professional judgment into the observation function, military, commercial, agricultural, and labor attachés are assigned to embassies, legations, and other missions. They are high-ranking officers and civil servants of the respective services and ministries. Army, air force, and naval attachés collect information about armaments, military organizations, and war planes; commercial attachés about industrial developments and economic trends; and other attachés about their own areas of specialization. They may carry out their observation functions by traveling about the country to which they are assigned—sometimes a hazardous undertaking in communist countries—or they may pick up information by visiting ministries and industrial fairs, or by conversing at cocktail parties.

Because the reports of diplomats on their observations are often significant raw material for the production of intelligence, they normally must fill out special reporting forms that systematize their observations and include judgments as to the reliability of sources and the substance of the observations reported. Thus, the diplomatic corps takes on the color of an elegant and yet sub rosa spy organization. Because all countries use their diplomats for this purpose, it is a generally accepted practice, which had its origin in the Middle Ages. In fact, the purpose of the first permanent embassies of the Italian city-state was to obtain timely information about impending aggression by stronger states. Because of this mission, diplomats were often regarded as a serious liability for the receiving state when the use of embassies began to spread in Europe during the 16th century.

Negotiation

Undoubtedly the most important function of diplomats is negotiation, which may pertain to formal long-term bilateral agreements or requests for short-term support of a particular policy of the diplomat's home country. The subject of the agreements being negotiated may vary: they may be comprehensive economic treaties or tariff agreements, arrangements for cultural exchange programs, extradition treaties, consular arrangements aimed at establishing consulates in the respective countries, the conclusion of alliances, and the like.

Short-term requests for policy support are exemplified by American endeavors in many capitals in 1971 to seek support for the U.S. policy of two Chinas, the People's Republic of China and the Republic of China on Taiwan. American ambassadors in many capitals urged the governments where they were accredited to cast a favorable vote in the United Nations General Assembly. At times this necessitated some concessions on the part of the United States, but these were considered an acceptable *quid pro quo*. In the end, however, the American efforts failed; the People's Republic assumed the official representation of the Chinese people in the United Nations, and the Chiang Kai-shek regime was expelled.

Many books and articles have been written about the art of negotiation, from the times of Machiavelli to the contemporary period.[1] Basically, *negotiation* involves a process in which a delicate balance is sought between giving what is asked and obtaining what is wanted.[2] The negotiation process must therefore begin with demands that are calculated to match in their excessiveness the perceived excessiveness in the opponent's position. If the process is carried out skillfully, the end result may be to "split the difference" and to conclude an agreement that is in the middle rather than one that reflects the "lowest common denominator." Somewhere, then, a compromise must be found between the bargainers' extreme positions. Every kind of persuasion, including withholding benefits or threatening harmful actions, may be used to influence the results of the negotiations, but the last vestiges of congeniality must not be swept away because the exchange of *quid pro quo*'s will be the basis for final agreement. Patience, therefore, is a great virtue, especially in negotiations with communist countries. These negotiations are often extremely tough and drawn out and prove a challenge for the most skillful of Western negotiators, as the Vietnam Peace negotiations and the Strategic Arms Limitation Talks (SALT) have demonstrated.[3]

So far we have focused mainly on diplomatic negotiation involving the embassy or legation staff and the host government, although the last examples were taken from multilateral or bilateral conferences (SALT) especially convened for negotiations. In fact, multilateral issues, such as international trade or disarmament, usually require special conferences or frameworks. An example is the so-called Kennedy Round of multilateral negotiations for the reduction of tariffs, which were conducted by fifty-five countries within the framework of GATT (General Agreement on Tariffs and Trade) in Geneva and in which the most influential participants were the United States and the European Common Market (technically, the European Economic Community) with Great Britain, Japan, and the Scandinavian countries. These negotiations lasted from 1964 to the middle of 1967 and were characterized by very tough bargaining tactics and strategies.

The Kennedy Round negotiations had all the trappings of a high-stake poker game; and every possible tactic, including threats of complete withdrawal from the negotiations, was used to influence their outcome. In addition to efforts by governments, nongovernmental groups were used to exercise subtle influences on similar groups in the member states sharing the same interests. For example, the Crotonville Conference of nearly 100 American businessmen and government leaders, held early in 1966, recommended that the American chambers of commerce be asked to appeal to their European counterparts for their vigorous support of the Kennedy Round negotiations. Private contacts were also maintained between farm groups in the United States and in the European Community, and joint meetings were held between American and European farmers on several occasions.

Some of the crisis tactics used were forced upon the negotiators because they had to establish their position vis-à-vis domestic political and economic groups and interests. In fact, the Community negotiators had to take into consideration six sets of domestic political and economic groups and interests. For example, the Germans were opposed to too much participation in a proposed food aid program, for which they would have had to foot a large part of the bill. The Italians, in turn, were set against too many concessions on chemicals. The clash of basic objectives between export-oriented Germany and the Benelux countries and the protectionist tendencies of France and to a lesser degree of Italy provided many opportunities for tenacious holdouts and stalling, sometimes supported by strong statements of influential Community interest groups.

It is noteworthy that Eric Wyndham White, the director general of GATT, on several occasions offered compromise solutions when the Kennedy Round seemed to be stalled during the final few weeks. Indeed, it was his package of compromises, submitted on the last morning of the negotiations, that served as the general framework for the settlement.

Diplomatic Behavior in IGOs

With the emergence of growing numbers of IGOs, individual countries have adopted the practice of establishing diplomatic missions to these organizations which have played increasingly larger roles on the international scene. Hence, every member of the United

Nations has a diplomatic mission accredited to this organization in New York, although smaller countries sometimes combine this function with their embassies in Washington. Similar diplomatic representatives are also assigned to the European Community, the North Atlantic Treaty Organization (NATO), the Organization for Economic Cooperation and Development (OECD), the Organization of American States (OAS), and other regional IGOs.

Diplomatic practice in these IGOs differs from that found in the embassies and legations in world capitals. While the role of a diplomat in the latter follows the tradition of straightforward representation of their country's interests, the role of a diplomat assigned to an IGO such as the United Nations tends to be more that of a parliamentarian. Issues in the United Nations are usually decided by a vote in the General Assembly, the Security Council, or other decision-making bodies; therefore, the game is to find a majority, simple or qualified, for the attainment of a country's foreign policy goals. As a consequence, the tactics and strategies that diplomats in the United Nations must use involve personal contacts, logrolling, and complex bargaining with payoffs for various countries willing to cosponsor or support particular resolutions. Hence, to be a good diplomat in this environment means to have the qualities of a successful parliamentary politician because, in accordance with the U.N. Charter, it is a vote that decides a matter in dispute.

Another factor producing a new element in U.N. diplomacy is the easy communication among diplomatic representatives in the corridors of the United Nations building and the many committee meetings of the General Assembly and the Economic and Social Council. Contacts between countries can be made easily and informally, and problems can be thrashed out without the constraints of traditional diplomacy. On the other hand, the high visibility of statements and actions in the General Assembly and the Security Council, while pleasing to those who advocate "spotlight" or "open" diplomacy, may cause rigidity of positions and thus render delicate international problems more difficult to solve.

Conditions similar to those in the United Nations and its various specialized agencies also prevail in the frequent conferences convened under the auspices of the United Nations or by a number of states for special purposes, such as the Conference on European Security which took place in Helsinki and Geneva. The stakes may be very high. An example of the latter is the Conference on the Law of the Sea, which has had several sessions in different cities over a number of years. In view of the high stakes involved and the length of the conference (several weeks), the demands on the stamina of the participating diplomats may be severe. They may have to attend plenary sessions and various committee meetings, and make the informal contacts necessary for logrolling tactics. Such "conference diplomacy" is often carried out without the benefit of rapid communications with the home ministry, although the larger countries, such as the United States, usually have embassies or consulates in the towns where conferences are held.

The Depreciation of Diplomacy

The often spectacular, brilliant, and always important role diplomats have played in the international arena in pursuit of their government's foreign policy goals began to decline following World War I and has further suffered since the end of World War II. There are two major reasons for this: (1) High-speed transportation has made it possible for chief executives and foreign ministers of all countries to travel anywhere in the world in a matter of hours; therefore, bilateral personal diplomacy between these individuals and multilateral summit conferences have pre-empted many of the traditional activities of diplomats for the implementation of foreign policy goals. (2) High-speed communications between the leaders of governments (hot lines) and among the foreign ministries and their diplomatic representatives all over the world have often reduced ambassadors or ministers of larger countries to glorified errand boys and transmitters of routine information. This development does not mean that the work of the diplomatic staff in the embassies has become superfluous. Many of the functions still performed by the staff require careful, personal attention, and the interpersonal relations an ambassador can develop with important governmental and political leaders in the country where he is stationed are important. But these changes have caused a recognizable erosion of morale among diplomats.

Before frequent personal diplomacy by chief executives and foreign ministers became popular after World War II, the groundwork for this development was laid by the claim voiced by Woodrow Wilson and other eloquent political leaders that secret diplomacy was inherently bad. It was asserted that the secret dealings of diplomats were responsible, at least in part, for the outbreak of World War I. Secret negotiations were an evil residue from an aristocratic world; a lasting peace could be achieved only when diplomatic negotiations were open to the scrutiny of a watchful public.

Whether this judgment is correct is, of course, uncertain. Nevertheless, there is a widespread feeling that difficult international problems can be solved by meetings on the highest level under the fanfare of the news media, although the meetings between President Eisenhower and top Soviet, British, and French leaders in 1955, or between President Johnson and Premier Kosygin in 1967, or between President Nixon and President Pompidou in 1973 offer only limited evidence to support this contention. On the other hand, the travels and activities of Henry Kissinger, often prepared and sometimes carried out in secrecy, were quite successful (although some of his "spectaculars" have been short-lived). One can conclude that summit meetings can be successful if they are prepared with care and secrecy, and the outcome is predetermined by agreements among the prospective participants.

ECONOMIC MEASURES

In view of the growing economic interdependence of the world, in which powerful multinational corporations play a significant role, the economic tools for policy implementation have to be examined in some detail. These tools need not be used only to attain foreign economic policy goals, but can also be used to achieve national security and political objectives as well. They assume special strategic importance when they involve the export of weapons and of nuclear power plants and fissionable materials. They may be employed as rewards for favorable international actions by other states, as punishment for adverse actions, and as a means of inducing a country to adopt a different behavior. They may also be used to persuade desired behavior by multinational enterprises (MNEs), either by providing incentives for foreign investment or by imposing constraints on the operations of MNE subsidiaries.

The most frequently applied economic device for policy implementation is the *tariff* of a country, which stipulates the amount of duty payable for the importation of goods from foreign countries. The effect of customs duties is to raise the price of imported products. In most instances, tariffs are used to protect domestic manufacturers, but sometimes their primary purpose is to raise revenues. If tariffs are reduced on specific items, the countries that are the leading suppliers of these items will benefit as more of these items are imported. If tariffs on particular goods are increased, the countries manufacturing these goods are apt to suffer.

Conventional Measures

From 1879 to 1934 tariffs steadily rose. Between 1913 and 1925 alone, the average percentage in duties assessed by sixteen of the leading industrial countries on the value of imported goods (*ad valorem* duties) had increased by one-third. After 1921 the British assessed 33.3 percent duty on certain items, and in 1930 the Smoot-Hawley Tariff of the United States stood at a general *ad valorem* level of 41.5 percent. As a consequence, American exports, which amounted to over $2.5 billion in the first half of 1929, fell below $1 billion by the same period in 1932. Other nations, of course, had resorted to retaliatory measures and hence tariff walls over the world rose higher and higher with the result that international trade took a nose dive.

A reversal of the protectionist economic foreign policy of the United States took place in 1934 when the government committed itself to an expansion of trade through a reciprocal trade program aimed at lowering tariffs worldwide. This program, technically known as the Trade Agreement Act of 1934, was renewed and modified at intervals during subsequent years until 1974. It permitted the president to reduce American tariffs providing that other countries made equivalent concessions on American goods.

The Most-favored-nation Clause   In addition to the policy of reciprocity embedded in the American legislation, the United States based its policy also on the so-called most-favored-nation clause, which has been inserted increasingly into commercial agreements. This clause provides that any reduction in duties stipulated in a commercial agreement between the United States and another country will also be made available to any third country with which the United States has most-favored-nation–type relations The most-favored-nation clause is also known as the principle of nondiscrimination and has become a cornerstone of American foreign economic policy.

General Agreement on Tariffs and Trade (GATT)   The principles of reciprocity and nondiscrimination are also the foundation of the General Agreement on Tariffs and Trade (GATT), which was drafted in 1947 and put into effect in 1948. The United States was an original signatory of this international treaty, whose purpose was to remove, as far as possible, restrictions on trade between the contracting parties. Almost all noncommunist advanced countries have become members of GATT, and a number of communist countries, including Czechoslovakia, Cuba, Poland, and Yugoslavia, participate in certain phases of the GATT machinery as well. Tariff concessions made between two parties to GATT extend to all other contracting parties as the result of the most-favored-nation principle. An important exception are customs unions and free trade areas within which tariffs are reduced to zero. The benefits to the participants of the customs unions and free trade areas, which flow from the elimination of tariffs, do not have to be offered to other GATT members.

A number of countries in varous parts of the world have taken advantage of this provision and have created regional customs unions and free trade areas. Examples of customs unions include, of course, the European Economic Community (or European Common Market), the Central American Common Market, the Andean Common Market along the northern and western shores of South America, and the East African Community. Examples of free trade areas are the European Free Trade Association, which has been partly dismantled with the entry of Great Britain and Denmark into the European Community,* and the Latin American Free Trade Association.

Preferential Trade Agreements   A special type of tariff reduction takes place when two countries enter into a preferential trade agreement. This is a clear violation of the GATT rules unless the signatories of the GATT treaty waive the application of the most-favored-nation clause. Preferential trade agreements have been used from time to time to expand the sphere of influence of economically advanced countries over less developed countries. As long ago as 1932, the members of the British Commonwealth introduced preferential tariffs for mutual trade, and these preferences were consented to by the GATT signatories in 1947. During the 1960s and 1970s, the European Economic Community has concluded a whole network of preferential agreements with African countries, various countries bordering the Mediterranean, and most recently, with Sweden, Norway, Austria, and Switzerland. They have been opposed generally by the United States as a violation of GATT and discrimination against third countries unless a germane free trade area was the ultimate objective of the agreement.

While preferential trade agreements remain a violation of GATT, amendments to the GATT treaty now make it possible for developed countries to extend general tariff preferences to imported manufactured and semimanufactured goods from the Third World. Some of the industrially advanced countries, including the United States, the European Community countries, and Japan, have installed generalized preference systems of varying dimensions. The European Community's limited system of general preferences benefits the

---

* The original members were Great Britain, Denmark, Norway, Sweden, Austria, Switzerland, and Portugal. The first two countries are now members of the Community or Common Market.

developing countries with which it does not have special preferential agreements.

Nontariff Barriers   A second economic tool for policy implementation is the imposition of nontariff barriers. These barriers stem from a variety of national laws, procedures, and regulations which tend to impair or nullify the reduction in duties for imports. They include laws giving preference to national sources of supply for official purchase (the Buy-American Act, for example), labeling regulations, health standards, quantitative restrictions, licensing controls, antidumping measures, tax discrimination between domestic and foreign goods, and customs valuations not reflecting actual costs. In terms of inducing desired behavior on the part of a foreign country, nontariff barriers produce effects much more quickly than do increased tariffs. On the other hand, lowering or eliminating certain quantitative restrictions for the imports from a particular country can be a significant reward.

Currency Regulations and Restrictions   Currency regulations and restrictions on capital flows are a third economic means of implementing foreign policy. Whenever the balance of payments of a country shows a deficit and it becomes necessary to stop the outflow of capital and other funds from that country, currency regulations and restrictions on capital movements constitute effective instruments of foreign economic policy. Because they impede the importation of goods into the country and the flow of tourists to other countries, and because capital investments abroad are reduced if not completely stopped, they have a variety of adverse effects on other countries. Western Europe protected its insufficient fund of dollars in this way during the immediate post–World War II period. The United States, during the past few years, has imposed temporary and "voluntary" restrictions on the outflow of private capital and has used the devaluation of the dollar to reverse its negative balance of payments and trade balance.

Clearly both nontariff barriers and currency regulations are much harsher instruments than changes in tariffs. A foreign manufacturer may accept a very low profit for his products to overcome a higher tariff, but he can do nothing against quantitative restrictions and currency regulations that prohibit his prospective customers from buying any of his goods at any price. An MNE can get around such restrictions by establishing manufacturing facilities in various countries so that its products are treated the same as those of national manufacturing firms.

Subsidies   Another economic instrument in the promotion of foreign policy goals is the granting of subsidies to national producers to enable them to compete better on the international market. Such subsidies may take the form of outright payments, lower freight rates for the transportation of exports, higher internal taxes on foreign produced goods, or tax credits or delays. Although these practices may violate certain provisions of GATT, some of the contracting parties have engaged in them. For example, the Common Market has paid extraordinarily high subsidies for the exportation of wheat, and the United States has permitted the creation of special export companies whose tax liabilities can be deferred.

Economic Warfare Measures

Pre-emption and Stockpiling   In times of war, it is often necessary to ensure a plentiful supply of critical materials. This can be done by pre-empting large quantities of the needed materials abroad before other countries can buy them. Examples are the large-scale purchases of rubber by the United States during World War II and the purchase and stockpiling of other strategic materials.

Embargo   A second economic warfare tool is the imposition of an embargo, which is the partial or total prohibition on trade with another state. U.S. embargoes on trade with China and Cuba have been examples of total embargo. The American and NATO policies of prohibiting the sale of strategic goods to the communist states in Eastern Europe constitute a partial embargo. The oil embargo imposed by Saudi Arabia on the United States and the Netherlands in the fall of 1973 is another example. In many instances, the effects of an embargo can be circumvented by sending prohibited goods to third countries which then resell them to the nation against which the embargo is being enforced. This has been done in Europe to circumvent the NATO embargo and was also done in Hong Kong to mitigate the embargo against China.

A more subtle form of an embargo, in fact not utilizing the term at all, is the imposition of export controls. For example, the United States during the last few years has utilized export controls for certain agricultural commodities to assure sufficiency of these foodstuffs for the American market. At the same time, a selective imposition of these controls, either in the form of licensing or by requiring that prospective sales be reported, can become a tool of economic warfare when it is directed against certain countries. The threat of such selective imposition provides leverage against countries that may threaten or apply embargoes of raw materials against other countries, or that form price cartels for the purpose of raising the cost of resources under their control. Petroleum is, of course, the outstanding example in our times.

Price and Marketing Cartels   Price and marketing cartels are another form of economic warfare in which countries that have within their territorial confines raw materials essential for the industrial economies of the developed countries and for the basic needs of many developing countries can engage. The creation of the Organization of Petroleum Exporting Countries (OPEC)* in 1960 is an example. OPEC has been utilized by the oil producers in the Middle East and in other parts of the world, especially Venezuela and Nigeria, to increase the price of oil well beyond the cost of producing it. As a consequence, a shift of wealth has taken place from the industrially advanced countries to the OPEC states and other producers of petroleum. While the consequences of this shift have initially been very beneficial to these countries, the ultimate result could be worldwide economic disaster.

Other countries producing natural resources, especially minerals, have attempted to form their own price cartels and emulate the success of OPEC. For example, Jamaica, a major bauxite producer, has led the effort to form a bauxite cartel. Countries with copper resources have formed an Intergovernmental Council of Copper Exporting Countries (CIPEC), which has attempted to devise a collective support system for the world market price of copper. Whether this kind of collaboration or perhaps collusion among countries to raise and maintain prices for these and other natural resources will be successful cannot be determined at this moment. Bauxite and copper are also found in some of the developed countries of the world and are not as essential for the welfare of the peoples of the globe as is the energy provided by petroleum.[4]

Boycott   Another economic warfare measure that can be very harmful is the boycott, which is the refusal to buy goods produced in a given foreign country. Sanctions by the United Nations include boycotts, but experience has shown that the self-interest of importers in many countries is so great that they will not obey the ordered

---

* Current members of OPEC include Algeria, Ecuador, Gabon, Indonesia, Iran, Iraq, Kuwait, Libya, Nigeria, Qatar, Saudi Arabia, the United Arab Emirates, and Venezuela.

boycott. The boycott imposed by the United Nations against Rhodesia is a case in point; in fact, the United States legislated an exception on chrome shipments from that country through the so-called Byrd Amendment, which, however, was rescinded in 1977. The boycott of Italian goods, which was ordered by the League of Nations in 1936 to stop Italy's aggression in Ethiopia, was not fully successful either.

Penetration by Multinational Enterprises   Economic warfare may also be employed in a very subtle manner through the penetration of foreign markets and control of foreign strategic industries by multinational enterprises headquartered in a particular country. Penetration of West European markets and control of certain industries in some European countries by American MNEs is an example. There may be "reverse economic penetration" as well, as indicated by the increasing establishments of European MNE subsidiaries in the United States. When large-scale economic interpenetration is accomplished by MNEs of one country, its government acquires political leverage on the penetrated countries and can induce or perhaps even compel desired behavior. The potential exercise of this leverage may be weakened, however, by cross-penetration, as has occurred between the United States and many Western European countries. In such instances, fears of counterretaliation against subsidiaries and markets established by its own MNEs serve as an effective brake on unfriendly political or economic acts. Subsidiaries and markets become hostages that raise the economic and political cost to countries contemplating the employment of economic warfare against each other.

Flow of Liquid Funds   Finally, the tremendous flow of liquid funds to the oil producing countries occasioned by the quadrupling of petroleum prices in 1973 has provided them with opportunities for economic warfare. The threat of massive shifts of funds—some estimates run as high as $650 billion by 1980—may spell economic disaster for the states that must pay these funds. This threat can give the oil producing countries leverage to compel the consuming countries to take actions not otherwise considered in their national interests.[5]

The range of economic warfare instruments has been expanded by such new economic entities as multinational enterprises and by the dire consequences of the growing demand for energy. The newer, though subtler, instruments of economic warfare are likely to be more effective and their effectiveness, more lasting. They may also produce substantial changes in the power status of individual countries. The fourfold rise in oil prices mandated by the producing countries within a span of one year has reduced Italy and some other industrialized countries to near-beggar status, while Saudi Arabia and Iran are moving toward middle-class power status. On the other hand, a number of developing countries, including India, which now possesses the technology for modest nuclear arms, have been declining into the destitute category by the huge bills they are forced to pay for energy.

Foreign Aid

Finally, an economic tool that has been utilized to a large degree since World War II is foreign aid. During the 1950s, when many countries of the world obtained their independence but were too weak to overcome the serious economic deficiencies from which they were suffering, foreign aid became a very popular way to influence Third World countries to attach their loyalty either to the Western or the Communist World. Hence foreign aid was not simply an instrument for assisting the poor countries, but was a means for seeking victory in the Cold War struggle. In fact, many of the newly independent countries became very adroit at playing the Western countries against the Soviet Union and China to obtain the highest level of foreign aid. In the late 1960s and early 1970s, the competitive factor in the dispensation of foreign aid subsided, and foreign aid is now being given by all economically advanced countries mainly to promote economic development in the Third World. Nevertheless, various political motivations remain important in most foreign aid programs, including those of the United States and Soviet Union. It is noteworthy that, in terms of percentage of Gross National Product (GNP) of the donor countries, the volume of aid has diminished over the past ten to fifteen years. Taking into consideration inflation, the net amount of aid has likewise decreased, although the net figures show an increase.[6]

Three Types of Economic Foreign Aid   Three types of economic foreign aid can be distinguished: (1) outright grants; (2) government loans; and (3) technical assistance. While *outright grants* were the preferred methods during the 1950s and early 1960s, *government loans* today play an increasingly significant role. Loans may be made in soft currency, that is, the currency of the recipient country, or in hard currency, which means that repayment must be made in convertible funds. Because the repayment of loans in soft currency may not be useful to the lending countries if they want to apply these funds for purchases in hard currency countries, some of these loans actually turn out to be grants. Most loans carry a relatively low interest rate and have very generous repayment provisions. While they are welcomed by the developing countries, they also impose a very serious burden on them because of the interest that must be paid, regardless of how generous the repayment schedule is. Because of the need of the less developed countries, loans continue to be granted even if, in some instances, they are used simply to repay previous loans. At the same time, outright grants are still made if for no other reason than to finance the continuous deficits in budgets of many newly independent countries.

The third type of foreign aid, *technical assistance*, has assumed a greater role during the past decade. It is a relatively inexpensive way of helping the developing countries and often provides the training necessary to enable native administrators, business managers, and engineers to run the more complex factories and institutions in their country by themselves. We should note that making available teachers and administrators is one way some former colonial powers continue the dependence of Third World countries on their former masters.

Bilateral versus Multilateral Aid   Foreign aid can be given either *bilaterally*, that is, from one economically advanced country to a Third World country, or *multilaterally* through the United Nations, the World Bank, or regional organizations. From the point of view of the recipient, multilateral aid of any kind is much more desirable because it avoids the creation of a dependency relationship with the donor country. But the economically advanced states do not share this preference. They often use foreign aid to promote not only humanitarian goals, but also specific foreign policy objectives as well and so prefer to give aid bilaterally. Bilateral arrangements may also be more efficient than multilateral programs, although some UN programs seem to be gradually becoming more effective.

PSYCHOLOGICAL WARFARE
AND PROPAGANDA

In the broad sense, *psychological warfare* consists of the application of psychological measures and techniques by a country to further its economic, political, or military policy objectives. The main tool is propaganda supplemented by economic, political, and military measures.[7] Examples of these measures are the creation of panics, the application of terror through bomb explosions, and causing pressures on currencies through large-scale border-crossing capital movements. Psychological warfare can be carried out during war and in times of peace. It is as old as mankind and is employed today to varying degrees by many countries of the world. The United States and the Soviet Union make frequent use of propaganda, but rarely employ other psychological warfare measures.

Propaganda

There are many definitions of *propaganda*. It may be understood as the planned use of any form of public or mass-produced communications designed to affect the minds and emotions of a given group for a specific public purpose, whether economic, political, or military. In international affairs, it seeks to influence politically relevant attitudes and actions on the part of target groups in foreign countries to compel their governments to adopt policies favorable to the government of the propagandist. The range of the media utilized is extensive. It includes radio broadcasts, television, films, loudspeakers, magazines, leaflets, libraries, information centers, scholarships, conducted tours for visitors, academic meetings, and even forgeries.

Three types of propaganda can be distinguished: *white propaganda*, which is issued from an acknowledged source, usually a government or an agency of government; *gray propaganda*, whose source is not clearly identified; and *black propaganda*, which purports to emanate from a source other than the true one. An example of the latter is radio broadcasts that claim to originate from within a particular country to obtain legitimacy, but actually come from a foreign station.

There are many reasons for the phenomenal growth in the use of political propaganda worldwide. In many countries the participation of the people in politics has increased, either through extension of the voting franchise or growing membership in one or more interest groups. Public opinion is more and more recognized as important by political leaders and therefore is a very frequent target of international propagandists. The rate of literacy has risen everywhere, even in countries that formerly were very backward. At the same time communications means and techniques have improved tremendously, and their use has expanded dramatically. In most places on this earth, nearly every family owns a radio, and in many countries people carry shirtpocket radios. Finally, one country can use electronic means to systematically and subtly inculcate its ideology in the population of another.

Effective propaganda must meet certain prerequisites. It must make use of phrases that are simple and easy to understand, such as "capitalist exploiters" or "godless communism." It must stimulate interest and avoid the impression of "propagandizing." It must create credibility. This latter can be accomplished by identifying the information disseminated with an actual experience of the group toward which the propaganda is directed. To be effective, propaganda must have a high level of constancy in terms of both dissemination and the theme being propagated. Finally, good propaganda must avoid promises that may not or cannot be kept. For example, the broadcasts made under the auspices of the Office of War Information in the United States never promised a definite government to the Germans during World War II. Unfortunately, however, individual transmitting facilities attached to the armed forces in the field during that same war made all sorts of promises that could not be kept. Voice of America broadcasts in the middle 1950s may have raised expectations for a change in government in Hungary in 1956 and contributed to the ill-fated uprising there in October of that year.

Effective propaganda should avoid fabrication. No greater misconception of propaganda exists than that it is simply "the big lie." Rather, good propaganda presents facts and depends on selection and emphasis for its effectiveness. The World War II BBC broadcasts from London used facts to influence the audience to support the British war effort. Even today, BBC broadcasts are held in high regard for their reliability and truthfulness.

International propaganda, as well as all aspects of psychological warfare, must be employed in close coordination with other instruments of foreign policy. It is insufficient to define audiences as hostile, friendly, or neutral; what is required is to be precise as to the desired ends, to prepare to cope with alternative reactions from the target group, and to keep always in mind the goals of the country's foreign policy.

In addition to the spoken word, actions and "demonstrations" can be propaganda. Actions, such as handing out free food packages to inhabitants of areas struck by disaster or making large-scale deliveries of wheat to countries that have experienced extensive droughts and poor harvests, can have more propagandistic value than millions of words flowing from different radio transmitters. Military demonstrations, such as fleet maneuvers and jet aircraft flybys in Moscow's Red Square or the Champs Elysee in Paris (the

First of May and Fourteenth of July celebrations, respectively), are also important means of propaganda. They furnish evidence of military power, which reassures allies and impresses foes.

Actions in the United Nations General Assembly by American and Soviet representatives are often designed to appeal to neutral countries in the hope of attracting them to their respective power blocs. Such actions thereby become tools of propaganda and have assumed increasing importance during the past two decades.

The Evolution of Propaganda \ Although propaganda dates back to the beginning of recorded history, the use of propaganda to influence mass popular opinion began with the French Revolution. During World War I, propaganda was used extensively by the European antagonists to influence neutral countries such as the United States to assist their respective efforts. When the United States entered World War I, a committee on public information was set up, and during the period from 1917 to 1919 it attempted to propagandize President Wilson's Fourteen Points.[8]

Between World War I and World War II, Lenin and Trotsky originated the first foreign language broadcasts from the Soviet Union. In Germany and Italy, respectively, Joseph Goebbels and Benito Mussolini became propaganda experts. In 1938 the BBC began broadcasting propaganda in German and Italian and by 1939 was transmitting in sixteen languages.

In the United States it was the Office of War Information that was given the task of employing psychological warfare and propaganda in World War II. By the end of that war, the United States had assembled a very capable corps of psychological warfare specialists.

Following World War II, the United States and Britain reduced the activities of their propaganda machines; however, with the spreading of the Cold War, the United States Information Agency (USIA) was established in 1953. Its mission was to explain United States actions and policy toward the world in a forceful and direct but not antagonistic manner. At the same time, it was to demonstrate and document the design of those forces that would threaten American security and seek to destroy freedom in general. Today, the United States Information Agency maintains nearly 300 posts in over 100 countries. It has established 200 libraries and 150 binational information centers. Each embassy and legation has at least one public information officer, who in turn may be assisted by other United States' Information Service (USIS) officials. In 1978 the functions of the USIA were taken over by the newly created International Communication Agency (ICA).

The main tool for major broadcasts of the ICA is the Voice of America, which has very extensive foreign language programs and whose broadcasts are relayed by local stations in important parts of the world. It has been estimated that 7 to 12 million people listen to the Voice of America worldwide, and 5 to 10 million listen daily behind the Iron Curtain. Other broadcasting facilities supported by the United States are Radio Free Europe, Radio Liberty, and RIAS (Radio Information in the American Sector in Berlin). Radio Free Europe broadcasts are designed primarily for the satellite countries of Eastern Europe, while Radio Liberty beams its messages to the Soviet people.

Soviet propaganda is handled by the Department of Propaganda and Agitation in the Soviet Union, known as AGITPROP. Its tasks cover media and content of mass communications, education, literature and art. In all these areas AGITPROP is responsible for carrying out Politburo directives. In this respect it is noteworthy that the party controls educational materials and curricula for institutions training future foreign policy decision makers. As agent for the Politburo, AGITPROP also supervises the content and dissemination of domestic propaganda on foreign affairs and Soviet foreign propaganda. Both *Pravda,* the Communist party's official daily spokesman, and *Kommunist,* the party's theoretical journal, are "sections" under AGITPROP.

The personnel of AGITPROP are highly trained, and its expenditures are enormous, although they may not equal those of the United States. It sponsors nearly as many foreign language broadcasts as the United States. In addition, the Soviet News Agency, TASS, as well as specialized film agencies, Soviet friendship societies, and other institutions in the Soviet Union, support the propaganda effort. Party personnel of all mass media, including the large number of *Pravda* correspondents, are expected to acquire information and to report popular attitudes abroad as they encounter them.

Many other large countries in the world also maintain an extensive propaganda broadcasting system. Foremost among those is Britain with its extensive BBC operation. In addition, the British Information Service operates in many countries similarly to the USIS. France and Germany also have developed efficient propaganda operations patterned after the American model; and French broadcasts, at least in Europe, seem to blanket the airwaves.

In summary, there is no question that effective propaganda and carefully devised psychological warfare are valuable instruments of policy implementation. Through them a government can sow division in foreign countries, confuse its enemies, increase the devotion of its allies, and win support of nations previously uncommitted.

POLITICAL WARFARE

Yet another category of instruments for policy implementation is *political warfare*. It can be defined as any means, short of actual war, that a state uses to weaken or exert pressure upon another state.

Subversion

The best-known political warfare measure is *subversion*. This type of political warfare, symbolized by the Trojan Horse in the times of ancient Greece, is as old as recorded history and has been utilized not only by communist and fascist countries, but by governments of democratic states as well. In subversion, a group allegedly loyal to the interests and values of one country is used to further the policy of a rival nation.[9]

Subversion often uses ethnic ties. For example, according to the Hitlerian doctrines, all Germans living outside the territory of Germany were duty-bound to advance the cause of Nazism and to assist the Fatherland in every way possible. In the United States, the German-American Bund was the vehicle for propagandizing the Nazi ideology and for fostering public opinion favorable to Hitler's Germany. In a similar manner, the Soviet Union has exploited Slavic populations in other countries not only to attract them to Soviet ideology, but also to use them to further Soviet policy.

In addition, the Soviet Union has also utilized Communist parties in Western countries for the support of its policies. The ideological ties with these parties and other left-wing groups at times became the vehicles for the establishment of so-called front organizations, which would ally themselves with socialist parties to form "popular fronts."

Democratic countries have also attempted to use subversion to lessen the totalitarian grip of communist governments. The United States and some of the West European countries have employed anti-Soviet emigrant groups for this purpose and, in some instances, have established governments in exile. The latter were to maintain contact with the dissatisfied elements in the Soviet Union in order to spread subversive influences in communist countries.

Subversive penetration is not an end in itself, but often serves to prepare the ground for coups d'etat (the overthrow of governments) and possible annexation. To prepare for coups d'etat, the communists have participated in coalition governments. In these governments they were anxious to control the ministries of interior and justice, which would give them a decisive influence on the administrations of police and law. Other ministerial posts were not considered to be as important and were allowed to go to noncommunist parties. These strategies were supported by the systematic use of terror which, of course, was tolerated by the communist-controlled police. The end result was the overthrow of the coalition government and the assumption of full control by the communist forces. An outstanding example of subversion operations along these lines was the communist coup d'etat in Czechoslovakia during February 1948.

The United States has also undertaken successful attempts at coup d'etat in foreign countries, although subversion may have played only a minor role. For example, with covert U.S. backing, in 1954 a revolt was led against President Arbenz of Guatemala, who had won the presidential election in 1950 but displayed communist leanings. In 1953 the Iranian Prime Minister Mohammed Mossadegh was ousted and sent to jail for three years, and it has been assumed that U.S. covert operations played a role in his ouster. Finally, in 1966 Western subversion efforts contributed to the overthrow of President Sukarno in Indonesia and the installation of General Suharto as his successor. Led by Muslim students, Indonesian masses engaged in an anti-communist campaign that eventually forced Sukarno to yield power to Suharto in March of that year. During the early 1970s, the CIA expended several million dollars to "destabilize" the socialist government of Allende in Chile by supporting groups and newspapers opposed to him. His final overthrow may well have been caused in part by these U.S. activities.

Subversion also can play a significant role in the annexation of foreign territories. One example is the Nazi annexation of a sector of Czechoslovakia in 1938 in which Germans living in the Sudeten region of that country played a major part. Ethnic minorities were also utilized as a provocation for Italy after World War I to annex part of formerly Austrian Tyrol. Thus the term *irredentism,* from the Italian words *Italia irredenta* ("Italy unredeemed"), came into being. It is still used to refer to the policy of seeking to incorporate within a nation any territory whose population is ethnically closely related to that nation.

The overthrow of governments and annexation efforts are often accompanied by large-scale sabotage activities and assassinations. Both of these activities spread terror among the target population and the government. Ultimately the desire for peace within the country weakens the resolve of the government and the population to continue resistance against the subversive and revolutionary forces.

Other Political Warfare Activities

In addition to the complex of subversive activities, a few other political warfare measures need to be mentioned briefly. One is the *blockade* of a particular country, which is undertaken usually by naval forces and attempts to stop all incoming and outgoing traffic of a third country. A blockade may be aimed at interdicting the influx of particular weapons, as was done by the American blockade of Cuba in 1962, or it may be used to inflict privations, including food shortages, on the civilians rather than damaging directly the military capabilities of a country.

Another means of political warfare is the *seizure of property owned by foreign nationals*. Cuba's seizure of American property led ultimately to the rupture of diplomatic relations between the two countries. It also has been employed again and again by Third World countries who have felt that the exploitation of their resources by the economically advanced countries was damaging to their national interests. The expropriation of copper mines in Chile is perhaps the best example.

Armed demonstrations may also be utilized as a political warfare device. For example in 1946 the Soviet Union moved troops to the Turkish border to put pressure on the Turkish government to adopt more favorable attitudes toward Soviet policies.

Finally, *guerrilla tactics* may be employed to attain foreign policy goals. The obvious case is the support given by Arab governments to the Palestinian guerrilla groups and specifically to the Popular Front for the Liberation of Palestine (PFLP). Their plane hijackings and kidnapings of foreign diplomats to exert pressure on the Israeli and other governments sympathetic to the Israeli cause are well known. Extreme left-wing urban guerrilla organizations, such as the Baader-Meinhof group in Germany, well-known for the daring manner in which it has carried out kidnapings and bank robberies and freed prisoners by force, may also receive indirect support from governments that regard such actions as aiding their overall goal of establishing a communist world order. The Soviet Union clearly falls into this category.

Political warfare in the United States during World War II was carried out by the Office of Strategic Services. Later the CIA became involved in these activities and participated in the Iranian, Guatemalan, Chilean, and most likely Indonesian actions related above. It appears that, in some instances, CIA personnel carry out political warfare operations directly; whereas in other instances, they are the guiding hand of indigenous forces or refugees, as seems to have been true during the 1961 abortive invasion of Cuba. To carry out their assignments, CIA personnel have had to learn how to gain control of civilian populations and to apply the principles and techniques of guerrilla warfare.*

In the Soviet Union, the KGB appears to control political warfare activities and to supervise training programs for agents to be used for this purpose abroad. The secret police representative, assigned to all Soviet embassies abroad although disguised as a minor diplomat, reports directly to the foreign section of the KGB. The Soviet government became involved in political warfare as early as 1919 when it initiated and supported the attempted overthrow of the governments of Germany and Hungary. In addition to the KGB, other organizations were tied in with political warfare activities. The best-known have been the *Comintern* and later the *Cominform* organizations, which were employed in the control of the machinery of international communism, including foreign Communist parties, and served as a transmission belt for communist propaganda. Although the Comintern has now been dissolved and the Kremlin has abandoned its policy of making detailed decisions for all foreign Communist parties, it insists that the Soviet Union be recognized as the leader of the Communist camp and continues to utilize foreign Communist parties wherever possible in support of Soviet foreign policy goals.[10]

Political warfare does not end with the outbreak of military conflict but normally continues and supports the military objectives of a country at war. Of course, it is war itself that is the ultimate tool of foreign policy implementation, to which we shall turn next.

WAR

Karl von Clausewitz, in his study on war, declared that "war is . . . a continuation of policy by other means. It is not merely a political act, but a real political instrument, a continuation of political intercourse, a conduct of political intercourse by other means."[11] War is a means for maximizing the power of a state if other means have failed; but it can also be a defensive tool for survival if a state is attacked by another country, or if overwhelming political and strategic pressures by one state upon another necessitate a pre-emptive

---

* *Guerrilla* is a Spanish word meaning "the small war." Guerrilla tactics were first used in Spain at the beginning of the 19th century when small units offered continuous resistance to the overwhelming power of Napoleon's invasion forces.

attack. Such pressures were exerted by Egypt and other Arab countries upon Israel in May 1967 and prompted the latter to initiate a war against Egypt, Jordan, and Syria.

It is difficult to define what constitutes an international war, the type with which we are concerned in this section. Clearly, it requires as a minimum two or more opposing states. In addition, more than occasional hostilities must occur. Singer and Small consider a war to exist when hostilities involving one or more states lead to a minimum of 1,000 battle fatalities among all participants. Any individual state could qualify as a participant by having a minimum of 100 fatalities. However, if under certain circumstances this figure is not reached, the 1,000 figure for total battle losses qualifies a country as long as it engages with armed personnel in an act of combat.[12] Singer and Small have carefully analyzed all of the wars fought between 1816 and 1965. Using their definition, they list 93 international wars with the two most violent being World Wars I and II, having 9 and 15 million battle deaths, respectively.[13]

We can distinguish among conventional wars, nuclear wars, and unconventional wars. Conventional war is the type of warfare developed over the past four centuries and excludes the use of nuclear weapons.

Conventional War

During the past four centuries, the size of the armies has grown tremendously. During the Thirty Years' War, the normal size of an army was 19,000 men. During the 16th century, it occasionally reached 30,000 men. During the 18th century, the average army grew to between 40,000 and 50,000 men, although in exceptional cases it may have reached 90,000. With the advent of the people's armies, Napoleon commanded as many as 200,000 men in some battles. By the end of the 19th century, the standing armies of the major powers in Europe averaged 500,000 men each; and by the outbreak of World War I, the number of men in these armies was even greater.[14] Present-day standing forces of the United States, Soviet Union, and China are between 2 and 3 million.

During wartime widespread conscription expanded the armed forces tremendously. During the Napoleonic times, France had about 800,000 men under arms. During World War I, the United States had 4.7 million under arms; Germany, 11 million; and Russia, 12 million. During World War II, these figures were 16.1 million for the United States and 20 million for Germany. No reliable figures are available for the Soviet Union; however, we can surmise from

Table 7.1: World-Record-Breaking Ranges of Projectiles 1,000,000 B.C. to
A.D. 1954

Date	Type of Projectile	Maximum Range, Miles[a]	Killing Area, Square Miles[b]
From before 1,000,000 B.C. to at least 200,000 B.C., nothing better than rock missile, thrown club, or simple javelin		0.01	0.0003
Period between javelin and arrow		0.03	0.005
Starting somewhere between 75,000 B.C. and 10,000 B.C. bow and arrow		0.10	0.09
From about 500 B.C. to A.D.1453, catapult and ballista		0.35	0.08
1453	Cannon	1.0	3.0
1670	Cannon	1.1	4.0
1807	Rocket	2.0	13.0
1830	Coast artillery	3.0	28.0
1859	Breech-loading rifle gun	5.0	78.0
1900	Coast artillery	6.3	125.0
1912	Coast artillery	11.4	408.0
1915	Zeppelin raid on London	200.0	126,000.0
1918	Bombing plane	280.0	246,000.0
1943	Bombing plane	1,200.0	4,480,000.0
1944	Bombing plane	2,050.0	12,900,000.0
1945	Bombing plane	5,000.0	69,000,000.0
·1954	Bombing plane refueled in flight	12,500.0	197,000,000.0

[a]Record-breaking range of projectiles (maximum range in miles) defined as "longest nonstop distance, from base to target, over which a missile intended to destroy life or demolish structures has been hurled or piloted through the air."

[b]Killing area (in square miles) defined as "maximum area within which lives and property may be destroyed by such projectiles."

SOURCE: Harold Sprout and Margaret Sprout, *Foundations of International Politics* (Princeton, N.J.: Van Nostrand, 1962), p. 253.

the more than 6 million battle deaths and 14 million wounded that the figure was enormous.

We have already briefly mentioned the tremendous advances in conventional weaponry during the past 400 years. Table 7.1 provides further evidence of this development in terms of destructive radius, distance, and speed of fire. With the increase in destructiveness of these weapons and air deliverability, the casualties among the civilian population and property damage have, of course, risen tremendously, although their scope is still small compared with nuclear damage. Yet such cities as Coventry in England and Dresden in Germany bear gruesome witness to the damage and casualties caused by "conventional" bombs.

In a conventional war, the primary mission of the attacking country's land, sea, and air forces is maximum destruction of the enemy. Although under the international rules of war the regular armed forces of a country are to combat only the regular forces of the opponent(s), both military and civilian targets may be attacked. The reason is not only that the civilian sector provides the economic and often logistic support for the military, that is, the manufacture of weapons, the provision of food for soldiers, and the like, but also that punishment directed at the civilian sector might raise the cost of the war to a country so high as to induce the leaders to surrender or ask for an armistice. In some instances, leaders of the opposing countries may agree to limit the geographic scope or military intensity of a conflict, as was done in Korea and Vietnam.

Nuclear War

The curtain was raised on nuclear war in 1945 when American bombers dropped atomic bombs on Hiroshima and Nagasaki in Japan. Since that time, no country has resorted to nuclear weapons despite the fact that more than 15 international wars have been fought.

Although the nuclear club at present includes six states, only the United States and the Soviet Union have the kind of nuclear weapons arsenal to make nuclear war a sophisticated instrument of policy implementation. Both of these countries have a variety of tactical and strategic nuclear weapons, which increases the chances that at first low-yield tactical nuclear weapons may be utilized and escalation of the nuclear conflict may be controlled, depending on what kind of counterweapon is used against a nuclear attack. Basically, both the United States and the Soviet Union seem anxious to adhere to a "no-first-use clause" for tactical nuclear weapons; but whether such a condition could be maintained in a conflict where one country found itself weaker in the total number of nuclear weapons than the other is very difficult to judge.

During the first decade of the nuclear era, the United States tended to rely for its security mainly on the deterrent effect of threatening to use nuclear weapons. Instant retaliation by means and at places of our own choosing in the event of aggression by an enemy country was seen as providing greater security at relatively low cost.

It was Henry Kissinger's famous book, *Nuclear Weapons and*

Foreign Policy,[15] that changed the strategic thinking of the United States. Kissinger pointed out that it was a very short-sighted strategy that would rely only on long-range, powerful nuclear weapons. It would deprive the United States of the needed flexibility to react with its armed forces successfully against limited brushfire wars, which were likely to be much more frequent than a challenge by the Soviet Union. Kissinger intimated that the reliance on what Secretary of State John Foster Dulles of the Eisenhower years called massive nuclear retaliation alone provided few options and basically implied an all-or-nothing response. Kissinger, therefore, argued for an expansion of conventional armed forces to fight limited wars and to avoid in the future situations such as the invasion of South Korea by the North Korean Communists in 1950. Despite the fact that the United States had a virtual nuclear monopoly when the Korean war broke out, the government was not prepared to use nuclear weapons at that time and had to rebuild quickly its army and air force to stave off defeat on the battlefield.

Closely related to the question of the size and composition of the armed forces was the very important issue of how to employ these forces and their weapons, which ranged from conventional arms to tactical and finally strategic nuclear weapons. Until 1961, the United States was committed to a strategy of massive nuclear retaliation. This strategy was seen by all NATO allies as the most credible means to deter Soviet aggression. Thus the threshold at which powerful nuclear weapons were to be introduced was low. Conventional forces were designed only to stop minor incursions. Conventional NATO forces in the European theater were to serve as a trip wire that would trigger a strategic strike by the American nuclear deterrent.

The Kennedy Administration brought to power a group of defense planners, including Secretary of Defense Robert McNamara, who were determined to reduce NATO's dependence on nuclear weapons and to emphasize instead the conventional aspect of the defense of Western Europe. As a result of their efforts, the official strategy of NATO was changed in 1967 to the policy of flexible or graduated response. Stripped to its bare essentials, this policy or strategy as developed by the Kennedy and Johnson administrations called for a distinct "fire break" between the conventional and nuclear phases of combat. To maintain the fire break, tactical nuclear weapons were given a primary deterrence role to prevent Soviet use of similar weapons. They were to provide a backstop if conventional defenses failed. Nuclear weapons were to be employed only after the conventional battle had actually been lost. Any escalation

of conflict was to be very deliberate because there was the fear
that, once the level of the strategic nuclear weapons was reached,
a worldwide nuclear holocaust would become inevitable.

An analysis of this *flexible response strategy* reveals advantages
as well as drawbacks. Effective implementation of this strategy in
Europe requires the maintenance of large troop contingents that
must be kept in a state of high military preparedness to defend
NATO's eastern boundaries successfully. Moreover, this strategy
must be able to cope with military actions of all kinds, ranging from
a minor and perhaps nonrecurring probe of NATO defense sectors
to a full-scale nuclear attack against the West.

Obviously the success of the flexible response doctrine depends
on the careful management of the military conflict. Political leaders
are given time to communicate, perhaps through the hot line
between Washington and Moscow, or through other facilities, to
prevent an all-out nuclear holocaust. It opens up the possibility of
setting limits to the war in terms of the geographical area involved
and in terms of the weapons employed, although serious difficulties
experienced by one side or the other can change this situation
rapidly. When such change may occur is very uncertain and adds
a highly speculative dimension to flexible response. At what point
would the U.S. government decide to use its strategic nuclear weapons against an enemy? Would the United States be willing to risk
destruction of its own territory to defend secondary cities in West
Germany or France that are about to fall to Soviet ground forces?
The European NATO partners are aware of the dilemmas that the
flexible response doctrine can create, and some responsible Europeans have argued for a return to the massive retaliation strategy,
which in their view would assure greater security for all of NATO.

Any of the strategic considerations discussed above may, of
course, be changed if one or the other nuclear power should pursue
efforts to acquire an overwhelming first-strike capability. A large
first nuclear strike must be able to destroy or neutralize all of the
opponent's nuclear counterforces and antiballistic missiles (ABMs).
Full success would also require a large ABM system designed to
shoot down any enemy missiles that survived the first attack. Any
country that acquired such capability could bring to its knees other
nuclear powers if they became convinced of its capability. If other
nuclear powers did not acknowledge this superiority, the first
country might consider the actual employment of a first strike as
opportune and beneficial. So far neither the United States nor the
Soviet Union has pursued this strategy; but despite the SALT agreements, apprehension continues to exist in some quarters in the

United States and Western Europe that the Soviet Union may develop delivery vehicles for nuclear weapons that are powerful enough to give her a decisive first-strike capability.

In the event of a nuclear attack, the consequences for the target area would be almost beyond comprehension. If a full-scale attack were made on the United States with 263 megaton bombs, which would be equivalent to one and a half billion tons of TNT, and 224 cities, military installations, and other targets were hit, 50 million deaths and 20 million additional casualties would result on the first day.[16] Such a catastrophe, which would transform organized society into a dazed mob, would tax the discipline of a people to the utmost. This kind of stress could most likely be borne only if extensive preparations for coping with such a disaster had been made in advance. Therefore, the nature and extent of civil defense and other disaster organizations may hold the key to survival of a country as an operating unit of the community of states. Any civil defense organization worth its name has a broad range of responsibilities, including giving first aid, inventorying skills, providing transportation, ensuring the continuity of government, and burying the thousands or millions of dead. It is a tremendous challenge, one that only the civil defense organization in the Soviet Union has begun to meet. In other countries, including the United States, civil defense has a very low priority. It may be that ABMs may reduce the horrible prospect described, but whether they can be perfected sufficiently to lower risks of nuclear attack is far from certain. Indeed it is quite doubtful when one considers that either the Soviet Union or the United States can mount attacks with about 20,000 megatons of warheads that would perhaps kill 95 percent of the American People. In the Soviet Union the percentage of casualties might be considerably lower because the population and industrial plants are more dispersed and civil defense agencies are more effective.[17]

Unconventional War

The conventional tactics of employing large formations of men and firepower to overcome and defeat the enemy normally have favored stronger over weaker states; however, special, unconventional tactics of rapidly moving small groups of men and weapons, quickly attacking violently under cover of stealth and with surprise and ruses, and then withdrawing just as quickly may offer weaker states military capabilities somewhat offsetting their lack of manpower and a broad arsenal.

Unconventional warfare, or "subversive" war, as it is sometimes called, can be as costly in battle losses as some conventional wars. In general, the state engaged in unconventional and especially guerrilla warfare minimizes direct military confrontation, which may subject its forces to quick annihilation. States using this type of warfare cannot count on a quick knockout of the enemy. They must be patient, and indeed it is this attribute that marks the national character of countries that employ these tactics. North Vietnam and China are excellent examples. The fact that unconventional warfare is a slow tool for fighting an opponent does not alter its ultimate effectiveness, as the Vietnam War illustrates.

A state may pursue conventional and unconventional warfare at the same time, as was done by the Soviet Union during World War II in fighting the Germans. Guerrilla tactics were used to supplement the conventional war effort, and the combination proved to be highly effective. The North Vietnamese and their Viet Cong allies began their military actions with guerrilla tactics and then gradually began to employ some conventionally organized formations. They appeared to follow tactics first conceived by Mao Tse-tung and later refined by Che Guevara and General Giap. According to classic Maoist doctrine, the war effort passes through three stages. The first stage is primarily guerrilla action. In the second stage, guerrillas may hold some areas and engage in some coordinated forms of military activity but avoid major combat. Terror is employed in both stages to compel behavior of resisting segments of civilian populations. In the third stage, the guerrillas are transformed into normal military formations that may cooperate with regular army units of allied countries (Viet Cong and North Vietnam, for example) in something approaching regular military combat. The strong political nature of unconventional warfare is obvious, and it is this factor that makes it so difficult for countries whose armed forces are accustomed to conventional, open warfare to devise effective countermeasures.

Although the normal traditional practice during war has been a complete rupture of communications and diplomatic relations between the warring states when hostilities broke out, this practice is being modified. Some indirect communications were carried out between the United States government and North Vietnam during the war through various unofficial intermediaries, and these were supplemented by trips to Hanoi by "peace" group representatives. In the event of a nuclear war, instant communications between the opponents may be of critical significance, and it is hoped that the hot line connecting the Kremlin with the White House would continue to operate in such a calamity to transmit clear signals of intentions on the part of the governments. Of course, third governments may also be used as intermediaries for message transmission. The International Red Cross has certain functions that touch warring nations, but cannot be used to relay governmental messages regarding strategic decisions of opponents.

SUMMARY

Policy implementation is a continuous process and is the major stimulus for interaction in international relations and politics. All international actors may be involved in the policy implementation process; however, the extent and intensity of their involvement varies, depending on what particular policy is to be implemented and which instrument is chosen for its implementation.

Diplomacy is the most commonly used instrument and is carried out chiefly by foreign service officers working in the foreign ministry at home and assigned to the embassies, legations, and missions of the country in the foreign capitals of the world. It is also carried out by diplomatic missions to IGOs, such as the United Nations and the European Economic Community. The functions of diplomats abroad can be classified as **representation, observation,** and **negotiation.**

A second instrument of policy implementation is the use of **economic measures.** They include tariff and trade agreements, nontariff barriers, currency regulations and restrictions, subsidies, preemption and stockpiling, embargoes and export controls, price and marketing cartels, boycotts, penetration by multinational enterprises, and foreign aid, and may be used to punish, persuade, or reward.

The principles of reciprocity and nondiscrimination form the foundation of the **General Agreement on Tariffs and Trade (GATT)** drafted in 1947. Recent amendments to this treaty make it possible for developed countries to extend general tariff preferences to imported manufactured and semimanufactured goods from the Third World.

Economic foreign aid may take the form of **outright grants, government loans,** or **technical assistance** and can be given either **bilaterally** or **multilaterally.** In some instances, former colonial powers have used teachers and administrators provided under the guise of technical assistance to prolong the dependence of Third World countries on their former masters.

Psychological warfare consists of the application of psychological measures and techniques by a country to further its economic, political, or military policy objectives. The main weapon of psychological warfare is **propaganda,** whether white, gray, or black. No greater misconception of propaganda exists than that it is simply "the big lie." Good propaganda presents facts and depends on selection and emphasis for its effectiveness. In terms of propagandistic value, actions and "demonstrations" may speak even louder than words. In the United States, governmental propaganda is prepared and disseminated primarily by the International Communication Agency (ICA). The Department of Propaganda and Agitation (AGIT-PROP) plays a similar role in the Soviet Union.

Yet another category of instruments for policy implementation is **political warfare,** which includes any means, short of actual war, that a state uses to weaken or exert pressure upon another state. The best-known political warfare measure is **subversion.** Others include **blockade, seizure of property owned by foreign nationals, armed demonstrations,** and **guerrilla and terrorist tactics.**

War is the ultimate tool of foreign policy implementation. It is an offensive tool in that it can be used to maximize the power of a state if other means have failed; but it is also a defensive tool used to ensure the survival of a state that has been attacked or put under overwhelming political and strategic pressures. Warfare may be **conventional, unconventional,** or **nuclear.**

The curtain was raised on nuclear war in 1945 when American bombers dropped atomic bombs on Hiroshima and Nagasaki in Japan. Immediately after World War II, the United States relied for its security on the deterrent effect of threatening instant and massive nuclear retaliation. Near defeat in Korea and Henry Kissinger's famous book, *Nuclear Weapons and Foreign Policy*, later brought about the adoption of a **flexible response strategy.**

The range of instruments for implementing foreign policy is considerable, and the proper choice may be crucial if policies are to have the intended effect. History is replete with examples of policy outcomes quite different from what was hoped for when a particular implementation instrument was selected. For instance, neither Kaiser Wilhelm II nor Hitler was able to use war to make Germany the dominant world power. While the negotiation of NATO in 1949 and the initiation of the Marshall Plan achieved their goal of containing Soviet expansion in Europe, the dispatch of American troops to Vietnam did not bring about the defeat of the North Vietnamese. France's careful diplomacy toward the Arab world combined with the use of selected economic policy tools has not won for her the privileged relationships with the Arab countries which she sought. The policy goal of the Afro-Asian countries to alter the political system in South Africa through pressure diplomacy in the United Nations has met with only limited success.

Transnational policy in general and foreign policy in particular provide the dynamics for the interaction process among the actors on the international stage. We turn now to the ways in which different international actors are reflected in, and make their imprint on, this process.

NOTES

1. Niccolò Machiavelli, *The Prince* (1531), reproduced by Modern Library (New York: Random House); Jules Cambon, *Le Diplomate* (Paris: Hachette, 1926); Adm. C. Turner Joy, *How Communists Negotiate* (New York: Macmillan, 1955); Raymond Dennett and J. E. Johnson, eds., *Negotiating with the Russians* (Boston: World Peace Foundation, 1951); Fred C. Ikle, *How Nations Negotiate* (New York: Harper & Row, 1964).

2. Frederick H. Hartmann, *The Relations of Nations*, 4th ed. (New York: Macmillan, 1973), p. 97.

3. See Joy, op. cit., p. 170.

4. Cf. Zuhayr Mikdashi, "Collusion Could Work," *Foreign Policy*, no. 14 (Spring 1974), pp. 57–67; Stephen D. Krasner, "Oil Is the Exception," ibid., pp. 68–83; and C. Fred Bergsten, "The Threat is Real," ibid., pp. 84–90.

5. Cf. Richard Rosecrance, *International Relations: Peace or War?* (New York: McGraw-Hill, 1973), p. 292.

6. See Joan E. Spero, *The Politics of International Economic Relations* (New York: St. Martin's Press, 1977), pp. 146–147.

7. Paul M. A. Linebarger, *Psychological Warfare* (Washington: Combat Forces Press, 1954), pp. 26 and 40.

8. Cf. *Selected Addresses and Public Papers of Woodrow Wilson*, edited by Albert Bushnell Hart (New York: Boni and Liveright, 1918), pp. 247–248.

9. Ernst B. Haas and Allen Whiting, *Dynamics of International Politics* (New York: McGraw-Hill, 1956), p. 200.

10. See Werner J. Feld, "National-International Linkage Theory: The East European Communist System and the EEC," *Journal of International Affairs*, vol. 22, no. 1 (1968), pp. 107–120.

11. Karl von Clausewitz, *War, Politics, and Power (On War)* (Chicago: Henry Regnery, 1962), p. 83.

12. J. David Singer and Melvin Small, *The Wages of War, 1816–1965: A Statistical Handbook* (New York: Wiley & Sons, 1972), pp. 35, 36.

13. Ibid., pp. 59–70. Battle deaths during Korea and Vietnam were 33,629 and 45,501, respectively. (See *Information Please Almanac* [1972], p. 701.)

14. Hartman, op. cit., p. 161.

15. Henry Kissinger, *Nuclear Weapons and Foreign Policy* (New York: Harper & Row, 1957).

16. Harold Sprout and Margaret Sprout, *Foundations of International Politics* (Princeton: N.J.: Van Nostrand, 1962), p. 253.

17. Donald G. Brennan, "When the SALT Hit the Fan" in Morton A. Kaplan, *Great Issues of International Politics*, 2nd ed. (Chicago: Aldine, 1974), pp. 548–564, on p. 562.

SUGGESTED READINGS

BELL, CORAL. *Negotiating From Strength.* London: Chatto & Windus, 1962.

CRAIG, GORDON A., AND FELIX GILBERT, eds. *The Diplomats: 1919–1939.* Princeton, N.J.: Princeton University Press, 1953.

ECKSTEIN, H., ed. *Internal War.* New York: Free Press, 1964.

GEORGE, A. L., D. K. HALL, AND W. R. SIMONS. *The Limits of Coercive Diplomacy.* Boston: Little, Brown, 1971.

HALPERIN, M. H. *Limited War in the Nuclear Age.* New York: Wiley, 1963.

HOLSTI, OLE R. *Crisis Escalation War.* Montreal and London: McGill-Queen's University Press, 1971.

IKLÉ, FRED C. *How Nations Negotiate.* New York: Harper & Row, 1964.

JOYCE, WALTER. *The Propaganda Gap.* New York: Harper & Row, 1963.

KAHN, HERMAN. *Thinking About the Unthinkable.* New York: Horizon Press, 1962.

QUALTER, TERENCE H. *Propaganda and Psychological Warfare.* New York: Random House, 1962.

SCHELLING, THOMAS C. *The Strategy of Conflict.* Cambridge, Mass.: Harvard University Press.

SCOTT, ANDREW M. *The Revolution in Statecraft: Informal Penetration.* New York: Random House, 1966.

SNYDER, GLENN H. *Deterrence and Defense.* Princeton, N.J.: Princeton University Press, 1960.

WHITAKER, URBAN G., JR., ed. and comp. *Propaganda and International Relations.* San Francisco: Chandler, 1963.

CHAPTER EIGHT
COLLABORATIVE
INTERNATIONAL
RELATIONS

In Chapter 1 we pointed out that transnational policies and especially foreign policy provide the dynamics for the interaction between states on the international stage. In the past six chapters we have looked at the various forces that shape policies, mainly from the perspective of the state as an international actor, and have examined the processes that determine how an individual state plans to and does interact with other states to attain its objectives in the international arena. Now we shall focus on the interaction among states and other international actors and try to capture the whole picture of purposeful behavior and movement on the international stage.

To analyze this behavior and movement, we shall approach the interaction among states in terms of *collaboration* and *conflict.* In almost any type of collaborative endeavor, there are aspects of conflict, which should not be surprising considering the great variety of interests individual states may seek to promote. Conversely, even the war filled with the utmost of hate and animosity is likely to contain some elements of collaboration, be it consent of the warring countries to permit sending Red Cross shipments of packages to prisoner-of-war camps or mutual respect for the rights of neutral countries.

In this chapter we shall concentrate mainly on collaborative interactions, such as the formation and functioning of alliances and the establishment of economic cooperative arrangements. In the next chapter we shall move to an examination of potential conflict situations and the means of preventing conflict from erupting into war.

ALLIANCES

The ability of international actors to attain their goals depends to a large degree on their power status; weak countries may increase their goal attainment potential by forming or joining informal, ad hoc coalitions or formal alliances. In many instances, the added power enhances the potential of the alliance-seeking country for self-preservation, but specific purposes vary widely and may include political and economic ends.

Alliances may be concluded by means of an international treaty between two or more states or they may take the form of an IGO; in the latter case an institutional structure is set up for the management of the alliance. During the 19th century and the first half of the 20th century, most alliances were merely contractual agreements. Examples are the Holy Alliance of 1815; the Three Emperors' League of 1873 joining Austria, Germany, and Russia; the Triple Entente of France, Russia, and Great Britain to counter the Triple Alliance of Germany, Austria, and Italy prior to World War I; and the Tripartite Pact between Germany, Italy, and Japan of 1940. After World War II, most alliances involving the Western World were cast as IGOs with an institutional framework, as NATO, SEATO, and CENTO* illustrate; however, communist alliances, such as the Chinese-North Vietnamese cooperative arrangement, did not have any institutional features.

Common and Diverging Interests

At the base of each viable alliance must be a community of major identical or converging interests, but this does not mean that certain interests of the alliance partners cannot be in conflict. For example, Japan's and Germany's interests were at odds in 1941 when Japan considered war between Germany and the Soviet Union as inimical

---

* Respectively, the North Atlantic Treaty Organization, Southeast Asia Treaty Organization, and Central Treaty Organization.

to her interests, while undoubtedly the Japanese attack on Pearl Harbor was upsetting to German interests, inasmuch as it brought the United States into the war against Hitler. Before these events, the so-called Pact of Steel concluded between Germany and Italy in May 1939 showed cracks, some of which stemmed from disparities of interests. Italian Catholics were upset by Hitler's antireligious tirades and the division of primarily Catholic Poland. Mussolini's designs on the French Navy and colonies clashed with Hitler's decision to conclude a moderate peace with France in June 1940. North Vietnamese and Chinese interests also clashed from time to time because, despite their need for help, the North Vietnamese were opposed to any predominant influence of the Chinese in any part of Indochina.

Conflicts of interest among alliance signatories may emerge after the alliance has been in operation for some time. In such cases, it may be necessary to redefine the alliance commonality of interests; otherwise, the alliance may collapse, or one or more of the partners may defect. A good example is NATO, which was formed in 1948 to counter what was perceived as the clear danger of Soviet aggression against Western Europe. As the magnitude of this threat diminished in the minds of many Europeans during the 1960s, segments of the elites and the mass public in several European countries and Canada began to doubt the need for the NATO alliance with its high cost to the taxpayer. In the United States, more and more persons advocated the withdrawal of American troops from Europe, or at least a reduction in these forces.

With the advent of détente, NATO leaders initiated studies to find new roles and new common interests, such as joint economic approaches to the problems of underdevelopment in the Third World or collaboration on antipollution measures, to keep the alliance together. Although the 1968 Soviet invasion of Czechoslovakia revived the spirit of military collaboration, the cohesion of NATO once again began to suffer and interests, to diverge. The negotiations for greater East-West economic cooperation and human contacts that led in 1975 to the Helsinki agreement, as well as the so far unsuccessful efforts toward a mutual and balanced reduction of NATO and communist forces in Europe, have stimulated new sets of common and converging interests, thereby diminishing the significance of existing conflicts of interest.

The rise of interest conflicts may lead to defection from alliances. For this reason France withdrew from collaboration in the NATO organization in 1967, although she remained a member of the alliance. A year earlier she had cut her tie to SEATO.

While the contemporary alliances discussed so far have mostly military purposes, others have additional or exclusive political and economic objectives. The Organization of African Unity, established in 1963, pursues primarily political goals. The Joint Defense and Economic Cooperation Treaty, concluded among members of the Arab League in 1950, emphasized economic purposes in addition to security tasks, but the economic program remained largely a paper operation.

Clashing ideologies are not necessarily an impediment to an alliance when powerful converging interests bring the alliance partners together, as can be seen, for example, in the Non-Aggression Pact of 1939 between Nazi Germany and the Soviet Union. This pact did not last more than two years and was terminated by Hitler's attack on Russia in June of 1941. On the other hand, identical or similar ideologies are no guarantee for the continuance of an alliance when the growing disparities of interests become burdensome. An example is the deterioration of military and economic cooperation arrangements between the Soviet Union and the People's Republic of China in the late 1950s, which led ultimately to the collapse of the alliance.

The Basic Commitment of the Alliance Partners

A difficult problem in any alliance is to define precisely the situation that is to bring obligatory action on the part of alliance partners. The question arises specifically as to how far the allies will be obliged to go in helping each other in case of attack on one or all of them by a third country. Should they automatically give military aid and assistance and thereby go to war, as stipulated in the Treaty of Brussels of 1948 joining Great Britain, France, and the Benelux countries, or should each alliance partner be obliged only to take "such actions as it deems necessary, including the use of armed force," as stipulated in Article 5 of the NATO Treaty.

There is a tendency to use great caution when the basic alliance commitment is drawn up and to seek minimal obligations. This has been especially true in Western alliances subsequent to the Treaty of Brussels and NATO, whereas the Axis pacts were more precise and compelling. Both the Pact of Steel and the Tripartite Pact insisted on military means of assistance and implied immediate responses by the allies in case of "warlike" complications or involvements with other powers. Despite the rigidity of terminology, however, Italy did not join Germany as a military partner in her war against France and Britain until June 1940, nearly ten months after the outbreak of war. On the other hand, flexibility in the definition of the alliance commitment, while initially inducing more countries to sign an alliance treaty, may create apprehension among some of the alliance partners as to the degree of security they have obtained by their signature. This has been a recurring problem among the NATO partners and can be overcome only when all alliance members have similar, if not identical, perceptions of the commonality of their interests.

The commonality of interests as seen by individual alliance partners is closely linked to the distribution of benefits and costs. Ideally there should be complete mutuality, but this is only possible in an alliance of countries that are more or less equal in power, which is rarely the case. In most instances of unequal power, the security achieved through an alliance offers equal benefit to all alliance members—it is an intangible "common good" that is indivisible[1]—despite the fact that member nations do not contribute equally. Smaller allies are guaranteed the same benefits but may pay proportionately less than the larger allies. On the other hand, the larger allies may be compensated by greater private individual benefits derived from the award of construction contracts for alliance infrastructure needs, such as the building of military facilities on their own territory and that of their allies and the supply of weapons and other military materiel.

Regardless of whether an alliance is served by an institutional structure or not, provisions must be made for periodic consultations among the allies. In some instances, special commissions are established for this purpose, as was done in the Tripartite Pact. As a minimum, regularly scheduled meetings of foreign ministers are essential for consultation; special personnel in the foreign ministries of the allies should be assigned to furnish continuity to the consultative activities.

A smooth-working consultation machinery can prevent conflicts of interest from arising and assures continued cohesion. Otherwise, as NATO has demonstrated again and again, complaints are often voiced that one of the partners, usually the United States, takes unilateral strategic actions without consultation, thereby undermining the morale and cohesion of the alliance. Unfortunately, *consultation* is an ambiguous term. To some it means simply to inform the alliance partners of a prospective decision and listen to their advice without being bound to follow it. To others it means a process of reasoning together and making joint decisions. The NATO history of consultation suggests that the United States leans toward the first interpretation, whereas the West European governments prefer the second.

Duration and Durability

Alliance treaties normally specify the duration of the collaboration of the partners: ten to twenty years seems to be normal. For instance, the Pact of Steel was concluded for ten years, and NATO had an initial duration of twenty years. Unless notice of withdrawal ("denunciation") was given by an alliance partner at least one year before the expiration of the twenty-year period, the contractual obligation of NATO continued. The ANCUS Mutual Security Treaty of 1951[2] between Australia, New Zealand, and the United States is unusual inasmuch as it is to be in force "indefinitely." In some cases, the duration of an alliance depends on external events such as the existence of a counteralliance, or on winning or losing a war, especially if it was formed for a particular military purpose.

No alliance can continue over an extended period of time unless protracted efforts are made to curb internal strains and to adapt it to external changes. Such adaptation is especially necessary when the alliance is composed of strong and weak states, because the unequal possession of resources usually entails differing perceptions of how much a country should contribute to the cost of an alliance. Cost-benefit calculations are apt to vary widely; and this problem is compounded by the fact that the larger powers in an alliance may have their way regardless of protests by the smaller allies. Machiavelli's warning to weak nations not to ally themselves with powerful ones except by necessity appears to be very sound advice.

If alliances are to last and be viable, it is necessary to operationalize the community of interests through the formulation and concrete pursuit of common policies and measures. This is not an easy task because the individual governments of alliance partners may give different priorities to their common interests in relation to other national interests; therefore, efforts to arrive at common policies may not be successful.

Problems for the maintenance of an alliance may also arise from a new interpretation of a country's interests, which may be the result of a major shift in government, changing perceptions of elites regarding their interests, changes of the power relationships within the alliance, and new alliances concluded by one ally in other parts of the world. General de Gaulle's assumption of power in 1958 did not immediately lead to a change in France's attitude toward NATO; but eventually it became clear that, for de Gaulle, other national interests, such as recapturing French glory through a policy of independence, outweighed full commitment to the common defense of the West through NATO.[3]

NATO is also a good example of changing attitudes of elites.

During the mid-sixties, influential groups in Europe began to doubt that the Soviet Union still constituted a threat and were wondering whether NATO had not lost its *raison d'etre.*

Not all changes in power relationships within an alliance challenge the maintenance of an alliance. Since its entry into NATO in 1955, Germany has increased its economic and military strength tremendously and has thereby strengthened rather than weakened the alliance. But a sudden decline in U.S. military might would undoubtedly jeopardize the functioning of the NATO alliance.

The dysfunctional effect of new alliances, such as the SEATO Treaty, is exemplified by the fact that many Europeans felt conclusion of this treaty demonstrated a de-emphasis of Europe in the global strategy of the United States in favor of Asia and the Pacific. It conjured up doubts in the minds of European elites as to whether continued reliance upon American men and weapons was justified, and these perceptions impaired the viability of the alliance even if they were completely unfounded.

To overcome these and other challenges to the operation of an alliance, continuous consultation and adjustment of policies are necessary. Communication among alliance partners must be open at all times. Erroneous impressions must be corrected; conflicting interests reconciled as much as possible; acceptable compromises worked out; and mutual understanding of problems assured. With rapid and multidirectional changes in the international arena and world politics becoming unavoidable, the management of an alliance is a difficult task that is made more difficult by the variety of governmental and private interests pursued domestically and transnationally in a highly complex world. Unless this management is handled capably, alliances may die quickly, or if their formal demise is avoided, they may lose their viability and remain as not much more than a skeleton. At present, CENTO fits this description, while SEATO was completely dismantled with the end of the Vietnam War.

ECONOMIC COOPERATION ARRANGEMENTS

A major purpose of alliances is to enhance a country's capability for self-preservation and survival; therefore, the accent is on sharing military resources. Another type of useful collaboration to bolster a country's power is economic cooperation through sharing enlarged markets, specialized manufacturing facilities and technologies, capital, and manpower resources. Many smaller and middle-sized countries in the world, whether in the developed or less developed areas, are no longer able to ensure the economic well-being of their people by providing full employment, adequate wages, and the proper assortment of foodstuffs. Economic collaboration with other countries may alleviate these deficiencies, thereby strengthening the countries involved. Of course, as with alliances, these economic collaboration arrangements require a basic community of interests among the participatory countries, but a number of conflicting interests usually are present also and must be taken into account when the arrangements are negotiated and begin to function. Compromises must be elaborated, and disparate interests have to be redefined or temporarily ignored, as in alliances. Continued efforts are required to keep collaboration arrangements from foundering.

Geographic Distribution and Problems

Economic cooperation arrangements may be cast in the form of IGOs or may merely be based on international agreements. In most instances, they establish customs unions or free trade areas in which a number of countries located in an international region participate; however, contiguity of the participating countries is not necessary, as membership in such organizations as the European Free Trade Association (EFTA) and the Latin American Free Trade Association (LAFTA) have demonstrated.*

In both customs unions and free trade associations, internal tariffs between member states are eliminated, but only the customs union has a common external tariff. Members of free trade associations maintain their individual tariffs for goods coming in from third countries.

Besides EFTA and LAFTA, established in 1959 and 1960, respectively, the best known economic cooperation arrangements are the European Coal and Steel Community (ECSC), established in 1952, and the European Economic Community (EEC), which went into operation in 1958. Both were originally composed of France, West Germany (the Federal Republic of Germany), Italy, Belgium, the Netherlands, and Luxembourg. Both organizations were joined in 1973 by Great Britain, Ireland, and Denmark and continue to exist at present. In Eastern Europe, COMECON—the communist regional trade organization—originated in 1949 and now has as members the

---

* Original members of EFTA were Great Britain, Denmark, Norway, Sweden, Switzerland, Austria, Portugal, and Iceland (an associate member). Great Britain and Denmark left EFTA in 1973 to join the European Economic Community (EEC). Mexico is part of LAFTA, but has no common border with its South American partners, all of which are LAFTA members.

Soviet Union, East Germany (the German Democratic Republic), Czechoslovakia, Poland, Hungary, Romania, and Bulgaria. Yugoslavia has observer status.

In the Western Hemisphere in addition to LAFTA, the governments of El Salvador, Guatemala, Honduras, and Nicaragua concluded in 1960 the basic treaty to establish a Central American Common Market to which Costa Rica acceded two years later. A more recent addition to the Latin American cooperation arrangements is the Andean Common Market, which comprises Venezuela, Colombia, Ecuador, Bolivia, Peru, and Chile.

In Africa the most important economic cooperation arrangement exists between Kenya, Uganda, and Tanzania. It is now called the East African Community and had its origins in a customs union of the three countries set up during the 1920s when they were colonies of Great Britain. There are other regional economic arrangements in West Africa, but they are insignificant.

A few additional economic cooperation agreements not cast in the form of IGOs include Australia and New Zealand, which concluded a free trade agreement in the late 1960s, and Great Britain and Ireland, which have a similar arrangement. Between the United States and Canada, a limited free trade area has been established which primarily provides for automotive products to be exempted from duties.

Without doubt the most successful endeavors of economic cooperation have been the EEC, ECSC, and EFTA. Their success reflects a high level of common interests and a minimum of conflicts of interests. Moreover, the distribution of benefits flowing from these arrangements to the governments and the people of these countries is fairly equitable. On the other hand, the Latin American efforts have met with many obstacles and have failed to produce the kind of forward movement in economic integration we have witnessed in Western Europe. A possible exception may be the Andean Common Market, but even there the final outcome is not certain.

Serious problems have also beset African efforts at regional cooperation. Although it appeared that the East African Community would be quite successful because the underlying customs union was originated several decades ago, the evidence suggests a deterioration of economic cooperation. In the Third World, the commonality of regional interests is undermined by the overriding domestic political concerns of leaders intent on holding onto their positions of power. The pursuit of narrow national interests predominates, and this trend has been reinforced by the unequal distribution of benefits derived from the Latin American and African cooperation efforts.

North-South Arrangements

While the economic cooperation arrangements discussed so far were carried out either completely among developed *or* developing countries, a number of attempts have been made to tie developed *and* developing countries together in so-called North-South arrangements. The most widespread of these arrangements exists among the European Economic Community and the Mediterranean and African countries, and some Caribbean and West Pacific states. The Common Market Treaty contains special provisions for setting up associations between the Community and other countries, and this device has been used extensively to establish economic cooperation with various countries.

Convention of Lomé   The best-known of these cooperation arrangements is the Convention of Lomé, which links nearly fifty African countries* with the Common Market. It provides lower, or no, tariffs for goods shipped from the African countries to the Common Market and provides preferential tariffs for Community exports to Africa. It also contains provisions for financial aid and technical assistance to the developing countries participating in the Convention and an elaborate institutional structure has been set up to manage the association. The most important element of this structure is the Association Council, which brings together representatives of the Community and the associated states. A parliamentary conference composed of members of the European Parliament and the parliaments of the associated countries has done much to intensify the relationship of the cooperating countries. Additional associations

---

* The following is a list of the 46 independent countries in Africa, the Caribbean, and the Pacific that have entered into the new agreement with the European Community: Nineteen states hitherto associated with the Common Market until January 31, 1975, by the Yaounde Convention: Burundi, Cameroon, Central African Republic, Chad, Congo, Dahomey, Gabon, Ivory Coast, Madagascar, Mali, Mauritania, Mauritius, Niger, Rwanda, Senegal, Somalia, Togo, Upper Volta, and Zaire. Twenty-one Commonwealth states, to which the EEC had offered special agreements on Great Britain's adhesion to the Common Market: in Africa—Botswana, Gambia, Ghana, Kenya, Lesotho, Malawi, Nigeria, Sierra Leone, Swaziland, Tanzania, Uganda, Zambia; in the Caribbean—Bahamas, Barbados, Guyana, Grenada, Jamaica, Trinidad-Tobago; in the Pacific—Fiji, Western Samoa, Tonga. Six countries of Africa with no special relationship with the countries of the EEC, which were invited to join the above-mentioned because their economies were "comparable": Ethiopia, Liberia, Sudan, Guinea, Equatorial Guinea, and Guinea-Bissau.

have been concluded with Tunisia, Morocco, Cyprus, Malta, Turkey, and Greece. Other special cooperation arrangements have been negotiated with most of the other countries rimming the Mediterranean. At present only Libya seems to be an exception.

Alliance for Progress   In the Western Hemisphere, a North-South economic cooperation arrangement was set up in the early 1960s between the United States and Latin America by the Alliance for Progress. Only Cuba was excepted from this arrangement. The program was developed within the framework of the Organization of American States (OAS), which aims not only at inter-American security but also seeks to solve economic, political, and juridical problems. Specifically, the Alliance for Progress called for the achievement of four major objectives:

1. A minimum inflow of $20 billion in capital to Latin America over a period from 1962 to 1972, with a major part coming from private sources in the United States and other industrially advanced countries and the remainder from governmental funds.
2. The implementation of various social and economic reforms within each of the recipient countries.
3. Strengthening of the democratic institutions and the role of private enterprise in Latin America.
4. Stabilization of markets and prices for Latin American primary commodities.

The priorities for expenditures of capital were to be determined multilaterally by a special panel of the OAS, with specific commitments made by the Interamerican Bank for Development, the Export-Import Bank, and the United States Agency for International Development. Despite the fact that, for the first four years, the United States poured more than $4 billion into Latin America, the results have been disappointing. Internal land and tax reforms have lagged in most countries, private investment did not measure up to expectations, and runaway population growth offset development gains. As a consequence, the Alliance for Progress program has been in limbo during the past few years. Very recently, however, the steady improvement in primary commodity prices, based largely on American and European prosperity and consequent increasing demand, has furnished much larger foreign currency earnings for Latin America and has contributed to improvement in the economic level of many countries in the southern part of the Western Hemisphere.

Asian and Pacific Council   Another North-South cooperative arrangement is the Asian and Pacific council, ASPAC, which joins industrially advanced Japan, Australia, and New Zealand to the less developed countries of South Korea, Taiwan, South Vietnam, the Philippines, Thailand, and Malaysia. Despite the fact that ASPAC was founded in 1966, it is difficult to judge how much the developing countries have benefited from this arrangement. Clearly, there exists a community of economic interests; however, Japan is still remembered as a conqueror during World War II, and this produces continuing psychological problems that might be overcome in time.

Colombo Plan   A similar arrangement between advanced and developing countries is found in the Colombo Plan aiming at development programs underwritten by the advanced Commonwealth states—the United Kingdom, Canada, Australia, and New Zealand—for the less developed Commonwealth states, India, Ceylon, Pakistan, Malaysia, and Singapore, as well as other Asian countries, such as Burma, Cambodia, and Indonesia. The Colombo Plan sought to achieve an ideal balance between a regional and bilateral approach to development. Institutional machinery was kept to a minimum. Contributions take the form of both grants and loans. They are provided through bilateral arrangements, but the distribution is based on multilateral consultation to coodinate the overall program.

Organization of Petroleum Exporting Countries   Finally, a relatively new organization in the field of economic cooperation is the Organization of Petroleum Exporting Countries (OPEC). It is headquartered in Vienna but consists primarily of the oil producing countries of the Middle East supplemented by Venezuela and Indonesia. Its main efforts have been to strengthen the power of these countries through successful endeavors to raise the price of crude oil, take over a majority share of the installations of the international oil companies engaged in petroleum extraction activities, and gradually to acquire marketing facilities in the oil consuming countries.[4] In addition OPEC has attempted to control the output of crude oil, which could be regarded either as a conservation measure or as an attempt to bring political pressure to bear on countries whose policies are disliked. Without doubt the latter objective has been very much in the mind of the Arab countries in order to see American foreign policy toward Israel changed.

Conference on International Economic Cooperation (CIEC)
Following the steep rise in oil prices and plagued by the continuing threat of another oil embargo against the Western industrialized world, efforts were undertaken in 1975 by the United States, the European Community countries, and Japan to open a North-South dialogue on energy problems. Because the developing countries insisted that not only petroleum, but other commodities, such as copper, bauxite, and food stuffs, should be included in this dialogue, the talks have been expanded. A Conference on International Economic Cooperation (CIEC) was convened in which oil consumers, oil producers, and other Third World countries were represented. Several committees have been formed to address themselves to the question of the supplies and prices of raw materials, including petroleum, and to the more general problem of trade and finances for the Third World. Progress has been very slow despite major incentives offered by the industrialized countries in the form of a large fund to help the poorest of the developing countries and of an additional, very extensive fund to stabilize the prices of commodities exported by the Third World countries to assure adequate foreign currency earnings for those countries.

The hope of the industrialized countries was to create a permanent organization in which oil and gas exporting and importing countries would consult on supplies, prices, and investments in new energy sources. It was anticipated that, through such an organization, it would be possible to guarantee adequate oil supplies and keep a lid on oil prices. But the result of CIEC was a disappointment to the Western countries, and OPEC's autonomy regarding supplies and prices was not impaired. In fact, CIEC may well disappear, and future negotiations take place in United Nations forums.

Economic cooperation arrangements are sometimes the cause for the creation of other similar arrangements, either in the same region or in another part of the world. There may be several reasons for this. A number of countries in the same region may feel threatened by the existing economic cooperation arrangements and compelled to establish a counterarrangement for their own protection. Another reason may be the success of the original arrangement, which prompts other countries to seek similar benefits through similar arrangements. In some instances, both of these reasons may be operative.

Two examples will illustrate the above cause-effect relationships. Great Britain was invited to be a charter member of the European Coal and Steel Community in 1951, and a few years later was asked to be an original member of the European Common Market and Euratom. Britain declined because she felt that her Commonwealth interests would not be served by joining either community, but later proposed that an All-European Free Trade Association be formed in which the prospective Common Market countries would partici- pate. Most countries that had signed the Common Market Treaty, especially France, were opposed to this approach. For France it would have meant a considerable loss of benefits from the forth- coming Common Market in terms of assistance to her farmers and a possible transfer to the Common Market of the burdens she was carrying in her colonies. When it became clear that the British proposal could not be realized, Great Britain established the Euro- pean Free Trade Association as a countermeasure against the Common Market and thereby split Western Europe into two trading blocs.

The creation of LAFTA and the Central American Common Market was motivated at least in part by the success of the European Common Market, as well as by the fear that this new economic cooperation arrangement might harm Latin American trade with Western Europe. Thus the two Latin American organizations owe their existence to the desire to emulate the success of economic cooperation in Europe and to the perceived need for countermea- sures against the operational effects of the European Common Market and the Coal and Steel Community.

SUMMARY

The interactions among states can be viewed in terms of **collabo- ration** and **conflict**. Collaborative interactions include the formation of **alliances** and the establishment of **economic cooperative arrange- ments.**

Alliances may be concluded by means of an international treaty between two or more states, or they may take the form of an IGO with consequent institutional framework. While conflicting ideolo- gies are not necessarily an impediment to an alliance, at the base of each viable alliance must be a community of major identical or converging interests.

Conflicts of interest among alliance signatories may emerge after an alliance has been in operation for some time. In such instances, the alliance or commonality of interests must be redefined to prevent defection of partners and collapse of the alliance itself. Moves toward détente have forced just such a re-examination of NATO, an alliance formed in 1948 to counter what was then perceived as the clear danger of Soviet aggression against Western Europe.

A difficult problem in any alliance is to define precisely the situation that is to bring obligatory action on the part of alliance partners. There is a tendency to use great caution when the basic alliance commitment is drawn up and to seek minimal obligations.

Regardless of whether or not an alliance is served by an institutional structure, provisions need to be made for periodic **consultations** among allies. No alliance can continue over an extended period of time unless protracted efforts are made to curb internal strains and to adapt the alliance to external changes.

A major purpose of alliances is to enhance a country's military and defense capabilities, but alliances may also be a means of achieving political and economic objectives. **Economic cooperation arrangements** may be cast in the form of IGOs or may be merely based on international agreements. In most instances, they establish **customs unions** or **free trade areas.** Examples of economic cooperation arrangements are those that established the European Free Trade Association (EFTA), the Latin American Free Trade Association (LAFTA), the European Coal and Steel Community (ECSC), the European Economic Community (EEC), and Comecon. The most successful of these are the EEC, ECSC, and EFTA.

A number of attempts have been made to tie developed and developing countries together in so-called **North-South arrangements.** Such arrangements include the Convention of Lomé, the Alliance for Progress, an Asian and Pacific arrangement known as ASPAC, the Colombo Plan, and the Conference on International Economic Cooperation (CIEC). The latter was an attempt by the United States, the European Community countries, and Japan to open a North-South dialogue on energy problems in response to the actions of the Organization of Petroleum Exporting Countries (OPEC). Through this conference, the industrialized world hoped to create a permanent organization in which oil and gas exporting and importing countries would consult on supplies, prices, and investments in new energy sources; but OPEC's autonomy regarding supplies and prices remains intact.

Most international relations are not exclusively collaborative or conflictual, but manifest varying degrees of each. In this chapter we have examined arrangements that were primarily collaborative. In the next chapter we shall look at those relationships characterized mainly by conflict.

NOTES

1. See Mancur Olson, Jr., and Richard Zeckhauser, "An Economic Theory of Alliances," in Bruce Russet, ed., *Economic Theories of International Politics* (Chicago: Markham, 1968), pp. 25–50.

2. Ernst B. Haas and Allen S. Whiting, *Dynamics of International Relations* (New York: McGraw-Hill, 1956).

3. See the De Gaulle news conference of February 21, 1966, in the *NATO Letters* of April 1966.

4. For details see Zuhar Mikdashi, *The Community of Oil Exporting Countries* (Ithaca, N.Y.: Cornell University Press, 1972); and Peter R. Odell, *Oil and World Power* (New York: Taplinger, 1970).

SUGGESTED READINGS

BERGSTEN, C. F., ed. *The Future of the International Economic Order: An Agenda for Research.* Lexington, Mass.: Lexington Books, 1973.

FEDDER, E. H. *NATO: The Dynamics of Alliance in the Postwar World.* New York: Dodd, Mead, 1973.

HEEGER, GERALD A. *The Politics of Underdevelopment.* New York: St. Martin's Press, 1974.

HOLSTI, O. R., P. I. HOPMANN, AND J. D. SULLIVAN. *Unity and Disintegration in International Alliances.* New York: Wiley, 1973.

NEUSTADT, R. E. *Alliance Politics.* New York: Columbia University Press, 1970.

TACHAU, FRANK, ed. *The Developing Nations: What Path to Modernization?* New York: Dodd, Mead, 1972.

CHAPTER NINE
CONFLICT IN INTERNATIONAL BEHAVIOR

Most international relations do not consist entirely of cooperation or conflict, but manifest varying degrees of each. Where relations are primarily in conflict, the relative power positions of the countries involved are of crucial significance. These positions are affected by alliances and by successful economic cooperation arrangements. Changes in perceived power positions may cause conflict, inasmuch as they create apprehension and frustration in the minds of governmental leaders in those countries who feel their power status has been lowered by the alliances and economic cooperation arrangements of others and who may seek to recoup their loss by forming similar alliances or participating in similar agreements. Their aim may be to "balance" through these agreements the increase in power accruing to the first group of alliance partners. The more a particular state feels threatened pursuing its own interests, the stronger will be its motivation for seeking such a power-balancing arrangement.

THE BALANCE OF POWER
AND INTERSTATE CONFLICT

The balancing of power as a tool in world politics is as old as recorded history. It is a prescription for action in the international arena and results in particular balance-of-power situations that may have regional or global implications. It may prevent wars when powerful antagonists perceive their power and aspirations check-mated, or it may precipitate war if a country bent on immediate expansion regards an emerging balance-of-power situation as a frustration to its aspirations. It may result in the development of economically competing trading blocs that later join politically and/or militarily to form opposing alliances that threaten armed conflict.

The impact of balance-of-power constellations upon the interaction between states has fascinated political scientists and international relations specialists for many years; therefore, we shall review the main concepts elaborated and offer some historical examples.

Concepts and Patterns

In Chapter 1 we discussed the notion of the international system and its subsystems, as well as the concept of *equilibrium*. When the equilibrium of a system composed of a number of elements or units is disturbed, either by an outside force or change in one of the component elements, the system tends either to re-establish the original equilibrium or to move toward a new one. Equilibrium in a system signifies stability; and just as the human body is characterized by a continuous quest to maintain equilibrium in case of internal disturbances or outside interferences, so the international system seeks to restore equilibrium and balance among its component parts. Equilibrium guarantees to the component parts, that is, mainly the different states, the right to exist: without equilibrium of the system, they might be destroyed by the ascendancy of one or several states over the others. The goals then are the preservation of the elements of the system, although some change is permissible, and the continuous maintenance of equilibrium and stability.[1]

Whether these goals can be deduced from the nature of the international system and whether the balance-of-power principle is an operating guide accepted by the leaders of states in the formulation and pursuit of their foreign policies are open to doubt. Certainly, during the first two to three centuries of the modern state system, which began in 1648, the balance-of-power concept was considered to be the guiding principle of international politics by theorists and monarchs alike.[2] But whether these dynastic leaders of the European states, who were also the policy makers, considered the balance of power to be an end in itself, as some of their rhetoric seemed to indicate, or merely a convenient technique for the maximizing of their own power, is uncertain.

At the base of any balance-of-power configuration is the struggle by one or more states to maximize power. In its simplest form, state *A* may pursue an expansionistic policy at the expense of state *B*, which may counter that policy with a similar policy toward state *A* or with a policy of the status quo. This pattern of direct opposition has been found in many instances of interaction, and relations between the Soviet Union and the United States since 1946, or between India and Pakistan, are good examples.

A more complex pattern emerges among three countries when state *A* follows a policy of tutelage toward state *C*, while state *B* either desires the status quo of state *C* or also seeks influence over the policies of state *C*. This then is a competitive situation for *A* and *B* with respect to *C* whereby the countervailing forces of *A* and *B* create a measure of security for *C* and thereby some kind of fragile stability in the relationship among the three countries. Of course, *C*'s security and the overall stability would be threatened at once if *A* could manage to increase its power rapidly. The situation regarding *C* may be repeated for many other smaller countries, and the competitive struggle, especially in the 1950s and early 1960s, between the United States and the Soviet Union for the allegiance of and influence over the policies of the newly independent states in Africa and Asia illustrates well this configuration of the balance of power. As Morgenthau points out, under such conditions the independence of $C_{1,2,3,n}$ is a function of the power relationship between *A* and *B*.[3] At the same time, this relationship also offers $C_{1,2,3,n}$ many bargaining opportunities vis-à-vis both *A* and *B*.

An interesting three-cornered balance-of-power relationship has developed among the United States, the Soviet Union, and China. While they are far from being equal in power, they have all passed the nuclear threshold and are large countries with substantial educated populations and substantial GNPs. Because the United States initiated quasi-diplomatic relations with China in 1972, any attempt at domination by one of the three countries can be met by a short-term coalition of the third country with the threatened state. Thus the possibility of shifting coalitions may bring a high degree of stability to the relationship among these three powerful states and reduce, if not eliminate, their dependence on other, less powerful states for assurance of their security.[4]

A fourth balance-of-power configuration, which has many historical examples, is the formation of an alliance by state *B* with *C*, *D*, *E*, and perhaps others against expansionist designs of powerful state *A*. The alliances formed by Francis I, king of France, with Henry VIII and the Turks against Charles V of Hapsburg to halt the expansion of his Spanish-based empire is a prime example of the balance of power operating between an alliance and a state bent on global expansion and domination. The formation of varying alliances by Great Britain, Prussia, Russia, Austria, and others against Napoleon's design of world domination is another example.

The most familiar and frequent balance-of-power constellation is that between two opposing alliances. States *A* and *B*, allied both to pursue expansionist policies and to strengthen their defensive capabilities, are opposed by an alliance formed by states *C*, *D*, and *E* to safeguard their territorial integrity and political independence. Perhaps the most active period of alliance and counteralliance in history was the 18th century when rapidly shifting coalitions, in which Great Britain, Russia, and Prussia played prominant roles, strengthened these countries and resulted in the decline of Swedish power.

The interaction between opposing alliances within various balance-of-power constellations continued through the 19th century to our times as one of the major factors in world politics. In fact, the Monroe Doctrine transformed an essentially European-oriented balance-of-power system to a worldwide system that has culminated in the post–World War II era of far-flung alliances.

A variation of the patterns of the opposing alliances for balance-of-power purposes is the addition of a single state that acts as a *balancer*. The function of the balancer is described well by Morgenthau:

> The balancer is not permanently identified with the policies of either nation or group of nations. Its only objective within the system is the maintenance of the balance, regardless of the concrete policies the balance will serve. In consequence, the holder of the balance will throw its weight at one time in this scale, at another time in the other scale, guided only by one consideration—the relative position of the scales. Thus it will put its weight always in the scale that seems to be higher than the other because it is lighter. The balancer may become in a relatively short span of history consecutively the friend and foe of all major powers, provided they all consecutively threaten the balance by approaching predominance over the others and are in turn threatened by others about to gain such predominance. To paraphrase a statement of Palmerston: While the holder of the balance has no permanent friends, it has no permanent enemies either; it has only the permanent interest of maintaining the balance of power itself.[5]

Great Britain, the Balancer

Great Britain played the role of balancer with consummate skill for three centuries, until World War I. She became a powerful factor in world politics by making it very difficult, if not impossible, for any state or combination of states to gain permanent dominance over the other states in the international system. Britain also gained, thereby, a rather unflattering reputation of letting other countries fight her wars, of keeping Europe divided in order to dominate the Continent, and of being an unreliable ally when she allied herself with another country. "Perfidious Albion"* became a label for Britain in the minds of many people. The British justified their balancing policy by pointing out that they always supported the weaker states against the strongest of the continental powers, although it may have been more tempting to join the stronger and share the profits of conquest. Taking the former course was the harder task, but it contributed to the preservation of liberties in Europe by defeating potentially dominating and tyrannical regimes, including those of the emperor of Spain during the 16th century, the French monarchy of Louis XIV, the French empire of the 19th century, and Germany's Emperor Wilhelm II and Hitler.[6]

Balance of power functioned most effectively to maintain peace between 1815 and 1914. The line of departure was a treaty complex, popularly known as the Holy Alliance of 1815, which obligated its signatories, most of the monarchs of Europe, to uphold the principle of monarchical legitimacy against the forces of nationalism unleashed by the French Revolution and to assure the inviolability of the frontiers of 1815. The main actors in the balance-of-power system during that period were Austria, Russia, Great Britain, France, and Prussia, which was replaced by a unified Germany in 1871. Initially, Prussia and Austria allied to balance the Russian empire; but all three, with the help of Great Britain, formed an alliance against a possibly resurging France. By the end of the 19th century, a new alliance emerged among Germany, Austria-Hungary, and Italy (the Triple Alliance), while the alliance among Germany (formerly Prussia), Austria, and Russia disintegrated under the inept diplomacy of Kaiser Wilhelm II. At the same time, France and Russia perceived an increasing commonality of interests and formed an alliance against the Triple Alliance in 1894. Initially, Britain played its role as a balancer but by 1904 had moved to the side of Russia, bringing about the Triple Entente of the two countries and France.

During the ninety-nine years between 1815 and 1914, general war was avoided, although six localized wars broke out, five of which were fought in connection with the unification of Germany and Italy. Some of the main actors in the balance of power participated in

---

* Albion is an ancient name for Great Britain and may have come from the Latin word *albus*, meaning "white," in reference to the White Cliffs of Dover. It was Napoleon who branded England *Albion Perfide*.

these localized wars, but no general conflagration occurred until World War I in 1914.

It would exceed the scope of this book to explore in detail the ways in which the balance-of-power system contributed to the avoidance of general war between 1815 and 1914. It may well have been the fluidity and flexibility of the shifting coalitions among the major powers and the astute skill of the balancer, Great Britain, that prevented any country in Europe from becoming so powerful that its leadership would believe that the benefits from a general war could outweigh the costs. Once shifting coalitions became difficult to achieve and perceptions of progress toward national goals through the balance-of-power mechanism vanished in the minds of the strongest actors, this mechanism was abandoned. For example, at the end of the 19th century, Germany decided to seek predominant power status in Europe for itself.

The Essential Rules for Balance-of-power Situations

Morton Kaplan has elaborated several rules that states involved in balance-of-power situations must follow if the balance mechanism is to function properly and the equilibrium is to be maintained or reconstituted, either in the old or a new form. He states that the minimum number of "essential" actors (states) must be five or preferably more. "Essential" appears to denote a major power, but not necessarily a superpower. France, Great Britain, and Italy would be equally acceptable. Sometimes one essential actor may drop out and be replaced by another essential actor. The important point is that the states involved must

1. Attempt to increase power status but negotiate rather than fight.
2. If necessary, fight rather than pass up a clear opportunity to increase power status.
3. Stop fighting rather than eliminate a state essential to the balance of power.
4. Act to oppose any coalition or single state which is in the process of assuming a position of predominance with respect to the rest of the system.
5. Permit defeated states to re-enter the balance-of-power system and play the roles described in the preceding points.[7]

Kaplan terms these rules essential. He holds that the number of the essential rules cannot be reduced and that the failure of one rule to operate will result in the failure of other rules. The result will be instability of the system.

What methods are available to a state that wants to increase its power status and become or remain a desirable and "essential" actor in a balance-of-power system?

Increased Armaments Perhaps the quickest way to gain a power advantage over a rival or to catch up with a successful competitor is to arm. As long as the balance-of-power system does not include war as a means of operation, the ability and suggested willingness to fight will be a source of power.

The Establishment of Buffer Zones To preserve a given distribution of power between two powerful countries, one or more neutral states may serve as buffer states. They are weak nations located between two large and not-too-friendly states. The function of the buffer state is to keep the two powers apart and thus reduce the chances of friction between them. Examples are Belgium and Holland, which have been buffers between France and Germany during the past hundred years. In some instances, buffer states may vanish when two large countries decide to divide the buffer states between them in equal shares. Poland, located between Russia and Prussia (later Germany), has been the victim of such a decision several times.

The Detachment of Allies If an ally can be detached from one of the opposing alliances in a balance-of-power situation, it will weaken that alliance and may in fact destroy it. Germany made many efforts to separate England and France in the years preceding each of the two world wars, and the Soviet Union has attempted during the past decade to alienate and detach some of the European members of NATO from that alliance and from the United States. If such efforts succeed, the power of the country encouraging the detachment may be correspondingly increased. The ultimate result, however, may be to make the balance-of-power system so unstable that it breaks down completely.

Destroying Hopes of New Allies An effective means of destroying a state's morale is to deprive it of allies it had hoped to gain from uncommitted states by persuading these to remain neutral. This will reduce the ability of that state to successfully counterbalance the opposing state or alliance and thereby undermine its potential strength. Bismarck's greatest successes stemmed from the persistent use of this technique. To loosen Austria's stranglehold on the members of the German Confederation, which hindered his efforts to unify Germany, Bismarck had to keep France and Russia from aiding Austria. Bismarck succeeded in these efforts and had little difficulty as a result in defeating Austria in the summer of 1866.

Summary   In most instances, states do not consider balance of power to be an end in itself but rather a means of maximizing their own power status. International society has not progressed much since the sovereign nation-state emerged in the 17th century. It is, in many respects, a competitive and anarchical society in which power is more important than justice, survival is often menaced, and the threat of violence is commonplace. Thomas Hobbes's description of the nature of man, characterized by competition, diffidence, and glory, set forth in 1651, is unfortunately even today applicable to the relations among nation-states. While an existing or changed equilibrium may be useful to aid a state in its quest for self-preservation and survival, it would be an error to assume that the balance-of-power system is a value in itself.

Participation in a balance-of-power situation requires a variety of power calculations on the part of each state, calculations that are difficult to make and may include serious errors. To have a margin of safety, these calculations cannot really be aimed at achieving a power status equal to that of other countries. Instead, superiority of power must be sought. As a consequence, miscalculations may lead to either a preventive or a pre-emptive war. Thus, one of the perceived virtues of the balance-of-power system, namely the prevention of general war, cannot be assured.

Finally, it seems clear that there is no inner logic in the system to return it to its old equilibrium or to produce a new equilibrium in the event of outside disturbances. As a consequence, while balance of power, especially the classical type of the 18th and 19th centuries in Europe, has produced some periods of peace and has prevented world domination by one powerful state, it requires skillful foreign policy formulation and manipulation of other states to achieve this objective.

Some international relations scholars have criticized the equilibrium notion and the prescriptive aspects of the balance-of-power concept as placing too much emphasis on the assumption that all states are bent upon maximizing their power through alliances, military aggression, and other means of expanding their territory.[8] As we have pointed out, states do indeed pursue certain interests that do not require an expansion of their power status; but if, through the successful attainment of economic and cultural goals by either domestic or transnational means, their power status rises, this increased power will influence the relative distribution of global power and affect balance-of-power situations.

Another criticism voiced is that nations are not free to make or break alliances at will for power considerations because they may well be tied to their friends by economic, political, or psychological ties.[9] However, these ties are part of the overall power calculations; and if certain strategic concerns predominate in the views of governmental and political elites, economic or psychological ties may be abandoned to enhance a country's power position in a particular balance-of-power situation. For example, if one were to look at NATO and the Warsaw Pact countries (the communist counterpart of NATO in Eastern Europe) as main elements of an East-West balance-of-power system, France's withdrawal from the NATO organization constituted a change, although minor, in the equilibrium. France took this step to gain strategic, political, and economic benefits from her increased independence from the United States, despite long-standing psychological and historical ties with America, as well as close economic ties with her Common Market partners, all of whom were also NATO members.

The Constellation of Power Since World War I

During the years between World War I and World War II, balance-of-power considerations continued to play a role in Western Europe. France attempted to construct an alliance system between herself, Germany's eastern neighbors (Poland and Czechoslovakia), and some of the Balkan countries (Rumania and Yugoslavia). On the other hand, Germany and the Soviet Union began to cooperate in 1923 under the Treaty of Rapallo, and this cooperation was extended in 1926 by the Treaty of Berlin. Overarching these two coalitions was the Treaty of Locarno signed by Germany, Belgium, France, Great Britain, and Italy, which aimed at guaranteeing the territorial frontiers Germany shared with Belgium and France.

These peace efforts, which initially seemed successful, later met with repeated failure. Nor did the attempt to introduce a system of collective security under the auspices of the League of Nations halt the erosion of peace. Under the concept of *collective security*, an attack on any one state is regarded as an attack on all states participating in the collective security system and requires repulsion of the attack by the combined forces of these states. The resort to collective security was based on the premise that it would do for the international society what police action could do for the domestic community. No serious application of the principle of collective security was attempted in Western Europe during the 1930s. Rather, Hitler's assumption of power in 1933 began to change the political map of Europe, and his quest for a place in the sun resulted in the outbreak of World War II.

Following that war, the political and strategic situation in Europe and the world was radically different. It was characterized by a system of two tightly organized opposing blocs, one of which was controlled by the United States and the other, by the Soviet Union. This bipolar system lasted until the end of the 1950s, when the tight control of the two superpowers over their blocs began to loosen. Some of the West European states that were part of the U.S.-controlled bloc became reluctant to accept this system and to follow the directions of American policy after their economies had been restored.

In the communist camp, the ideological and strategic struggle between the Soviet Union and the People's Republic of China created an increasingly wider rift between the two principal communist powers. At the same time, the East European satellites began to show signs of independent national aspirations, which slowly began to loosen the tight control that the Soviet Union had initially exercised over these countries. In addition, many of the newly independent countries of the world began to form a nonaligned bloc, which was joined by some of the older countries, such as Yugoslavia and India. Finally, the two superpowers lost their nuclear monopoly. Britain, France, the People's Republic of China, and India became members of the nuclear club, with other countries also approaching the threshold.

A number of power centers have emerged in what was once a bipolar world. These power centers, which include not only blocs but also single states, are playing an increasingly important role in the international arena; and as we suggested earlier, a new triangular balance-of-power system has been established among China, the Soviet Union, and the United States. The government of each of the three countries may throw its support to the government of one of the other two countries in the pursuit of its national interests or to balance the dominant position of another country in the triangle. If one takes into account the emergence of the European Community of Nine and Japan as major independent economic and political powers, the balance-of-power system could be visualized as double triangles (see Figure 9.1) with the United States alone holding positions in both triangles.[10] In any event, international society is becoming more polycentric, but the full implications of this development are still obscure.

Figure 9.1: Double Triangle, Balance-of-power System

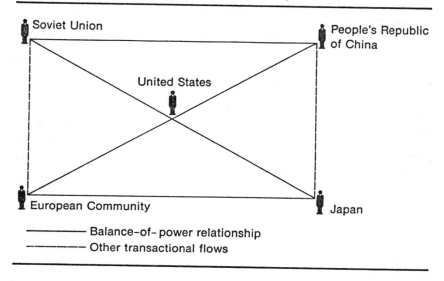

Balance–of– power relationship
Other transactional flows

It would be erroneous, however, to assume that the two opposing blocs or the balance-of-power constellations have kept world peace. Nor was the United Nations, a renewed effort at collective security, able to maintain a peaceful world. Rather, what kept the world from sliding into another tragic conflagration during that time was the mutual deterrence stemming from the powerful nuclear weapons possessed by both the United States and the Soviet Union. As a result of this "balance of terror," both superpowers have been fully aware that, in a nuclear holocaust, nobody would be a victor. To maintain the necessary deterrent to restrain the other from initiating a nuclear attack, each superpower has had to build a credible retaliatory counterstrike nuclear force sufficient to rain vast destruction on the people and weapons of the initiator of nuclear warfare.

The Problems of Nuclear Weapons Employment

Assured Destruction Capability and Overkill   There is much argument about exactly what it takes in the way of *assured destruction capability* to deter, but it generally is accepted that only a few hundred warheads exploding over population and industrial centers would be sufficient. In fact, a strong *overkill* is likely, especially because, in the future, all or most missiles will be equipped with MIRV (Multiple Independently-targeted Reentry Vehicles) warheads, which will permit each missile to deliver individually targeted nuclear weapons. What is meant by "assured destruction"? According to American policy during the postwar period, assured deterrent strategy rested on the basic assumption that what is necessary to deter a nuclear war is the ability without question to destroy the enemy society *after* receiving an all-out attack. Success in this strategy depends on two questions: (1) how much force is necessary to deter; and (2) whether it is possible to limit damage in the event of war. The specific aim of this strategy must be to convince the potential enemy that one is not threatening his deterrent by developing a first-strike capability and that, in the event of nuclear war, both countries would be destroyed. If such a war should break out, an effort would be made to use nuclear weapons in a controlled way, but with little expectation that an all-out nuclear war could be avoided.

How much of a strategic force is enough for deterrent purposes and how much may constitute an overkill is very difficult to answer.[11] Clearly, just as important as the quantity of the strategic forces is the quality of those forces, as measured by their accuracy, their ability to survive an enemy attack, and finally, their ability to penetrate enemy defenses.

Another important aspect of deterrence is communicating to the opponent one's policy about general nuclear war. American officials have emphasized the traditional American reluctance to initiate a general war, nuclear or conventional, and have stated again and again that the United States would never be the aggressor. On the other hand, the NATO commitment requires the United States, at least implicitly, to defend Europe by the eventual deployment of nuclear weapons against the Soviet Union if the latter should attack Western Europe, even if initially only nonnuclear weapons are used. Another issue in communicating policy is whether either opponent will bomb cities in addition to missile sites and submarines equipped with nuclear weapons. The United States has stated that it might not strike Soviet cities, particularly if the Soviet Union would refrain from attacking American cities, but how long the United States will maintain this position is uncertain, especially in view of Soviet assertions that cities, as well as strategic targets, would be struck in the event of a nuclear war.

While deterrence of a deliberate attack would be strengthened by emphasis on the hair-trigger nature of immediate retaliation with nuclear forces, U.S. policy has stressed that American nuclear weapons are under such tight command and control that they would not be used in provocative ways and would only be launched after a number of Soviet missiles had exploded in the United States. This would mean that the accidental firing of a few Soviet missiles or an attempt by a local Soviet commander or a third country to simulate an all-out Soviet attack would not be sufficient to stimulate a counterstrike by the United States.

Antiballistic Missiles (ABMs) An important difference in the deterrence picture may be made by the introduction of antiballistic missiles (ABMs). The question has been raised whether the installation of such missiles would strengthen or reduce the deterrence factor in the relations between the two superpowers. Two situations must be distinguished. In one situation ABMs would be used only to defend population centers. If the deployed ABMs were effective, it seems likely that a country attacked by a first strike might be able to ride out a strategic nuclear exchange without catastrophic damage. In such an event, the deterrence factor might lose much of its effect because, if both the United States and the Soviet Union knew they could protect their populations with a high degree of certainty, they would not need to fear retaliation. The result of effective ABMs for the defense of population centers may therefore be to increase the arms race to find means to reconstitute a balance between first strike and counterstrike. On the other hand, using ABMs to defend sites for retaliatory missiles would reduce the chances of a successful first strike and make retaliation more certain. Viewed in this way, ABMs become a stabilizing influence as they increase the deterrence effect. At the same time, they might be a cost alternative to multiplying ICBMs or building more missile-carrying submarines.[12]

Strategic Arms Limitation Talks In May 1972 an agreement was reached between the Soviet Union and the United States in the Strategic Arms Limitation Talks (SALT). This agreement consists of an ABM treaty, which provides that the United States and the Soviet Union will limit their ABM deployment to only two sites: their national capitals and one ICBM field each. Each site will have no more than 100 ABMs. This treaty is of unlimited duration, but so far the United States has not installed an ABM system around Washington and is unlikely to do so in the future. In addition, an interim agreement has been concluded, which was to run for five years and provides for a freeze on ICBMs and submarine-launched ballistic missiles (SLBM). The ICBMs may be modernized and equipped with MIRVs, and the submarine systems may also be improved. This agreement stimulated Paris and London to improve European nuclear capabilities because of the fear that the SALT Agreement may lower the effectiveness of the United States nuclear guarantee; how-

ever, whether the British and French governments will be able to combine their very limited nuclear capabilities and create meaningful
nuclear deterrents is doubtful in view of the conflicting trends in
British and French defense policies. Moreover, the Federal Republic
of Germany has to be considered in such an arrangement. It is
difficult to anticipate the attitude of the West German government,
which has as one of its main aims to improve its relationship with
the Soviet Union and other East European countries. There is also
a question whether the smaller NATO allies would look with favor
on the emergence of Britain and France as the dominant partners
of the NATO alliance in Europe.

The SALT Agreement, now labeled SALT I, was followed by
new talks between the United States and the Soviet Union to define
further the strategic relations between the two countries. In November 1974 an interim agreement was reached in Vladivostok in
the Soviet Union between then President Ford and Chairman Brezhnev that fixed the ceiling for strategic weapons with multiple warheads at 1,320 and the ceiling for all strategic weapons systems,
including heavy bombers, at 2,400. It was hoped the ceilings would
end the strategic competition in numbers for a ten-year period,
but details were to be worked out in a second SALT Agreement.[13]

The Ford administration was not able to come to an agreement
with the Soviet government, partly because there was uncertainty
as to whether such weapons systems as the Soviet Backfire bomber
(medium-range) and the subsonic American cruise missile (to be
launched from surface ships, submarines, and aircraft and having
a range of 1,500 miles) were to be included in SALT II. Another
problem was the development and deployment of increasingly
heavier and more powerful Soviet delivery vehicles for nuclear warheads (SS-17, -18, -19), which made it possible to increase an individual missile's payload. Submarine-launched missile strength has also
risen, thereby contributing to the maintenance of the balance envisaged by the United States; however, the United States has also
replaced older ICBMs with newer models during the past few years
and may be developing a movable missile launcher, the MX-1.

Historical changes in U.S. and Soviet strategic power are compared in Table 9.1, which shows that American missile strength has
remained static in terms of numbers, although the development of
very sophisticated MIRVs has markedly increased the power of the
American missile force. As already noted, however, the Soviet Union
has now also acquired the MIRV technology, and the slight decrease
in ICBMs in 1977 is compensated for by the expansion of SLBMs.

When the Carter administration took office, it approached the
SALT talks with a strong intention for genuine reductions and strict

Table 9.1: U.S. and Soviet Strategic Weapons Inventory, 1962–1977 (mid-year)

	1962	1965	1970	1971	1972	1974	1975	1977
United States								
ICBM[a]	294	894	1054	1054	1054	1054	1054	1054
SLBM (submarine-launched)	144	496	656	656	656	656	656	656
Long-range bombers[c] (ballistic missles)	600	630	550	505	455	437	432	441
Soviet Union								
ICBM	75	270	1300	1510[b]	1527[b]	1575	1618	1477
SLBM	Some	120	280	440	560	720	784	909
Long-range bombers[c]	190	190	150	140	140	140	135	135

[a]ICBM range = 4,000+ miles

[b]A version of the SS-11 with three MIRVs replacing some of the single-warhead versions in the SS-11 force.

[c]Long-range bomber = maximum range of 6,000+ miles; medium-range bomber = maximum range of 3,500 to 6,000 miles, primarily designed for bombing missions. Backfire is classified as a medium-range bomber on the basis of reported range characteristics.

SOURCE: International Institute of Strategic Studies, *The Military Balance 1975–76*, p. 73.

limitations of weapons strength, while maintaining the basic strategic balance. As a consequence, U.S. proposals included deep reductions in the arsenals of both sides, freezing of deployment and technology, and avoiding steps that might destabilize the existing balance. But new developments continued to create new concerns, especially U.S. development of the cruise missile and the buildup of Soviet strategic offensive weapons forces. Nevertheless, the United States goal is to reach agreements that will not be overturned by the next technological breakthrough but will stabilize competition in these weapons in such a way as to provide a sound basis for improvement in the political relations between the two countries. In President Carter's words:

> What matters ultimately is whether we can create a relationship of cooperation that will be rooted in the national interests of both sides. We shape our own policies to accommodate the changing world, and we hope the Soviets will do the same. Together we can give this change a positive direction.[14]

Although the SALT I provisions regarding the freeze of ICBM and SLBM strength expired on October 1, 1977, the U.S. and Soviet governments declared in unilateral statements their continued respect for the agreement.

Nuclear Test Ban Treaty   The United States and the Soviet Union have also tried to limit by treaty atomic tests and the employment of nuclear weapons. The Nuclear Test Ban Treaty, concluded in 1963, prohibits atmospheric tests of nuclear weapons and has been adopted by 113 countries, including the United States; however, France and the People's Republic of China, both nuclear powers, have refused to sign or to be bound by this treaty. Another important agreement prohibits nuclear development in outer space. Signed by both the United States and the Soviet Union, it requires the signatories not to place in orbit around the earth any objects carrying nuclear weapons or any other kind of weapons of mass destruction, or to install such weapons on satellite bodies and outer space stations. However, the Soviet Union may have developed satellite "killers" that, operating from ground facilities, could play havoc with U.S. military satellite communications and prompt the American government to build similar devices.

Nuclear Nonproliferation Treaty   Finally, the last general agreement has been the Nuclear Nonproliferation Treaty negotiated by the United States and the Soviet Union to which most major powers have acceded. Notable exceptions are again France and China. This treaty obligates the signatories not to transfer nuclear weapons or supply weapons technology to any nonnuclear weapons state, and it requires nonnuclear weapons states not to receive such weapons.

Considering the awesome power of nuclear weapons, it is not surprising that most efforts at arms limitations should first be directed toward these weapons; however, conventional weapon systems cannot be entirely neglected in the negotiations. During the past few years, the Soviet Union has made tremendous strides in building up its navy. The number of tanks in the hands of Soviet and other Warsaw Pact forces has been expanded markedly and speedily. This rapid growth of strength on the ground and at sea has been matched by an increase in fighter and medium-range bomber aircraft. In the meantime, the negotiations for the mutual and balanced reduction of conventional forces by NATO and Warsaw Pact countries has made very little, if any, progress. What to count and how to count different arms presents major obstacles. The widely heralded neutron bomb, if it should be put into production by the United States, will complicate things further. But some kind of balance in the nonnuclear field must be achieved to everybody's satisfaction, as otherwise apprehension about the security of the NATO and the Warsaw Pact countries will adversely affect efforts to limit the nuclear arsenal.

CAUSES AND EFFECTS OF WAR

Eighteen wars have been fought since 1967, many of them minor hostilities in terms of involvement of combatants, but nevertheless causing a substantial number of casualties.* We described the characteristics of war as a policy instrument in Chapter 7. Now we shall examine its causes and effects.

Causes

Many scholarly efforts have been made to identify the causes of war,[15] and peace research institutes established in many countries (the best known is in Norway) pursue the same goal. Some periodi-

---

* These wars are: Arab-Israeli (1967); Czechoslovakia (1968); Malaysia, El Salvador, Chad, Northern Ireland (1969); Ethiopia/Eritrea (1970); India/Pakistan/Bangladesh, Cambodia (1971); Burundi (1972); Arab-Israeli (1973); Iraq (Kurdish), Cyprus (1974); Angola, Timor, Lebanon (1975); Morocco/Spanish Sahara (1976); Zaire-Angola, Ethiopia-Somalia (1977).

cals, such as the *Journal of Conflict Resolution*, are also devoted
to this subject; and this overall effort is highly praiseworthy, considering the misery wars have brought to mankind throughout
history. But while it is possible to pinpoint particular behavior patterns and sequences of actions and events that have eventually led
to the outbreak of hostilities, strict cause-effect relationships can
rarely be established, and similar circumstances do not always produce the same outcome. Nevertheless, the probability of war is increased by power disparity, power miscalculations, communications
failure, liberation wars, separatism and irredentism, social superiority syndromes, and economic causes.

Power Disparity   In our analysis of the balance-of-power
system, we have suggested that this constellation tends to maintain
peace among the states that are participants in this system. On the
other hand, a wide disparity of power between states without an
equilibrating mechanism may invite aggression. Italy's attack on Ethiopia in the middle 1930s, Hitler's aggression against Poland in 1939
unleashing World War II, India's attack and annexation of the small
Portuguese colony of Goa in the 1960s, and Morocco's attack on
the Spanish Sahara fall into this category. Of course, there are also
many instances where two states, very disparate in power, have lived
peacefully side by side. France and Monaco, as well as Italy and
San Marino, are but two of many examples.

Power Miscalculations   In some instances, governmental
leaders overrate the power of their own states and underrate the
power potential of others. Such perceptions have prompted states
to go to war, when the anticipated outcome would either be increased dominance by the attacking state or when war seemed to
be the only way to settle a vital dispute between two countries.
Germany's miscalculation of power of potential enemies may have
triggered her attacks in August of 1914 starting World War I, and
American misperception of North Vietnamese prowess may have
been a contributing factor in our involvement in the Vietnamese
quagmire.

Communications Failure   When disputes between states es-
calate, communications between them become critical. Ideologies
and stereotyped images may color messages from one government
to the other: the message recipient hears what he *wants* to hear
and acts accordingly. The result is communications failure and initiation of military action.

Liberation Wars   Liberation wars are a mixture of internal guerrilla action and external support and/or intervention. The demise of colonialism following World War II has not always proceeded rapidly enough for black Africans. The Portuguese tried to hold onto their colonies long after Great Britain and France largely dismantled their colonial empires. In Rhodesia and South Africa, white minority governments have attempted to hold onto their power through very discriminatory policies such as apartheid. This has prompted internal riots and uprisings with widespread external involvement and implications. Especially in Angola, formerly under Portuguese control, outside forces, including large numbers of Cuban soldiers, participated in the bloody struggle for independence. Neighboring African states have given strong support to efforts of the black inhabitants of Rhodesia to topple the white minority regime of Prime Minister Ian Smith.

Separatism and Irredentism   Many countries have substantial ethnic, linguistic, tribal, and religious minorities within their boundaries and sometimes within special regions of their territory. In some instances, these minorities cover areas in two states. Examples in the industrialized world are the Welsh and Scots within Great Britain, the Bretons and Corsicans in France, the Sicilians and Sardinians in Italy, and the Catalans in Spain. The Basques are found in both Spain and France. The most violent religious minority in Europe is the Ulster Catholic group in Northern Ireland; the French in Quebec have come into the limelight recently as a linguistic minority. In the Soviet Union, the Latvians, Estonians, Lithuanians, and Ukrainians are prominent ethnic and cultural minorities.

In the Third World, and especially in Africa, we also find a large number of ethnic and tribal minorities. When the colonial powers drew boundaries, ethnic and tribal lines were largely ignored. Indeed, many precolonial societies did not have officially drawn borders. Examples of restive minorities in the Third World are the Ibos in Nigeria, the Arabs of Eritrea in Ethiopia, the Bugandians of Uganda, the Baluchis in Pakistan, and the Kurds in Iraq. Again, in some instances, minorities cover areas in two or more countries: the Kurds live not only in Iraq, but also in Turkey and Iran.

Minorities can become causes of war in two ways: they may want to secede from one state to form a new one, or an existing state may lay claim to a territory containing a minority group presently living within another state. The first is called *separatism*, and the second is known as *irredentism*. Separatism produces violent struggles for independence, while irredentism produces violent struggles for reunification, inasmuch as the area desired is regarded as lost or stolen.[16] Wars of secession to achieve independence have often failed. A successful effort has been the secession of East Pakistan to form Bangladesh. Irredentist claims have also often met with failure. A typical case is the abortive attempt to capture the Ogaden province of Ethiopia by the Somalis.

Social Superiority Syndromes   People in a particular country may feel at times that their nation deserves a higher place in the hierarchy of states than it is perceived to have. They may consider themselves superior, in terms of culture, economic achievement, organizational skill, or even race, to the people in most other countries. If the proper recognition is denied, they may resort to military action to obtain their "place in the sun." This is what happened in Germany prior to World Wars I and II when many Germans were stirred up to fight for the glory of the Fatherland. Many Italians similarly viewed the attack on Ethiopia.

In a more general way, superiority syndromes reflect the competitive, glory-seeking nature of man as described by Thomas Hobbes in the 17th century and Charles Darwin's concept of the survival of the fittest and the elimination of the weak. Transposed to the nation-state, this concept provides a strong motivation for war to transfer the reins of power from the inferior and perhaps decaying nations to the strong and young states. The perceived need for more "living space" also offers an additional motivation for possible military action. Thus aggression is rationalized and conflict, glorified. This may explain, at least in part, the Japanese invasion of China and later Southeast Asia. Combined with sentiments that "we" are not only better but also different from "they" (the people in other countries), superiority syndromes may offer some insights into the causes of the India-Pakistan War of 1971 and the Eritrean liberation struggle against Ethiopia.

Economic Causes   Specific economic advantages or economic desperation can be direct causes of war. The invasion of Spanish Sahara by Moroccan forces in 1976 was prompted by the existence of large phosphate deposits in that area, and the attack on Southern Zaire by Angola-supported forces was motivated by the hoped-for capture of copper-rich Katanga province. Many of the colonial wars of the 18th and 19th century were fought to gain specific economic advantages.

A war whose origin was basically economic desperation was fought between Honduras and El Salvador in 1969. As a consequence of the Central American Common Market, Honduras was flooded by goods from El Salvador. In addition, Salvadorian land squatters had intruded on Honduran soil, to the displeasure of the Honduran people. Honduran mobs attacked the Salvadorian aliens, diplomatic relations were suspended, and the armed forces launched full-scale attacks.

Shortly after the Arab oil embargo in 1973 and the sharp rise in oil prices, there was talk in the United States in official quarters and elsewhere that the Arab stranglehold on oil deliveries could be broken only by military intervention. No such action was taken. It is conceivable, however, that a country might undertake military action against a state responsible for either withholding urgently needed raw materials or imposing a painful boycott on goods produced in that country.

Large expenditures for military hardware normally benefit many, though not all, industries in a country, and thereby reduce unemployment. Shortly before and during World War II, the American economy moved rapidly from the depression of the 1930s to prosperity. Similarly, German industries were greatly aided when Hitler, in the second half of the 1930s, expanded the German armed forces in preparation for eventual offensive actions. Does this mean that the initiation of war can become a purposeful policy for economic well-being? There is no clear evidence to support such an assumption, although the economic benefits of a war initiated for other reasons may well be taken into consideration by policy makers as a not undesirable side effect.

What is the role of the so-called military-industrial complex in unleashing a war? Manufacturers of military hardware from rifles to naval vessels to airplanes are said to have a deep interest in military spending, which normally is substantially increased during times of international tensions. These manufacturers often gain support for the pursuit of their business interests from professional soldiers, legislators in whose districts producers of military goods are located, high civil servants in defense and economic ministries, labor unions operating in plants producing war material, and veterans organizations. The common interests of these groups prompt them to promote or perpetuate a philosophy of conflict and to emphasize in all international dealings the overriding need for security. They are the hardliners or hawks in most industrialized countries, including the communist states. In the Soviet Union, a natural alliance exists among the managers of heavy industry, the top echelons of the armed forces, and the hard-line wing of upper-rank party functionaries. While these groups undoubtedly support warlike policies and may well oppose peaceful, "weak" solutions to international conflicts as threatening national security or survival, they contribute to conditions conducive to war initiation, but are not a direct cause of war. Moreover, there is now considerable doubt whether the production of war material is the profitable business that it used to be before World War II. A careful analysis of the balance sheets of major arms manufacturers in the United States suggests that companies supplying the civilian markets have earned higher profits than firms mainly engaged in the delivery of goods to the armed forces. The financial problems of the Lockheed Corporation, a major supplier of military products, are an example. Since the mid-1960s, many defense firms have sought to enter the civilian markets.

A probable consequence of the industrial-military complex and potentially a contributory economic factor to new wars is the extensive trade in arms. Both governments and private firms sell weapons. Among developed countries, arms trade is carried on within the NATO and Warsaw Pact alliances, but a substantial number of arms shipments also go to the developing countries. Between 1964 and 1973, arms worth more than $38 billion were sold to these countries,[17] and the trend continues upward with the Arab oil producing states buying an increasing share of highly sophisticated weapons. While the latter can afford these purchases and have the means to train operators and maintenance personnel for these weapons, most Third World countries really cannot afford these items, and their acquisition represents a waste of funds that could be better used for economic development. Nevertheless, many developing countries now possess extensive arsenals of modern weapons, and if disputes and conflicts should arise with their neighbors, the temptation may be great to employ them for military action.

Sales of weapons are also made to guerrilla groups through various intermediaries. This trade leads to heightened instability in different countries, deeper conflict situations, and greater likelihood of outbreaks of war. The activities of the Palestine Liberation Front and other anti-Israel guerrilla groups are obvious examples, and another illustration is the violence in Northern Ireland.

Effects

The effects of war may range from complete extinction of the defeated country to the payment of reparations. The division of Poland in 1772, 1793, and 1795 among Prussia, Russia, and Austria, and the partition of that unfortunate country again in 1939 between Germany and the Soviet Union are examples of extinction, albeit only temporary. In most instances, however, defeated states remain members of the society of nations, but are forced to accept territorial losses. For example, Germany, after World War I, lost Alsace-Lorraine to France and parts of her eastern territory to Poland. In addition, reparations may be required and limitations may be imposed on the size of the armed forces and armaments. These were also conditions for Germany in the Peace Treaty of Versailles ending World War I.

In general, the effects of war as spelled out in peace settlements conform with the perception of changes in the distribution of power of the countries involved in the hostilities. The magnitude of power is not only reflected in the actual battle losses and occupation of territory by the victor, but also depends on the influence of alliances victors and defeated countries may have with powerful third countries and on the distribution of global power and interests. Thus, the victories of Israel over its Arab enemies are not likely to result ultimately in large acquisitions of territories that were or are now occupied by Israeli forces. Rather, the interests and influences of the superpowers are such that, despite the close ties between Israel and the United States, the final settlement of the Israeli-Arab conflict may see very little change in the territories of former combatants.

Another factor bearing on the final settlement is the domestic political situation in the victorious or defeated countries, as well as in influential third countries. Some domestic groups in the victor state may insist on very harsh terms for a peace settlement, while others see virtue in leniency. In the defeated nation, those who are willing to make concessions may be accused of being traitors by those insisting on continuing the struggle. In influential third countries, some domestic political forces may want the government to exert pressure on the victor to be restrained with respect to territorial changes, while others would like to see all claims of the victorious nation accepted and supported. The latter is the attitude of most American Jews with respect to Israel.

Finally, territorial changes and other conditions imposed by the victor may not be lasting. Poland rose from the ashes of extinction again and again, mainly because of power distribution concerns on the part of third countries. Germany and Japan, stripped of their power status following defeat in World War II, have again risen rapidly on the ladder of power, partly because of their own industry and economic skills and partly because of changed global power constellations, and now possess more power than some of the nations that helped in their vanquishment.

INTERNATIONAL LAW

In the preceding sections we have discussed the various aspects of conflict among states, including balance-of-power problems and selected issues related to war, and mentioned some of the international agreements designed to curb the dangers of nuclear war. We shall now briefly examine how far interactions among states are governed by legal rules and how effective these rules are. This brings us to the subject of international law.

International society as a whole lacks the institutional framework of the state. Under this framework, peaceful changes can be initiated and carried out through legislation and enforcement of laws by the state's government. International law is, in many ways, less perfect than the national (sometimes called municipal) legal system. It is a body of rules accepted as binding on states and other international legal entities, such as IGOs, for orderly management of their mutual relations. Because all states are sovereign equals and therefore do not tolerate superior external control, the enforcement of these laws poses a logical contradiction. Either the states are truly sovereign and recognize no superior, in which case no enforcement of any norm from the outside can be accepted, or enforcement against the will of the states is recognized, and then the states are no longer sovereign. Indeed, most states jealously guard their own autonomy in the international arena; therefore, a few scholars argue that there is no such thing as international law.[18]

Despite the fact that historical experience has shown again and again that states will, on occasion, disobey international law—for example, Hitler violated the German-Soviet Nonaggression Pact when he attacked Russia in June 1941, and the United States violated the U.N.-ordered boycott of Rhodesian goods by importing chrome from that country—in most instances, international law is observed. The ultimate explanation for this, as J. L. Brierly declares in his *Law of Nations,* is that

> man, whether he is a single individual or whether he is associated with the men in a state, is constrained insofar as he is a reasonable being, to believe that order and not chaos is the governing principle of the world in which he has to live.[19]

This attitude translated into political terms means that states find it more convenient to follow certain rules than to live in utter anarchy. They follow these norms usually in areas of minor significance, such as commercial and diplomatic intercourse, because they derive mutual benefits from the orderly conduct of such relations. For fear of retaliation, other international rules—for example, those pertaining to the treatment of prisoners of war—are also adhered to in most instances. When vital interests of a state are involved, however, governments may be prompted to disregard international law and pursue courses of action that, in their opinion, will best serve their own interests. In such cases, for instance, the legal machinery for the settlement of international disputes as provided by the United Nations is largely ignored. This should not be surprising so long as the concept of sovereignty prevails.

In national legal systems, the main source of law is usually the legislature. In the international arena, a universal legislature does not exist; therefore, other sources for international law must be identified. Five basic sources can be listed:

1. Custom
2. International treaties and agreements
3. National and international court decisions
4. The writings of legal authorities and specialists
5. The general principles of law

These are also the sources of international law recognized by the Statute of the International Court of Justice (Article 38).

Customary Law

Customary international law consists of rules that have been established by custom, use, and practice over many decades, if not centuries. They have been firmly accepted and are so generally applied that they ultimately have emerged as rules of law. Customary international law has the disadvantage of developing slowly, although there are exceptions. An example is the rule of national sovereignty over superjacent airspace. This became recognized as law very quickly and became codified into international treaties later.

One of the most important international laws with customary origins is the maxim of *pacta sunt servanda*, which means that treaties, once concluded and ratified, must be observed.

International Treaties and Agreements

The treaties themselves are a second source of international law. They are formal agreements among states setting forth the rules, obligations, and rights that are to govern the mutual relationships among the contracting parties. Treaties may be bilateral, creating what is called *particular* international law; or multilateral, creating *general* international law. Treaty law is sometimes referred to as conventional law, and multilateral treaties are sometimes called law-making treaties because of their wide application.

Treaty law is binding only upon the signatory states, but when a large number of states have agreed to similar provisions, a general international law may be said to have emerged. Furthermore, especially in the rules applying to warfare, a treaty may be temporarily adhered to by a number of nonsignatory states if it is in their interest to do so. We should note that, in many instances, treaty law may consist merely of codified rules that already had been accepted as customary law.

National and International Court Decisions

While without doubt custom and treaties are the two most important sources of international law, court decisions have played an increasingly significant role. Although decisions are binding basically only in the case before the court, rulings in crucial cases become accepted as law. It is interesting to note that most of the cases involving international law questions are decided by national courts, because international disputes are not often submitted to international courts. The national court decisions arise from a wide variety of circumstances, but all have in common the fact that some elements of the case turn on the interpretation of a point in international law. Hence they frequently contribute to the crystallization of customary law and help to formulate new international law rules. While there is no legal requirement for a court to accept a decision rendered by another court in a different country, the arguments presented are often so persuasive that judges will feel compelled to apply them in their own country. As a consequence, international case law is being developed.

The Writings of Legal Authorities and Specialists

Legal writers have exerted considerable influence on judicial matters of every kind, national and international, but especially in international law their statements have had pronounced effects. Like court decisions, statements of legal commentators are essentially persuasive arguments and interpretations. They are used as evidence in court cases and are quoted in diplomatic discussions between governments as being descriptive of current international usage. They thus move from an authoritative scholarly judgment to the realm of law itself.

In a landmark decision by the U.S. Supreme Court in 1900 dealing with fishing vessels *Paquete Habana* and *Lola,* Justice Gray said:

It is necessary to resort to the works of jurists and commentators, who by years of labor, research and experience have made themselves peculiarly well acquainted with the subjects of which they treat. Such works are resorted to by judicial tribunals, not for the speculation of their authors concerning what the law ought to be, but for trustworthy evidence of what the law really is.[20]

The General Principles of Law

The principles of law may flow either from *natural law* or from *Roman law*. Natural law is based on the immutable principles of morality and justice embedded in the human heart or derived from "right reason" or from the Bible. Natural law goes back more than 2000 years and was one of the principal sources of law during the Middle Ages. Judges were instructed to "find the law," which was all around them. Natural law principles are said to be of a much higher authority than the decrees and statutes promulgated by earthly institutions.

The principles of Roman law date from the time Rome ruled much of the world. Roman law upheld the principle that a state, having entertained certain claims indisputably for a particular period of time, establishes thereby a legal right to the substance of this claim. It was Hugo Grotius, an outstanding Dutch legal scholar, who analyzed and synthesized the many strands of Roman and natural law into a comprehensive and systematic legal compendium early in the 17th century. Grotius's work is a classic in international law and continues to be the basis of contemporary international law rules and decisions.

As long as rules of international law are observed by states, they are indeed an effective mechanism governing the relationships among countries. But what happens if international disputes arise about the application of law? Is there an effective court system to deal with such problems? We have already mentioned that national courts frequently decide disputes involving international law and that, in many instances, these decisions become the basis for further decisions by courts in third countries. However, we are concerned primarily with interstate relationships, and for this reason, we must examine whether international tribunals constitute an adequate method for the settlement of international disputes. Two possible methods exist for the settlement of disputes by international institutions: *adjudication* and *arbitration*. In both, a tribunal hands down a decision that is binding upon the parties to the dispute.

Adjudication   Adjudication presupposes a permanent tribunal with permanent judges who carry out functions similar to those of their counterparts in national courts. Up to now, only five attempts at creating international courts have been successful, and only one of these five courts functions successfully in a way similar to a national tribunal. Two of these courts have a global jurisdiction. They are the Permanent Court of International Justice created under the League of Nations Covenant in 1920; and its successor, the International Court of Justice established under the United Nations Charter in 1945. The latter court is also known as the World Court. The other courts are regional in nature. They are the Central American Court of Justice established in 1907 and dissolved in 1917, the Court of Justice of the European Communities, which began to function in 1952 and has successfully decided an increasing number of cases, and the European Court of Justice of Human Rights established in 1959.

The Permanent Court of International Justice decided its first case in 1923. By the time it ceased to function in 1945, it had rendered judgments on 57 cases. The International Court of Justice, the present World Court, operates as an integral part of the United Nations. It normally consists of fifteen judges, no more than one of whom can be from a single state. There is also a provision for ad hoc national judges from countries involved in the litigation before the court if these countries are not already represented by a judge of the court. The judges are elected by the General Assembly and the Security Council.

Only states may bring cases before the Court, but it is not necessary that the states be members of the United Nations. Cases may be brought by mutual consent or by one litigant against another when both have declared in advance that "they recognize as compulsory and without special agreement the jurisdiction of the court." This clause is known as the optional clause of the Court, and its acceptance implies automatic future acceptance of the jurisdiction of the World Court. Unfortunately, only a minority of the states of the world have adopted this clause and thereby the jurisdiction of the Court. By the end of the 1960s, a mere 48 states had declared themselves ready to accept the Court's jurisdiction, and many of these declarations contained reservations. The United States is a typical case, inasmuch as her acceptance of the Court read as follows:

. . . The United States of America recognizes as compulsory *ipso facto* and without special agreement, in relation to any other state accepting the same obligation, the jurisdiction of the International Court of Justice in all legal disputes hereafter arising concerning: (a) the interpretation of a treaty; (b) any question of international law; (c) the existence of any fact which, if established, would constitute a breach of an international obligation; (d) the nature or extent of the reparation to be made for the breach of an international obligation, *Provided*, that the declaration shall not apply to

a. disputes the solution of which the parties shall entrust to other tribunals by virtue of agreements already in existence or which may be concluded in the future; or

b. disputes with regard to matters which are essentially within the domestic jurisdiction of the United States of America as determined by the United States of America; or

c. disputes arising under a multilateral treaty, unless (1) all parties to the treaty affected by the decision are also parties to the case before the Court, or (2) the United States of America specially agrees to jurisdiction . . .[21]

Even a cursory reading of this declaration suggests that the United States can find many reasons to avoid jurisdiction of the Court. Declarations of most other countries are equally punctuated with exceptions; therefore, the World Court as such has remained a very ineffective instrument of adjudication. As a consequence, the World Court decided fewer than fifty cases between 1945 and 1976. On the other hand, the Court of Justice of the European Communities, endowed with extensive compulsory jurisdiction, has rendered more than 1,000 judgments since 1952.[22]

Arbitration   Arbitration is a process by which the parties to a dispute agree to submit issues in question to one or more judges or umpires for a binding decision. Such decisions need not necessarily be based on law, but might be rendered in terms of equity or even in a spirit of compromise. What method is to be applied depends on the agreement between the parties setting up arbitration.

In contrast to the permanency of the Court and the judges when the chosen method for settlement is adjudication, the characteristic of arbitration is the free ad hoc selection of arbitrators, who may be lawyers, judges, or even laymen. The important point is that the parties agree on who the arbitrators should be. A permanent panel of arbitrators was set up in 1899 in The Hague in the form of the Permanent Court of Arbitration, which provided the administrative machinery for arbitration. When a dispute was referred to the Court, each party would select two arbitrators from the panel, who in turn would select an umpire.

Arbitration was practiced in ancient Greece and Rome and

during the Middle Ages as well. Although mostly utilized for economic and less important political disputes, arbitration has been used to settle important political issues from time to time. For example, the question of German minorities in Italy was amicably handled through arbitration between the two world wars.

We should note that, despite the voluntary nature of arbitration agreements, the awards of the arbitrators to the parties involved in a dispute are at times rejected. States may also refuse to comply with judgments rendered by the International Court of Justice. Although the United Nations Charter (Article 94) provides for the enforcement of such judgments through the Security Council, enforcement action by means of sanctions or other measures is most unlikely. While the weakness of the enforcement system may not affect compliance with the vast majority of international law rules, with regard to high politics and grave strategic concerns, it may make the difference between peace and war.

SUMMARY

Most international relations do not consist entirely of either cooperation or conflict, but manifest varying degrees of each. Where relations are primarily conflictory, the relative power positions of the countries involved are of crucial significance. These positions are affected by **alliances** and by **successful economic cooperation arrangements.**

In Chapter 1 we discussed the concept of **equilibrium.** Equilibrium in a system signifies stability. When the equilibrium of a system is disturbed, either by an outside force or by a change in one of the component elements, the system tends either to re-establish the original equilibrium or to move toward a new one.

Closely related to the idea of equilibrium is the **balance-of-power concept,** which has been a guiding principle of international politics since the advent of the modern state system in 1648 and functioned most effectively to maintain peace between 1815 and 1914.

The most frequent balance-of-power configuration is that between two opposing alliances. A variation is the addition of a single state that acts as a **balancer.** Great Britain played this role with consummate skill for three centuries, until World War I, and gained thereby the label of "Perfidious Albion."

A state that wants to increase its power status and become or remain a desirable and, to use Morton Kaplan's term, "essential" actor in a balance-of-power system can do so by increasing its armaments, establishing buffer zones, detaching allies from opposing alliances, and/or destroying hopes of allies by persuading uncommitted states to remain neutral. Bismarck's greatest successes stemmed from his persistent use of this latter technique.

Following World War I, the League of Nations was founded in an effort to use the **collective security** principle to guarantee peace. No serious attempt was made to apply this principle in Western Europe during the 1930s, and Hitler's quest for power resulted in the outbreak of World War II.

After that war, the world political and strategic situation was characterized by two tightly organized opposing blocs, one of which was controlled by the United States and the other by the Soviet Union. This bipolar system lasted until the end of the 1950s, when international society become more polycentric.

It has not been the United Nations, a renewed effort at collective security, that has kept the world from sliding into another tragic conflagration, but the **balance of terror,** a mutual deterrence stemming from the powerful nuclear weapons possessed by both the United States and the Soviet Union.

There are frequent discussions about how much **assured destruction capability** is necessary to deter and how much constitutes **overkill,** and many of the world powers have sought to limit the massive arms buildup. In May 1972, the **Strategic Arms Limitation Talks** (SALT) resulted in an agreement between the United States and the Soviet Union limiting antiballistic missile (ABM) deployment and providing for a freeze on intercontinental ballistic missiles (ICBMs) and submarine-launched ballistic missiles (SLBMs). Efforts to conclude additional arms limitation agreements have been unsuccessful so far, but the United States and the Soviet Union have tried to limit by treaty atomic tests and the employment of nuclear weapons. Examples are the Nuclear Test Ban Treaty of 1963 and the Nuclear Nonproliferation Treaty.

While it is not possible to list the precise **causes of war,** it is possible to state that the probability of war is increased by **power disparity, power miscalculations, communications failure, liberation wars, separatism and irredentism, social superiority syndromes,** and **economic advantage or desperation.**

The **effects of war,** as spelled out in peace settlements, range in severity from complete **extinction** of a defeated country to the **payment of reparations.** In most instances, however, defeated states remain members of the society of nations but are forced to accept territorial losses.

International law is a body of rules accepted as binding on states and other international legal entities, such as IGOs, for orderly management of their mutual relations. Because all states are **sovereign**

equals, the enforcement of these laws poses a logical contradiction; however, states find it more convenient to follow certain rules than to live in utter anarchy.

The five basic sources of international law are **custom, international treaties and agreements, national and international court decisions, the writings of legal authorities and specialists,** and **general principles of law.** The principles of law may flow either from **natural law** or from **Roman law,** which Hugo Grotius synthesized into a comprehensive compendium early in the 17th century.

Two possible methods exist for the settlement of disputes by international institutions: **adjudication** and **arbitration.** In arbitration, the parties to a dispute agree to submit issues in question to one or more judges or umpires for a binding decision. Adjudication takes place before an international court.

Only five attempts at creating international courts have been successful, and only one of these courts—the Court of Justice of the European Communities—functions successfully in a way similar to a national tribunal. Because most countries do not accept without reservations the **optional clause** of the International Court of Justice and find many reasons and ways to avoid its jurisdiction, it has remained a very ineffective instrument of adjudication.

Clearly, the high-sounding slogan of "World Peace through World Law" can become meaningful only when compliance with world law can be assured effectively. Attempts have been made to use the collective security principle to attain this objective through intergovernmental organizations (IGOs), and it is to an examination of these organizations that we now turn.

NOTES

1. Hans J. Morgenthau, *Politics Among Nations,* 5th ed. (New York: Knopf, 1973), pp. 167–169.

2. For example, Frederick the Great cited in Morgenthau, op. cit., p. 189. See also David Hume, "Of the Balance of Power," in *Essays Moral and Political,* 3rd ed. (London, 1748); E. Kaeber, *Die Idee des Europaeischen Gleichgewichts in der publizistischen Literatur vom 16. bis zur 18. Jahrhunderts* (Berlin: A. Dunker, 1906); A. J. Grant and Harold Temperley, *Europe in the Nineteenth and Twentieth Centuries,* 1789–1939 (New York: Longmans, Green, 1940); and Bernadotte E. Schmitt, *Triple Alliance and Triple Entente* (New York: Holt, 1934).

3. This discussion generally follows Morgenthau, op. cit., p. 174.

4. See Z. Brzezinski, "The Balance of Power Delusion," *Foreign Policy,* no. 7 (Summer, 1972), pp. 54–59.

5. Morgenthau, op. cit., pp. 183–184.

6. Cf. Winston S. Churchill, *The Second World War,* vol. 1, *The Gathering Storm* (Boston: Houghton Mifflin, 1948), pp. 207–208.

7. For details see Morton A. Kaplan, *System and Process in International Politics* (New York: Wiley & Sons, 1964), p. 23.

8. See A. F. K. Organski, *World Politics* (New York: Knopf, 1967), pp. 296–298.

9. Ibid.

10. Some students of international politics have asserted that the five powers form a pentagonal system, but this is an inaccurate picture because the games played on the two triangles are different. One is strictly a balance-of-power game in the military-strategic sense in which the loss of one of the parties results in gain for the other (zero-sum game). The second triangle (United States–European Community–Japan) concentrates on economic relations, and benefits for all can flow from particular patterns of interaction (positive-sum game). Cf. J. S. Nye, "Innovative Foreign Policies for the Solution of Transatlantic Economic Problems," paper delivered at the Tensions Across the Atlantic conference held at Louisiana State University in New Orleans, December 1, and 2, 1972 (mimeographed), pp. 41–53. See also Brzezinski, op. cit.

11. For additional details see Morton H. Halperin, *Defense Strategies for the Seventies* (Boston: Little, Brown, 1971), esp. pp. 1–9, 20–24.

12. For a full discussion of these issues, see L. W. Martin, *Ballistic Defense and the Alliance* (Paris: The Atlantic Institute, 1969), and Wynfred Joshua, *Nuclear Weapons and the Atlantic Alliance* (New York: National Strategy Information Center, 1973).

13. Regarding details of the SALT I Agreement and the possible future agreements, see Mason Willrich and John B. Rhinelander, eds., *SALT, The Moscow Agreements and Beyond* (New York: The Free Press, 1974).

14. Speech to the Southern Legislative Conference, July 21, 1977, Charleston, S.C. (Department of State News Release).

15. For example, Kenneth Waltz, *Man, the State, and War* (New York: Columbia University Press, 1975); and Quincy Wright, *The Study of War* (Chicago: The University of Chicago Press, 1965).

16. For details see Steven J. Rose and Walter S. Jones, *The Logic of International Relations,* 2nd ed. (Cambridge, Mass.: Winthrop, 1977), pp. 286–292.

17. Ibid., p. 132.

18. Cf. William L. Tung, *International Law in an Organizing World* (New York: Crowell, 1968), pp. 18–19.

19. J. L. Brierly, *The Law of Nations,* 4th ed. (Oxford: Clarendon Press, 1949), p. 57.

20. U.S. Supreme Court Reports, vol. 175, p. 677 (1900).

21. Department of State *Bulletin,* no. 15 (September 8, 1946), pp. 452 ff. See also, for text, Frederick H. Hartmann, ed., *Basic Documents of International Relations* (New York: McGraw-Hill, 1951), p. 221.

22. See A. W. Green, *Political Integration by Jurisprudence* (Leyden: A. W. Sijthoff, 1969); and Werner Feld, *The Court of the European Communities: New Dimension in International Adjudication* (The Hague: Martinus Nijhoff, 1964).

SUGGESTED READINGS

BLAINEY, G. *The Causes of War.* New York: Free Press, 1975.

HALPERIN, MORTON H. *Defense Strategies for the Seventies.* Boston: Little, Brown, 1971.

HIGGINS, ROSALYN. *The Development of International Law Through the Political Organs of the United Nations.* London: Oxford University Press, 1963.

RAKOVE, MILTON L., ed. *Arms and Foreign Policy in the Nuclear Age.* New York: Oxford University Press, 1972.

SCHEINMAN, LAWRENCE, AND DAVID WILKINSON, eds. *International Law and Political Crisis: An Analytic Casebook.* Boston: Little, Brown, 1968.

WILKENFELD, JONATHAN, JR., ed. *Conflict Behavior and Linkage Politics.* New York: McKay, 1973.

WILLRICH, M., AND J. B. RHINELANDER. *SALT: The Moscow Agreements and Beyond.* New York: Free Press, 1974.

YOUNG, O. R. *The Politics of Force: Bargaining During International Crises.* Princeton, N.J.: Princeton University Press, 1969.

PART III
The Dynamics
of
Transnational Networks

CHAPTER TEN
INTERGOVERNMENTAL ORGANIZATIONS

NATURE

Since World War II, cooperation among nation-states with common interests has become increasingly institutionalized in the form of intergovernmental organizations (IGOs), which are established by two or more states for the attainment of common objectives. In many instances they constitute the framework for military and political alliances or economic cooperation schemes. IGOs possess a number of characteristics which we shall examine briefly:

1. Intergovernmental organizations are entities set up by sovereign states. This distinguishes them from international nongovernmental organizations (NGOs), which have sprung up in large numbers during the past fifty years. There are also mixed organizations in which both states and private entities take part. An example is the Global Commercial Communications Satellite System in which the United States and private companies both participate.

2. The pursuit of common interests and the achievement of common purposes and common objectives for which the IGO is set up are theoretically carried out with the equal participation of all states, although in practice this is not always so. The activities of the states may be best described as a round-table operation in

contrast to a normal international treaty through which two states may also pursue common purposes but for which the basis is a trade-off of advantages and disadvantages. Moreover, the purposes and objectives pursued by IGOs are normally long-range and long-lasting.

3. The most distinguishing feature of an IGO is its institutional framework. This framework may be very simple and consist of nothing more than a lightly staffed secretariat; or it may be complex and comprehensive, approximating the legislative, executive, and judiciary branches of a national government. In most instances, however, the legislative functions are quite limited. Representatives of the member states of the IGO normally meet in an annual conference that makes general policy. Decisions usually require a two-thirds majority and in special circumstances, unanimity. A council is frequently entrusted with the executive functions of the IGO. It meets more frequently than the conference and almost always decides questions by unanimous vote. The performance of judicial functions is normally carried out by an international tribunal, such as the International Court of Justice of the United Nations, to which other IGOs may also assign jurisdictional competences.

4. IGOs are always established by a multilateral international treaty. This treaty is often called a charter or a constitution. It stipulates the competences of the organs of the IGO, the interrelations among them, and sets up the basic norms of procedure for the operations of the organization.

5. IGOs are considered to have international legal personality, which means that, under international law, they can act similarly to a state: they have standing to sue or be sued in the International Court of Justice, they can conclude international treaties in their own name, and diplomatic missions from their own member states, as well as from third countries, can be accredited to them.

IGOs may be classified into several categories. First, their geographic spread may be global, as is that of the United Nations, or extend only to a particular region, for example, Western Europe or Central America. Second, in terms of functions, they may be classified as security, political, economic, or technical IGOs. In some instances, several of these functions may be combined. Third, their competence may be general or limited. For example, the European Coal and Steel Community is a regional IGO with economic functions, but its competence is limited to the coal and steel sectors. Fourth, IGOs differ in their degree of integration. Some IGOs may be very loosely integrated with a minimum institutional framework. Others may be on the other end of the spectrum of integration and may, in fact, have reached *supranational* status. This term means that the member states of the IGO have transferred to the organs of the organization some of the powers usually exercised only by sovereign states. In addition, the organs of the IGO have been given the authority to issue certain legal rules that are binding upon the population of the member states without having obtained the force of law through national legislative procedures. A supranational IGO, then, is the nearest unit to a state.

A BRIEF HISTORICAL REVIEW

Although IGOs have purposes and objectives of their own, it must be recognized that, for the member states, the establishment of an IGO represents a tool for the achievement of their own individual foreign policies. When governments are not able to attain their foreign policy goals on their own, they hope the establishment of an IGO will constitute an extension of their power. This was recognized increasingly during the latter part of the 19th century and especially after World War II when the number of IGOs rose dramatically, as can be seen from Table 10.1. The number if IGOs had reached 195 by 1964 with a total membership of 4,436, or 22.7 nations per IGO.

The Congress of Vienna

The first organization that attempted to institutionalize regular consultations among the great powers was the Congress of Vienna.* It was convened in 1815 to lay the diplomatic foundations for a new European order amid the ruins left by the Napoleonic Wars. Although four major conferences were held between 1815 and 1822, severe differences in policies and objectives among the great powers made it clear that the time had not arrived for institutionalized collaboration and management in Europe. Nevertheless, the leaders of the major states involved had constituted themselves as the Concert of Europe, which met sporadically to deal with pressing political issues.

---

* Great Britain, Russia, Austria, Prussia, and France were the members.

Table 10.1: Growth of IGOs

Period	Number of IGOs	Number of Memberships	Mean Number of Nations per IGO	Mean Number of IGOs per Nation	Mean Number of Shared Memberships	Number of Nations
1815-19	1	6	6.1	0.3	--	23
1820-24	1	6	6.1	0.3	--	23
1825-29	1	6	6.1	0.2	--	25
1830-34	1	6	6.1	0.2	--	28
1835-39	2	18	9.0	0.6	--	31
1840-44	2	18	9.0	0.5	--	35
1845-49	2	18	9.0	0.5	--	38
1850-54	2	18	9.0	0.5	--	40
1855-59	3	24	8.0	0.6	--	42
1860-64	3	21	7.0	0.5	--	44
1865-69	6	54	9.0	1.4	0.5	39
1869-74	7	65	9.3	1.9	0.8	34
1875-79	9	106	11.8	3.1	1.4	34
1880-84	11	136	12.4	3.9	1.8	35
1885-89	17	203	11.9	5.3	2.6	38
1890-94	21	267	12.7	7.0	3.1	38
1895-99	23	299	13.0	7.3	3.4	41
1900-04	30	412	13.7	9.6	4.0	43
1905-09	44	639	14.5	14.2	6.8	45
1910-14	49	753	15.4	16.7	7.9	45
1915-19	53	826	15.6	16.2	7.6	51
1920-24	72	1336	18.6	21.2	9.4	63
1925-29	83	1528	18.4	23.5	10.2	65
1930-34	87	1639	18.8	24.8	10.5	66
1935-39	86	1697	19.7	25.3	11.0	67
1940-44	82	1560	19.0	24.0	10.9	65
1945-49	123	2284	18.6	30.5	13.0	75
1950-54	144	2684	18.6	32.7	14.2	82
1955-59	168	3338	19.9	37.1	15.7	90
1960-64	195	4436	22.7	36.4	14.3	122

SOURCE: *Yearbook of International Organizations, 1972–73,* 14th ed. (Brussels, Belgium: Union of International Associations), p. 885.

The Rhine Commission

The Congress of Vienna established a subordinate organization, the Rhine Commission, whose purpose it was to regulate traffic and trade along the Rhine River. The members of this commission were the littoral states of the Rhine, each of which had one vote. The commission was given considerable powers to amend its own rules and to act as a court of appeals for decisions of local courts regarding river problems or issues. Similar commissions were established later for the Danube, Elbe, Douro, and Po rivers.

Public International Unions

While the various river commissions dealt at times with politically sensitive issues, another type of IGO sprang up in the middle of the 19th century which was concerned primarily with nonpolitical, technical matters. These IGOs were known as public international unions, and the most important of these were the International Telegraphic Union (1865), the Universal Postal Union (1874), and the International Union of Railway Freight Transportation (1890). Other IGOs of a very nonpolitical nature established during that period dealt with such diverse fields as agriculture, health, standards of weights and measurements, patents and copyrights, and narcotics and drugs. Some of these IGOs had elaborate institutional frameworks: for example, the Universal Postal Union had a Congress of Plenipotentiaries that met every five years, a Conference of Delegates of Administrations, and a Permanent International Bureau. The Conference had amendment powers and frequently used majority vote.

The Zollverein

The first attempt at economic integration in Europe came with the establishment of the German Zollverein in 1834. This organization was a loosely joined customs union and lasted until 1867. Initially, only eighteen of the thirty-eight German states—kingdoms, duchies, and free cities—participated; but by 1867, almost all states had become members. Prussia was the moving spirit and overall manager of the Zollverein. The General Congress was the chief organ; decisions were made by unanimity.

THE LEAGUE OF NATIONS

The first major effort to organize a universal security IGO for the maintenance of international peace was the establishment of the League of Nations. Following the extraordinary losses of life and property suffered during World War I, the time was ripe to set up the League. World War I aroused the nations to their responsibility for preventing the recurrence of war and finding ways to avoid blundering again into hostilities. The principle underlying the League of Nations was the notion of *collective security*, under which all member states of this IGO were obligated to come to the aid of a member country that was the victim of military aggression.

Both private and public endeavors during the period between 1914 and 1918 contributed to the creation of the League. Prominent and influential citizens in the United States formed the League to Enforce Peace, and similar groups of citizens in Great Britain set up the League of Nations Society. On the official side, the British government established a cabinet-level committee to draft proposals for a collective security organization, and the French government set up a similar planning body. In the United States, President Woodrow Wilson gave strong support to the concept of a League of Nations as early as 1916. He later included an explicit commitment to the formation of a "general association of nations" as the ultimate objective in his famous list of Fourteen Points.[1] Finally, Jan C. Smuts, a distinguished and prestigious South African statesman, published an imaginative and yet down-to-earth treatise, *League of Nations—A Practical Suggestion*, which not only became the organizational basis for the Covenant of the League, but also for many other important IGOs, including the United Nations. Smuts's ideas were not only on a high humanitarian plane, but reflected first-rate organizational thinking. For him, the League was to be the organizational center of international life. He insisted on a strong and elaborate structure that could ensure the League's collective security function, regulate all international activities, and become the center for world public opinion.

The Covenant was rapidly drafted in a special committee established by the Paris Peace Conference of 1919 and ably chaired by President Wilson. It was accepted as a part of the Peace Treaty of Versailles on April 28, 1919. The League became operational on January 10, 1920, but it suffered from a grave flaw, inasmuch as it was part of the Versailles Treaty, which was full of internal conflicts and was a victor's document. The fact that the Covenant was incorporated in the Treaty of Versailles was a major reason the United States did not join the League. Despite President Wilson's tremendous efforts to persuade American public opinion to subscribe to the League, domestic political considerations associated with the presidential elections and complex manipulations in the Senate when the Peace Treaty came up for ratification resulted in the tragedy of the United States's refusal to join.

The Covenant of the League was a relatively short document containing only twenty-six articles. It established four major organs:

the Assembly, in which all states were represented; the Council, in which only the major powers and some smaller countries were seated; the Secretariat, which was the administrative heart of the League and was headed by a secretary general; and the Permanent Court of International Justice.

The Council of the League was a revised edition of the Concert of Europe and was the main organ for collective security action. All great powers belonging at a particular time to the League were permanent members of the Council; they included France, Great Britain, Italy, Japan, and later Germany and the Soviet Union. The nonpermanent members numbered originally four, but this figure was later raised to eleven. The Assembly was a body with broad competences which could deal with any issue affecting world peace or otherwise within the sphere of action of the League. It therefore competed at times with the Council in handling the same matters, and ad hoc arrangements were necessary to delineate the activities of both organs in a particular case. Voting in both the Assembly and the Council was by unanimity except where, in isolated instances, the Covenant authorized majority vote. For example, admission to membership and election of a member to the Council could be voted in the Assembly by a two-thirds majority.

The core of the League was an elaborate procedure for collective security. Actually two procedures were available. Under a so-called short procedure, every member of the League was permitted to call to the attention of the Assembly or the Council any circumstances that threatened to disturb international peace. Moreover, a member who felt threatened could request a meeting of the Council. Under the long procedure, the Council was authorized and, in fact, obligated to recommend to the member nations that military action be taken by them against a state, whether or not a member of the League, that had resorted to war in disregard of the provisions of the Covenant. Such a state was branded as having committed an act of war against all members of the League. The other League members would be requested to impose on the aggressor a complete boycott and to isolate it from any kind of intercourse with any other member of the community of nations. At the same time they were obligated to give each other all financial and economic assistance in the execution of collective actions.*

While these obligations at first glance appear to provide immediate action on the part of each member state to oppose the lawbreaking state, the Council could only *recommend* what member states

---

* Article 16.

were to do, and according to authoritative interpretation of the pertinent provisions, the member states themselves had discretion over the particular actions they would take. Moreover, the Covenant contained a domestic jurisdiction clause (Article 15, section 8), which permitted a state to claim that a particular violation of the Covenant charged against it was a matter solely within its *domestic jurisdiction* and that therefore no collective security measure could be taken against it. Although it was up to the Council to make a definitive determination as to whether a case of domestic jurisdiction existed, such a claim tended to delay enforcement action considerably.

As a consequence of the internal weakness of the collective security provisions and the interpretation given to these provisions, the League of Nations was not able to maintain international peace. Although during the period from 1920 to 1930 the League dealt successfully with international disputes and aggressive actions by minor countries—an example is the invasion of Bulgarian territory by Greek forces in 1925—the decade of the 1930s produced mostly failures. Despite long discussions in the League of Nations Assembly regarding the far-flung hostilities Japan had initiated against China, the Assembly found that Japan had not resorted to war in violation of the Covenant. In 1934 when Paraguay continued hostilities against Bolivia initiated two years earlier, a limited arms embargo proved ineffective. Only the invasion of Ethiopia by Italy brought forth a full application of the collective security provisions of the League. In 1935 the Assembly found that this invasion constituted resort to war within the meaning and in violation of the Covenant and that collective economic sanctions were to be imposed against Italy. Yet while some sanctions were indeed initiated, the measures that might have been most effective, such as closure of the Suez Canal or an embargo on oil shipments to Italy, were not taken. In fact, after the imposition of sanctions against Italy, France and Great Britain conspired to bypass them and to assist the Italian economy to a large degree.

During the 1930s it became evident that the system of law enforcement under the collective security provisions of the Covenant was largely a failure. Most major powers disregarded this procedure when it did not suit their purposes. The League was an instrument of policy of the major powers when it assisted them in attaining specific objectives, and the authority of the Covenant was undermined when a country felt that the League of Nations was impairing the pursuit of its own foreign policy.

There have been many explanations for the failure of the League of Nations. Some analysts have argued that the absence of the United States dealt the League a fatal blow. Others have blamed the lack of sharply defined responsibilities for the major League organs. Again others have expressed doubt that sovereign states can collaborate successfully and have asserted that only a world government can guarantee peace. They argue that international peace and security cannot be maintained by imposing legal restrictions on states but requires an appropriate balance of power based on the necessary military means and capabilities. Yet, whatever weaknesses the collective security system of the League manifested, and clearly they were profound, the statesmen of the world turned again to this system when they established the United Nations after World War II.

THE UNITED NATIONS

The first mention of a new postwar organizational effort toward collective security was made in a Declaration by United Nations issued in January 1942, after the United States had joined the countries fighting the Axis powers (Germany, Italy, and Japan). This declaration made reference to the Atlantic Charter of August 1941, in which Great Britain and the United States had put forth a number of proposals to be followed after the war. This charter inferentially recognized the need for some form of permanent international organization for the disarmament of aggressive nations and the establishment of a wider and permanent system of general security. About fifty nations had expressed support for the Declaration by United Nations.

The governments of the United States and Great Britain had come to an agreement by the summer of 1943 to seek the creation of a permanent international organization for the maintenance of international peace and security; however, the position of the Soviet Union was not clearly defined until October of that year when, during a conference of foreign ministers, the Soviet government gave its consent in principle to such an organization.

The major foundation for the Charter of the United Nations was laid during a lengthy conference at Dumbarton Oaks outside Washington. Representatives of the United States, the United Kingdom, the Soviet Union, and China accepted as a basis for further discussions for an international organization a draft proposal that had been prepared in the U.S. Department of State and had received the general approval of important congressional leaders. Several important points emerged during the Dumbarton Oaks Conference:

1. The new organization would not only be dedicated to the task of maintaining security and international peace, but a major part of its efforts was to be directed toward the promotion

of international cooperation to solve economic and social problems. In this respect the new organization was to be much more elaborate than anything attempted by the League of Nations.

2. Following up this dual thrust of activities, the functions of the former League Council were to be divided among a council dealing with security affairs and one dealing with economic and social affairs.

3. A clear-cut distinction of functions was to be made between the Council and the Assembly. As we had mentioned earlier, the League Covenant was ambiguous on this point.

4. The enforcement powers of the United Nations Security Council were to be much stronger than those of the League Council.

While the Dumbarton Oaks negotiators had learned from the experiences of the League, in some respects their proposals remained incomplete. The greatest gap to be filled later was the voting in the Security Council and specifically the kind of veto that would be acceptable to the major powers. It was during the Yalta Conference of 1945 that the important compromises regarding Security Council voting were made. It should be pointed out that the veto was *not* added at Yalta because the Big Three (United States, Soviet Union, and United Kingdom) already had agreed on the need for the veto. What remained in question was the type of veto. Stalin wanted an absolute veto, whereas President Franklin Roosevelt preferred only a limited veto. The question was settled in favor of an absolute veto, which has been limited over the years by interpretation and certain customary practices.

Another decision made during the Yalta Conference pertained to the status of colonies and other non-self-governing territories. A trusteeship system was introduced with a Trusteeship Council becoming the third council in the United Nations framework.

The final drafting work on the United Nations Charter was done during the San Francisco Conference, which began in April of 1945. Fifty countries participated in this conference which was begun before either Germany or Japan had been defeated. All states that had signed the Declaration by United Nations of 1942 were invited to this conference. There was some disagreement between the United States and the Soviet Union on the one hand, and the United States and the United Kingdom on the other, regarding invitations to certain governments. Finally, an agreement was reached that permitted the United States to invite Argentina, while the Soviet Union insisted on the invitations and membership of the Byelorussian Soviet Socialist Republic and the Ukrainian Soviet Socialist Republic. The latter two states were admitted as members of the United Nations despite the fact that they cannot claim the status of international sovereignty.

The Charter of the United Nations was signed in June 1945 in San Francisco. With 111 articles, it was a much longer document than the Covenant of the League of Nations. There was no particular reason to call this document a charter; no special legal connotation can be attributed to this name. As a result of pressure exercised by the smaller states attending the San Francisco Conference, the economic and social functions of the United Nations were expanded beyond the Dumbarton Oaks proposals. Moreover, the functions and powers of the General Assembly were more clearly defined. Finally, the amendment procedures were revised to facilitate a later review of the Charter.

Nature and Purposes

Despite the fact that the preamble of the Charter states that "We the peoples of the United Nations . . . have resolved to combine our efforts to accomplish [certain] aims," we must re-emphasize that the members of the United Nations are the states and not the peoples of those states. In fact, the basic principle of the Charter is the sovereign equality of all its members; however, the veto in the Security Council places certain countries above others. On the other hand, the principle of sovereign equality is anchored in the authority of each state to insist that its domestic jurisdiction not be violated by United Nations action. It is interesting to note that the inclusion of the domestic jurisdiction clause in the Charter was largely the result of a United States initiative. It was done to satisfy the special concerns of the United States congressional delegation to the San Francisco Conference that there would be no United Nations interference in matters considered to be domestic in nature.

The United Nations is clearly a multipurpose organization. Although the maintenance of international peace and security is the primary purpose of the organization, the achievement of international cooperation in dealing with economic and social matters, the development of friendly relations among all countries of the world, and the harmonizing of national actions in the attainment of common ends are explicit purposes listed in Article 1 of the Charter. To emphasize the economic and social functions, we find subordinate objectives listed specifically in Article 55 of the Charter. They include:

1. higher standards of living, full employment, and conditions of economic and social progress and development;

2. solutions of international economic, social, health, and related problems; and international cultural and educational cooperation; and
3. universal respect for, and observance of, human rights and fundamental freedoms for all without distinction as to race, sex, language, or religion.

Structure, Functions, and Powers

In addition to the Security and Economic and Social Councils mentioned earlier, the Trusteeship Council, the General Assembly, the Secretariat, and the International Court of Justice constitute the principal organs of the United Nations.

General Assembly   The General Assembly was conceived as approximating a representative legislative body, although we must stress that it does not have major legislative powers. Each member country has one vote in the General Assembly. A mere majority is sufficient to make decisions. Certain questions classified as important issues in the Charter require a two-thirds vote for favorable decision, for example, recommendations with respect to the maintenance of international peace and security. Any other item may be made an "important issue" by a majority vote of the Assembly and then substantive decisions require a two-thirds majority.

It is in the Assembly that discussion takes place and recommendations are made. Any matter may be discussed as long as it is within the scope of the Charter. It should be noted that recommendations are not binding because action and pertinent decisions for action are exclusively the responsibility of the Security Council. This fact places a limitation on the General Assembly, inasmuch as it must refer to the Security Council any question on which enforcement action is necessary. Moreover, the General Assembly must refrain from making any recommendation on any dispute or situation in respect to which the Security Council is in the process of exercising its function under the Charter.

Security Council   The Security Council is a body of fifteen members with China, France, the Soviet Union, the United Kingdom, and the United States having permanent membership. Until 1971 the Chinese seat was occupied by the Republic of China on the island of Taiwan; but in the fall of that year, the Communist People's Republic of China was given this seat by a vote in the General Assembly. The vote reversed the long-standing American policy of denying diplomatic recognition to the regime of Mao Tse-tung, which had been in full control of the Chinese mainland since 1949. Normally the nonpermanent members are elected for two years, but under certain conditions the term may be split between two countries with each country serving only one year.

Any decision on a substantive question taken by the Security Council requires the affirmative vote of the permanent members. This then is the veto power of the Big Powers. The impact of the phrase "affirmative vote" has been somewhat softened by the interpretation that a permanent member who abstains or who is absent from a vote is not considered to have cast a veto.

It should not be surprising that the Charter devotes more space to the Security Council than to any other organ. It stipulates that, as a first step, U.N. member states should attempt to settle disputes by peaceful means of their own choice with the Security Council assigned a prodding and investigating role. Disputes may be brought to the attention of not only the Security Council but also the General Assembly. The Charter makes it clear, however, that in event of a threat to peace, a breach of the peace, or an act of aggression, the Council is the organ to take prompt action. The Council may at first try peaceful means of settlement or proceed at once to enforcement action. Such action may include partial or full economic boycott, rupture of all types of communications, and/or severance of diplomatic relations. While the member states are required to give these measures their full support when decided upon by the Council, they cannot be ordered to take military action unless they have previously undertaken by agreement to place military forces and facilities at the disposal of the Security Council. No such agreements have been concluded up to now, but member states have provided military contingents on an ad hoc basis in specific instances, such as the Congo crisis of 1960 and the Cyprus dispute of 1968.

Economic and Social Council   The Economic and Social Council was originally composed of eighteen members but now has a membership of fifty-four. The Council members are elected for three-year terms by the General Assembly; and their choice, according to the assumption made by the framers of the Charter, is to be guided by the contribution they can make to the work of the United Nations in the social and economic fields. As a consequence, the United States, the Soviet Union, the United Kingdom, and France have always been represented on the Council. The Charter gives the Council a variety of powers, which include the initiation of studies, the making of recommendations, the preparation of draft conventions, and the negotiations of agreements with the numerous specialized agencies of the United Nations, such as the United

Nations Educational, Scientific, and Cultural Organization (UNESCO), the World Health Organization (WHO), and the Food and Agricultural Organization (FAO), all of them IGOs in their own right.

Trusteeship Council   The Trusteeship Council, another major organ in the Charter, is today an anachronism. The drafters of the Charter in 1945 did not anticipate the colonial revolution; therefore, the elaborate system of supervising the administration of non-self-governing territories and the assurance of the welfare and advancement of dependent people now applies to only very few countries of the world. Almost all former colonies and dependencies are now independent states and attempt to use the machinery of the General Assembly and Security Council to bring autonomy to what is left of the colonial world.

International Court of Justice   The fifth principal organ of the United Nations organization is the International Court of Justice, whose functions in international disputes were discussed briefly in Chapter 9. It is composed of fifteen judges elected concurrently by the General Assembly and the Security Council. In addition to rendering decisions in litigations between states, it also issues advisory opinions on legal questions referred to it by the General Assembly. The Security Council and other organs or specialized agencies authorized by the General Assembly may request such opinions.

Secretariat   The last principal organ, the Secretariat, directs the activities of an extensive international civil service. The position of secretary general is more powerful in the United Nations than it was in the League. He is not only the chief administrator and executive, but has also important political functions. He can bring to the attention of the Security Council any threat to international peace; he may make recommendations to all U.N. organs; and he sits in all bodies of the United Nations and may speak whenever he wishes to do so.

Problem Areas

The Veto   As many observers feared, the veto in the Security Council constitutes a serious problem for the proper functioning of the United Nations. More than 100 vetoes have been cast in the Security Council, most of them by the Soviet Union but recently some by the United States.

Perhaps the majority of vetoes cast by the Soviet Union pertained to the admission of new members. Between 1946 and 1955, the Soviet Union wanted to admit a number of the communist states; and to assure their admission, she insisted on a package deal for the balanced admission of countries proposed both by the Free World and her own candidates. To obtain her goals, the Soviet Union vetoed the applicants proposed by the West, whereas the Western countries exercised their influence in the General Assembly to withhold approval of the Soviet candidates. As a consequence, the deadlock for admission of new members was complete for all admissions from 1949 to 1955. Before that date only a few new countries had been admitted. Finally, in 1955 the United States agreed to a package deal, and the deadlock was broken. As of 1977, 151 countries have become members of the United Nations, tripling the membership since 1945.

In the collective security field, the veto also represented a serious impediment to the fulfillment of the Security Council's mission. In December of 1946, Greece complained that her northern neighbors were threatening the peace by giving aid to guerrillas in northern Greece. Security Council action was vetoed by the Soviet Union. The Council was blocked again by a number of Soviet vetos when it attempted to deal in 1948 with a complaint of Soviet intervention in Czechoslovakia. Later in 1950 the Security Council could take positive action on the invasion of South Korea by North Korean forces only because the Soviet representative was absent, having withdrawn from the Security Council in January of that year in protest against the seating of the delegation of the Chinese Nationalist government. When the Soviet representative returned, on August 1 of that year, the permanent members were in conflict over the continuation of the United Nations label under which the United States and South Korean forces fought against the North Koreans.

It was the deadlock over Korea that prodded the United States to propose in the General Assembly the Uniting for Peace Resolution of November 30, 1950. In this resolution, the Assembly asserted its right to exercise a residual responsibility in any threat to or breach of the peace. In the event that the Security Council was prevented from exercising its chief responsibility because of a veto, the General Assembly was to consider the matter with a view to making appropriate recommendations for collective measures, including the use of forces, in any breach of the peace or act of aggression. The resolution also provided for peace observation committees and missions, as well as a collective measures committee to study and make reports on methods to be used to maintain and strengthen international peace and security. The resolution was adopted by a large majority in the General Assembly, and action was taken under this resolution following the intervention in Korea by Communist China in late 1950.

The Uniting for Peace Resolution was also the basis for the creation of the United Nations Emergency Force (UNEF) to deal with the Suez crisis of 1956 precipitated when Israel, Britain, and France invaded Egypt. The Security Council was unable to act because of British and French vetoes. It was the Assembly that appealed for a cease-fire and withdrawal of forces from Egypt. The proposal for UNEF aimed at stationing it in the area of conflict between the contending states to supervise the implementation of a cease-fire and arrangements for the withdrawal of the invading forces, to ensure the pacification of the borders, and to stabilize the situation until a more desirable settlement could be negotiated. The Assembly accepted this proposal and asked Secretary General Dag Hammarskjöld to carry out its implementation. In an extraordinary display of rapid political and administrative initiative, Hammarskjöld offered a detailed plan to the Assembly, obtained contributions of troops from several states, and carried out the delicate negotiations with Egypt for putting UNEF into the field. Twenty-five states offered to contribute military contingents. Hammarskjöld declined troops from any of the permanent members of the Security Council and accepted approximately 6,000 men for UNEF. Although the number of men was reduced later, UNEF remained in place and in operation until May 1967 when it was withdrawn by Secretary General U Thant on the demand of President Gamal Abdel Nasser of Egypt. While UNEF guaranteed stability in the area for more than a decade, its withdrawal cleared the way for military confrontations in 1967 and 1973. In October of 1973, United Nations forces were reintroduced into the troubled Middle East—this time, however, on the basis of a Security Council resolution.

The consequence of the Uniting for Peace Resolution combined with the weakness of the Security Council represented the political reality of the immediate postwar world and altered the constitutional scheme of the Charter by introducing a new legal dimension through customary law. The result was the decline of the Security Council's importance and prestige and the ascendancy of the General Assembly. The shifting balance and the comparative importance of the Security Council and the General Assembly can be seen by the quantitative changes in the activities of the two organs between 1948 and 1964. Beginning in July, 1948—after the veto by the Soviet Union in the Czechoslovakian coup matter—the political issues considered by the Security Council peaked and then began to decrease in number, while the number of those considered by the General Assembly rose. Toward the end of this period, the General Assembly began to decline in importance and the Security Council to become more influential once again.

The revival of the Security Council began in 1960 when the Congo crisis erupted. The Belgians had given the Congo independence, but the newly established republic was wracked by mutiny and disorder. This prompted Belgium to reintroduce troops into the territory that had just been relieved from its colonial rule. Secretary General Hammarskjöld called the Security Council into urgent session for consideration of the crisis and received a mandate to organize a United Nations program of assistance. He promptly moved into the Congo both military and civilian elements of a United Nations force, which was known as ONUC, reflecting its French title. The military force was gradually built up to a maximum strength of approximately 20,000 men with personnel from more than thirty states participating at one time or another. The civilians drawn into ONUC were primarily administrators, and it was the first time that the United Nations introduced into a country critical services in such fields as transportation and communications, health, agriculture, education, public administration, and finance. The operations in the Congo were terminated in mid 1964.

Although initially the Soviet Union concurred in the Congo operations and gave her affirmative vote in the Security Council, she later turned against the operation when she considered ONUC as impairing her own interests in Africa. Although the Soviet government used the veto to oppose some of ONUC's activities, it began to abstain on issues it might have vetoed before. The reason was most likely that, from the experience of preceding years, the Soviet government knew that, in the event of too many vetoes, the Assembly might step into the breach and run the operation under the Uniting for Peace Resolution. By this strategy, the Soviet Union kept decisions in the Council where she could exercise more influence than if the Assembly or the Secretary General were in control. The result was that, while between 1946 and 1959 the Soviet Union cast eighty-eight vetoes, or approximately 6.3 per year, she cast only twenty-one vetoes from 1960 to 1973, or 1.5 per year.[2]

In the middle of the 1960s another peace-keeping operation of the United Nations was originated in the Security Council. Cyprus, torn by ethnic conflicts which implicated Greece, Turkey, and Britain, threatened to bring on an international war of unpredictable proportions. To prevent such a development, the Security Council created the United Nations Forces in Cyprus (UNFICYP) in March of 1964. This force, which at its maximum included 6,500 military personnel and civilian police from nine Western European and Commonwealth countries, has been successful in preventing a major conflagration and continues to function. Finally, the Security Council resolution of November 1967 dealing with the seven-day war between Israel, Egypt, Jordan, and Syria, introduced United Nations observer teams into the Middle East. They have contributed to stabilizing a very explosive situation, but could not prevent the October 1973 war between Israel and Egypt, Syria, Iraq, and other Arab states. On October 22, 1973, the Security Council ordered a cease-fire, and United Nations forces were again sent to the Middle East to maintain and supervise a fragile armistice.

Although the Soviet Union clearly has been the most prolific in the use of the veto, the United States has recently also begun to employ this tool to promote or protect her policies. On March 17, 1969, the United States cast her first veto in support of Britain against an Afro-Asian resolution that would have condemned the United Kingdom for not using force to outlaw the white government in Rhodesia. Although there was no need actually to utilize the veto because Great Britain had already exercised this prerogative, the casting of the veto on the part of the United States represented an important signal that the Security Council was becoming a more important forum for the pursuit of American foreign policy than it had been heretofore. Other occasional American vetoes, including the blockage of new members such as the unified Vietnam in 1976, have been cast since 1969, and this new policy is likely to continue. One reason for the change in the American attitude has been the membership explosion in the United Nations, which has made it increasingly difficult for the United States to protect its vital national interests through successful political action and diplomacy in the General Assembly.

The Membership Explosion and the Political Process   The significant aspect of the growth in U.N. membership (from 50 in 1945 to 151 in 1977) is not only simply a larger number of member states, but a changed distribution. The number of industrially advanced countries of the world increased only slightly with the addition of the Federal Republic of Germany (West Germany) and the German Democratic Republic (East Germany) in 1973. It is the developing world that has showed the largest growth in membership, and it is especially the African countries whose membership has brought about a remarkable change in the pattern of the United Nations. Africa has now more than forty states in the United Nations (this includes one developed state, South Africa) and thereby has become the largest group of countries. Asia, with thirty-two members, represents the second largest group of countries. In fact, the Asian and African countries together constitute a majority in the United Nations at present.

Similar to a national legislature the politics in the United Nations revolve around the various groups and blocs that have been formed on the basis of common interests and geographic contiguity. The Afro-Asian countries form such a group and represent the largest proportion of the world population (66 percent). Within the Afro-Asian group, however, the African and Asian countries also have formed subgroups; in addition, the Arab countries have constituted themselves as a special group with special interests. Other groups are the Latin American countries, Western Europe, the Soviet bloc of East European countries plus Mongolia, the Commonwealth countries, and Scandinavia. These groups are the main political interest groups that operate in the Assembly and are involved in behind-the-scenes negotiations on most issues whose resolution is strongly contested. To some extent they resemble the political parties in a national legislature. We should note that some countries, including the United States, Israel, Yugoslavia, and China, have refrained from belonging to any of these groups; however, this does not mean that these countries are not politically active. On the contrary, they are often very active and seek to influence group policies by informal negotiations. Finally, some of the regional organizations, such as NATO, the European Community, and the OAS, also engage in specialized politics, attempting to promote their particular interests despite the fact that their memberships overlap to a great extent that of the main groups.

With the exception of the East European Soviet Bloc (consisting of the Soviet Union, Ukraine, Byelorussia, Bulgaria, Czechoslovakia, Hungary, Poland, Romania, East Germany, plus Mongolia), the various groups identified above do not vote generally as a unit. In fact, the scope of group action varies considerably. The Afro-Asian and Latin American groups discuss a large variety of issues, but the scope of uniform decision-making is limited. Regional issues, such as colonial questions, apartheid, and economic matters, predominate. Nuclear tests and disarmament are rarely subjects of consultation. The Afro-Asian countries are often joined by Yugoslavia when questions of nonalignment are discussed. When the Asian and West European groups caucus, they are primarily intent on making common decisions on candidacies for the Security Council and ECOSOC. But none of the groups makes decisions by majority vote that are binding on all members. Indeed, individual groups possess very little power vis-à-vis recalcitrant members; and unless a compromise is unanimously accepted, no official group action can be expected. As a consequence, the chief business of the group is consultative and the creation of a limited consensus within the confines imposed by individual sovereignties. However, caucus leaders emerge frequently, drafting committees are appointed to formulate compromise resolutions, and at times negotiating committees are set up to deal with other groups. The process is often frustrating and the result meager.

Both the United States and the Soviet Union, as well as other major powers, utilize the United Nations General Assembly and its committees, as well as the Economic and Social Council, as forums to promote their foreign policies. All kinds of parliamentary tactics are used, including logrolling, trade-offs, personal favors, and the like. The fact that sometimes an individual delegate sits next to another in a committee may become the means for informal negotiations and politicking. The authorship and sponsorship of proposals are key factors in the politics of the General Assembly. In some instances, proposals contain clear statements of policy preferences regarding a certain issue; in others, proposals may be introduced to influence, warn, embarrass, propagandize, or simply harass. Sponsors of proposals may seek additional sponsors to stimulate proposals by other delegations in support of their original sponsored statement. At times countries do not want to make proposals openly and choose to work through other nations in getting their policies before a committee or the General Assembly in the form of draft resolutions. The United States and the Soviet Union have made use of this type of indirect sponsorship on occasion. For example, the United States utilized Latin American countries in 1946 and in 1950 for proposing resolutions regarding the relations of the United Nations with Spain.

As we mentioned earlier, the United States has been very astute in its politics in the United Nations. As a consequence, in the early years of the United Nations, Western voting victories occurred with almost monotonous regularity. During these years the United States found it relatively easy to secure overwhelming support in the General Assembly on issues considered important by the American government. Although intense efforts were often necessary to achieve these goals, the United States had every reason to regard itself as the established leader of the United Nations majority, and as a consequence developed enthusiasm for majority rule which reflected American ideological sympathy for majoritarianism.

Inis Claude states that during these years, the United States tended to exploit its capacity to inflict defeats upon the Soviet Union to the point of undermining the potential usefulness of the United Nations as a mediating force between the Cold War antagonists. During that period the Soviet Union began to develop the conviction that the United Nations was an instrument of American foreign policy, devoted primarily to supporting American interests;[3] however, the increase in numbers of Third World states in the

General Assembly created conditions much more favorable to the interests of the Soviet Union. Tendencies toward neutral attitudes among the new members have made it more difficult for the Western powers to mobilize overwhelming majorities in support of anti-Soviet resolutions. The Soviet Union has more often opted for aid to developing countries than the United States, although much of the assistance proposed proved to be more rhetoric than genuine interest in implementing action. The coincidence of Soviet anti-Western attitudes with Afro-Asian contempt for colonialism has provided many opportunities for the Soviet Bloc to align itself with the majority of members in the United Nations General Assembly and other bodies. It has curtailed American influence and increased Soviet capacity to play a more positive role in the United Nations. Only on the question of peace-keeping have the Western powers continued their predominance, but there is no assurance that this condition will continue.

It is for these reasons that the United States has looked for ways to change the present system of one-state-one-vote in the United Nations and to resort more to the Security Council for the protection of its vital interests. Many United States leaders have said that, with the tremendous disparity in the financial support given to the United Nations and the tremendous disparity in population, some kind of weighted voting should be introduced. As long as the United States provides 25 percent of the United Nations budget (it used to provide 39 percent and further cuts may be made), while more than 100 countries contribute less than 30 percent of the cost, they have considered it unfair that each of these small contributors should have the same voting power as the United States. However, whether criteria such as financial support and population—China and India would benefit from the latter criteria considerably—or literacy and per capita income would produce a more equitable solution is difficult to say. In any event, the establishment of a new weighted voting system would require a Charter amendment; and whether the approval of not only the Soviet Union, China, and other permanent members of the Security Council, but also two-thirds of the members of the General Assembly could be obtained for such an amendment is exceedingly doubtful.

Economic and Social Progress   While the collective security and peace-keeping functions of the United Nations have always attracted the attention of the world public much more than the economic and social activities, the United Nations has made important progress in the latter areas. The many specialized agencies of the United Nations, dealing with every facet of economic and social life, have made successful inroads into many problems of world

Figure 10.1: Associated Agencies and Institutes of the United Nations

The Specialized Agencies, listed chronologically according to date of entry into force of respective agreements with the United States.

International Labor Organisation
International Institute of Labour Studies
International Occupational Safety and Health Information Centre
International Centre for Advanced Technical and Vocational Training
Food and Agriculture Organization of the United Nations
U.N. Educational, Scientific and Cultural Organization
    International Institute for Educational Planning
World Health Organization
    International Agency for Research on Cancer
International Bank for Reconstruction and Development
    International Monetary Fund
    International Finance Corporation
    International Development Association
International Civil Aviation Association
Universal Postal Union
International Telecommunication Union
    International Frequency Registration Board
    International Telegraph and Telephone Consultative Committee
    International Radio Consultative Committee
World Meteorological Organization
Inter-Governmental Maritime Consultative Organization

Other Members of U.N. Family:

Office of the U.N. High Commissioner for Refugees
International Narcotics Control Board
U.N. Children's Fund
U.N. Conference on Trade and Development
International Trade Centre UNCTAD/GATT
U.N. Development Programs
U.N. Industrial Development Organization
U.N. Institute for Training and Research
U.N. Research Institute for Social Development
World Food Program

SOURCE: *Yearbook of International Organizations, 1972–73,* 14th ed.
       (Brussels, Belgium: Union of International Associations), p. 855.

society. In an indirect manner, finding solutions for these problems through intergovernmental and transnational organizations may have done more for world peace than the successful organization of United Nations emergency forces. While it would exceed the scope of this book to examine in any detail the activities of the manifold specialized agencies and organizations created either under the auspices of the United Nations or associated with it, they are listed in Figure 10.1.

One particular problem that has produced tensions and frictions in the world and must be looked upon as a potential source for future disturbances of international peace has been the inability of Third World countries to overcome their poverty and unstable economic and political conditions. More than 100 member countries of the United Nations fall into the category of underdevelopment, although the extent of their economic, social, and political difficulties varies widely. Most of the developing countries are located in the Southern Hemisphere and look toward the industrially advanced and wealthy countries of the North for assistance. To resolve this awesome problem, the United Nations Conference on Trade and Development (UNCTAD) was organized in Geneva in 1964. The major impetus for this conference came from the developing countries, which had been dissatisfied with the unfavorable economic trends in the later 1950s. The preparations for this conference took place in the Economic and Social Council in 1962 and 1963 and gave birth to UNCTAD as an organization a year later.

During the Geneva conference, 120 countries, both developing and developed, participated. The major goals of the conference were to expand international trade in such a way as to benefit mainly the developing countries, to find solutions to the violent fluctuations in the prices of international commodities, to permit greater access of manufactured and semimanufactured goods produced in the developing countries to the markets of the industrially advanced states through special tariff concessions, and to find new methods of financing the international trade of the Third World.

UNCTAD is now an organ of the United Nations General Assembly with a specific institutional framework. It consists of a triennial conference open to all United Nations member states, a trade and development board elected by the conference and meeting twice a year, and four permanent committees dealing with the problems of commodities, manufacturing, financing, and shipping.

Despite the fact that four conferences have been held so far—in addition to the Geneva conference, a conference in New Delhi in 1968, in Santiago, Chile, in 1972, and in Nairobi, Kenya, in 1976—and despite the fact that each of these conferences was a huge affair attended by approximately 1,500 delegates from more than 120 countries lasting for several weeks, the results of UNCTAD have not been spectacular. In fact, while the Geneva conference appeared to usher in a very fruitful period of cooperation between developing and developed states, the New Delhi, Santiago, and Nairobi conferences were generally disappointing. Perhaps the most important aspect of these conferences has been the establishment of a high level of solidarity among the developing countries and a means of producing common stands on many problems. However, even reaching agreement on various issues required some compromises, and the acceptance of the positions of the developing countries by the industrially advanced states of the world has been very slow. Perhaps the greatest success so far has been the tariff concessions made by some developed countries, such as the Common Market member states, Japan, and the United States, in offering generalized tariff preferences to the importation of manufactured and semimanufactured goods from these countries. These concessions have not fully satisfied the developing countries because they have been emasculated by quantitative restrictions of the Common Market countries and the ineligibility of certain important products for tariff concessions by the United States.

In terms of world politics, UNCTAD meant Third World unity on many economic issues which placed both the Western and communist developed countries nearly always in minority positions and in turn provided an incentive for Western countries to strengthen their own group solidarity. One consequence of UNCTAD may be that a number of Western countries look upon Third World states with less compassion and humanitarian concern than they had before. Some of the major nations have adopted an attitude of benign neglect toward the Third World; and Werner Levi, an acknowledged authority on Third World problems, has stated that, in the foreseeable future, this trend on the part of the industrially advanced countries will continue and worsen rather than improve the disadvantageous position of the Third World states. He observed that the Third World countries

> find themselves in a vicious circle: their poor condition makes them unattractive to the major nations, but without the (favorable) attention of the major nations, these states will find it very difficult to improve their condition. It will take much more self-reliance and a greater effort at self-improvement in many of the Third World states to make themselves more attractive to the major and some important other nations and thereby to improve their status in the society of nations. Stating this is not implying that the major nations are without guilt, contemporary guilt, in perpetuating the poor condition of some of the Third World states. In other words, it takes a change of behavior among all concerned and a joint effort to improve the condition of the states in the Third World, which is one prerequisite for improving their status in the international society.[4]

The political realities reflected in Levi's comments regarding the developing countries and, indirectly, UNCTAD, as well as the attitudes of many industrially advanced countries, should not lead us to overlook certain solid achievements of the United Nations and some of its specialized organizations in the Third World. Economists of the U.N. Industrial Development Organization have provided invaluable services to some of the newly independent countries in Africa and Asia. Administrative experts of the U.N Development Program and other United Nations agencies have assisted Third World governments in strengthening their public administration processes and procedures. Technical assistance teams and other experts from the Economic Commission for Latin America (ECLA), for Africa (ECA), and for Asia and the Far East (ECAFE) have improved skills and expertise in agriculture and industry. The employment of the United Nations organization in all activities within their competences to aid the Third World has steadily grown in both absolute and relative terms. By 1970 annual contributions to the U.N. Development Program had exceeded $200 million, and the United Nations system was devoting about 80 percent of its personnel and budgetary resources to economic advancement.

In the eyes of Third World leaders, however, these achievements are only a start toward meeting demands for the improvement of their economic conditions, which they now consider to be their right through redistribution of world resources between their countries and economically advanced nations. In 1974 they succeeded in passing two U.N. General Assembly Resolutions aimed at creating a New International Economic Order and setting up a Charter of Rights and Obligations of States for this purpose. Although these resolutions have no binding force on U.N. member states, they do have an important effect on world public opinion. Moreover, they require the governments of the Western advanced countries to take the new demands inherent in their resolutions seriously and come up with proposals for compromise solutions to the obviously serious problems besetting many developing countries.

REGIONAL IGOs

Because it would be impossible to examine the manifold regional IGOs within the scope of this book, we shall only discuss in this chapter three predominately security and political IGOs in different parts of the world. The first IGO to be reviewed will be the North Atlantic Treaty Organization (NATO), followed by the Organization of American States (OAS) and the Organization of African Unity (OAU).

North Atlantic Treaty Organization

At its inception, the North Atlantic Treaty Organization (NATO) represented a collective response to the threat of a Soviet military attack on Western Europe. Its legal basis was Article 51 of the United Nations Charter, which authorizes collective self-defense until the Security Council has taken measures for the maintenance of international peace and security. Its members are the United States, Canada, the United Kingdom, France, the Federal Republic of Germany, the Netherlands, Belgium, Luxembourg, Italy, Denmark, Norway, Iceland, Portugal, Greece, and Turkey. Although reference is made in the NATO Treaty to encouraging economic cooperation and promoting friendly relations generally, the principal commitments relate to military security.

The members of NATO agree (1) to "develop their individual and collective capacity to resist armed attack," (2) to "consult" whenever the security of any of them is threatened, and (3) to "assist" any member subjected to armed attack in Europe or North America. Two qualifications limit this commitment. The protection given by the treaty does not extend to any possessions of the NATO member states outside Europe, North America, and the North Atlantic area. The second qualification refers to the action that must be taken. It is described only as "such action as [a country] deems necessary," which is a very minimal obligation.*

Organization   Although the NATO Treaty itself does not provide the details for an institutional framework beyond requiring a Council, a Defense Committee, and any other subsidiary bodies, a complex organizational superstructure has been erected. Figure 10.2 provides a picture of the civilian and military structure with its many committees.

At the heart of the structure is the North Atlantic Council, which is the main policy-making organ and at the same time is also responsible for the implementation of policy. Consensus must be reached by discussion, and decisions are made by unanimous vote. If it is not possible to reach full consensus, those members who have reservations but do not want to prohibit action for others go along with policy matters of interest to the latter.

The routine work of the Council is carried out by Permanent Representatives of ambassadorial rank assigned by the member

---

* Articles 3–5, NATO Treaty.

Figure 10.2: NATO's Civil and Military Structure

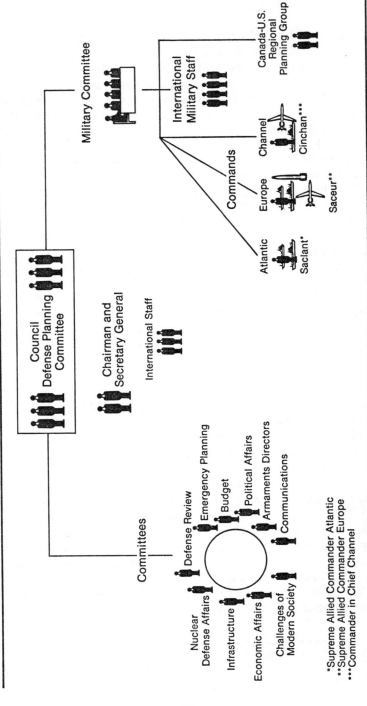

Council
Defense Planning
Committee

Chairman and
Secretary General

International Staff

Committees

Defense Review
Emergency Planning
Nuclear Defense Affairs
Budget
Infrastructure
Political Affairs
Economic Affairs
Armaments Directors
Challenges of Modern Society
Communications

Military Committee

International
Military Staff

Commands

Atlantic
Saclant*

Europe
Saceur**

Channel
Cinchan***

Canada-U.S.
Regional
Planning Group

*Supreme Allied Commander Atlantic
**Supreme Allied Commander Europe
***Commander in Chief Channel

SOURCE: The *NATO Handbook*, (March 1977), p. 36.

242

states to the NATO Headquarters in Brussels. They meet at least weekly, but the more important issues tend to be reserved for the ministerial meetings of the Council, which are held twice a year and are attended by the foreign ministers, defense ministers, and sometimes also the finance ministers of the member states. The Council deliberates in private, and its proceedings are never published except for an official communiqué issued at the end of the meeting.

A Secretariat headed by a secretary general (at present Joseph Luns of the Netherlands) functions under the Council and is organized into seven major divisions. Some of these divisions are concerned with political, economic, and financial matters, and all of them serve the Council and its committees through studies and reports.

The military command structure is kept separate from the civilian organization of the Secretariat and the Council committees. The coordination and integration of civilian and military policies within NATO takes place primarily at the Council level. The Military Committee, the highest military authority in the Alliance, is responsible for making recommendations to the Council and the Defense Planning Committee on military matters and for supplying guidance on military questions to allied commanders and subordinate military authorities. It is composed of the chiefs of staff of all member countries, except France, which has withdrawn from NATO's military organizational structure, and Iceland, which has no military forces. The chiefs of staff meet at least twice a year and whenever else it may be found necessary. To enable the Military Committee to function in permanent session with effective powers of decision, each chief of staff appoints a permanent military representative. Liaison between the Military Committee and the French High Command is effected through the chief of the French military mission to the Military Committee.

Taking account of geographical and political factors, the strategic area covered by the North Atlantic Treaty is divided among three Commands: the Atlantic Ocean Command; the European Command; and the Channel Command. (Defense plans for the North American area are developed by the Canada-U.S. Regional Planning Group.) Of the various commands, only the European Command has military forces assigned in time of peace, although forces for the other commands are earmarked. However, even most of the forces assigned to the European Command remain under the residual control of national general staffs. As France and others have demonstrated, these forces may be withdrawn at will. The full integration of the units assigned to NATO takes place only when war breaks out; in the meantime, the NATO Command must secure national government consent for the deployment of troops. The only exception has been the integration of air surveillance units in the Mediterranean necessitated by the increasing presence of Soviet naval units. Despite these limitations, the NATO military headquarters has functioned effectively as a unit of joint command and military planning operations, exercising day-to-day control over as many as twenty-four divisions from seven countries.

A number of specialized agencies have been created by NATO to assure logistic support. They manage fuel pipelines, maintain a common system for the supply of spare parts, coordinate the production of certain aircraft and missiles, and have established the NATO Defense College.

It is evident from the descriptions of the NATO structure that the patterns of decision making and influence are highly complex. Moreover, since the inception of NATO, the relationship between the United States and its partners has changed. Although American predominance in military strength remains a continuing political reality, the revival of European economic strength and the perception that the Soviet threat to Europe is receding has produced frictions and tensions. While all alliance members, including the United States, realize that consultation is the name of the game, it has been at times difficult for the American government to recognize that consultation requires more than simply informing the NATO partners. To minimize the trauma of intra-NATO disputes, the secretary general himself has been formally authorized to use his good offices in such disputes. This gives the secretary general a very important role in addition to his administrative function.

Decision-making performance has been enhanced at times by utilizing the expedient of shunting difficult problems to committees or to technical experts in the hope that, in this way, a compromise solution can be found more easily than in the more rigid atmosphere of the NATO Council. This has indeed been a useful method and has contributed to the overall success of the NATO Alliance.

Problems   There can be little doubt that NATO has a record of impressive accomplishment. Without the NATO organization, the peace of Europe and the world may well have been jeopardized. Yet very real problems beset the alliance. One of the most difficult problems stems from the disparity of support for the alliance. If you will refer to Table 3.13, you will find the defense share of GNP by the NATO countries. The data show that in overall terms the United States is spending a larger part for defense than its allies. The repeated threats of the United States Senate to withdraw part of the American ground forces and U.S. insistence on compensatory measures, such as special purchases of American military products to remedy part of the United States balance-of-payments deficit caused by the stationing of American troops in Germany, highlight the frictions stemming from this particular problem. However, we must also note the complexity of NATO "burden sharing." The United States is not contributing a disproportionate share in all categories of the common effort. European NATO members provide 90 percent of the ground forces, 75 percent of the air forces, and 80 percent of the naval forces.

Another problem has been caused by the perception of many Europeans that the Soviet Union wants to achieve a more cooperative relationship with the West and that therefore the threat of Soviet aggression has diminished if not disappeared. During the past few years, NATO has become an important cog in the attempt to reduce tensions between East and West by participating as a unit in the negotiations with the Communist Bloc countries regarding the mutual and balanced reductions of forces. The NATO countries also adopted a common position in the negotiations leading to the Helsinki agreement on détente in 1975, which is aimed primarily at establishing a higher level of economic cooperation between East and West and bringing about closer person-to-person contacts between the countries of Eastern and Western Europe.

The problems of NATO reflect the difficulty of meshing national interests and policies, for which an IGO is an instrument, with the common interest that has led to its creation in the first place and through which it has become an independent actor. As perceptions of these interests shift and priorities change, the tensions within alliance members are a natural result. The management of these tensions and recurring crises demands the highest statesmanship and diplomatic skill, and administrative as well as executive expertise on the part of the NATO civil service. It is perhaps not surprising that these tensions and frictions exist in view of the differing economic and political progress made by the Alliance members; what is astonishing is that, despite these frictions, NATO has continued to fulfill its major functions.

Organization of American States

The Organization of American States (OAS) has primarily security and political aims; but economic objectives have received increased emphasis since 1970, while social and cultural concerns play a minor role. It differs from NATO because many of its activities and most of its organs evolved during the sixty years between the First Conference of American States (1889–90) and the formal establishment of the OAS in 1948, whose charter was later modified in 1970. To a considerable extent, therefore, the OAS Charter restates commitments, formalizes institutional relationships, and confirms procedures that have been in existence for some time.

The cornerstone of inter-American peace and security arrangements is the Treaty of Reciprocal Assistance of 1947, the so-called Rio Pact, forerunner of the NATO and SEATO treaties. It brings together and makes explicit mutual security commitments agreed upon at Buenos Aires in 1936 after the United States, following President Franklin D. Roosevelt's initiation of the "Good Neighbor" policy, had renounced unilateral intervention in affairs of Latin American states. Other mutual security commitments were negotiated in Havana in 1940 and at Chapultepec in 1945. Members of the inter-American community agreed that an armed attack on one is an attack upon all, regardless of whether it originates within or outside the American region, which includes Canada, Greenland, and certain Arctic and Antarctic areas, although Canada and Greenland are not members of this community. In such an event, each state is bound to "assist in meeting the attack," but is left free to "determine the immediate measures which it may individually take" until the members decide upon collective action.* If the territorial integrity or political independence of an American state is affected by an aggression short of an armed attack or any other situation endangering the peace including subversion, the member states are only obligated to consult; however—and this is a crucial difference from the NATO Treaty—a two-thirds vote of the member states may authorize collective sanctions ranging from the recall of the chiefs of diplomatic missions to the use of armed force. While consent for the latter can be denied by a member state, other sanctions must be undertaken, even if a state has voted against them.

These comprehensive pledges have been reaffirmed by the OAS Charter. They have been supplemented by the Pact of Bogotá concluded the same time as the charter. This pact contains an unqualified commitment for the pacific settlement of inter-American disputes and an obligation to use these settlement procedures before referring a dispute to the Security Council of the United Nations. This provision conforms with Article 52 of the U.N. Charter.

The supreme organ of the OAS is the General Assembly, formerly the Inter-American Conference, which is convened annually.

---

* Article 3 of the Inter-American Treaty of Reciprocal Assistance (Rio Treaty).

But the key in urgent situations is the Organ of Consultation of Ministers of Foreign Affairs. This body, in turn, may be summoned by the chairman of a third institution, the OAS Council, which is composed of the permanent representatives of the member states and at present is located in Washington, or by a majority of the council on the initiative of a member state.

The charter provides for the establishment of an Advisory Defense Committee to aid the Organ of Consultation in military operations arising from collective defense actions. A permanently functioning Inter-American Defense Board coordinates planning for hemispheric defense, but can deal only with threats from outside the hemisphere. Meeting in Washington, the chairman, director of the staff, and the secretary have always been American officers. An Inter-American Peace Committee also functions permanently; it carries out "watchdog" activities and undertakes studies in advance of possible controversies arising from likely subversion or attempts in one state to overthrow the government of another state.

The Secretariat of the OAS, headquartered in Washington, is the former Pan American Union, which, prior to 1910, was the Commercial Bureau of the American Republics. An Economic and Social Council, to which not much attention was paid in 1948, has been strengthened in 1970 by stressing greater united efforts of the member states in the economic sphere and more intensive cooperation in the use of resources. The Inter-American Development Bank is an important cog in their endeavors.

The Inter-American system characteristically looks toward international law for the settlement of disputes. The Inter-American Council of Jurists, assisted by a Judicial Committee headquartered in Brazil, has encouraged the progressive enlargement of the scope of international law in matters ranging from the traditional rights and duties of states to the more novel international concern for fundamental human rights.

Although the regional OAS peace-keeping machinery has been bypassed occasionally with an immediate appeal to the U.N. organs—the 1954 Guatemala situation surrounding the activities and overthrow of President Arbenz is an example*—the Inter-American

---

* In 1973 the U.N. Security Council held a meeting in Panama with respect to the renegotiation of the treaties between the United States and Panama regarding the Panama Canal. Panama complained that the United States impinged on Panamanian sovereignty in the Canal Zone. The United States cast a veto against a resolution in the Council which aimed at assuring effective Panamanian sovereignty over "all its territory." The United States contended that the treaty negotiations should proceed without "outside pressures."

system has a good record of accomplishment in the field of peace and security when faced with problems arising within the hemisphere. It has helped to prevent or stop armed conflict between American states and has applied sanctions against violators of the principle of peaceful relations. In 1960 the OAS foreign ministers voted to apply diplomatic and partial economic sanctions against the Dominican Republic for acts of indirect aggression against Venezuela. In 1962 they expelled the Castro government from the OAS and voted to impose limited economic sanctions upon Cuba although only the bare minimum of favorable votes required were cast. In 1964 these sanctions were expanded, and OAS members were ordered to break diplomatic relations with Cuba, which was done by all member states except Mexico. In 1975 a few other Latin American states resumed again diplomatic contact with Cuba. During the 1962 Cuban missile crisis, the OAS Council supported the United States naval blockade of Cuba and her demand for the removal of Soviet missiles.

Undoubtedly the most far-reaching application of the inter-American security system has been the decision of the OAS Council, taken again with the minimum required voting, to create an inter-American peace force following the 1965 revolt in the Dominican Republic. It was a means to legitimize the unilateral intervention by the U.S. government with more than 20,000 troops in apparent violation of the OAS Charter. The council decision brought 2,500 Latin American soldiers, mostly Brazilians, to the Dominican Republic to share peace-keeping activities with the American forces and permitted the latter to wear OAS armbands.

Finally in 1970, an OAS police force was established to assure a return to peaceful relations between El Salvador and Honduras. El Salvador had invaded the latter country in 1969, and the ensuing fighting left 1,000 dead and many more homeless. By threatening economic sanctions and military intervention, the OAS Council induced El Salvador to withdraw. Despite two more border flare-ups, the two countries negotiated a peace settlement in 1971.

The Dominican Republic affair and the action against Cuba spotlight the predominance of the United States in the American security system and the support by the OAS of the U.S. government's militant stand against the spread of communism in the Western Hemisphere; however, the positions of the OAS, adopted sometimes under heavy pressure by the United States, must not be permitted to conceal the strong aversion of most Latin American countries toward military interventionism and the general apprehension over Yankee imperialism. Despite the overwhelming influence of the United States in Latin America, the U.S. government must increasingly pay attention to the views and concerns of its neighbors to the south because ignoring them is likely to affect the implementation of foreign policies adversely.

There are growing indications that many Latin American and Caribbean governments are seeking to reorient their economic relations more toward Europe where an enlarged European Community with tremendous economic power is able to offer investments for new markets for Latin American products. Such a shift in economic orientation would be assisted by long-standing cultural ties with Europe, which the Community countries have carefully sought to intensify during the last years. The disappointments both in Latin America and the United States with the many failures of the much-heralded Alliance for Progress and the adverse public reaction to interference by American multinational corporations in the domestic affairs of certain South American countries are likely to reinforce this trend.

Organization of African Unity

The third regional organization to be examined is the Organization of African Unity (OAU), which was established in 1963 in Addis Ababa. Its members are all independent countries in Africa except South Africa and Rhodesia and the islands of the Malagasy Republic and Mauritius in the Indian Ocean. The purposes of the OAU go beyond the assurance of the security and independence of the member states and aim at the eradication of colonialism in Africa, as well as intense cooperation among the members to improve the standard of living of the African people.

The main organs of the OAU are the Assembly of Heads of State and Government, which meets at least annually; the Council of Ministers, usually attended by the foreign ministers but sometimes also by other ministers; the General Secretariat, located in Addis Ababa; and the Commission of Mediation, Conciliation and Arbitration. The basic voting procedure in the OAU requires a two-thirds majority for taking decisions.

The OAU charter does not have the specific security commitments of NATO and the OAS. It obligates the member states to coordinate and harmonize their policies for defense and security and to settle all disputes among themselves by peaceful means with the help of the Commission for Mediation, Conciliation and Arbitration. The establishment of a Defense Commission by the Assembly in case of need is also authorized.

Since its inception the OAU has become involved in several

cases of hostilities. The first was a border dispute between Algeria and Morocco in the fall of 1963, which led to open fighting and casualties. OAU representatives induced the warring parties to agree on a cease-fire, and the OAU Council, meeting in special session, appointed an ad hoc commission to settle the dispute. The commission was unsuccessful, but by 1968 de facto border lines were accepted by the two countries during the OAU Assembly meeting in Algiers.

Two cases of OAU intervention in African conflicts were precipitated by interstate guerrilla fighting. In one case, Ethiopia, Somalia, and Kenya were involved during the period from 1964 to 1967, with regular Ethiopian and Somali armies also participating in the fighting. Through the initiatives of a special OAU Council meeting, a cease-fire was arranged, and ultimately a joint commission to supervise the withdrawal of forces performed its task. The guerrilla war and hostile relations persisted until 1967, when reconciliation between Kenya and Somalia was accomplished. The second case involved Rwanda and Burundi in 1967, and OAU conciliation efforts isolated and abated the conflict.

Three other OAU involvements pertained to internal conflicts, namely, the Congolese, Nigerian, and Angolan civil wars. In the Congo, rebellions in rural areas began to spread rapidly after the U.N. forces (ONUC) had withdrawn in 1964 and Tschombe had become premier. A ten-nation conciliation commission appointed by the Assembly meeting in July 1964 was ineffectual, and an OAU Council meeting in March 1965 was so severely split over the legitimacy of intervention that not even a cease-fire resolution could be passed. Equally fruitless was the OAU involvement in the Nigerian civil war during 1968 and 1969, which consisted primarily of OAU-sponsored talks resented by Biafra as being partial to the Lagos government.[5] The involvement in the Angolan affair in 1976 did not produce a solution by itself but aided indirectly in the establishment of the Marxist-leaning government of the MPLA (Marxist Popular Movement for the Liberation of Angola).

We should note that, in all instances, the primary role of the OAU was that of a forum rather than that of an administrator of peace-keeping operations. Whatever operations were carried out consisted mainly of observation missions. While the solution of interstate conflicts was relatively successful, the attempts to solve internal conflicts were failures.

The struggle against colonialism is carried out by a ten-nation Liberation Committee directly under the control of the OAU General Secretariat. Its main tasks are to coordinate military and financial aid to African liberation movements in the Portuguese colonies of

Angola and Mozambique, Rhodesia, and South Africa* and to administer the funds contributed by member states for this purpose. This struggle, although undertaken with great zeal and aggressiveness, has suffered from the necessities of economic reality.Large-scale unemployment has compelled Zambia and Malawi to continue economic intercourse with Rhodesia and South Africa. Nigeria and Uganda have tempered their antiapartheid positions because economic benefits from trade with South Africa seem at times to have outweighed the ideological Pan-African considerations that are the foundation of the OAU.

In the economic sector, subregional endeavors at obtaining benefits from economic integration have been made by several groups of countries; however, the OAU plays only a minor supervisory role through its Economic and Social Commission. It also attempts to unify the African labor movement (split into opposing labor federations), seeks to coordinate the policies of the member states toward UNCTAD, and has established a Scientific and Technical Commission to promote coordinated progress in these fields in Africa.

In contrast to her roles in NATO and the OAS, United States influence in the OAU is minimal; however, President Julius Nyerere of Tanzania has complained, perhaps with some exaggeration, that France and Great Britain have more power in the OAU than the whole of Africa put together.[6] There is no question that many of the economic patterns and relationships between the two countries and their former colonies persist and that much of the African trade, as well as many governmental and administrative practices, remain oriented toward their former colonial masters. The OAU had financial trouble, and its membership has been split between more conservative and radical members. The attendance of heads of state or government at the annual meeting of the Assembly has been low in recent years, which might reflect the low regard of the OAU as a major instrument for national policy implementation. Nevertheless, the ideological impetus of Pan-Africanism remains significant as a source of strength for the OAU, and in terms of conflict control in Africa, the OAU has had a measure of success.

SUMMARY

Since World War II, cooperation among nation-states with common interests has become increasingly institutionalized in the form of **intergovernmental organizations (IGOs),** which are founded by two

---

* There are also liberation movements in such countries as French Somaliland and the Canary Islands.

or more states for the attainment of common objectives. Established by multilateral treaty, IGOs are considered to have international legal personality. They may be **global** or **regional** in scope; may involve themselves in **security, political, economic,** or **technical** functions; and may be of general or limited competence. A **supranational** IGO is the nearest unit to a state.

The first organization that attempted to institutionalize regular consultations among the great powers was the Congress of Vienna in 1815. It was followed by a series of river commissions and public international unions. The German Zollverein, a loosely joined customs union established in 1834, was the first attempt at economic integration in Europe.

The **League of Nations** was the first major effort to organize a universal security IGO for the maintenance of international peace. Its underlying principle was **collective security.** Its Covenant was drafted by a special committee and accepted as a part of the Treaty of Versailles on April 28, 1919. It established four major organs: the **Assembly,** the **Council,** the **Secretariat,** and the **Permanent Court of International Justice.**

The League of Nations failed, and some analysts have argued that U.S. refusal to join dealt the fatal blow. Others have blamed the lack of sharply defined responsibilities for the major League organs. Still others have expressed doubt that sovereign states can collaborate successfully and have asserted that only a world government can guarantee peace.

Yet, the statesmen of the world turned again to the collective security system when they established the **United Nations** after World War II. According to its Charter, the principal organs of the United Nations are the **Security Council,** the **Economic and Social Council,** the **Trusteeship Council,** the **General Assembly,** the **Secretariat,** and the **International Court of Justice.**

Although drafters of the U.N. Charter learned a lesson from the League failure, the United Nations is not without problems. One is the **veto power** of the big powers exercised in the Security Council. More than 100 vetoes have been cast, and they have proved an impediment to the admission of new member states and to U.N. peace-keeping efforts. An attempt to remedy the veto-induced paralysis was the **Uniting for Peace Resolution.** In any threat to or breach of the peace, it allows the General Assembly to exercise a residual responsibility if the Security Council is prevented from exercising its chief responsibility because of a veto.

U.N. membership has grown from 50 nations in 1945 to 151 in 1977. A significant aspect of this growth is the changed distribution: the Asian and African countries together now constitute a majority.

More than 100 member countries are underdeveloped. To decide how their problems might be resolved, the **U.N. Conference on Trade and Development (UNCTAD)** was organized in Geneva in 1964, but the results have been disappointing.

Three regional IGOs that are predominately concerned with security and politics are the North Atlantic Treaty Organization (NATO), the Organization of American States (OAS), and the Organization of African Unity (OAU). While NATO and the OAS have been quite successful in meeting their security obligations, the OAU has been faced with much internal dissension. Nevertheless, the record of the OAU has shown some successes.

We agree with Inis Claude that a distinction must be made between IGOs and international organization as an approach to the solution to the problem of world peace and order and that this is an important distinction. He observes that

> Particular organizations may be nothing more than playthings of power politics and handmaidens of national ambitions. But international organization, considered as an historical process, represents a secular trend toward the systematic development of an enterprising quest for political means of making the world safe for human habitation. It may fail, and peter out ignominiously. But if it maintains the momentum that it has built up in the twentieth century, it may yet effect a transformation of human relationships on this planet which will at some indeterminate point justify the assertion that the world has come to be governed—that mankind has become a community capable of sustaining order, promoting justice, and establishing the conditions of the good life which Aristotle took to be the supreme aim of politics.[7]

NOTES

1. Cf. R. S. Baker and William E. Dodd, eds., *The Public Papers of Woodrow Wilson, War and Peace* (New York: Harper & Row, n.d.), p. 16.

2. John G. Stoessinger, *The United Nations and the Superpowers*, 3rd ed. (New York: Random House, 1973), p. 20.

3. Inis L. Claude, Jr., *Swords into Plowshares: The Problems and Progress of International Organization*, 4th ed. (New York: Random House, 1971), pp. 129–130.

4. Werner Levi, "Third World States: Objects of Colonialism or Neglect?" *International Studies Quarterly*, vol. 17, no. 2 (June 1973), pp. 227–248, on p. 248.

5. For details see Joseph S. Nye, *Peace in Parts* (Boston: Little, Brown, 1971), pp. 154–159.

6. Ibid., p. 134.

7. Inis L. Claude, Jr., *Swords into Plowshares: The Problems and Progress of International Organization*, 4th ed. (New York: Random House, 1971), pp. 447–448.

SUGGESTED READINGS

BALL, MARGARET M. *The OAS in Transition*. Durham, N.C.: Duke University Press, 1969.

CLAUDE, I. *Swords into Plowshares*. New York: Random House, 1971.

GOODRICH, L., E. HAMBRO, AND A. SIMONS. *Charter of the United Nations: Commentary and Documents*. 3rd ed. New York: Columbia University Press, 1969.

HAAS, E. B. *Tangle of Hopes*. Englewood Cliffs, N.J.: Prentice-Hall, 1969.

JACOB, P. E., A. ATHERTON, AND A. WALLERSTEIN. *The Dynamics of International Organization*. Rev. ed. Homewood, Ill.: Dorsey Press, 1972.

THARP, P. A., JR., ed. *Regional International Organizations: Structures and Functions*. New York: St. Martin's Press, 1971.

CHAPTER ELEVEN
NONGOVERNMENTAL ORGANIZATIONS

Nongovernmental organizations (NGOs) with international interests and transnational objectives have become ever more numerous
during the past hundred years. The variety of objectives pursued
is extensive. Examples are the International Chamber of Commerce,
representing business and trade interests; the World Confederation
of Labour, consisting mainly of Catholic unions and promoting their
goals; the International Union of Architects; the International Federation of Teachers; the Afro-Asian Peoples Solidarity Organization,
coordinating the struggle of its members against "imperialism"; and
the African Football Confederation. Fields in which NGOs are active
are listed in Table 11.1.

To be genuine international NGOs, these organizations must
meet certain criteria regarding aims, membership, governance, and
financing postulated by the Union of International Associations.
They must engage in activities in at least three countries, their membership must be drawn from at least three countries, and substantial
financial contributions to the budget must come from three countries
as a minimum. As a consequence, many "international" societies
and unions in North America are excluded because their funds are
usually derived wholly from U.S. members. No attempt must be made
to make profits for direct distribution to the members of the NGOs,
but this does not mean that members may not be helped to increase

Table 11.1: Functional Breakdown of International NGOs

Category	1909-10	1956-57	1966-67	1970-71	Dead or Inactive	
					1966-67	1970-71
Bibliography, press	19	26	58	63	28	31
Religion, ethics	21	70	93	109	60	62
Social sciences	10	57	80	95	34	35
International relations	12	61	111	127	101	102
Politics	3	13	15	22	21	30
Law, administration	13	28	48	54	31	29
Social welfare	10	52	76	95	50	51
Professions, employers	2	67	93	112	34	34
Trade unions	1	48	63	70	21	22
Economics, finance	3	15	35	45	15	15
Commerce, industry	5	123	211	239	31	34
Agriculture	5	27	76	83	24	26
Transport, travel	5	40	72	82	15	15
Technology	8	36	83	113	26	28
Science	21	69	137	174	49	53
Health, medicine	16	100	173	225	35	37
Education, youth	10	56	91	106	31	35
Arts, literature, radio	6	34	70	80	28	27
Sport, recreation	6	51	90	99	16	18
European Common Market and EFTA business and professional groups	--	--	245	288	--	2
National organizations in consultative status with United Nations	--	12	15	15	--	--
Total NGOs	176	985	1935	2296	650	676

Note: The compilers of the 1909-10 edition of the *Yearbook* defined "international" in a more restricted sense than is customary today. After discussions with ECOSOC officials in 1950, the Union of International Associations adopted criteria allowing the inclusion of regional bodies (involving three countries or more), which had been excluded in 1909-10.

SOURCE: *Yearbook of International Organizations,* 1st, 6th, 11th, and 13th eds. (Brussels, Belgium: Union of International Associations).

their profits or better their economic organization through the activities of the NGOs.[1]

GROWTH AND DISTRIBUTION

International NGOs as delineated above are generally assumed to date back to 1846 when the World's Evangelical Alliance was founded.[2] The dramatic growth of international NGOs from 1860 to 1970 is illustrated in Figure 11.1. The number of NGOs founded increased sharply in the period immediately following major wars (for example, the Russo-Japanese War and World Wars I and II) and decreased during periods of rising international conflict and wars, such as the time spans from 1911-1920 and from 1931-1940. This suggests that international strife and turmoil impede the establishment of international NGOs,[3] while the settlement of devastating wars coupled with the bitter memories of misery and deprivation seems to stimulate the formation of international NGOs reflecting a revived spirit of border-crossing cooperation. It is interesting to note that a very similar situation prevails in the growth pattern of IGOs since 1860, also shown in Figure 11.1. Expanding international cooperation after World Wars I and II is clearly evidenced by the sharp increases in the founding of IGOs during the periods from 1921 to 1930 and from 1941 to 1960. Equally visible is the distinct drop in increases between 1931 and 1940.[4] It has been estimated that by 1980, NGOs should reach a total of about 2,600 and by the year 2000, a total of approximately 4,000.[5]

Table 11.1 provides a functional breakdown of international NGOs for selected years. Commerce and industry groups lead the field followed by health and scientific organizations. It is also noteworthy that NGOs in the economic sector show a much higher growth rate from 1909-10 to 1970-71 than do other groups. According to the 1970-71 compilations, a substantial number (676) of NGOs were inactive or completely dead. While not all disappearances of NGOs may become a matter of record, the figures shown are at least suggestive, and it may be a symptom of our troubled times that in this category fall 102 groups in the field of international relations, a figure not much smaller than those that are active (127). Even worse is the situation with organizations concerned with politics where inactive organizations outnumber the active ones. The high percentage of inactive NGOs in these two fields and the much smaller percentage of inactive NGOs in all other fields may offer some indirect evidence for the argument that the dynamics of functionalism are more effective when pragmatic, "low politics," interests, and objectives are pursued and less effective when the pursuit

Figure 11.1: Growth Pattern of International NGOs Compared with IGOs, 1860–1970

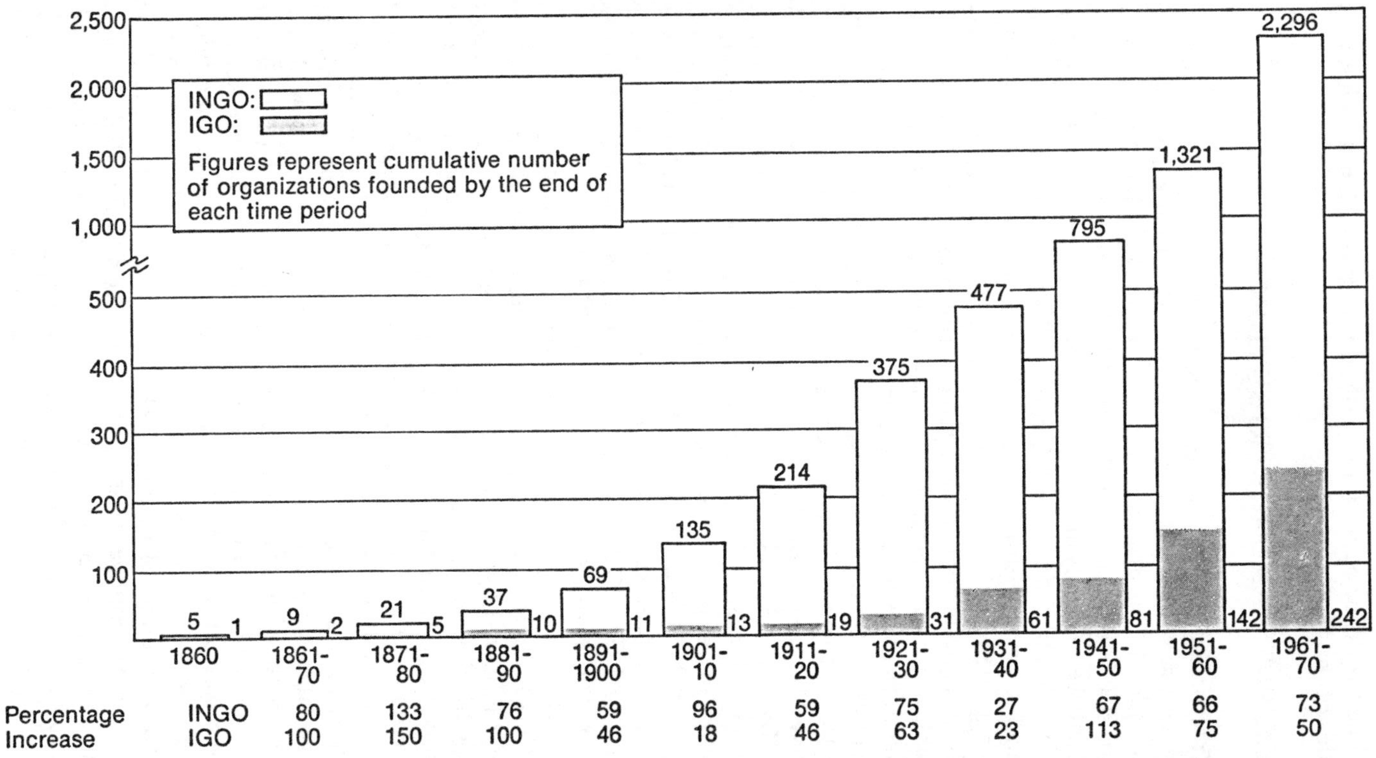

	1860	1861–70	1871–80	1881–90	1891–1900	1901–10	1911–20	1921–30	1931–40	1941–50	1951–60	1961–70
INGO:	5	9	21	37	69	135	214	375	477	795	1,321	2,296
IGO:	1	2	5	10	11	13	19	31	61	81	142	242

Figures represent cumulative number of organizations founded by the end of each time period

Percentage Increase		1861–70	1871–80	1881–90	1891–1900	1901–10	1911–20	1921–30	1931–40	1941–50	1951–60	1961–70
INGO		80	133	76	59	96	59	75	27	67	66	73
IGO		100	150	100	46	18	46	63	23	113	75	50

SOURCE: Werner J. Feld, *Nongovernmental Forces and World Politics* (New York, Praeger, 1972), p. 177.

is concerned with "high politics" and strongly opposed ideological commitments.[8]

Table 11.2 furnishes data regarding the number of states from which members are drawn and the geographical distribution of NGOs by continents and international regions. A substantial majority (1,123) of NGOs draw their members from twenty-five or fewer states, while only a small number (70) have members in 76 or more states of the world.[7] As to distribution by continent, 1,604 NGOs draw members from Europe, while only 722 have memberships in Australia. Of course, many NGOs have members on more than one continent, and this distribution is found in the second section of Table 11.2. Roughly one-quarter of the NGOs (550) cover all five continents, and may therefore be considered as truly universal. At the other end of the scale are NGOs limiting themselves to only one continent; and in view of the large number of European IGOs, it is not astonishing that 454 NGOs in this category operate exclusively in Europe. On the other hand, only very few NGOs have confined their activities to Australia, Asia, and Africa. Most of the organizations operating there have links with other continents; in fact, a large majority of them are in the four- or five-continent category, attesting perhaps to the need for international linkages which the economic and other sectors of the society on these continents have for the pursuit of their overall goals.

Table 11.3 shows the location of headquarters of international NGOs. In keeping with the distribution of NGOs by continent, Europe is the undisputed leader in the number of headquarters locations. France heads the list followed by Belgium and the United Kingdom. The Soviet Union is the headquarters for only four nongovernmental organizations, but its citizens are members in about 200 NGOs. Table 11.4 shows that since 1954 a number of countries in Black Africa have become hosts of NGO headquarters, which is not surprising in view of the sharply rising African representation in NGOs. Also, there are small increases in headquarters in Latin America, the Arab countries, Western Asia, and East Europe, with a corresponding percentage decline in Western Europe and North America.

ORGANIZATIONAL EFFECTIVENESS AND FINANCIAL REVENUES

While it is obviously difficult to make a comprehensive judgment regarding the organizational effectiveness of individual NGOs or of the totality of NGOs compared with other nongovernmental forces,

Table 11.2: NGO Membership Distribution by Number of States, Continents, and Regions

Number of States From Which NGO Members are Drawn (1968)[a]				
	0–25	26–50	51–75	75+
Number of NGOs	1123	394	137	70

Distribution of NGO Membership by Individual Continents (1968)[a]					
	Europe	America	Asia	Africa	Australia
Number of NGOs	1604	1160	1021	830	722

Distribution of NGOs by Membership Coverage of One or Several Continents

Africa-America-Asia-Australia-Europe	550
Africa-America-Asia-Europe	167
America-Asia-Australia-Europe	103
Africa-America-Australia-Europe	23
Africa-America-Asia-Australia	7
Africa-Asia-Australia-Europe	4
America-Asia-Europe	105
Africa-America-Europe	29
America-Australia-Europe	16
Africa-Asia-Europe	14
America-Asia-Australia	4
Africa-America-Asia	4
Africa-Australia-Europe	2
Asia-Australia-Europe	1
America-Europe	80
Asia-Europe	39
Africa-Europe	15
Asia-Australia	9
Africa-Asia	5
Australia-Europe	2
America-Asia	1
Europe	454
America	71
Africa	10
Asia	8
Australia	1

[a]The data in the *Yearbook* for individual NGOs are not always complete; therefore, the figures given in the first and last sections of the table do not add up to the total in Table 13.1. Of course, the figures in the middle section cannot be added because individual NGOs may have members on several continents.

SOURCE: *Yearbook of International Organizations, 1968–69,* 12th ed., pp. 52–240.

Table 11.3: Location of Headquarters of International NGOs, 1956

Country	Number of NGO's	Country	Number of NGO's
Africa, French West	1	Japan	1
Africa, North	3	Luxembourg	14
Argentina	10	Mexico	15
Australia	2	Monaco	3
Austria	26	Netherlands	85
Belgian Congo	1	Norway	3
Belgium	245	Pakistan	2
Bolivia	1	Panama	2
Brazil	8	Peru	7
Bulgaria	1	Philippines	3
Canada	4	Poland	9
Chile	6	Portugal	1
Colombia	5	Romania	2
Crete	1	Salvador	3
Cuba	14	Silesia	1
Czechoslovakia	13	Soviet Union	4
Denmark	18	Spain	9
Egypt	3	Sweden	23
Finland	1	Switzerland	184
France	428	Turkey	3
Germany	110	Union of South Africa	1
Greece	2	United Kingdom	189
Guatemala	2	United States	129
Hungary	10	Uruguay	5
Iceland	1	Venezuela	1
India	8	Yugoslavia	2
Iran	1		
Italy	84	Total	1710

SOURCE: J. J. Lador-Lederer, *International Non-Government Organizations: and Economic Entities* (Leyden: A. W. Sythoff, 1963), p. 74.

it seems reasonable to hypothesize that the larger the paid staff, the greater the annual budget, the larger the number of secondary offices, the more numerous the membership meetings, and the more numerous the publications issued, the higher is the organizational effectiveness. Data on these variables are often unavailable, and it goes without saying that they differ greatly with respect to individual NGOs. For example, the International Chamber of Commerce, headquartered in Paris, has a paid staff of fifty, an annual budget of $500,000, three secondary offices, holds biannual congresses, has council, committee, and commission meetings several times a year, and publishes a periodical and many specialized studies. On the other hand, the International Judicial Organization for Developing

Table 11.4: Locations of Headquarters in Percentages per Region, 1954–68

	1954	1958	1962	1964	1966	1968
Western Europe and						
North America	93.2	92.0	90.8	89.4	88.7	87.1
Latin America	3.1	3.7	3.7	4.4	4.8	5.4
Arab Countries	.4	.5	.5	1.1	.9	1.1
Asia, Western	1.3	1.5	1.8	1.7	1.7	2.1
Asia, Communist	.0	.0	.0	.0	.0	.0
Eastern Europe	1.3	1.6	1.8	1.8	2.1	2.1
Black Africa	.5	1.6	1.2	1.4	1.5	1.9
All Others	.3	.1	.1	.1	.1	.2
Total	100.1	100.0	99.9	99.9	99.8	99.9
N	1198	1257	1549	1758	2207	2663

Note: This table includes IGOs, but since their number is so very small compared with NGOs, the trend visible in the table remains significant.

SOURCE: Adapted from *International Associations*, no. 11 (1954), pp. 548–549; no. 6 (1969), pp. 446; no. 2 (1965), pp. 86–89, no. 2 (1967), pp. 166–169; *Yearbook of International Organizations*, 12th ed.

Countries, headquartered in Rome, has a paid staff of four, a budget of $20,000, no secondary offices, no regularly scheduled meetings, and no publication.[8] Many NGOs do not have any paid staff, only volunteers, and their finances are extremely precarious.

CONTACTS AND COALITIONS

The major vehicles for successfully attaining NGO objectives are formal and informal contacts with IGOs and governmental agencies. In this endeavor the formation of coalitions among NGOs has also proven to be beneficial. As a consequence, access to the decision-making process of intergovernmental organizations is valued highly and regarded as very important by the NGOs in the pursuit of their international objectives. The remarkable increase in the number of NGOs that have been accorded some kind of consultative status with different universal and regional IGOs is shown in Table 11.5. It should be noted that not only international but also a few national NGOs have been admitted as consultants.[9] The largest increases of consultation relationships with NGOs have been recorded by the ILO and the Food and Agriculture Organization (FAO).

The financing of NGOs has produced a number of problems. On the one hand, the basic principle of NGOs requires that these organizations be independent of any government influence. Clearly

Table 11.5: NGOs Accorded Consultative Status by Intergovernmental Organizations[a]

International Organization[a]	1951–52	1958–59	1962–63	1966–67	1970–71	Growth[b]
ECOSOC	212	302	332	360	352	166
ILO	5	47	58	81	92	1840
FAO	10	40	51	79	106	1060
UNESCO	99	125	200	250	264	266
WHO	26	46	57	68	82	315
ICAO	17	26	27	28	28	164
ITU	18	23	28	30	31	172
WMO	--	11	11	15	15	136
IMCO	--	--	11	11	21	190
IAEA	--	--	19	19	19	100
UNICEF	--	57	70	75	77	135
IRO	9	--	--	--	--	--
UNCTAD	--	--	--	17	35	205
UNIDO	--	--	--	--	16	N.A.
CL of E	--	--	--	76	106	139
OAS	--	--	--	48	46	95
Total	396	677	864	1157	1290	

[a]Most of these NGOs are of the international kind, but a few national NGOs have also been granted consultative status: 12 in 1956–57, increased to 16 in 1968–69. They include some important American organizations, for example the U.S. Chamber of Commerce, the Committee for Economic Development, and the Carnegie Endowment for International Peace.

[b]Base = 100 for first year organization appears on this chart.

SOURCE: Adapted from the *Yearbook of International Organizations* of the years shown.

if secret governmental finances are furnished, this may imply that these organizations are to be induced to undertake actions that might be contrary to the purposes and principles of the Charter of the United Nations.[10] On the other hand, most of the NGOs are strapped for money, and consequently any kind of financial support may be most appealing to the management of NGOs.[11] As a consequence, efforts have been made by the Economic and Social Council of the United Nations to require periodic disclosures of sources of funds. Voluntary contributions by amounts and donors are to be revealed faithfully, and financing from sources other than individual members or national nongovernmental affiliates must be explained, especially those that suggest direct or indirect governmental support. If an NGO cannot furnish a satisfactory explanation, its consultative status may be terminated.

There has been criticism by delegates of some developing countries against NGOs currently enjoying consultative status that they were predominantly "Western-oriented." On the other hand, committee members from the Third World have shown a tendency to vote admission on the basis of the policies and capabilities of consultative status-seeking NGOs with respect to providing assistance to developing countries.[12]

It is obvious that the various types of consultative relations with intergovernmental organizations give the NGOs opportunities to exert influences for the attainment of their goals. Moreover, United Nations bodies make available to NGO representatives reports of special studies, notices of forthcoming events, and summary records of debates and decisions which, although it may be a time-consuming task to select relevant materials, provide an important source of information necessary for the lobbying activities of NGOs and for the statements of NGO representatives before IGO bodies. It should be noted that the overwhelming majority of NGOs do not have special U.N. representatives but dispatch ad hoc representatives to the IGO sessions pertinent to their interests.* To influence the policies of the United Nations and other IGO bodies effectively, it is necessary to exert pressures at the national as well as the international level.[13] In this connection, another aspect of the consultative relationship must be mentioned. NGOs may often become the instruments of implementation which stand at the disposal of IGOs. Such action can add power to the NGOs' goal attainment potential. Moreover, because of sometimes close NGO relations to national authorities, which use NGOs occasionally for carrying out technical and administrative matters, IGOs may gain special means of influencing national governmental agencies.[14] All this points up the importance for NGOs to have good connections to the governmental decision makers and other elites in the countries where they have offices and members and the usefulness of contacts with other NGOs.

International and national NGOs may also form coalitions for the pursuit of their international objectives, thereby enhancing their goal attainment potentials. These coalitions may be on a horizontal basis, whereby NGOs pursuing goals in the field of law may form an alliance with NGOs in the fields of economics and finance or technology. It is also possible for NGOs to form vertical coalitions that may lead to the creation of umbrella-type NGOs seeking to coordinate and promote in a more effective manner the interests

---

* Sixty-one NGOs have one special representative; twenty-seven NGOs, two representatives; and only two have as many as six representatives.

and objectives of similarly situated NGOs. Thus the interconnections among NGOs, as well as overlapping memberships of individual members in various NGOs, produce a worldwide ever-expanding network whose growth is likely to continue in the future.

Although in many instances the objectives and interests of NGOs are conflicting and antithetical, international NGOs have found it useful to form an umbrella group of their own, the NGO Conference. This group seeks to coordinate the activities of all NGOs, promote interaction among NGOs, facilitate the contacts between IGO bodies and NGOs, and seek ways by which the NGOs might give more "collective" as distinctive from "individual" advice on matters relating to the consultative process. The conference meets triennially in Geneva and elects a president and vice president and an executive bureau of fifteen members. The hope it to create a more functional and efficient relationship in particular areas of concern to NGOs and to improve the representation of NGOs in the United Nations.[15]

EFFECTS ON IGOs

What has been the impact of international NGOs on intergovernmental organizations? No systematic study exists so far dealing with the effect of the NGO consultative relationship on United Nations policies and programs. To come up with some kind of evaluation, it might be helpful to consider views expressed by various member states and by the staff of the United Nations Secretariat. The secretary general, addressing a Conference of NGOs in May 1969, stated that he wanted to express his

> very sincere thanks to all of you, not only for your magnificent work for the United Nations and the peoples of the United Nations but also for your consistent understanding, cooperation and support, and your very sincere spirit of dedication and devotion to the principles of the Charter. As a matter of fact, the United Nations owes all of you a deep debt of gratitude.

A different aspect of NGO activity was expressed by President Kenneth Kaunda of Zambia in 1968 at a NGO-sponsored conference on human rights:

> We are still too national in our thinking and outlook. . . . the efforts of NGOs . . . must be directed towards strengthening the world body and increasing its capability to solve problems which continue to bedevil human development . . .

He also expressed the "sincere hope that NGOs will continue to assist in whatever way to shed more light on possible solutions to current problems facing the United Nations and the world."[16] Finally, during an ECOSOC debate of 1969, a delegate from Norway said it was certain that in the future the Economic and Social Council would have to rely more on cooperation with NGOs having consultative status. These optimistic and euphemistic statements must be juxtaposed to the actual attitudes in the United Nations vis-à-vis NGOs. Walter R. Sharp reports that few of the speeches delivered before ECOSOC by NGO representatives appear to be taken very seriously. For the most part, they are considered dull, while some have a definitely propagandistic flavor. As a consequence, according to Sharp, delegates of national governments frequently read newspapers or absent themselves during NGO presentations. At times the representatives of closely related NGOs insist they all hold forth on the same issue instead of authorizing one to speak in behalf of the group. This tendency might suggest vanity or the need of each to justify his presence as an NGO representative.[17]

While Sharp's comments may reflect the views of many observers of NGO activities in New York and Geneva, his judgment may be overly critical. The fact that delegates may not always listen to the statements of NGO representatives might not, in fact, be convincing evidence that these statements are not being taken seriously. Certainly in every national legislature of the world, as well as in the state legislatures in the United States, statements by interest groups may not arouse the greatest enthusiam on the floor, yet behind-the-scene contacts based on the statements made officially might well produce an impact. Moreover, United Nations officials and delegates are showing an increasing interest in the value of cooperation with NGOs that can and are willing to help inform the public on the activities and goals of United Nations agencies and are able to exert influence on both the public and national governments in support of these goals. As a consequence, greater emphasis is being placed on liaison between United Nations agencies and NGOs, which suggests a greater acceptance of the value of the NGOs. One example is the major effort made to accommodate 200 to 300 observers from NGOs at the U.N. Conference on Human Environment in June 1972 in Stockholm to ensure maximum participation in the proceedings of the meeting.[18] Another example is the cooperation between United Nations officials and NGOs to promote the goals and achieve the targets of the Second Development Decade. A number of NGOs are taking steps to schedule seminars, initiate training programs, and provide fellowships to assist the United Nations efforts.

THE CONSEQUENCES FOR
THE INTERNATIONAL SYSTEM

What can one say about the consequences of NGO activity for the global interaction process in the international system? In terms of collaboration and conflict, the transnational contacts of NGOs in the technical field have promoted and are likely to promote in the future an increasing amount of collaboration among states. In this field, NGO activity is mostly unobtrusive, and governmental decision makers do not consider such activity as building a competing base of power. However, when NGOs pursue primarily economic goals, the results in terms of collaboration are more difficult to discern as the activities of these NGOs might run counter to the declared objectives of national governments.

Some NGO activities in the human rights field have been viewed as infringements on sovereignty, especially, but not exclusively, by totalitarian governments; however, even these infringements produce only very gentle waves of conflict and are not very significant for changing the global interaction pattern. Of course, the more ideological the goals of NGOs are, the greater the conflict that may be caused among individual governments. Because the majority of NGOs recruit members and operate according to functional needs, political and ideological barriers may be overcome and a contribution made to collaboration.[19] A further favorable factor is the fact that memberships of individuals in various organizations are frequently overlapping and therefore, as Kjell Skjelsbaek points out,[20] adversaries and competitors in one connection might be allies and collaborators in another.

An interesting question to conjecture upon is whether the growing net of international NGOs has consequences for bringing about better prospects for international peace. Skjelsbaek reports[21] that an analysis of international NGO representation of the divided countries of the world—Germany, China, Korea, and Vietnam—shows that in each instance there were *more* co-memberships among them than expected on the basis of each country's total number of co-memberships. This is particularly significant inasmuch as IGO co-memberships are almost nonexistent. Especially pronounced was the relationship between the two Germanies: in 1964, West Germany was represented in 93 percent of the international NGOs in which East Germany was represented. While there is no positive knowledge that these channels are used for interaction between national delegations, they have at least potential importance. Another interesting element of the East-West relationship is the fact that East-West co-memberships in international NGOs are higher than those for intra-East connections. From this, one could deduce that East European countries generally have more NGO contacts with Western states than with each other.

From the foregoing discussion the impression emerges that NGOs succeed in bringing about some changes in the global interaction pattern of the international system; however, their impact is undramatic, diffuse, and slow, and does not suggest any single direction. Although one might be tempted to speculate that the spreading web of NGO activity might produce the basis for greater integration of mankind and thereby contribute to higher prospects for international peace, little concrete evidence is available to sustain genuine hopes for the latter. Nevertheless, as was observed earlier, the number of NGOs continues to grow and their activity continues to increase, and therefore they will become an increasingly important factor in world politics.

SUMMARY

Nongovernmental organizations (NGOs) with international interests and transnational objectives have become more numerous during the past hundred years. To be classified as genuinely **international,** they must meet certain criteria regarding aims, membership, governance, and financing established by the Union of International Associations. They must engage in activities in at least three countries, their membership must be drawn from at least three countries, and substantial financial contributions to the budget must come from a minimum of three countries.

International NGOs are generally assumed to date back to the founding of the World's Evangelical Alliance in 1846. Their formation has been stimulated by the devastation and settlement of wars, and their number increased dramatically between 1860 and 1970 and should reach 2,600 by 1980.

The purposes of NGOs vary widely and may be economic, political, or technical. The formulation and implementation of appropriate IGO transnational policies often requires pertinent information and other inputs from particular nongovernmental organizations (NGOs), and the use of the United Nations or its agencies as instruments of national external policies may be aided by NGOs.

Although it is difficult to assess the impact of NGOs, their number continues to grow and the area of their activity widens. For these reasons they are bound to play an increasingly important role in the international arena.

NOTES

1. Cf. *Yearbook of International Organizations, 1970–71*, 13th ed. (Brussels, Belgium: Union of International Associations).
2. According to Lyman C. White, *International Non-Governmental Organizations* (New York: Greenwood Press, 1968), p. 279, fn. 5, the first international NGO was founded in 1855 and was the World Alliance of the YMCAs. White contends that the Evangelical Alliance was not a truly international NGO because "its so-called members . . . [were] mere subscribers to its publications, without any voting rights." Others believe that the Rosicrucian Order founded in 1674 was the first international NGO. Cf. Kjell Skjelsbaek, "The Growth of International Nongovernmental Organization in the Twentieth Century," *International Organization*, vol. 25, no. 3 (Summer 1971), p. 424.
3. Ibid., p. 425.
4. We should note that J. David Singer and Michael Wallace in "Intergovernmental Organization and the Preservation of Peace, 1816–1864: Some Bivariate Relationships," *International Organization*, vol. 24, no. 3 (Summer 1970), pp. 520–547, use slightly different data for IGOs founded from those used in Figure 9.1. These disparities, perhaps due to definitional differences, do not, however, affect the general growth trend.
5. Werner J. Feld, *Nongovernmental Forces and World Politics* (New York: Praeger, 1972), p. 179.
6. Cf. Ernst B. Haas, *The Uniting of Europe* (Stanford, Calif.: Stanford University Press, 1968), p. xxxiii.
7. Skjelsbaek, "The Growth of International Nongovernmental Organizations," op. cit., pp. 425, 426, using different data sources, states that the mean of the number of countries that have individual citizen, national organizations, and/or governmental agencies affiliated with international NGOs has risen from 21.0 in 1951 to 25.7 in 1966. Of the NGOs surveyed on this subject, 61 percent expect the number of their national branches to rise in the future.
8. *Yearbook of International Organizations, 1970–71*, 13th ed., pp. 311, 312, 452, 453.
9. Cf. Article 71 of the United Nations Charter.
10. It has been alleged that funds have been provided by the CIA to certain international NGOs. Cf. Persia Campbell, "Do NGOs Have a Role?" *International Development Review*, vol. 11, no. 3 (1969), pp. 34–39, on p. 36.
11. Cf. James E. Knott, *Freedom of Association* (Brussels, Belgium: Union of International Associations, 1962), pp. 67–83.
12. See Walter R. Sharp, *The United Nations Economic and Social Council* (New York: Columbia University Press, 1969), pp. 37, 38, and 42; Campbell, "Do NGOs Have a Role?" op. cit.; and Kiichiro Nakahara, "International Pressure Groups and the UN Enlarged ECOSOC," *Behavioral Science Research* (Tokyo), no. 7 (1970), pp. 39–49. For a particular roll call vote on admission of three NGOs, see page 47. For distribution of voting

power in the NGO committee of ECOSOC, see Table 5, page 40. It shows overrepresentation of Western and Eastern Europe. See also Table 4, p. 39.

13. Campbell, "Do NGOs Have a Role?" op. cit., p. 39.

14. For examples see J. J. Lador-Lederer, *International Non-Governmental Organizations: And Economic Entities* (Leyden: A. W. Sythoff, 1963), p. 75.

15. Campbell, "Do NGOs Have a Role?" op. cit., p. 39; and Sharp, *The United Nations Economic and Social Council*, op. cit., pp. 41–42. See also "The Use of 'Multi-Meetings,'" *International Associations*, no. 6 (1971), pp. 354–359.

16. Quoted by Campbell, "Do NGOs Have a Role?" op. cit., pp. 34 and 37.

17. Sharp, *The United Nations Economic and Social Council*, op. cit., pp. 39 and 40, and fn. 15. Sharp also points out that sometimes delegates simply come "just for the ride" with expenses paid.

18. U.N. Conference on Human Environment, *Information Letter*, no. 1 (June 30, 1971), p. 7. See also "UN-NGO Relations: A New Departure," *International Associations*, nos. 8–9 (1973), pp. 421–423.

19. Cf. David Mitrany, *A Working Peace System*, 4th ed. (London: National Peace Council, 1946).

20. Skjelsbaek, "The Growth of International Nongovernmental Organizations," op. cit., p. 439.

21. Ibid., p. 440.

SUGGESTED READINGS

Cox, Robert W., and Harold K. Jacobson. *The Anatomy of Influence: Decision-making in International Organizations.* New Haven, Conn.: Yale University Press, 1973.

Feld, Werner J. *Nongovernmental Forces and World Politics.* New York: Praeger, 1972.

Skjelsbaek, K. "The Growth of International Nongovernmental Organization in the Twentieth Century." *International Organization*, vol. 25 (Summer 1971), pp. 420–442.

White, Lyman C. *International Nongovernmental Organizations.* New York: Greenwood Press, 1968.

CHAPTER TWELVE

REGIONAL INTEGRATION AND TRANSNATIONAL COALITIONS

In Chapter 10 we have learned that IGO policies or the use of these organizations as instruments for transnational policy implementation of the member states can make salient contributions to the dynamics of international relations. In this chapter we will focus mainly on those regional IGOs in the economic sector for which a more intensive level of transnational collaboration was considered desirable and necessary by the member states to achieve the postulated goals. This brings us to the degree of integration among the member states which, at the beginning of Chapter 10, we considered as one of the criteria by which to evaluate the nature of a particular IGO. Our main concern in this chapter will be the process of integration as it relates to the transformation of conventional regional IGOs to supranational IGOs and perhaps the creation of a regional state composed of the former member countries of an IGO. Such transformation is likely to have significant effects not only on the region itself, but also on global international relations and politics.

The term *integration* in an international context refers broadly to intensified collaboration among states in a region which might culminate in the establishment of a common regional government. Following generally Joseph Nye[1] we will conceive this term in three different meanings and distinguish basically between economic, social, and political integration.

ECONOMIC INTEGRATION

Economic integration is understood not only as the abolition of discrimination, especially tariff and nontariff barriers, between national economic units, but also as a "growing together" of the national economies of several states to ensure the optimal operation of the total economy in an international region.[2] Several levels of economic integration can be distinguished. The lowest level is the creation of a *free trade area* by several states leading to the elimination of tariffs for goods shipped between these states. The second higher level is the establishment of a *customs union,* which adds a common external tariff for goods shipped from outside countries into the unified market of the participating states. The creation of a *common market* raises the level of economic integration further by providing unimpeded flows of labor, capital, and other economic factors between the member states. The next higher level is *economic union,* which requires the harmonization of economic policies of its member states. A final step upwards would be the unification of these policies and *monetary union.* If this were accomplished, the member states might be very close to political unification, but this final step might not really be possible without the unification of political institutions.

SOCIAL INTEGRATION

Regional *social integration* may be defined as the development of a transnational society within a region whose members share values, goal preferences, symbols of identity, and modes of communication.[3] To achieve social integration requires a learning process of collaboration among nationals of different states in the region in which well-developed communication nets and shared goals play a major part. As a consequence, a subtle socialization process is put in motion through which a gradual adoption of regional values and beliefs may take place. Of course, the experiences flowing from the collaborating activities may not always be recognized as having a socially significant effect; nevertheless, these social effects exist and may spill over into the political sphere, inasmuch as many of these experiences are likely to relate to the political environment in which the collaborating activities are carried out.

We should stress that this process of socialization will be particularly effective in pluralistic societies typical of the Western developed countries where its impact may spread to the populace at large. In the Third World the wide gap between elites and masses acts as a strong impediment to the socialization process. In fact, whatever socialization might occur would widen this gap and thus have deleterious effects on the political stability of countries in the area.

POLITICAL INTEGRATION

Political integration has four subcategories, which are institutional, policy, attitudinal, and security integration. *Institutional integration* refers to the process of transferring decision-making powers and activities from the national units to the institutions of the regional IGOs. *Policy integration* is conceived as the endeavor to make policy jointly by all governments within the region and create a framework for the coordinated formulation of these policies. Because decision-making authorities and machinery require legitimization to function smoothly, support must be forthcoming by the political and other elites in the region. This support, in turn, depends on favorable attitudes not only of the elites, although this is most important, but also of the mass public and can become effective only if the elites and the public have a commitment to regional ideals, look toward the regional institutions for economic and other rewards, and slowly shift loyalties and expectations from the national units to the regional institutions. In most instances, then, *attitudinal integration* is a precondition for the first two subcategories of political integration; but in some instances, policy integration may engender increased attitudinal integration. In turn, progress in both attitudinal and policy integration is likely to lead to further institutional integration, which is characterized by expanded involvement of the regional authorities in terms of scope, level, and competences in regional decision and policy making.[4]

It is quite obvious that socialization plays an important role with respect to attitudinal integration, inasmuch as it may lead to the adoption of favorable political attitudes and values for the regional integration process. Particularly important is the emergence of business elites committed to regional ideologies, inasmuch as they have the capability through cross-communications with other elites in the region to generate support for the regional decision-making process and thereby enhance its legitimacy.

The fourth category of political integration, *security integration*, refers to the expectation of nonviolent relations and the concept of building a security community to assure such relations. Expectation of security through the creation of a community may pertain to peace within the region, as well as to the prevention of aggression and defeat by outsiders. How far the perception of outside threats stimulates the emergence of common symbols and identities is difficult to judge. Experiences with security IGOs, such as NATO and the OAS, suggest that, while the common goal of protecting collectively the integrity of the member states is regarded highly in time of major threat perceptions, its value diminishes rapidly during periods when elites and public have little concern about security. As a consequence, the processes of institutional and attitudinal integration are likely to receive little impetus, although policy integration may persist as a long-term assurance against future external threats.

Although we do not have precise knowledge about the impact of economic integration on political integration, we can hypothesize that progress in both economic and social integration will produce tendencies for the promotion of the other aspects of political integration, but progress of the latter may be impeded, as we shall see, by strong countervailing forces and factors.

STIMULANTS FOR THE INTEGRATION PROCESS

Does some kind of stimulus exist to push the process of integration to higher levels? What are the incentives of states in an international region to integrate their economies and perhaps move toward the economic and political unification of their separate national units? What sets into motion the learning and socialization processes leading to the creation of a single community?

The loyalties that citizens attach to their state are based at least in part on the implied assumption that the state will provide certain services in return. Among these services are protection from hostile external forces, military as well as economic, and assurance of the necessary conditions for economic well-being and for steady improvement of living standards. Traditionally, protection from external forces presupposed that the government had full control over the state's territory and could prevent hostile penetration of the territorial boundaries. Economic well-being was closely linked to economic self-sufficiency in terms of supply and markets and to assured lines of transportation for needed raw materials.

The tremendous advances made by science and technology during the 20th century and especially since World War II have cast doubt on the continuing validity of these assumptions. Consequently, the frontiers of a state have been losing their meaning as lines delineating a territory under the complete sovereignty of its government. The main challenges have come from technological developments in warfare discussed earlier—bombers, long-range ballistic missiles, and orbiting space platforms possibly linked with nuclear weapons. Even the superpowers (the United States and the Soviet Union) cannot prevent such intrusions into their territories. Other challenges to the sovereign control of territories have come from psychological warfare and changing economic conditions. Industrialization and mass production have greatly increased the economic vulnerability of states because of their dependence on external sources of supplies and markets, from which they could be cut off by military and economic warfare.[5]

Another problem impairing the capability of many nation-states to provide full economic welfare to their citizens has been the small size of the market. Developed countries, such as Belgium, the Netherlands, or Denmark, are unable to accommodate many factories that can take advantage of the economies of scale and thereby provide the most efficient production facilities with the lowest cost for their products. As a consequence, the standard of living of their citizens may lag behind, and unemployment problems may crop up. This situation is even more serious in the Third World, where incomes are so low that market demand is severely restricted. The problem of unemployment in these countries is considerably more serious than what is found in some of the smallest countries of the developed world. As a consequence of these conditions, social services may have to be limited, and it is evident that the economic well-being of the citizens must suffer.

What have been the responses of the nation-states to meet some of these challenges? The most prominent device to overcome the military deficiencies and vulnerabilities inherent in the new technology has been the formation of regional security units, some of which were discussed in Chapter 10. When some of these units such as NATO were formed shortly after World War II, it was thought that they might offer good prospects for increased integration of the member states. However, the integration process among these regional security units did not make any progress. Two reasons may account for this: first, military and political matters may be too controversial to foster the upward movement of integration; and second, the growth of military and political regional organizations has depended heavily on shocks from their environment and on hegemonic leadership. both of which are often uneven over time.[6]

FUNCTIONALISM

Regional integration may have better prospects when the impetus comes in the less politicized fields of the economic and technical service sectors of a society. The economic and social needs of the peoples of a region could perhaps be met through border-crossing collaboration, and it is upon this premise that the theory of functionalism is built. This theory stresses the creative work of solving common problems and the building of habits of cross-national cooperation through which the expectation of future constructive and beneficial collaboration will replace the selfish quest for power as a dominant motive in international relations. International agencies will create through their work a system of mutual advantages which will assume too great a value in the eyes of their beneficiaries to be disrupted by war. Men will recognize transnational collaboration and international organization as providers of goods that their states can no longer provide by themselves. Men will no longer apprehensively look at the diminution of their country's sovereignty as a dangerous national sacrifice but come to think of it as a beneficial investment in economic well-being and better services. As a result, loyalty will be increasingly divided between the state and institutions engaged in transnational collaboration. As this process progresses, people participating as well as benefiting from transnational collaboration will learn not only to accept this collaboration as useful and beneficial, but also to work for further and more effective cooperation among the peoples of the world. This, in turn, will deepen the feeling of human solidarity. This line of thought is the theory of functionalism initially developed by David Mitrany in his stimulating book, *A Working Peace System.*[7] Functionalism thus shaves off successive layers of sovereignty from the nation-state and eventually produces a world thoroughly oriented to peace.

Whether this general transformation process stimulated by cross-national satisfaction of economic and social needs can in fact produce an ever higher level of integration among states in a region and culminate ultimately in regional states and perhaps some kind of world government eliminating all interstate conflicts is far from certain. Functionalist theory presumes that transnational collaboration for the solution of economic and social problems is sufficiently divorced from politics to permit governments and private groups operating in transnational coalitions to pursue their common welfare interests without the troublesome conflicts of power politics. Functionalists also stress the importance of learned habits of cooperation, which are presumed to be readily transferable from one sphere of activity to others. Finally, functionalists insist that special international institutions are better capable of coherently attacking extensive economic and social problems than the nation-state system. Artificial national barriers impair rooting out these problems, and only international agencies can perform this task effectively. As a consequence these institutions become the focus of human loyalties and support.

This separation of politics from welfare may not reflect reality. As we will see, the impelling forces of functionalism are often impeded by emotion-laden and ego-interest-oriented politics. Moreover, while collaboration habits can indeed be learned and socialization processes can be set in motion, they may also be placed in limbo by powerful contrary political forces. And while the transfer of functions from national governments to international institutions may result in the corresponding transfer of loyalty and support within the states making up the region, overriding national loyalties and attachments may continue. These realities make us question the assertion that the integration process will be more or less automatic and will spread continually from economic sector to economic sector, gradually, but inexorably, enlarging the authority of international institutions at the expense of the national governments.

NEOFUNCTIONALISM

To give functionalism a definitive forward thrust in a particular region, the school of neofunctionalism has advocated a number of strategies:

1. Regional institutions must be specifically designed to further the process of integration and have a high level of authority for collective decision making.

2. Instead of seeking transnational collaboration in matters that are not very relevant in political terms as suggested by Mitrany, social and economic sectors must be chosen that are politically important, yet can be planned and carried out by civil servants involved in the performance of technical tasks (technocrats).

3. The tasks given to the regional institutions must be inherently expansive, culminating in "spillover," or must be designed in such a way to cultivate "spillover." This term refers to a situation that is created when the attainment of an original goal within the regional integration context can be assured only by taking further actions, which in turn may create additional situations needing further action to attain regional goals. Spillover may take place from one sector

of the economy to another, or from one economic sector to a political sector, or through the expansion of authority in one of the regional institutions, or by creating additional institutions.

4. Decisions made jointly by nation-states in a region and the regional institutions must lead to an upgrading and the promotion of the common interests of the region.

5. Technocrats must have political "savvy" and skills to help with spillover and to move integration processes forward. They are expected to have close links with the traditional centers of national power, but rather than making frontal attacks on national sovereignty, must move integration forward by stealth.

6. Deliberate linkages between economic and political sectors must be sought to ensure the full working of "the expansive logic of sector integration." The mix of economic and political factors may generate controversy regarding the integration process and thereby lead to a widening of the audience that would be interested and active in integration. The integration process may also be aided by the formation of transnational groups and coalitions that perceive the upward movement of integration to be in their interest and thus strengthen their legitimacy. Many of these groups are likely to consist of business elites whose shared goals and common interests in integration tend to assist in the adoption of regional values[5] and aid in the socialization process.

Several or all of the above strategies have been employed in regional integration schemes since World War II. Whether or not these strategies have been successful can only be gleaned from individual case studies. In the following pages we will concentrate on the description and analysis of three examples of regional integration: the European Community, the Latin American Free Trade Association, and the East African Community. There are many more regional economic organizations aiming at regional integration in Europe, Asia, Africa, and Latin America. Figure 12.1 is a list of these organizations by geographic area.

THE EUROPEAN COMMUNITY

The European Coal and Steel Community

The first experiment in broad economic integration in Western Europe was the European Coal and Steel Community (ECSC), consisting of six countries, France, Germany, Italy, the Netherlands, Belgium, and Luxembourg. The establishment of this Community

Figure 12.1: Regional Economic IGOs

Europe	
Benelux	Belgium, Netherlands, Luxembourg
European Communities (EEC, ECSC, EURATOM)	France, Germany, Britain, Italy, Belgium, Netherlands, Denmark, Ireland
European Free Trade Association	Britain, Sweden, Norway, Denmark, Austria, Switzerland, Portugal
Council for Mutual Economic Assistance (COMECON)	Soviet Union, Poland, East Germany, Czechoslovakia, Bulgaria, Hungary, Romania
Asia	
Asian and Pacific Council (ASPAC)	Japan, South Korea, Taiwan, South Vietnam, Australia, New Zealand, Philippines, Thailand, Malaysia
Mekong Basin Committe	Thailand, Cambodia, Laos, South Vietnam
Africa and Middle East	
Arab League	Algeria, Iraq, Jordan, Kuwait, Lebanon
East African Community (EAC)	Kenya, Tanzania, Uganda
Conseil de l'Entente	Ivory Coast, Niger, Dahomey, Upper Volta, Togo
Union Douaniere et Economique de l'Afrique Centrale (UDEAC)	East Cameroon, Gabon Central African Republic, Congo (Brazzaville)
Union des Etats de l'Afrique centrale (UEAC)	Zaire, Central African Republic, Chad, former Belgian Congo
Union douaniere des etats d'Afrique occidentale (UDEAO)	Dahomey, Ivory Coast, Mali, Mauritania, Niger, Senegal, Upper Volta
Economic Community of West Africa (ECWA)	Dahomey, Ghana, Ivory Coast, Liberia, Mali, Mauritania, Niger, Senegal, Upper Volta
Western Hemisphere	
Organization of American States	United States, Trinidad-Tobago, and the 20 Latin American states (Cuba is excluded)
Central American Common Market (CACM)	Guatemala, El Salvador, Honduras, Nicaragua, Costa Rica
Andean Common Market	Venezuela, Colombia, Ecuador, Peru, Chile, Bolivia
River Plate Basin Group	Argentina, Uruguay, Brazil, Bolivia, Paraguay
Caribbean Free Trade Association	Trinidad-Tobago, Jamaica, Barbados, Guyana, Leeward and Windward Islands

followed a proposal of French Foreign Minister Robert Schumann on May 9, 1950, to merge the entire France-German production of coal and steel. The constituting treaty was signed in April of 1951, named the Treaty of Paris, and the Community entered into force in July of 1952.

Objectives and Purposes   The ECSC included a previous experiment in economic integration undertaken by three small countries, Belgium, Luxembourg, and the Netherlands. In 1944 these three countries signed a customs union agreement; however, their action did not produce the economic union that had been anticipated. The principal economic objective of the new Community was to establish a single market for coal, iron, and steel and eliminate all barriers to free competitive trading, such as tariffs, quantitative restrictions, all forms of price discrimination (including those in transport), and agreements restricting trade and cartels. Overarching the Community was an important political goal, which was to gain a rapprochement between France and Germany and at the same time to control the war-making potential of the latter. On a more visionary plane was a desire to create a unified Europe.

Organization and Structure   The ECSC had four major organs: the High Authority, the Special Council of Ministers, the Common Assembly, and the Court of Justice. The High Authority was one of the executive agencies of the Community and had supranational powers. Decisions rendered by the High Authority, acting by majority vote, could bind directly enterprises in the territories of the six member states, and these decisions could be enforced by the imposition of fines and penalties. The nine members of the High Authority were prohibited from accepting directions from the member governments and were to act only in the general interest of the Community.

The Special Council of Ministers performed two functions. It collaborated with the High Authority in the governance of the Community and at the same time represented the interests of the six member states. It was authorized to issue ordinances in conjunction with the High Authority affecting directly coal and steel enterprises. It was composed of those ministers of the member states especially interested in decisions before the Council. As a consequence, in some instances the ministers represented the foreign ministries; in other instances, they were the economics ministers. The voting procedure in the Council varied from unanimity to two-thirds or simple majority as specified in the treaty.

The Common Assembly had no legislative powers but possessed a limited measure of control over the High Authority. The Assembly could force the resignation of the entire High Authority by a vote of censure and could request the High Authority to reply to all questions put to it by individual Assembly members. The members of the Assembly were elected by their respective parliaments but were not seated in accordance with their nationality, but by political alignments, that is, Christian Democrat, Socialist, and Liberal.

The Court of Justice had and continues to have exclusive jurisdiction for the settlement of disputes between the member states regarding the interpretation and application of the treaty. In addition, private persons and enterprises are permitted to file suits with the Court under certain conditions and obtain judgments when they have suffered damages through acts of the Community.

The European Economic Community and Euratom

By 1955 the ECSC was considered a success. Despite this somewhat premature assessment, it was a partial motivation for political leaders in the six member states to begin planning for a broader European market. Another reason for moving ahead with a more extensive integration scheme was the failure of France to ratify the European Defense Community Treaty, which would have contributed to further political unification through the creation of an integrated armed force of the Six. In 1956 a very important conference took place in Messina, Italy, in which Paul-Henri Spaak, a prominent Belgian statesman, played a leading role, and which produced the blueprint for the European Economic Community (EEC). The basis of this Community was a customs union with gradual elimination over a transition period of twelve years of internal tariffs and nontarrif barriers, as well as the phased establishment of a common external tariff. In addition, a "common market" was established in which labor and capital were to be given free movement, uniform antitrust regulations were to be promulgated, and broad economic policy harmonization was to be attempted. In the agriculture field special schemes were to be instituted to assure a higher income for farmers of the six member states.

Besides the economic aims of increasing the standard of living of the people living in the Community of the Six and making it possible to employ the economies of scale in an enlarged and unified market, political considerations also played a role in the establishment of the EEC. It was hoped that, through the establishment of the Common Market, the Six could gain sufficient strength to compete economically with the United States and perhaps also with the

Soviet Union. It was felt that increased economic strength would eventually give the Six, and later the whole of Western Europe, a political position equal to that of the two superpowers. Moreover, as far as the Atlantic relationship was concerned, Europe would become an equal partner with the United States in the defense of the Free World. Finally, the problem of a divided Germany was given careful thought, and it was anticipated that tying the Federal Republic of Germany closely to the West would reduce, if not eliminate, the feared possibility of Germany either orienting herself toward the East, as she had done after World War I, or adopting a more or less neutral attitude.

At the same time as plans for the EEC were made, favorable consideration was given to the establishment of the European Atomic Energy Community (Euratom). The major reasons for the creation of this Community were apprehension that the present energy sources, mainly coal, would soon be exhausted and nuclear energy would have to take its place in due time. Euratom, therefore, was to coordinate research and technological development for the construction of nuclear power plants, assure the availability of nuclear fuel, and seek to avoid costly duplication of effort among the six member states. For the purpose of achieving its goal, Euratom was to become the basis of a common market for fissionable materials and the center of an extensive supply operation for these materials.

The treaties establishing both Communities were signed in Rome in March 1957 and are frequently referred to as the Treaties of Rome. Both Communities became operational in January 1958. Their institutional framework made use of some of the organs set up earlier for the ECSC. The responsibility of the Court of Justice was broadened to become the judicial arbitrator for the interpretation and application of the two new treaties. The membership of the Common Assembly was enlarged and became the European Parliament. The new name should not lead us to believe that the expanded body had been given additional legislative powers. The only new competences added were a minimal power of debating the budget and very minor control over the executive bodies of the two new communities.

The major executive and legislative functions were vested in a Commission for each of the two Communities and in a single Council of Ministers. In fact, this Council became the common body for all three Communities. According to both the EEC and Euratom Treaties, a finely drawn balance was established between the powers of the two Commissions and the Council. The Commissions were given the right of proposing ordinances and decisions, but the Council was to have the last word in translating these proposals into effective Community orders. Two types of orders were to be distinguished: *regulations*, which had the force of law upon people residing in the six member states and which were directly applicable without any assistance from the national legislatures; and *directives*, which were orders only to the governments of the member states to translate the orders of the Community institutions into law through the normal legislative processes. Proposals were adopted by the Commission by a majority vote. In the Council, however, the initial rule was unanimity, for which a qualified majority was to be substituted in many instances after eight years. We see then that under the two Treaties of Rome the Commissions were to be the motors of the Community decision-making processes and were expected in this particular function to promote the Communities' interests. The Council, on the other hand, performed two functions: it governed with the Commission the operations of the two Communities and, at the same time, represented the interests of the member states.

Britain and the European Community

When the ECSC Treaty was negotiated, Great Britain was invited to join the Community as a charter member. Again during the 1955 and 1956 negotiations aiming at the establishment of the EEC and Euratom, Britain was asked to become a charter member. Concerned that participation in the EEC structure would harm the relations between the United Kingdom and the Commonwealth countries and apprehensive about the supranational aspects of the proposed treaties, the British declined both invitations. However, to the surprise of many on both sides of the Atlantic, the British government announced on July 31, 1961, that it had changed its mind and now wanted to become a member of the Community. The reasons for this change of heart were both political and economic. Britain felt that she would be increasingly affected by whatever happened on the Continent and that she had to take her place in the movement toward greater unity in Europe and perhaps ultimately in the Free World. She was concerned about serious balance-of-payments deficits caused in part by a sharp drop of exports to the Commonwealth countries. Moreover, the European Free Trade Association (EFTA), which had been established under the leadership of Great Britain as an economic response to the EEC, was only a moderate success as a trading group. After long and difficult negotiations in 1961 and 1962, the prospects seemed good that an agreement could be reached for Britain to join the EEC. It was at that time, specifically on January 14, 1963, that General Charles de Gaulle cast his famous veto on the entry of Britain. General de Gaulle's professed reasons were grave doubts about Britain's readiness for membership because her main orientation was insular and directed toward the other shore of the Atlantic, as well as to the Commonwealth countries. But perhaps the most significant considerations for the de Gaulle veto were strategic and political. The membership of Great Britain was likely to threaten France's leadership in the EEC and, in his views, Britain could constitute a Trojan Horse for the American government, on the one hand impeding Western Europe's emergence as a unified power under French leadership and on the other, leading ultimately to an Atlantic Community under American hegemony.[9]

The Status of the Community at the End of the Transition Period (1958–70)

Assessing the integration process at the end of the twelve-year transitional period, we find that, in some sectors, this process had made greater progress than anticipated, while in others, the objectives of the treaties have not only not been reached, but in fact have been aborted.

Spectacular progress had been made in the implementation of the Common Market. The internal tariffs were eliminated completely eighteen months ahead of schedule and the common external tariff put in place at the same time. Although a few problems cropped up occasionally, the cross-national movement of labor, capital, and other economic factors was introduced successfully in accordance with the expectations of the treaties, and the EEC antitrust regulations were applied Community-wide.

Intra-EEC trade grew from $7.5 billion in 1958 to $24.5 billion in 1967, an increase of 326 percent. There was little doubt that the standard of living in the Community had moved upward dramatically and that the general economic posture of the six member states had reached impressive dimensions.

A common agricultural policy (CAP) was instituted, which provided high target prices for basic agricultural commodities to be applied equally in all six member states. To protect these target prices, the conventional machinery of customs duties and quotas was replaced by a scheme of variable import levies for a large number of important agricultural products, including grain, beef, pork, and dairy products. These levies were designed to cover the gap between world prices and the prices fixed for the internal market and to prevent low-priced imports from upsetting the high guaranteed prices of agricultural products.

To assure full success of the CAP, a European Agricultural Guidance and Guarantee Fund (EAGGF) was set up. This fund was used to provide subsidies for restructuring inefficient farms and to finance farm exports that, because of high internal prices, were not competitive on the world market.

While the CAP did indeed increase the incomes of farmers, it also produced large-scale surpluses of such commodities as wheat and butter because no restrictions on acreage were included. Because these surpluses could not continue to grow indefinitely without imposing a tremendous burden on storage facilities in the Community, large subsidies from the EAGGF were required to move these surpluses through sales abroad. The result was that the cost for the operation of the fund soared to $14 billion a year. These foreign sales highlighted the problems of the consumer in the European Community. On the one hand, prices were artificially raised every year and the cost of living increased appreciably; but at the same time, some of the commodities had to be sold at bargain prices abroad. Complicating this problem was the fact that some countries, such as France and the Netherlands, benefited greatly from the system of high prices and subsidies because they produced a large part of the agricultural commodities. On the other hand, Germany, especially, was forced to pay a high share for the support of the Agricultural Fund and received only minor benefits from its payments. Finally, the devaluation of the French franc and the revaluation of the German mark in the second part of 1969 caused havoc in the smooth functioning of the CAP and required new border adjustments in the form of compensatory payments to assure the continued equality of farm prices in all member states.

In July 1967, a major reshuffling took place in the institutional structure of the three Communities. The High Authority of the ECSC and the two Commissions of the EEC and Euratom were merged into one unified Commission. The result was that four major organs were now operating the three Communities, but each one was continuing to function under its own constituent treaty.

While the establishment of the unified Commission appeared to be progress on the path to integration, other developments had a negative effect on the functioning of the institutions and the manner of decision making as laid out by the treaties. De Gaulle's 1963 veto of British membership in the Community ushered in an at first imperceptible shift in the exercise of powers from the Commission to the Council. This became much clearer during a

serious Community crisis in the summer of 1965 when France boy-
cotted the proceedings in the Community organs for six months.
The official reason given was that France's EEC partners had not
fulfilled their promises with respect to the financing of the CAP,
but the real reason for the boycott was the general's violent resistance
to any extension of the EEC Commission's decision-making authority
and his fear that France might lose some of her national prerogatives.[10] Although the crisis was settled in January 1966 by the Foreign
Ministers' Conference of the Six in Luxembourg, the powers of the
Community Commission did not escape unscathed. And the qualified
majority voting procedure in the Council of Ministers, which, according to the EEC Treaty, was to go into effect with respect to many
important issues at the beginning of that year, replacing the unanimity voting requirement, was emasculated by an ambiguous and inconclusive compromise.

Other factors were also responsible for the shift of power from
the Commission to the Council. Nationalism began to be revived
not only in France but in all other Community member states, rekin-
dled principally, but not exclusively, by the actions and philosophies
of General de Gaulle. Another factor was a slowly rising opposition to the progress of political integration on the part of basically
nationalistic-oriented bureaucracies in the member states. As a
consequence of all these factors, the Committee of Permanent
Representatives, composed of national civil servants and subordinated to the Council as an agency responsible for the preparation
of Council decisions, had assumed an increasingly larger role in the
decision-making process of the Community. On the other hand, the
Commission had been limited more and more to technical operations
and the collection of information, with its political influence cut
substantially. Of course, the Commission continued to perform the
functions assigned to it by the treaties, but with considerable reserve
and a measure of passivity. At the same time the morale of the
more than 5,000 civil servants of the Community plummeted, and
by the beginning of 1969 nearly two out of three of these officials
were looking for other jobs.[11]

Relations with Third World Countries

When the six member states decided in 1957 to establish the
Common Market, several of them had possessions in overseas areas,
especially in Africa. France still possessed a considerable colonial
empire on the Dark Continent and had special relations with Tunisia
and Morocco. Algeria, in fact, was part of metropolitan France.

Belgium was installed in the Congo and Rwanda-Burundi. Although Italy had lost its colonial possessions as the result of her defeat in World War II, she was authorized to administer her former possession of Somaliland as a trust territory for the United Nations. In addition, she had special relations with Libya. The Netherlands had no colonial territories in Africa, but had possessions in Southeast Asia (Dutch New Guinea) and in the New World (Surinam and Curaçao). France also had a few overseas territories outside Africa, some of them in the Caribbean and others in the Southwest Pacific. Only Luxembourg and Germany did not have any overseas possessions: Germany was deprived of her colonies after World War I.

In view of the traditionally close economic and cultural relationship between France and her dependencies, the French government threatened to abandon the Rome Treaty negotiations at a rather late stage unless the question of the overseas possessions of the member states was on the negotiating agenda. France wanted either to extend the Common Market to the overseas territories or accord them some sort of preferential treatment. Having guaranteed its possessions a market for tropical commodities at prices often above the world level, France felt that she could not join the EEC if it meant that the African dependencies were to be completely separated from France in the economic sphere.*

Reluctantly, France's partners, too far committed and too eager to get started with the common venture to risk a breakdown of the whole Common Market project, agreed to accommodate the French demand. The formula found was the establishment of an association with most of the overseas territories, especially those located in Africa, which was to be embodied in the EEC Treaty.** The first period of the association was to run for five years. After that the association could be renewed or revised, taking into account the changed circumstances. In addition, a Declaration of Intention opened the way for future negotiations on association agreements with the autonomous parts of the Netherlands (Surinam and the Antilles) that had not been included in the original association, as well as with the independent countries of Morocco, Tunisia, and Libya.

---

* For the guarantee of higher prices, the so-called surprix system, the French required the African countries concerned to buy their capital and consumer goods from France.
** Articles 131–136 of the EEC Treaty. Annex IV of the treaty lists the overseas dependencies included in the association. An implementing convention and a number of special protocols annexed to the EEC Treaty provide the details of the association.

When most of the associated countries in Africa obtained independence in the early 1960s, it became clear that, after the expiration of the first affiliation, the associational relationship with these countries could not be continued by a unilateral decision of the Council of Ministers, as was stipulated by the EEC Treaty. Rather, the associational arrangement had to be based on an international law treaty with full equality accorded to the African states in their negotiations and relations with the Community and the member states. The result was a new association agreement named the Convention of Yaoundé, which was signed on July 20, 1963.*

The broad aims of this convention, concluded for a period of five years, were to expand trade between the associated African states and the EEC members, strengthen the economic independence of the African associates, and contribute thereby to the development of international trade. To accomplish these goals the Convention basically continued the special preference system between the Community and the Associated states established in 1958 by the EEC Treaty, which provided not only for preferential access of goods from the African countries to the Community, but also for Common Market merchandise to the associates.** In addition, financing for development projects and technical assistance in the associated countries was to be made available in the amount of $730 million from the European Development Fund (EDF).

On February 1, 1970, a second five-year agreement was concluded. It continued the two-way preferential trade arrangement although the tariff preferences for the associate countries have been somewhat reduced in comparison with the nonassociated Third World countries. It also continued development aid administered by the EDF, which was increased to $1 billion.

In 1963 negotiations were also initiated for the conclusion of an association agreement with Nigeria. The agreement was signed in 1966, but the content of this association was considerbly less extensive than that of the Yaoundé Convention. No financial aid

---

* The African states involved in this association are Burundi, the Federal Republic of Cameroon, the Central African Republic, the Republic of Chad, the Republic of the Congo (Brazzaville), the Congolese Republic (Leopoldville), the Republic of Dahomey, the Gabon Republic, the Republic of the Ivory Coast, Madagascar, the Republic of Mali, the Islamic Republic of Mauritania, and the Republics of Niger, Rwanda, Senegal, Somalia, Togo, and the Upper Volta.

** Technically, the Convention of Yaoundé arrangements aim at the ultimate creation of individual free trade areas between each associate country and the EEC.

from the EDF was stipulated.[12] However, this agreement never entered into force because several of the parliaments of the Community member states refused ratification in view of the civil war that had broken out as a result of the attempted Biafra secession.

Negotiations were also undertaken to associate the East African Commonwealth countries of Kenya, Tanzania, and Uganda. The content of this agreement was similar to the Nigerian Association. It was concluded in 1968 but did not go into effect until January 1, 1971.

Since 1975 all the associated African countries as well as Nigeria have become affiliated with the EC through the Convention of Lomé, which added a number of former Commonwealth countries in Africa, the Caribbean, and the Western Pacific to the former associates and consolidated the benefits for all affiliates.

In the Mediterranean area the Community also extended its influence by concluding a number of associations and special preferential arrangements. The first of these associations was concluded with Greece and Turkey in the early 1960s. They were followed by preferential agreements with Morocco, Tunisia, Israel, and Spain. Although these agreements were not full-fledged associations, they offer mutual advantages to the Mediterranean countries listed and the Community.

The Community policy toward the Mediterranean was supported by the elites and public opinion in general in the member states. Elite surveys conducted in 1965 and 1970 suggested that the overwhelming majority of the respondents (nearly 97 percent) perceived the associations and other preferential agreements as useful instruments of policy, fully justified in view of the historical ties of these countries to Europe.[13] As such they constituted a positive factor in the integration process, inasmuch as they strengthened the legitimacy of the Community institutions and endowed them with increased utilitarian value in the eyes of the people of Community member states.

DEVELOPMENTS IN THE 1970s
AND PROSPECTS FOR THE FUTURE

At the end of the EEC transition period, it became clear that not all the objectives outlined in the Treaty of Rome had been accomplished and that some policies, such as the CAP, required adjustment. To prepare the path for the EEC to move into the "final" phase, a Summit Conference of the Heads of State and Government was convened in The Hague on December 1 and 2, 1969, and played a decisive role in setting the policy line and development pattern for the 1970s and beyond.

The conference addressed itself to several issues. Until the end of the transitional time, the operations of the Community, including the support of the EAGGF and EDF, had been financed by annual contributions of the member states with amounts determined by their size and economic strength. The conferees agreed to replace progressively the contributions of the member states for the operation of the EAGGF by assigning independent financial resources to the Community, "taking into account all the interests involved," and to strengthen the budgetary powers of the Parliament. This decision was one of the most important decisions made at the conference. Of equal significance was the agreement reached on the principle of admitting new members provided that the applicant countries accepted the provisions and tenor of the Community Treaties. This meant that French opposition to the admission of Great Britain had finally been overcome and the Community membership could be enlarged not only by the accession of Britain, but of other qualified European countries as well. A third significant agreement was to move forward on the path toward economic and monetary union and work toward more intensive technological cooperation. Finally, the Heads of State and Government reaffirmed the will of their governments to pass from the transition period to the final stage of the Communities. In a communiqué issued at the end of the conference, the participants expressed their desire to build a Europe which, "assured of its internal cohesion, true to its friendly relations with outside countries, conscious of the role it has to play in promoting the relaxation of international tension . . . is indispensable if . . . world equilibrium and peace are to be preserved."[14]

There can be no doubt that the Summit Conference at The Hague signified a change in the political direction of Europe. A new spirit, dubbed the "Spirit of The Hague," began to pervade the European Community. The emotional climate and the morale among the civil servants of the community took a turn for the better, and those in the member states who saw in a united Europe the only hope for the future breathed easier. However, while the leaders of the six member states agreed on many issues, many divergent interests and attitudes, as well as dissatisfied forces, remained. A close reading of the final communiqué revealed many ambiguities, although of course by their very nature communiqués are made up of compromises of various kinds. But nowhere in the communiqué was it spelled out what form a united Europe would take. De Gaulle's vision of a Europe of the Fatherlands seemed to continue to lurk in the background as the emphasis on several occasions was on political cooperation among independent states rather than on political integration, a term that was never mentioned. On the other hand, we should note that the extent of cooperation envisaged in the communiqué goes beyond the text of the Community Treaties and as such it must be viewed as progress of sorts toward a unified Europe. Whatever the shortcomings of the conference may have been, one thing was clear: a new political will on the part of the member governments had emerged to intensify the integration of their economies which, by necessity, would also require a strengthening of the institutional machinery beyond the declared objective of increasing the budgetary powers of the Parliament. In addition, the removal of all obstacles to the initiation of the negotiations with the countries seeking membership in the European Community (EC) opened the vista of an enlarged Europe moving toward unification, although it was not certain whether the increased number of EC members would produce more and deeper disparities of objectives and thereby constitute a hindrance to effective political integration.

Some of the fruits of The Hague Conference were not long in coming. On December 22, 1969, the Community was authorized to acquire its own financial resources, and the budgetary powers of the European Parliament were strengthened. For the Community to acquire its own financial resources, a gradual approach was employed. During an interim period from January 1, 1971, to the end of 1974, all levies on agricultural imports into the Community were to be turned over to the EC institutions immediately, while a gradual transfer to the Community institutions was put into effect for customs duties on other imported goods. Beginning in 1975 a certain percentage of the internal tax receipts of the member governments were also turned over to the Community so that by 1978, all expenditures of the Community, that is, the EAGGF and the operating expenses of the institutions, could be met from the above revenues.

The budgetary powers of the Parliament were only increased modestly and again this was done on a gradual basis. The Council, and to a lesser degree the Commission, retain much of the budgeting authority, but the parliamentary deputies are given the significant opportunity to modify the budget presented to them and in fact may increase its overall amount within certain narrow limitations.

The grant by the EC member states of clearly defined financial resources accruing directly to the Community and the expansion of the Parliament's budget authority are major steps on the path toward political integration. Only four years earlier, the Community came close to collapse and passed through nine months of almost complete stagnation over the issue of autonomous financial resources and an increase in the budgetary powers of Parliament when de Gaulle strenuously objected to them. Now, new institutional and operational principles have been introduced into the Community framework which raise the position of the Parliament to that of a more important partner of the Council and Commission in fiscal affairs. When linked to the creation of independent Community resources, it is evident that a highly political problem has been solved in favor of the common interest. This recognition of the common interest was made possible to a large degree by the convergence of national interests in the agricultural field. The need for financing the CAP and agreement on the terms for carrying out this task were important motivations and the impetus for a renewed political integration movement. The meeting of this need is an excellent example of the process of functional "spillover," a vital element for the progress of integration. To accomplish the objective of financing the agricultural program in the Community, in which all member states were interested because of domestic political considerations, a broadening of the powers originally assigned to the Community institutions was regarded as necessary, and the appropriate decisions were made for this purpose.[15]

Another result of the Summit Conference at The Hague has been progress in the coordination of the economic and monetary policies of the member states. Motivated largely by the currency disturbances in 1968 and 1969, which were, to a considerable extent, the consequences of divergent economic trends within the Community and ultimately led to the devaluation of the French franc and the revaluation of the German mark, the Council of Ministers recognized on January 26, 1970, that the harmonization of these trends was the only alternative to a constant repetition of these undesirable events. As a move toward common economic and monetary policies in the Community, the Council adopted a program consisting of establishing definitive economic guideposts for the period from 1970 to 1975 and working up an inventory of the main structural reforms to be accomplished at the national and Community levels. In addition, a joint currency float was instituted (the so-called snake arrangement) under which the currencies of the EC member states were to fluctuate only within a 2.25 percent margin. Some member states (Great Britain, Ireland, and Italy) did not participate, however, and France has moved in and out of the snake.

Of course, these were only the first, far from perfect, steps on a long political journey. While the immediate aim had to be the prevention of greater divergencies of the economic policies pursued by the member countries, the more significant task for the future is to ensure the convergence of the broad trends of national economic policies and their mutual compatibility. This means that the purely national definition of policy objectives must give way to policy decisions arrived at in common and with strict attention to the common interest of the Community. Experience during the past decade has shown that this is not an easy undertaking, particularly since it may well involve added delegation of normally national authority to the central institutions of the Community and restraint on the part of the member governments in the exercise of their national prerogatives. Even in crucial areas such as energy, full agreement on a common policy has not been possible so far, despite very comprehensive and reasonable proposals by the Commission to the Council of Ministers.[16]

Because the economic and monetary unions need to be achieved simultaneously if they are to provide maximum benefits for the member states as well as the Community as a whole, the Commission elaborated a three-stage plan for their implementation. This plan, which includes the creation of a unified financial market and fiscal harmonization, set 1978 as the primary target date, although the final stage may be continued to 1980.[17] Basically the Commission plan reflects the needs of the member states to avoid currency disturbances of the kind that took place in 1968–69, because the proper functioning of the CAP is dependent upon holding currency fluctuations to a minimum. Similarly, the free movement of industrial goods is hampered by major deviations from traditional currency levels.

The plan for the 1970s developed by the Commission at the beginning of the period has been complicated by the entry of Great Britain, Ireland, and Denmark into the Community. Great Britain made its second application to full membership in May 1967. Although initially de Gaulle rejected again Britain's membership, President Pompidou took a more favorable attitude in 1969, and negotiations initiated in 1971 culminated in the accession of the United Kingdom beginning January 1, 1973.

To ease the economic problems for the new members caused by their entry into the Community, a five-year transitional period was worked out during which the three countries were to adjust themselves to the Community system. Moreover, some concessions were made by the Community for some of the specific problems that British membership would generate for the economies of some of the Commonwealth countries, especially New Zealand. To assist the developing countries of the Commonwealth in Africa, the Caribbean area, and the Pacific, an opportunity was provided for them to negotiate association agreements with the enlarged Community during the transitional period. The Convention of Lomé, signed in

1975 and briefly discussed earlier, added these countries to the association arrangement established under the Yaoundé system and brought the number of EC affiliated countries in Sub-Saharan Africa, the Caribbean, and the Pacific to over fifty.*

It is important to note that, while public opinion in the late 1960s was favorable toward Britain's joining the Community, by 1970, 63 percent of Britishers queried were opposed to such a move. The main concern of many Britishers was an expected increase in the cost of living as a result of the Community's Common Agricultural Policy. There was also fear that the traditional sovereignty of Parliament would be undermined by the powers given to the Community institutions. As a consequence, entry into the Community aroused an intensive political battle. The Conservative Government of Prime Minister Edward Heath was pushing for accession, while the bulk of the Labour Party attempted to prevent membership in the Community. Nevertheless, the British Parliament approved by a relatively narrow margin Britain's membership in the Common Market, and a constitutionally unusual referendum, held subsequently, showed that a substantial majority of Britishers supported this step.

In Denmark the proposed entry into the Common Market also aroused considerable opposition. However, a referendum indicated that a majority of the Danes favored membership although many Danish people continued to have reservations about their country's new relationship with the Community even after Denmark became a member in 1973. Only in Ireland did public opinion express itself generally in favor of membership because the Irish people felt that they could gain major advantages from the Community's Agricultural Policy and were anticipating Community funds for promoting regional development schemes within Ireland.

The concerns of the British and Danes began to generate frictions almost from the day the Community was enlarged. Although the new members had accepted the Community rules and proce-

---

* Bahamas, Barbados, Benin, Botswana, Burundi, Cameroon, Cape Verde, Central African Republic, Chad, Comoros, Congo, Dahomey, Djibuti, Equatorial Guinea, Ethiopia, Fiji, Gabon, Gambia, Ghana, Grenada, Guinea, Guinea-Bissau, Guyana, Ivory Coast, Jamaica, Kenya, Lesotho, Liberia, Madagascar, Malawi, Mali, Mauritania, Mauritius, Niger, Nigeria, Papua New Guinea, Republic of Seychelles, Republic of Surinam, Rwanda, Samoa, São Tomé and Principe, Senegal, Sierra Leone, Somalia, Sudan, Swaziland, Tanzania, Togo, Tonga, Trinidad-Tobago, Uganda, Upper Volta, Western Samoa, Zaïre, Zambia.

dures, the British government attempted to initiate changes in the CAP. In this effort it found a willing ally in the German government. Another problem for the Community was the continued weakness of the British pound, which was apt to hold back the EC plans for an economic and monetary union. Although the majority of the Community members agreed on a common currency alignment, the British insisted on keeping the pound sterling out of this arrangement, and here they were joined by the Italians and the Irish. Obviously, as long as a common agreement on currency arrangements of *all* Community members cannot be achieved, progress toward the economic and monetary union is in jeopardy.

Because of the anxieties described above, the "Spirit of The Hague" and the consequent forward movement toward political integration has lost some of its momentum. The surpluses generated by the CAP, which led to large accumulations of butter that had to be sold at cut-rate prices to the Soviet Union in 1973, deepened the unhappiness over the many undesirable consequences of the agricultural policy. While public opinion surveys suggest continuing support for the unification of Europe, few of the respondents really understand the full meaning of this process. On the other hand, important political and administrative elites in all member states have anxieties and reservations about the process of political integration, although they do not always express them explicitly.[18] The anticipated favorable impact of the superior technological knowledge and political skill of the Community civil servants on the process of integration has not materialized. On the contrary, many of the national civil servants in the member states show animosity and low esteem for the technocrats in the Community service. While business and agricultural elites look toward the Community as offering many rewards for their economic interests, their attitudes provide only limited support for the legitimacy of the Community and do not translate themselves in broad ideological acceptance of a region-state. Nationalistic tendencies, reinforced by perceptions that business and agriculture receive the lion's share of the benefits flowing from the integration process, have been successful in halting the "expansive logic of integration" and have cast doubt on the adequacy and explanatory powers of functionalist and neofunctionalist theories. Despite the fact that the European Parliament has received a small increase in powers, and its members will be elected by direct suffrage beginning in 1979, it is uncertain how much elections will aid the prestige and legitimacy of the European Parliament.[19]

The application by Greece for EC membership and the likely requests for accession later by Portugal, Spain, and Turkey may result in a Community of thirteen members with quite different political backgrounds and differing economic levels. Thus the Community might become a very unwieldy organization in which progress toward political integration is most doubtful. Enlargement, on the other hand, could be a long-run positive factor for integration because of the tremendously increased economic power of the Community.

The economic strength of the EC exceeds that of the United States in certain areas. In international trade the Community has become the most powerful unit in the world, and this position has been strengthened further by the free trade arrangements made with the remaining members of EFTA, Norway, Sweden, Austria, Switzerland, and Portugal. This newly found strength, applauded by the people in all Community countries, has generated perceptions of pride and aroused strong sentiments that this economic strength should be transformed into political power and that this political power in turn may require the harmonization of foreign and defense policies. It is premature to speculate on the precise effects these aspirations may have on the process of political integration, but we should note that efforts to develop common foreign policies by the EC have made progress. Two methods have been employed for the coordination of these policies. First, the Community treaties, especially the one establishing the Common Market, contain specific provisions for a common commercial policy which, despite earlier resistance by the member states, are nearing full implementation. These provisions also form the legal basis for the association agreements discussed earlier, and because these agreements are exclusive Community foreign policy instruments, they have served as an important tool for the formulation of a common foreign policy approach toward the Third World. Second, and perhaps most important, the EC member states have created a policy-coordinating mechanism outside the Community treaties through the establishment of periodic institutionalized meetings of foreign ministers of the Nine. The staff work for these meetings is being handled by the so-called Political Committee, which consists of the political directors of the foreign ministries of the member governments. This intergovernmental policy-coordinating mechanism has been very useful in the harmonization of foreign policies and continues to be employed extensively. The common stands of the EC countries regarding the negotiations on European Security and Cooperation in Helsinki and Belgrade and with respect to the North-South dialogue on raw materials of the Third World were the result of this mechanism.

THE LATIN AMERICAN
FREE TRADE ASSOCIATION

While economic integration in Western Europe has been a resounding success and political integration has made some progress, the situation in Latin America with respect to regional integration has been generally disappointing. Basic economic and political differences between the two regions account in part for this dissimilarity. Western Europe is marked generally by a high level of homogeneity in social achievement, substantial, although somewhat uneven, economic development, and a fair amount of political stability; in Latin America the opposite is true. Social inequality is pronounced; the illiteracy rate varies from 14 percent in Argentina to 89 percent in Haiti; GNPs and per capita incomes in Latin America differ widely; overland transportation facilities between most countries are poor; and political instability is proverbial.

Integration Motivations

The intellectual leadership for understanding the need for regional integration in Latin America came from the U.N. Economic Commission of Latin America (ECLA) and especially its Secretary General, Dr. Raul Prebisch, who headed ECLA from 1950 to 1963. There were no political pressures for integration in Latin American as existed in Europe after World War II, but there were forces tending in the direction of continental solidarity. These forces were matched by equally strong feelings of nationalism. Thus, the initiation of integration in Latin America had to depend much more on economic arguments than it did in Europe.[20] Dr. Prebisch and his ECLA staff were able to present these arguments convincingly, partly because almost every government in Latin America had at least one prominent member, often at cabinet level, who had served on the ECLA staff or in an ECLA training course. ECLA was highly respected all over Latin America, which helped to convince doubting national politicians and administrators.

An impelling force for regional integration was the decline of trade among Latin American countries from 1955 to 1961. While in 1955 this trade amounted to $700 million, it dropped to $510 million in 1961 or 25 percent, yet during the same periods imports from the rest of the world increased by more than 20 percent.[21] Moreover, existing trade consisted mainly of primary products, whereas economic integration might lead to the creation of region-wide markets for manufactured goods.

The LAFTA Treaty Provisions

The negotiations leading ultimately to the establishment of the Latin American Free Trade Association (LAFTA) began in 1958 with consultation among only four countries, Argentina, Brazil, Chile, and Uruguay. These negotiations were later joined by representatives of Bolivia, Paraguay, Peru, and Mexico. Understandably, the Central American states stood aside as they were in the process of initiating their own integration experiment, the Central American Common Market.

In February the Treaty of Montevideo was signed setting up LAFTA. Argentina, Brazil, Chile, Mexico, Paraguay, Peru, and Uruguay were the charter members. Colombia and Ecuador acceded in 1961, and Venezuela and Bolivia, in the middle of the 1960s. The objectives of the treaty were the creation of a regional unified trading area through the gradual elimination of tariffs and other trade barriers, the coordination and harmonization of the national economies, and ultimately the establishment of a "common market" with a common external tariff and cross-national free movement of economic factors.

The gradual elimination of tariffs was to be accomplished by 1973 after a twelve-year transitional period and was to be carried out through two different negotiating processes. One set of negotiations pertaining to the so-called National Schedules was to be conducted bilaterally every year on an item-by-item basis. These negotiations were to produce tariff reductions of not less than 8 percent of the weighted average tariff applicable to third countries and the elimination of individual nontariff barriers. The concessions did not need to be granted to all members of LAFTA simultaneously, but only to one or more for reciprocal concessions. The potential for protracted haggling inherent in this arrangement is obvious.

The second set of negotiations involved the so-called Common Schedule made up of those products on which the LAFTA member states agreed to remove all restrictions irrevocably. These negotiations were to be held every three years, and each negotiating session was to account for 25 percent of all trade between LAFTA members resulting in restriction-free trade of substantially all items shipped by the end of the transitional period.

One of the most important provisions of the Treaty of Montevideo is for joint industrial planning for the Latin American region as a whole. A major instrument for this purpose is the negotiation of complementarity agreements for particular industrial sectors. The main objective of these agreements is the coordination of the manufacturing facilities of individual companies and industries in two or more countries in such a way as to bring about the specialized production of particular parts in different countries to be assembled later in one of these countries or a third country. It was hoped that such specialization would produce a larger flow of industrial products across national borders and promote economic integration. While industrial integration was given major emphasis, the Treaty of Montevideo largely neglected agriculture and limited itself to exhortatory rhetoric.

In view of the widely differing levels of economic development among its members, the LAFTA Treaty contains a number of escape clauses and special exceptions. Some of these provisions offer special advantages and progress to the countries of lowest development—Bolivia, Ecuador, and Paraguay—and the treaty recognizes that certain countries, such as Chile, Colombia, Peru, Uruguay, and Venezuela, have "insufficient markets."

The LAFTA Institutions

Two major organs serve LAFTA: the Conference of Contracting Parties and the Standing Executive Committee. The Conference is required to meet at least once a year, makes general policy, and makes decisions by a minimum of two-thirds vote of the member states, "providing that no negative vote is cast" (Article 38). In practice, then, unanimity in decision-making prevails.

The Standing Executive Committee is responsible for supervising the implementation of the Montevideo Treaty. It is composed of one delegate and one alternate appointed by each member government. It should be stressed that these delegates function as representatives of their governments and, as a collectivity, do not possess supranational power.

The Committee is served by a Secretariat headed by a secretary general and staffed by an international civil service to carry out technical and administrative duties. A number of study and planning commissions have been created, and ad hoc committees are used for special purposes. The staff of the Secretariat is small compared with the civil service of the European Community, and its office facilities are tiny in comparison with the imposing edifices in Brussels.

Disappointing Results

Despite the good intentions reflected in the Treaty of Montevideo, the progress of integration in LAFTA has been minimal and faltering. The annual negotiations on tariff and nontariff reductions under the National Schedules have become less meaningful each year and now accomplish virtually nothing. Initially, the emphasis in these negotiations had been on products that were customarily imported from outside the region and therefore could not affect the flow of internal trade. Other items whose tariffs were cut were mainly primary products that already were shipped traditionally within Latin America. When it came to additional products, economic and political vested interests in the member states made themselves felt and opposed any decision in National Schedule negotiations for reducing barriers. The situation turned out to be even worse in the Common Schedule negotiations. After restrictions were removed on 200 items, subsequent attempts to expand the list failed completely.[22]

Despite these failures, the dollar value of intra-LAFTA trade expanded in the early 1970s and nearly tripled from the low point of 1961. The composition of this trade has also changed and includes now a larger share of manufactured and semimanufactured goods. Yet even this increased intraregional trade remains a small percentage of the LAFTA members' total trade with the world.

In the field of industrial complementarity, progress has also been very meager. Only four complementarity agreements have been signed involving mostly American firms in the data processing and electronic industries. Agreements regarding fertilizers, paper products, glass, and agricultural machinery have been under discussion and are to be executed in the future.

A bright point in LAFTA's activities has been the establishment of a regional payments system which should make it easier for intraregional trade to expand. Another possible benefit flowing from the efforts of LAFTA is the spawning of subregional organizations aimed at economic integration: the Andean Common Market joining Chile, Peru, Bolivia, Ecuador, Colombia, and Venezuela; and the River Plate Basin Group comprised of Argentina, Brazil, Bolivia, Paraguay, and Uruguay. The prospects for successful economic integration appear to be better for the Andean than the River Plate organization, but if even mediocre success could be achieved, it might aid the fortunes of LAFTA.[23]

Prospects

Despite LAFTA's failure to attain its objectives, the chiefs of state of the OAS nations convened in 1970 in Punta del Este and advocated the creation of a full-scale Latin American common market to be operative by 1985. The Declaration of Presidents of America resulting from this meeting proposed a full-scale customs union, free movement of capital and labor, freely convertible currencies, policy harmonization in all economic and related social areas, and institutions endowed with supranational powers.[24] This declaration is of course not a treaty with binding obligations and represents nothing more than pleasing rhetoric for the future. The much less pleasant reality is that the future of LAFTA is bleak as far as can be judged at present. The annual negotiations on the National Schedule have been stretched out, and the obligatory reduction of 8 percent has been lowered to 2.9 percent. The work on the Common Schedule has been postponed again and again, and the chances are not bright that the objectives of the LAFTA Treaty can be attained by 1980. The prospect of a full-blown common market appears nebulous indeed.

Why have the forces of functionalism and the neofunctionalist strategies been so ineffective in LAFTA? Perhaps the most obvious reason integration has not moved forward vigorously is the asymmetry in economic development of the LAFTA member states. The more developed member countries have more access to foreign capital for investment purposes and possess greater managerial resources and higher technological capabilities. For this reason, they are in a better position to penetrate and dominate the regional market. This potential penetration, however, creates apprehension in the less developed countries of Latin America that their industries are too weak to compete with those of the more affluent sister nations and that their economies may suffer from the impact of integration. Governmental leaders and other elites therefore tend to gain the impression of an unequal distribution of benefits and costs flowing from the integration scheme, which prevents full support of this scheme by all LAFTA countries and severely impairs its functioning.

Another reason for the LAFTA failure is the conviction of many business executives that the reward in profits and enlarged sales from the enlarged regional market involves high risks and perhaps a slow return from invested capital. They prefer a quick return and maximum security with strong protection from foreign competition, advantages they have traditionally received from their governments. Moreover, there is always the pervasive fear that the United States was promoting a common market in the Southern Hemisphere to better "exploit" Latin America.

Although a large number of meetings convened during the early years of LAFTA discussed possible profit and marketing benefits for specific industries and advocated transnational coordination of industrial plans and policies, there were few concrete results. While during these years LAFTA officials were successful in stimulating the formation of transnational business and professional groups, their impact on corporate and governmental decision making was minimal. On the contrary, LAFTA goals were often identified with possible loss of jobs and reduction of profits by nationalistic governments, and none of the news media made any sustained efforts to oppose this kind of thinking by explaining in popular terms the idea and benefits of a unified Latin America.

As in Europe, LAFTA technocrats and officials have not been able to sell their national colleagues on the advantages LAFTA could bring through an expansion of functions and an increase in living standards in all the member states. Rather, the LAFTA idea has remained an inspiration only for the LAFTA civil servants themselves. On the other hand, influential military leaders in Latin America have spread the belief that integration is a communist plot. They have given as one reason for this belief the fact that the integration movement was largely the brainchild of ECLA, a U.N. organization, and they stressed the similarity of some of the LAFTA concepts to the Soviet plans for the specialization of industries in Eastern Europe.[25] Whatever credence may be given to the claims of Latin American military leaders, it is clear that national rivalries and the concerns of governmental leaders to retain their position of power by being able to point to economic successes in their own countries have diminished Latin American hopes for economic integration for the future and that political integration is completely out of the question.

It is interesting to note that the Central American Common Market (CACM), consisting of Guatemala, San Salvador, Honduras, Nicaragua, and Costa Rica, ultimately suffered a fate similar to that of LAFTA, although it enjoyed considerable success and vigor during the first seven or eight years of its existence. Internal tariffs were eliminated rapidly, and the carefully planned and coordinated establishment of various industrial plants in the five member states to assist in the regional integration process seemed to take hold. But national rivalries and jealousies, caused in part by perceptions of unequal distribution of benefits and costs for individual member countries, led to virtual disintegration, although the CACM framework continues to operate.

THE EAST AFRICAN COMMUNITY

Integration Motivations

Like its Latin American counterpart, the U.N. Economic Commission for Africa (ECA) has been a major stimulator for regional integration schemes in Africa. In view of the fragmentation of previous colonial areas into many very small countries, some of the newly independent governments, faced with very limited national markets, have found it difficult to "go it alone" economically. Broad studies of the ECA have suggested possibilities of major industrial development if carefully selected industries for wider regional markets could be established. In Central and West Africa, four organizations primarily devoted to regional economic integration exist at present. They are the Central African Customs and Economic Union (UDEAC, Union Douanière et Economique de l'Afrique Centrale); the Union of Central African States (UEAC, Union des Etats de l'Afrique Centrale), set up in 1968; the West African Customs Union (UDEO, Union Douanière des Etats de l'Afrique Occidentale); and the Economic Community of West Africa (ECWA), cutting across divisions of language and colonial history, set up in 1967.* There are other regional IGOs in Central and Western Africa, but their interest in regional economic integration is only peripheral.

In East Africa economic integration efforts date back to colonial times and have been more intensive than in West and Central Africa. The East African Community (EAC), consisting of Kenya, Tanzania, and Uganda, is an excellent example of African regional integration; therefore, the remainder of this section will be devoted to a brief review of its history and contemporary development.

EAC Backgrounds

The foundation of the EAC was laid by the British colonial regime when in 1917 a customs union was set up between Kenya and Uganda. By 1927 the British had created a common market in which

---

* For the composition of these IGOs see Figure 12.1.

Tanganyika, the forerunner of present-day Tanzania, joined the first two East African countries. In the 1930s functional cooperation was broadened to include postal and telecommunications administration, meteorology, locust control, air service, and higher education. After World War II, a regional bureaucracy and a special legislature were provided for the common services, and by 1961, when independence was approaching, the structure was given the name of East African Common Services Organization (EASCO).

EASCO consisted of an Authority composed of the three heads of government which made decisions by unanimity and a Central Legislative Assembly indirectly elected by the legislatures of the three countries. A secretary general aided by 300 senior civil servants was headquartered in Nairobi, Kenya's capital, to furnish the necessary administrative support. The three most important services were the East African Railways and Harbors, East African Airways, and East African Posts and Telegraphs. Total full-time employment of EASCO in the early 1960s was nearly 21,000 people.

In their common market the East Africans enjoyed almost free movement of goods, labor, and capital. After World War II trade among member states grew more rapidly than did East African trade with the outside world and reached about 20 percent of external exports by 1964. At the same time, Kenya's exports of light manufactured goods to Uganda and Tanganyika rose impressively. When this caused loss of customs revenue for the latter two countries because goods imported from Kenya were not subject to duty payment, a fund based on 40 percent of company income taxes and 6 percent of customs and excise revenues was established to compensate Uganda and Tanganyika.

Despite these efforts to equalize benefits and costs flowing from economic integration, Uganda and Tanzania have become increasingly dissatisfied with the common market. Although proposals for an East African federation were discussed after all three countries had obtained their independence by the end of 1963, and Tanzania's President Nyerere was especially enthusiastic about such a development, the project was abandoned in May 1964.[26] At the same time the tendency of new industries to cluster in Kenya, which had better managerial and labor resources than her partners, a more centralized location, and a more developed transportation net, aroused growing misgivings and apprehension. Friction also developed from the coordination of development plans, and disputes arose over the distribution of benefits from the various services. Existing regional links were broken in such key fields as currency administration and tourism, and restrictions were imposed unilaterally on intercountry trade. After Tanganyika merged with Zanzibar and became Tanzania, her government, previously the strongest advocate of cooperation and federation, threatened to withdraw from the common market because of the inequalities of benefits and costs, and the whole integration structure was close to collapse. It received, however, a new lease on life with the signing of the Kampala Agreement in 1964, which was modified in 1965 in the Ugandan town of Mbale.

The Kampala-Mbale Agreement sought to redress the balance between the three partners by rectifying trade inequities through the imposition of quotas on specified items, encouraging increased production in a deficit country by firms operating in two or more countries, and by stressing allocation of new industrial plants in Uganda and Tanzania. However, the Kampala-Mbale effort did not prove effective in stemming disintegration. In fact, by 1966 Kenya's share of intraregional shipments had climbed to 66 percent. Whereas Kenya's common market trade showed a favorable balance of nearly $50 million, Tanzania had a deficit of nearly $30 million and Uganda $15 million.[27]

Establishment and Institutions of EAC

It was obvious that a new approach to integration was needed if the climate of doom and uncertainty in East Africa was to be changed. This new approach was realized when, in December 1967, a fifteen-year East African Cooperative Treaty was signed establishing the EAC. This new organization supersedes EASCO and sets up an East African Common Market. To achieve a measure of equality in benefits, it provides for a complex transfer tax system to by imposed temporarily on intraregional imports under specific conditions by those states that have a deficit in total trade of manufactured goods with the other two member states.[28] Moreover, fiscal incentives for industrial development were designed to benefit Tanzania and Uganda with each to receive 38.75 percent of total investment and the remaining 22.5 percent going to Kenya. The common services, hitherto administered by EASCO, are now in the hands of the Community, but the headquarters of the individual services, such as Posts and Telegraphs, are distributed among the three member states.

Several organs have been established for operation of the EAC. An East African Authority, consisting of the presidents of the three member states, has general direction and control over the executive function of the Community. Five councils consisting of various ministers from the three governments supervise the execution of specific functions, such as Common Market operations or finance. All decisions are made by unanimous votes in these bodies. An East African Legislative Assembly provides territorial representation; each country appoints the same number of members to the Assembly. A Common Market Tribunal has the task of adjudicating disputes between the member states arising from the operation of the common market. Finally, an East African Development Board has been set up. None of the EAC institutions has supranational powers, and state sovereignty of the member countries has not been seriously challenged by the EAC system.

Problems and Results

Although the East African Cooperative Treaty aimed at producing a viable institutional framework accepting the reality of national interests and attempted to reduce centrifugal tendencies through an equalization of opportunities in the integration scheme and the Common Services, success in achieving these objectives remains elusive. Not only has the percentage share of intraregional exports in relation to total EAC exports been falling after reaching a peak briefly in 1967, but Uganda's and Tanzania's shipments to Kenya have also shown considerable decreases and continued deficits since then.[29] Moreover, the industrialization scheme weighted in favor of the two less developed partners does not appear to work well, and strong grievances have been voiced about Kenyans taking away jobs of Ugandans in Uganda where unemployment is higher than in Kenya. Clearly, investors cannot be forced to construct plants in Uganda or Tanzania when they consider market and labor conditions more favorable in Kenya.

Pure political problems also contribute to the Common Market difficulties. In 1971, after General Idi Amin took over the presidency in Uganda following a military coup, Uganda claimed that the whole Community was threatened by "ideological hardliners"[30] in Tanzania. The military hostilities between the two countries in 1972 have not helped the situation, although the relationship seems to have improved now. All three countries, independent only a little more than a decade, are still engaged in nation-building, and political independence is a prime consideration for governmental leaders who wish to retain power. It is obvious that the civil servants of the EAC have not been able to convince their national colleagues and the national political leadership of the value of political integration for the promotion of common East African interests. But undoubtedly the greatest drawback in the whole EAC system is the perception and reality of the unequal distribution of benefits and costs stemming from the integration process, which has resulted in renewed fragmentation and disintegration after a well-functioning common market existed under the former colonial rule.

The same problem has beset the operation of the Central and West African regional integration schemes. UDEAC, which attempted to equalize benefits and costs through the creation of a Solidarity Fund and the appropriate distribution of a special tax (*taxe unique*) to the member states, has achieved limited progress. But dissatisfaction about the distribution of benefits, especially the allocation of industrial projects, persists, and domestic political problems render the outlook cloudy. The future of UEAC is even less clear and UDEAO has been largely ineffective. Although the ECWA has a much larger potential market and more widespread trading links than the other groupings, it is too early to assess whether this IGO can overcome the differences in development levels of its members and make a real contribution to regional integration.

SUMMARY

Integration in an international regional context may be **economic, social,** or **political.**

Economic integration is understood not only as the abolition of discriminatory practices between national economic units, but also as a "growing together" of the national economies of several states to ensure optimal operation of the total economy in an international region. The levels of economic integration are, from low to high: **free trade area, customs union, common market, economic union,** and **monetary union.**

Regional **social integration** may be defined as the development of a transnational society within a region whose members share values, goal preferences, symbols of identity, and modes of communication.

The four subcategories of **political integration** are **institutional, policy, attitudinal,** and **security** integration.

Necessary for the achievement of increased integration is the process of **socialization.** Functionalists such as David Mitrany postulate that states may be pushed to higher levels of integration by **functionalism,** a process of cross-national satisfaction of economic and social needs that will transcend political problems and national loyalties. Basic to functionalism is the separation of welfare from politics. The **neofunctionalist** school advocates a number of strategies to give functionalism a thrust in particular regions, and all have been employed in regional integration schemes since World War II.

Three examples of regional integration are the **European Community,** the **Latin American Free Trade Association (LAFTA),** and the **East African Community (EAC).** In each of these instances a purposeful scheme was elaborated to initiate the integration process. Institutions were set up to guide this process, and the force of **functionalism** began to become operative initially and succeeded in satisfying some economic needs through cross-national collaboration. In the European Community, at least, the expansive logic of functionalism produced **spillover** across economic sectors and, to a lesser degree, in the institutional framework. In the EAC case the broadening of the functional context occurred during colonial rule and was perhaps inposed rather than evolved. In the LAFTA experiment sectoral spillover did not take place to any extent.

The basic functionalist tenet of separating welfare from politics was confirmed initially in all three cases; however, when efforts were made to apply the neofunctional strategy of linking economic and political sectors, it failed completely in LAFTA and the EAC, although it is not quite clear how intentional the application of this strategy was in these instances. In the European Community, these efforts led to a broadening of the audience and clientele and increased the politicization of the integration process in some instances, but it did not seem to help in advancing the total integration process. The reason may well be that those groups whose political sensitivities had been aroused, such as farmers in France, were concerned only with obtaining short-range material benefits and had no desire to commit themselves to political integration. Any efforts to broaden the audience in order to strengthen the integration process in East Africa and Latin America failed because most business and political elites in Latin America and governmental leadership groups in Africa were strongly opposed.

Whatever strategy was introduced to utilize the civil services of the regional institutions to persuade national administrative and political elites in their region of the value of political integration and to advance the cause of political unification was unsuccessful. Even in the European Community, where such a strategy seemed to have initial chances of success, it failed because national civil servants perceived their self-interests to lie with the continuance and strengthening of national institutions, while most elected and political leaders could not see major advantages in political integration for their own interests and careers.

While there is no doubt that, especially in Europe, cross-national collaboration has set in motion a **socialization** process favoring the adoption of regional values and norms that could increase support for political unification, it has not produced a sufficiently strong ideological commitment to overcome the powerful nationalistic tendencies pervading the member countries of the European Community. In the developing countries, this socialization process, if it got started at all, has been extremely weak.

Finally, perhaps the strongest impediment to the process of economic integration and even more so of political integration is the inequality in the distribution of benefits and costs to the member states. In this connection, we should note that the trade and investment patterns differ between Western Europe and the two Third World regions. Intraregional trade in Western Europe has always been very high, but in the LAFTA and EAC regions this trade is limited, while external trade with Europe and the United States is much more substantial. Regional investment is spread more or less evenly throughout Western Europe, while within LAFTA and the EAC, the more economically advanced parts of the member states are preferred. These factors, coupled with the relatively equal level of economic development in the European Community, have resulted in a distribution of benefits and costs that may have aroused occasional expressions of dissatisfaction by the member governments, but has generally been viewed as acceptable. The trade and investment patterns prevailing in much of the Third World have contributed to the inequality of distribution of benefits and costs in LAFTA and the EAC and have generated fragmenting and disintegrating tendencies in these regions.

All in all, our case studies demonstrate that the pragmatic-interest politics associated with the satisfaction of social and economic needs, which are the heart of the functional theory, are too frail to overcome powerful emotion-laden political interests, reinforced by strong nationalistic commitments. The instinct for self-preservation of political and governmental leaders can constitute a powerful impediment to the forces of functionalism, and such an impediment may grow even more powerful if it is related to concerns regarding the integrity and national security of individual member states.

Thus we must conclude that, while functionalism is indeed a force for change in international relations, it appears to be too weak to bring about by itself far-reaching changes in the political map of the international arena.

Nevertheless, despite the limited success in political integration in Western Europe and failures in economic integration in various parts of the Third World, regional integration constitutes a rational means to surmount the economic shortcomings of individual nation-states and therefore remains an attractive mechanism for such countries to reach higher levels of economic development, as recent efforts at regional organization in Africa and Asia have demonstrated. The long-range consequences are a gradual transformation of existing international relations primarily in the important economic sphere and a shift in the global distribution of economic and political power that may well accelerate in the future. An example of these changes can be seen in the relative distribution of economic power between the United States and the European Community. In spite of the lag in political integration in the EC, its economic power and worldwide influence have grown appreciably during the 1970s while the corresponding international economic influence of the United States has declined somewhat.

NOTES

1. Joseph S. Nye, "Comparative Integration: Concept and Measurement," *International Organization,* vol. 22, no. 4 (1968), pp. 855–880. See also Nye's "Comparing Common Markets: A Revised Neo-Functionalist Model," *International Organization,* vol. 24, no. 4 (1970), pp. 796–835.

2. Cf. Bela Balassa, *The Theory of Economic Integration* (Homewood, Ill.: Richard D. Irwin, 1961), pp. 10–14, 21–25, 102–104, 118–134, 163–167. See also Jan Tinbergen, *International Economic Integration,* 2nd rev. ed. (Amsterdam, N.Y.: Elsevier, 1965), pp. 57–62.

3. Cf. Claude Ake, *A Theory of Political Integration* (Homewood, Ill.: Dorsey, 1967), p. 11.

4. Cf. Nye, "Comparative Regional Integration: Concept and Measurement," op. cit., pp. 874–877.

5. Further cogent observations are found in John H. Herz, *International Politics in the Atomic Age* (New York: Columbia University Press, 1959).

6. Joseph N. Nye, *Peace in Parts* (Boston: Little, Brown, 1971), p. 22.

7. David Mitrany, *A Working Peace System* (Chicago: Quadrangle Books, 1966).

8. An extensive literature exists on the various strands of the functionalist theory. The seminal work regarding regional integration is Ernst B. Haas's *The Uniting of Europe* (Stanford, Calif.: Stanford University Press, 1958). Other important works are Leon N. Lindberg, *The Political Dynamics of European Economic Integration* (Stanford, Calif.: Stanford University Press, 1963); Philip C. Schmitter, "A Revised Theory of Regional Integration," in Leon N. Lindberg and Stuart A. Scheingold, eds., *Regional Integration: Theory and Research, International Organizations,* vol. 24, no. 4 (Autumn 1970), pp. 836–868, and other articles in this issue.

9. For additional details see Werner Feld, *The European Common Market and the World* (Englewood Cliffs, N.J.: Prentice-Hall, 1967), pp. 71–76.

10. For a fuller discussion of the crisis provoked by France, see John Lambert, "The Constitutional Crisis 1965–66," *Journal of Common Market Studies*, vol. 6, no. 3 (May 1966), pp. 195–228; and John Newhouse, *Collision in Brussels: The Common Market Crisis of 30 June 1965* (New York: Norton, 1967).

11. Cf. *Le Monde*, April 27–28, 1969.

12. See John Costanis, "The Treaty-Making Power of the European Economic Community: The Perspectives of a Decade," *Common Market Law Review*, vol. 5, no. 4 (March 1968), pp. 421–457.

13. For more details on these agreements see Feld, *The European Common Market and the World*, op. cit., pp. 59–60 and 114–134.

14. For the full text, see *Agence Europe Bulletin*, December 3, 1969.

15. For a discussion of the spillover hypothesis see Schmitter, op. cit., pp. 837–846.

16. For details, see Feld, *The European Community in World Affairs*, op. cit., pp. 277–295.

17. See Supplements to the *Bulletin of the European Communities* 3–70 and 5–73; also *Fifth General Report on the Activities of the Communities* (1971), pp. 145–169.

18. See Werner Feld, "The National Bureaucracies of the EEC Member States and Political Integration: A Preliminary Inquiry," in Robert S. Jordan, ed., *International Administration: Its Evolution and Contemporary Applications* (New York: Oxford University Press, 1971), pp. 228–244.

19. Werner J. Feld and John K. Wildgen, *Domestic Political Realities and European Unification* (Boulder, Colorado: Westview Press, 1977).

20. Sidney Dell, *A Latin American Common Market?* (London: Oxford University Press, 1966), p. 25.

21. Ibid., p. 27.

22. Richard D. Baker, "Latin American Integration," in Paul A. Tharp, *Regional International Organizations* (New York: St. Martin's Press, 1971), pp. 230–242, on p. 235.

23. For an excellent analysis of the Andean Common Market, see William Average and James D. Cochrane, "Innovation in Latin American Regionalism," *International Organization*, vol. 27, no. 2 (Spring 1973), p. 181.

24. Baker, op. cit., p. 236.

25. *Journal of Commerce*, July 15, 1971, p. 2. This specialization was part of the East European integration scheme known as the Council for Mutual Economic Assistance (COMECON). For details on this organization see Michael Kaser, *Comecon* (London: Oxford, 1965). COMECON members are listed in Exhibit 12.1. Although the Soviet Union wanted COMECON to be seen as the counterpart of the European Community in Eastern Europe, the structural and functional differences between the two organizations are wide. COMECON has no supranational features and has not created a unified market as has been done by the EC.

26. See Joseph N. Nye, *Pan-Africanism and East African Integration* (Cambridge, Mass.: Harvard University Press, 1965).

27. See Donald Rothschild, "Experiment in Functional Integration," *Africa Report*, vol. 13, no. 4 (April 1968), pp. 42–47, on p. 45.

28. Ibid., p. 46.

29. *Uganda Argus*, July 30, 1971.

30. Ibid.

SUGGESTED READINGS

CANTORI, L. J., AND S. SPIEGEL. *The International Politics of Regions.* Englewood Cliffs, N.J.: Prentice-Hall, 1970.

GALTUNG, J. *The European Community: A Superpower in the Making.* London: Allen & Unwin, 1973.

HAAS, E. R. *The Uniting of Europe: Political, Social and Economic Forces, 1950–1957.* Stanford, Calif.: Stanford University Press, 1968.

———. *Beyond the Nation-State: Functionalism and International Organization.* Stanford, Calif.: Stanford University Press, 1968.

LINDBERG, L. N., AND S. A. SCHEINGOLD. *Europe's Would-Be Polity.* Englewood Cliffs, N.J.: Prentice-Hall, 1969.

NYE, J. S. *International Regionalism.* Boston: Little, Brown, 1968.

SEWELL, J. P. *Functionalism and World Politics.* Princeton, N.J.: Princeton University Press, 1966.

PART IV
New Forces
in
International Relations

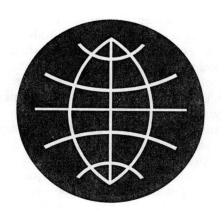

CHAPTER THIRTEEN
THE MULTINATIONAL ENTERPRISE AS AN INTERNATIONAL ACTOR

When we considered which entities should be accorded international actor status, the great economic power of multinational enterprises (MNEs), at times exceeding that of the smaller nation-states, prompted us to include them among these actors. In our discussion of transnational policy analysis as a conceptual framework to understand and explain interaction patterns in the international arena, we also recognized the capabilities of MNEs to exert significant influences on transnational policy making and implementation. In this chapter we shall explore in some detail the underlying reasons for the influence MNEs wield not only in the economic sector, but often also in the political sphere, and in the next chapter we shall assess the impact of transnational MNE operations on international relations and give special consideration to their effects on development in the Third World.

During the past few years much more has been written about the multinational enterprise than about any of the other nongovernmental entities. As a result, by now a very respectable literature has been developed on this subject, both in terms of books and even more so in scholarly and popular articles.[1]

The rise of the MNE and its worldwide expansion has indeed been spectacular. American and European giant firms such as Unilever, IBM, Nestle, Exxon, or Philips are able to obtain capital from anywhere in the world if they need it, although many of these giants not only generate sufficient revenue to be self-financing, but on occasion lend money to banks. Moreover, these large MNEs have developed worldwide production and distribution systems which make it possible to launch new products anywhere in the world and reach millions of customers all over the globe. They have the financial resources to undertake research and development activities necessary to make and exploit breakthroughs in science and technology. They can diversify their risks by global investment patterns, reducing their vulnerability to the economic and political cycles of a given state and to takeovers or acquisition moves by other companies.

The scenario of the future, suggested in the second chapter of this book, whereby 300 MNEs control a large part of world production and employment does not negate the ability of undersized or small regional or "microglobal" multinational companies to find a positive niche in the world economy.[2] At the same time, it demonstrates forcefully the dynamic nature inherent in large-scale, profit-oriented, entrepreneurial activities supported by powerful resources. Employment of 20 percent of the world's labor force by a relatively small number of MNEs could have interesting implications for a shift of loyalties of these workers from national governments to new corporate bodies that might be in a better position to fulfill their economic and social needs and expectations than state authorities.

WHAT IS THE MNE?

Despite the fact that so much ink has been expended on examining the MNE, there is little agreement as to its definition, nor in fact as to its name. Some authors talk about international corporations,[3] others speak of multinational firms or corporations, and even of supranational firms. Howard Perlmutter has prepared a list of definitions[4] which include

> An *international firm* is one in which international operations are consolidated in a particular division and which, as a matter of policy, is willing to consider all potential strategies for entering foreign markets *except* direct investment.
> A *multinational firm* is one in which foreign operations are co-equal with domestic, and management is willing to allocate company resources without regard to national frontiers to achieve corporate objectives. Decisions remain nationally biased for

ownership and headquarters management remains uninational.

A *supranational firm* is legally denationalized in that it is permitted to register with, be controlled by, and pay taxes to, some international body established by multinational convention.

Other authors such as Jonathan F. Galloway consider multinational enterprises only those that have twenty-five subsidiaries,[5] while Jack N. Behrman prefers a very restricted definition according to which an MNE is characterized by central control of a parent company, a common strategy for the entire enterprise, and *integration of operations of affiliates with each other and the parent.*[6] We prefer a broader definition that does not place the emphasis on integration of production. We regard an MNE, a term basically equated with multinational corporations, as a number of affiliated business establishments that function simultaneously in different countries, are joined together by ties of common ownership or control, and are responsible to a common management strategy. From the headquarters company (and country) flow direction and control, and from the affiliates (branches, subsidiaries, joint enterprises), products, revenues, and information. Management may be organized in either monocentric or polycentric fashion. In the former case, top management is centered in one headquarters company; in the latter case, management has been divided into geographic zones, and a separate headquarters company has been established for each zone.[7]

THE PATTERN OF GROWTH

The degree of impact which MNE transnational activities have on national governments and the consequences of their activities for the international system obviously are closely related to the phenomenal growth of multinational enterprises, especially during the past twenty-five years. The rate and geographic pattern of this growth and the type and nature of the expanding multinational operations may suggest in a general way the directions and intensity of present and future effects on nation-states and IGOs caused by these activities and their eventual consequences for the international system and its subsystems. One may also hypothesize that the growing incidence of multinational business enterprises is an indirect indicator of relative success in the attainment of international goals pursued by these entities.

The growing incidence of multinational enterprises can be seen from case studies of 187 U.S. corporations with subsidiaries in at least six foreign countries undertaken by Raymond Vernon at Harvard Graduate School of Business. Table 13.1 shows the increase in the number of these corporations that have expanded beyond the national boundaries since 1901 and the proliferation in the number of their foreign subsidiaries. While the number of parent systems engaged in activities outside the United States rose by about 800 percent, their foreign subsidiaries exhibited a phenomenal sixtyfold expansion.

Analyzing Table 13.1 we find that the earlier very rapid rate of the parent system expansion has slowed down since 1955, while subsidiary proliferation has continued to move upward. In fact, a saturation point in the number of large U.S. multinational parent systems seems to have been reached, but most of these corporations have continued to enlarge their foreign operations, perhaps to preempt international production and marketing opportunities and to stifle the aspirations of ambitious newcomers. The proliferation has been greatest in Europe (about 43 percent), followed by Latin America (23 percent) and Canada (13 percent). More recently, the proliferation of subsidiaries of U.S. MNEs has also slowed; indeed, some subsidiaries have been sold to national companies or have been closed down.

Although American multinational corporations have shown the most spectacular growth during the past fifty years, multinational parent companies are now found in many countries. Table 13.2 shows the number of parent companies in the United States and the major countries of Western Europe, as well as the number of countries where affiliates are located. Table 13.3 provides a geographic distribution of the countries in which parent companies in the countries listed in Table 13.2 have subsidiaries and affiliates. Note that the figures given in both tables are for the number of countries, not the number of subsidiaries and affiliates in an individual country, which may be considerable.

From Table 13.3 we can gather that there are 3,357 parent companies in fifteen European countries and in the United States with affiliates in one foreign country only, and 3,919 with affiliates in two or more. Of these parent companies, U.S. corporations constitute 36 and 33 percent, respectively. Parent companies having affiliates in at least ten countries number 678, and 177 have affiliates in twenty or more countries. Of these, U.S. parent companies constitute 21 and 42 percent, respectively. These percentages suggest that the multinational operations of individual U.S. corporations cover a larger number of countries than those of European companies, but it says nothing about the size of individual corporations. Considering that the 7,276 parent companies have a total of 27,310 links

Table 13.1: Increase of Multinational Corporations and Their Subsidiaries of Selected U.S. Corporations (187)

Country or Region	1901	1913	1919	1924	1929	1939	1950	1955	1960	1965	1967
Expansion in Number of Parent System											
Outside U.S.	23	47	74	93	123	153	168	182	186	187	186
Canada	6	27	54	65	92	123	137	158	176	179	174
Latin America	3	9	16	23	36	72	113	143	179	185	182
Europe	22	37	45	64	95	116	129	154	180	187	185
EFTA	18	29	38	50	86	102	113	130	166	183	181
European Community	15	25	29	47	63	80	84	116	166	185	179
Southern Dominions	2	8	14	21	34	63	77	95	129	154	154
Asia and Other Africa	0	4	8	12	23	33	51	71	103	153	158
Japan	0	1	3	3	7	10	9	26	50	111	117
Other Asia and Africa	0	3	7	11	23	30	49	63	87	123	133
Arab World	0	2	2	2	4	7	11	17	26	32	37
Black Africa	0	0	0	1	4	4	3	8	24	53	62
The Proliferation of Foreign Subsidiaries											
Outside U.S.	107	255	390	591	987	1763	2289	3114	4796	7379	7927
Canada	9	36	86	123	215	353	473	600	792	1017	1048
Latin America	12	27	49	86	139	315	606	856	1341	1813	1924
Europe	83	173	218	327	530	883	904	1165	1872	3140	3401
EFTA	36	80	104	136	242	419	449	562	881	1335	1405
European Community	43	83	101	156	238	370	397	513	869	1540	1675
Southern Dominions	3	13	22	33	53	120	172	250	399	639	648
Asia and Other Africa	0	6	15	22	50	92	134	243	392	770	906
Japan	0	1	3	4	8	11	11	57	68	197	233
Black Africa	0	0	0	1	6	4	9	42	65	142	166
Arab World	0	3	3	3	7	16	29	43	56	77	88

SOURCE: James W. Vaupel and John P. Curran, *The Making of Multinational Enterprise* (Boston: Division of Research, Graduate School of Business Administration, Harvard University, 1969), pp. 11, 123.

Table 13.2: Number and Location of Parent Companies and the Number of Countries (Excepting the Country of the Parent Company) in which Parent Companies Have Affiliates (Data as of 1970)

Country of Parent	Number of Countries												Total Parents[a]	Total Countries[b]
	1	2	3	4	5	6	7	8	9	10-14	15-19	20+		
Austria	21	5	6	1	1	1	2	0	--	2	--	--	39	105
Belgium	137	41	12	14	7	8	2	4	--	7	1	2	235	594
Denmark	54	36	19	13	4	3	--	1	3	4	--	1	128	354
France	211	107	55	45	24	14	14	7	9	32	10	10	538	2023
Germany (FR)	448	196	89	53	38	23	22	18	13	31	12	11	954	2916
Italy	57	17	12	9	9	4	2	1	--	1	2	6	120	459
Luxembourg	10	1	1	1	1	2	--	1	--	1	--	--	18	55
Netherlands	92	50	34	15	24	9	6	6	5	17	3	7	268	1118
Norway	54	16	6	6	4	4	--	--	--	3	1	--	94	220
Portugal	3	1	1	--	--	--	--	--	--	--	--	--	5	8
Spain	11	1	2	--	--	--	1	--	--	--	--	--	15	26
Sweden	93	42	38	9	16	6	8	3	7	17	7	9	255	1159
Switzerland	213	74	34	41	21	8	10	5	9	19	7	6	447	1456
United Kingdom	725	289	163	100	85	57	55	34	26	85	23	40	1692	7116
United States	1228	335	175	115	82	76	58	72	36	146	70	75	2468	9691
Total	3357	1201	647	422	316	215	180	152	108	365	136	177	7276	27310

[a]Total number of parent companies established in a given country.

[b]Total number of links from parent companies in the country to foreign countries. Two or more affiliates of a particular company in a given foreign country are counted as one link.

SOURCE: *Yearbook of International Organizations*, 13th ed. (Brussels, Belgium: Union of International Associations).

Table 13.3: Number of Parent Companies for Each Major Industrialized Country Having Subsidiaries and Associates in a Given Foreign Country (Data as of 1970)

Country of Parent

Country of Subsidiary or Associate	Austria	Belgium	Denmark	France	Germany (FR)	Italy	Luxembourg	Netherlands	Norway	Portugal	Spain	Sweden	Switzerland	United Kingdom	United States	Totals
Europe and USA																
Austria	—	4	4	43	297	10	43	19	1	—	—	27	83	54	100	645
Belgium	2	—	9	136	138	25	3	141	4	1	2	39	87	233	460	1280
Denmark	2	3	—	10	39	3	2	16	24	—	—	104	18	80	100	401
France	3	101	24	—	387	58	7	90	9	1	4	55	158	340	575	1812
Germany (FR)	27	31	58	153	—	39	17	136	21	2	3	111	260	337	702	1887
Italy	11	26	13	136	183	—	5	44	3	—	—	38	137	158	455	1211
Luxembourg	1	31	6	20	39	18	—	6	1	—	—	2	14	39	52	229
Netherlands	2	42	19	58	191	10	6	—	10	—	2	60	73	247	464	1184
Norway	1	3	24	14	16	2	1	7	—	—	—	104	14	46	63	295
Portugal	—	14	2	24	24	6	—	18	1	—	4	19	19	60	54	245
Spain	2	28	4	138	148	24	2	33	2	—	—	26	47	134	249	837
Sweden	2	5	46	15	63	5	2	20	44	—	—	—	32	107	175	516
Switzerland	11	24	11	116	291	36	5	43	13	—	1	57	—	183	421	1212
United Kingdom	5	29	39	118	179	14	3	83	22	—	3	91	99	—	1362	2047
United States	4	18	13	84	145	20	1	46	12	—	—	66	67	482	—	958
Subtotal	73	361	272	1065	2140	270	47	702	167	4	19	799	1109	2500	5232	14759

Source: *Yearbook of International Organizations, 1970–71*, 13th ed.

320

Table 13.3: *Continued*

Country of Subsidiary or Associate	Austria	Belgium	Denmark	France	Germany (FR)	Italy	Luxembourg	Netherlands	Norway	Portugal	Spain	Sweden	Switzerland	United Kingdom	United States	Totals
Other Europe																
Cyprus	:	1	:	:	:	1	:	:	:	:	:	:	:	21	4	28
Finland	:	2	8	2	11	:	:	4	3	:	:	74	10	21	41	176
Greece	1	5	1	13	25	7	:	13	2	:	:	3	9	21	33	133
Ireland	:	6	:	9	22	1	:	14	1	:	:	5	9	368	80	516
Turkey	4	2	2	10	18	5	:	6	:	:	:	5	7	10	18	87
Other Western Europe	1	:	1	5	4	2	:	1	:	:	:	1	6	64	23	108
East Europe	7	:	:	:	1	1	:	1	:	:	:	3	1	1	:	15
Subtotal	13	16	13	39	81	17	:	39	6	:	:	92	42	506	199	1063
Africa	2	132	20	564	171	52	3	118	18	3	1	33	52	1417	378	2964
Americas (excluding U.S.)	10	59	23	251	325	92	5	158	16	1	6	164	160	1117	2744	5131
Asia	6	13	22	76	155	18	:	80	10	:	:	47	61	712	707	1907
Australasia and Oceania	1	13	4	28	44	10	:	21	3	:	:	24	33	864	431	1476
Total	105	594	354	2023	2916	459	65	1118	220	8	26	1159	1456	7116	9691	27310

Country of Parent

321

with foreign countries in which they have affiliates, the average company has links in about four countries.

The geographic distribution of the links of the parent companies with foreign countries as shown in Table 13.3 reveals that 57 percent of these links are with Europe; 19 percent with the Americas (excluding the United States, which is listed under Europe because it relates more to the developed European countries than to the developing countries of Latin America); 11 percent with Africa; 7 percent with Asia; and 5 percent with Australia. These percentages indicate that the majority of multinational corporations are concentrated in the developed countries but that the Third World has begun to attract a growing number of MNE affiliates. While the United States has the largest number of multinational corporations with affiliates in most countries, followed by the United Kingdom and West Germany, it is not surprising that in Africa, because of former colonial ties, affiliates of MNEs based in the United Kingdom and France exceed those of the American MNEs by 300 percent and 150 percent, respectively. In Australia the U.K. firms have twice as many affiliates as those of the United States.

It should be pointed out that reliable and pertinent figures for Japan and Canada were not available and had to be omitted from Tables 13.2 and 13.3. While this omission obviously causes a certain distortion in the overall picture presented, the tables provide useful data regarding the extensive network of multinational corporations in the contemporary international arena. Japan's corporations have been increasing rapidly in size; 79 of these corporations, some of them perhaps not falling in the MNE classification, are among the 300 largest industrial companies outside the United States as listed by *Fortune* in September 1973. They represent the largest national group followed by Britain, which has 61 firms listed. More Japanese companies joined the "300" during 1972 than those of any other country. It is also noteworthy that during the period from 1946 to 1958, Japanese MNEs established 21 subsidiaries. Between 1968 and 1970, the number was 532.[8]

Recapitulating the statistical information regarding the growth and geographical distribution of MNEs presented in the preceding pages, one finds the parent system headquarters of these enterprises concentrated in the advanced countries of the world, although it should be noted that a few large firms, mostly Western-controlled, have established corporate headquarters in Latin America and Africa. While the increase in the creation of MNEs in the United States seems to have stopped, it continues in other developed countries, presenting a challenge to the dominance of American MNEs. At the same time, the proliferation of new subsidiaries continues with multinational operations in the developing nations slowly catching up with those carried out in the advanced countries.

Turning now to an examination of specific initiatives for transnational interaction by MNEs, it should be stressed from the outset that, in most instances, these initiatives will not be "politically" motivated per se, but are actions to enhance the economic potential of the individual MNE in terms of profits, markets, research and development (R&D), or finances. In fact, interviews with top executives of large multinational corporations by this author and others[9] have revealed again and again that most of these executives consider themselves apolitical and only engaged in activities to promote the growth and profits of their firms. They are anxious to project the image of the good citizen in parent and host countries and to have close relations with the agencies of the host government as "friend of the regime."

To systematize this examination of transnational initiatives by MNEs, it is useful to group them into several categories: (1) private foreign investments, (2) transfer of technology, and (3) lobbying activities in support of specific MNE demands. The last category clearly has the strongest direct political thrust, but the first category, foreign investments, is likely to have the most far-reaching and diverse effects and consequences.

FOREIGN INVESTMENTS

As Agents of Change

International investments are potentially powerful agents of economic, social, and political change, regardless of whether they are made in developed or developing, Free World or communist, countries. Their manifold effects on states, IGOs, and indirectly on the international system can offer advantages or create conflicts. The investments influence the balance of payments of the countries involved, may lead to the control of strategic industries often considered undesirable by national governments of the host countries, may add to the export totals of the countries in which new factories are built, and provide investing corporations with bargaining leverage regarding prospective host country laws and regulations, particularly if the infusion of capital can be shifted to a neighboring country with impunity, as is possible in a customs union or free trade area. Moreover, they may affect domestic politics because wage scales and working conditions may improve in the countries where investments are made and job opportunities may be impaired in the countries where the parent company is located. Also, bidding up labor costs may cause inflation, and borrowing of multinational companies in countries with weak currencies may tend to weaken these currencies further. Finally, investments abroad may reduce parent government control over the corporation and thus give management greater operational latitude to, for instance, circumvent export embargoes through shipment from foreign subsidiaries. At the same time, a multinational corporation may appeal to its parent government to intervene through diplomatic channels or even stronger means to protect it against unfriendly action by host governments. But international investments may also supplement the foreign policy goals of the parent government by helping developing countries to achieve a higher economic level and thereby attain greater political stability, or by promoting national security by ensuring the flow of needed raw materials.

As Indicators

Investments are useful indicators to measure the thrust and intensity of economic and perhaps social changes effected or expected in various parts of the world. An overall view of direct foreign investments by major countries and certain broad industrial sectors can be gained from Tables 13.4 and 13.5. Table 13.4 shows international investments by the United States, Canada, Western Europe, and Japan broken down by developed economies and developing regions, including investment percentages in these regions. Table 13.5 identifies investments in the major industrial sectors in the developing countries. The highest percentage of total investments in the Third World (nearly 50 percent) is devoted to oil and other extractive industries, and only about 22 percent to manufacturing industries for whose establishment a particularly urgent need exists in the developing nations. Since 1966 investments in the Third World by MNEs have risen substantially from about $2 billion a year to more than $10 billion in 1975.[10] These figures do not reflect, however, the diminishing value of the dollar as a consequence of substantial inflation. Moreover, investments from some industrialized countries, such as France and Italy, have in fact decreased, while United States and German firms have made above-average investments.

Investments and Exports

Another dimension of direct foreign investments by multinational corporations can be seen when these investments are related to exports and the GNP of the country where the parent system is

Table 13.4: Estimated Stock of Foreign Direct Investment, by Country of Origin and Region of Investment, End 1967

Country of Origin	World Total[a]	Developed Countries[a]	Developing Countries[a]	Developing Countries[b]					
				Africa	Central America	South America	Middle East	Asia	Total Developing Countries
United States	59,486	42,783	16,703	2.3	7.4	12.4	3.0	3.0	28.1
United Kingdom	17,521	10,939	6,582	11.3	4.7	5.0	4.8	11.8	37.6
France	6,000	3,311	2,689	28.8	1.0	6.8	2.7	5.5	44.8
Netherlands	2,250	556	1,694	14.4	8.2	33.6	7.7	11.4	75.3
Canada	3,728	2,275	1,453	1.5	13.3	22.7	0.2	1.3	39.0
Germany (FR)	3,015	1,997	1,018	4.6	3.4	22.8	0.8	2.2	33.8
Japan	1,458	758	700	0.9	6.9	20.9	5.8	13.5	48.0
Italy	2,110	1,414	696	11.7	1.0	17.6	1.2	1.4	33.0
Belgium	2,040	1,427	613	23.6	--	5.5	0.1	0.8	30.0
Switzerland	4,250	3,685	565	1.4	3.4	6.7	0.1	1.7	13.3
Sweden	1,514	1,334	180	5.3	0.8	4.6	--	1.2	11.9
Australia	380	280	100	--	--	--	--	26.3	26.3
Portugal	200	101	99	--	--	3.0	--	--	49.5
Denmark	190	161	29	8.7	1.5	1.2	1.0	2.7	15.3
Norway	60	51	9	5.0	--	10.0	--	--	15.0
Austria	30	25	5	--	--	16.7	--	--	16.7
Total	104,232	71,097	33,135	6.3	6.1	11.6	3.0	4.8	31.8

[a]Total book value, millions of dollars

[b]Percentage share

SOURCE: Centre for Development Planning, Projections and Policies of the Department of Economic and Social Affairs of the United Nations Secretariat, based on Table 5 and Organisation for Economic Co-operation and Development, *Stock of Private Direct Investments by DAC Countries in Developing Countries, End 1967* (Paris, 1972).

Table 13.5: Direct Foreign Investment, Accumulated Assets, by Major Countries, End 1966 (book value, in millions of dollars)

	Less Developed Countries (Percent)	World	United States	United Kingdom	France	Germany	Sweden	Canada	Japan
Petroleum		25,942	16,264	4,200	d	200	a	a	a
(LDC)	45.84	(11,892)	(6,975)	(2,167)	(670)	(65)	a	a	(222)
Mining and Smelting		5,923	4,135	759	a	100	a	250b	a
(LDC)	47.45	(2,801)	(1,827)	(298)	(200)b	(38)	(65)	(202)	(71)
Manufacturing		32,246	22,050	6,028	a	1,800	a	2,988b	a
(LDC)	22.2	(8,047)	(4,124)	(1,471)	(1,230)b	(645)	(96)	(332)	(270)
Other		21,472	12,113	5,015c	a	400	a	a	a
(LDC)	33.67	(7,230)	(3,915)	(2,255)	a	(97)	a	a	(33)
Total		89,583	54,462	16,002	4,000	2,500	793	3,238	1,000
(LDC)		(29,970)	(16,841)	(6,184)	(2,100)	(845)	(161)	(534)	(605)
LDC percent of Total by Country		33.45	30.92	38.64	52.5	33.8	20.3	16.49	60.5

Note: Italy, Holland, Switzerland, and Belgium data not available; Australia total investment is $300 million.

aNot available.

bEstimate.

cIncluding agriculture of 1,022 (864 in the less developed countries, or LDCs).

dTotal French oil production estimated at 57.2 million tons in 1966.

SOURCE: Compiled from OECD, DAC (68) 14, Annex C (April 23, 1968).

located. Both foreign investments and exports are, to a large extent, manifestations of nongovernmental initiatives capable of influencing the international system.* For illustrative purposes let us compare the United States and Germany. In 1976 the book value of total direct foreign investments by U.S. firms was $137 billion, or about 8.1 percent of GNP, which was about $1.7 trillion. American exports were $108 billion, or 6.4 percent of GNP. In Germany total foreign investments had reached only $13 billion by 1976, which represented 3 percent of GNP amounting to $451 billion. However, exports were $90 billion and constituted 20 percent of GNP.**

While the capability of the United States to influence the international system through foreign investments and exports is highest in net terms, only a relatively small percentage of GNP has been employed for this purpose. On the other hand, Germany's corresponding capability through exports is very large, and despite the relatively small total of foreign investments, the sum of exports and investments represents 23 percent of GNP, almost twice as much as the U.S. percentage. Moreover, the foreign investment trend of German firms is steeply upward and therefore augurs well for a rise in Germany's potential to influence the international interaction process through nongovernmental initiatives.

This figure dramatizes an ongoing revolution in world economics. From a trade standpoint, American participation in the world economy appears as very limited while that of Germany looms very large; but as Richard J. Barber points out,[11] trade statistics actually mask the realities of the new globalism in economics flowing from increasing foreign investments. Instead of shipping goods to purchasers from production facilities in one country, for instance automobiles from Detroit, plants are established in low-cost locations around the world from which potential customers are served. From a business standpoint, this makes perfectly good economic sense, but it could also mean that exports from the United States may suffer.

On the other hand, investment in a foreign country may often face greater resistance than the importation of goods because it presents a more direct challenge to established prices. Companies that were previously prepared to tolerate some competition in the form of exports by foreign firms may not be willing to tolerate com-

---

* This statement does not apply to communist countries, where exports are governmental activities and whatever few foreign investments may be made *outside* the communist world are also controlled by state agencies.
** See OECD, *Observer*, May 1977, pp. 15 ff. and U.S. Department of Commerce, *Survey of Current Business* (1977, vol. 57, #8), pp. 32 ff.

petition by direct investment and will seek to drive the intruder out of the market before he becomes too strong. Nevertheless, the firm making the foreign investment can win this struggle if it has the necessary financial resources, as has been proved many times by the experiences of American MNEs. With the increasing financial strength of European firms, the tempting benefits of foreign investment will serve as a strong inducement for the latter to expand their transnational production and marketing facilities.[12] Of course, the availability of financial resources may not be the only limitation to foreign investments. Balance-of-payments problems may also impede the flow of international investments, as the American experience has shown. This points up another relationship between investment and exports inasmuch as vigorous export trade is at least in part the foundation for the continued outpouring of foreign investments.

Profitability

Although marketing strategies, tariff barriers, the ease of technological research, and production and transportation costs are important motivations for business enterprises to multinationalize their operations, the maximization of profits remains always a pervasive catalyst for investments in different parts of the world. As a consequence, a major motivation for the initiation, continuation, and enlargement of foreign investments is the degree of their profitability.

Foreign earnings for some American corporations have been very significant over the years. For example, Exxon, Ford, Anaconda, and H. J. Heinz often obtained a higher percentage of income abroad than from U.S. operations, although with the exception of Ford their sales were greater in the United States than in foreign countries.[13]

THE TRANSFER OF KNOWLEDGE

Transfer of knowledge as an MNE initiative for transnational interaction consists of the transmission of either technological knowledge or management skills across national boundaries.

As Peter Drucker has pointed out, in our age of rapid change, understanding the dynamics of technology and applying the proper technological strategy are essential for the success and indeed, the survival, of a business and perhaps even of an industrial nation.[14] Businessmen and also governments must be able to anticipate the direction and speed of technological change and take advantage of the opportunities that technological developments offer. With innovation often being the crucial variable for economic success in production and marketing, as well as for the military-strategic security of nation-states, it is obvious that transfers of technology can play a vital role in the fortunes of MNEs and states.

Technology can be transferred by *licensing agreements* and through the medium of the MNE either by the use of existing multinational facilities or investment in a new facility in a foreign country. Licensing agreements, which do not require any border-crossing capital or foreign ownership of industrial installations, have been successful vehicles for large numbers of patents and technological know-how transfers.

Midway between the transfer of technology by an MNE to a wholly owned affiliate and licensing agreements is the *joint equity venture* formed by a multinational corporation and a host-country company. While under this arrangement the involvement of MNE management is reduced, there is likely to be a better appreciation of local economic conditions and needs, thereby enhancing the relations with the host government.[15]

For the transfer of managerial skills across national boundaries the MNE is also a potent agent. These skills are in short supply in many industrially advanced countries, but are most urgently needed in the Third World. Few business executives even in Europe are trained to meet the problems of rapid technological change and the demands of competitive markets. American management methods and training have proved to be most successful in solving modern business problems.

Skills within an MNE can be transferred in several ways. Management personnel and instructors can be sent from the parent company to affiliates in the host countries, and potential managers in the affiliates can be sent for training to the parent company headquarters. Management conferences in which personnel from affiliates in different countries participate may be scheduled and handbooks and guides distributed by the parent company. This leads to the adoption of new management techniques on a company-wide basis, benefiting the operations in all affiliates.[16]

LOBBYING AND EXERTION OF INFLUENCE

The final initiative available to MNEs for setting into motion transnational interactions is lobbying to press national governments and IGOs for the acceptance of their demands and objectives. As has already been observed, many business executives claim to be "apolitical," interested only in the pursuit of greater profits and wider markets; however, they are not adverse to using various channels to bring their needs and demands to the attention of the authorities for favorable consideration. In fact, it is precisely the multinational opportunities offered MNE executives, which permit close coordination of lobbying activities in several countries, that ultimately may lead to the harmonization of national policies and laws and, in turn, to greater political integration in areas where regional economic unions have been instituted.[17]

While undoubtedly many MNEs want to project or retain the image of the "corporate good citizen" and therefore avoid any adverse publicity associated with "lobbying," some corporations and their affiliates may not be disturbed by aggressively seeking their political ends. The story of ITT political activities in Chile is well known; large amounts of money were spent to assure Chilean governmental support for ITT subsidiaries; and when President Allende, an avowed Communist, came to power, help was sought from American governmental agencies for his overthrow. Characterized by Charles T. Goodsell as "Back Room Heavies," executives of subsidiaries in foreign countries may engage in large-scale bribery, such as paying large commissions or giving gifts to governmental leaders or their families, induce concessions by promising to make new investments if certain conditions are met, or threaten the intervention of the parent company government if the host government takes specific actions or refuses the demands of the MNE.[18]

Some of Goodsell's examples illustrate these activities. In the 1920s, the Electric Boat Company paid huge commissions to the Peruvian president to sell submarines to the Peruvian Navy. In 1965 an Italian construction consortium probably bribed the minister of development and public works, along with several Peruvian congressmen, to obtain the Mantaro hydroelectric contract, previously assigned to Anglo-German interests. In 1967 the presidents of three U.S. mining companies—Cerro de Pasco, American Smelting and Refining, and Anaconda—arranged a private, joint meeting with President Fernando Belaunde Terry, at which they showed him several projects they had in mind for Peru, but only if Article 56 of the Mining Code were liberalized (it was, shortly thereafter). ITT, for years the majority stockholder in the Peruvian Telephone Company, launched telephone expansion projects in the 1960s and then deliberately halted them, making resumption of the work contingent on a rate increase. In 1967, the president of ITT cabled Secretary of State Dean Rusk regarding a pending telephone bill in the Peruvian Congress which threatened ITT's control, requesting the intervention of the State Department at the highest level. In 1969, California tuna interests did their best to generate pressure in the U.S. Congress to provide naval escorts to their tuna clippers when they invaded Peru's 200-mile coastal fishing jurisdiction; and in 1971, W. R. Grace proposed to a U.S. congressional committee that part of Peru's sugar quota payments be held back as a fund to compensate victims of nationalization. The extensive bribery attempts through the payments of enormous commissions by nearly 200 American firms to high-ranking officials in foreign countries—perhaps you remember the Lockheed and United Brands scandals in the 1970s—have become a matter of official record[19] and have made the front pages of newspapers all over the world.

To achieve lobbying objectives, MNE headquarters and especially affiliate executives may determine important target groups in the host country with which they maintain continuing relationships. The targets are not only government officials, but also general public and special interest groups, trade unions, news media, shareholders, supplier and customer organizations, universities, and last but not least, other companies. Functional departments within the MNE and its affiliates are assigned the task of dealing with various target groups. This means that, for example, the marketing department would deal with customer organizations; the personnel department, with trade unions; the financial department, with shareholders; and the public relations department, with the news media and the general public. Some large corporations, such as Royal Dutch—Shell or Exxon, have set up large-scale organizations resembling the foreign ministries of national governments. These organizations engage in carefully coordinated information- and intelligence-gathering operations through a network of representatives in the major capitals of the world. At the same time, these representatives present their companies' viewpoints on pertinent issues to the national governments in whose countries they are stationed and seek to influence national decision-makers in the direction desired by the corporation management. Periodically, these representatives are called back to headquarters to discuss foreign policy problems and to receive new instructions.

The formulation of foreign policy objectives by MNEs is not always easy. Different regional headquarters, especially in polycentrically organized corporations, may have conflicting policy priorities stemming from varying economic and political activities in the countries in which they operate. For example, one regional subsidiary may advocate flexibility or concessions with respect to a particular national government demand, while other subsidiaries may insist on a hard-nosed attitude worldwide, arguing that flexibility in one country may induce other governments to request equal concessions.

In fact, such differences of opinion can emerge within the MNE management of one country subsidiary, as Goodsell relates with respect to the problems of the International Petroleum Company (IPC) in Peru. The IPC management was split into behavioral camps, unofficially known as "Hawks" and "Doves." The first group opposed innovative concessions to the Peruvians on the grounds that some of the more than 100 governments with which IPC's parent, then the Standard Oil Company of New Jersey, had to deal would demand the same. The Doves believed that appropriate flexibility was the only way to save the company in Peru. The Hawk leadership was in part comprised of former managers of IPC's field operations at Talara (rather than the Lima office). As it happened, several former Talara managers had been promoted in recent years to the top echelons of Standard Oil, which may help to explain why the hawk approach prevailed, although at the end it had to be modified.[20]

To make the lobbying process effective and successful a variety of frequently overlapping coalitions need to be formed. These coalitions are not limited to intranational groups, but may reach regional and worldwide dimensions. They may be formed vertically embracing the MNE's customers as well as suppliers and their trade associations, and they may reach out horizontally to companies with related or common interests and again their trade associations.

The closest allies for the MNE are the specialized interest groups in their own industries. For example, in the oil industry, the American Petroleum Institute (API) is the permanent basis of useful intercorporate alliances. The API serves as a meeting ground for some 8,000 individual members from most segments of the industry. While much of its efforts are devoted to technical research, there is also continuing concern with fundamentals of national oil policy and the behavior of governmental agencies in Washington and in state capitals. The policies, financial contributions, and leadership of the API are clearly dominated by the large international oil companies, and API statements of position generally echo their interests. However, the international oil companies do not rely solely on the API; rather, they form coalitions with such groups as the National Foreign Trade Council, the Committee for Economic Development, the Chamber of Commerce of the United States, and the Venezuelan Chamber of Commerce, whose objectives the international oil MNEs frequently support.* Depending on the particular goals the oil corpora-

---

* During the energy crisis created by the worldwide shortage of petroleum in 1973, the large oil companies were suspected of cooperating clandestinely with the OPEC countries in raising the price of crude oil and thereby increasing their own profits.

tions pursue, they may also seek support from such diverse groups as teachers' associations, the Congress of Parents and Teachers, state bar associations, the American Legion, the Veterans of Foreign Wars, water conservation associations, soil conservation district supervisors, and the Federation of Women's Clubs.[21]

MNEs also engage in formal and informal government alliances in order to press the pursuit of their objectives. This does not mean that the oil companies or other MNEs should be viewed simply as Machiavellian manipulators and the governments, as innocent bystanders or agents. Rather, in many instances, alliances stem from an assumption of mutual needs. Nevertheless, returning to the example of the international oil companies, it appears that, on many occasions, the State Department has taken its policies right out of the executive suites of these companies. This process has been helped by the fact that a close, informal relationship has existed between a number of public officials with oil business backgrounds and their friends in the industry.

Another potent ally of MNEs may be national and international professional business associations, which bring together executives engaged in international business and in which MNE executives may be able to play a policy-determining role. Other professional associations in the fields of technology, science, economics, finance, and law may also be used as coalition partners in support of MNE demands. Finally, possible allies for MNEs may be national or international labor organizations; however, in view of the very complex, often hostile, attitudes of organized labor toward MNEs, alliances with labor organizations may be effective only in very specific cases.

SUMMARY

When we considered which entities should be accorded international actor status, the great economic power of **multinational enterprises (MNEs)**, at times exceeding that of the smaller nation-states, prompted us to include them among these actors. A multinational corporation or enterprise is a number of affiliated business establishments that function simultaneously in different countries, are joined together by ties of common ownership or control, and are responsible to a common management strategy.

Transnational initiatives by MNEs may be grouped into three categories: **private foreign investments, transfer of knowledge,** and **lobbying activities** in support of specific MNE demands.

International investments are potentially powerful agents of economic, social, and political change. They may reduce parent government control over a corporation and thus give management greater operational latitude. The major motivation for their initiation, continuation, and enlargement is their degree of **profitability.** The major limitations on them are the availability of funds and balance-of-payments problems, as the American experience has shown.

In our age of rapid change, **transfers of knowledge** play a vital role in the fortunes of MNEs and nation-states. Knowledge can be transferred by **licensing agreements** and the formation of **joint equity ventures.** MNEs may transfer technology to a wholly owned affiliate by exchange or training of personnel and are potent agents for transferring managerial skills across national boundaries.

While many MNEs want to project an image of the "corporate good citizen" and therefore to avoid any adverse publicity associated with lobbying some corporations and their affiliates do not hesitate to use bribery and other heavy-handed tactics to gain the desired political ends or corporate advantage. MNEs also form coalitions and formal and informal government alliances to press the pursuit of their objectives.

The successes of lobbying efforts are always difficult to determine and frequently do not become visible until considerable time has elapsed. In many instances, lobbying agents do not want to trumpet their successes to the world, as such publicity may be counterproductive. Of course, they are also anxious to conceal failures whenever possible.

However, whatever determination can be made of the effective influence exerted by the MNEs through lobbying must be seen in the context of the overall effects on governmental and intergovernmental actors produced by transnational MNE initiatives. Indeed, an effect one government may perceive as a benefit, another may view as a drawback because each government operates under different economic, cultural, and political conditions. In fact, even individual political and administrative leaders within a particular government may disagree on this score. Frequently, benefits and drawbacks need to be balanced carefully before conclusions can be drawn. This brings us to an overall assessment of the impact of MNE operations on the international arena, which is the subject of the next chapter.

NOTES

1. Representative works are: Stefan H. Robock and Kenneth Simmons, *International Business and Multinational Enterprises* (Homewood, Ill.: Irwin, 1973); Jack N. Behrman, *National Interests and the Mul-*

tinational Enterprise: Tensions Among the North Atlantic Countries (Englewood Cliffs, N.J.: Prentice-Hall, 1970); Raymond Vernon, *Sovereignty at Bay: The Multinational Spread of U.S. Enterprises*, Harvard Multinational Enterprise Series (New York: Basic Books, 1971); Abdul A. Said and Luiz R. Simmons, *The New Sovereigns* (Englewood Cliffs, N.J.: Prentice-Hall, 1971); R. J. Barnett and R. E. Muller, *Global Reach* (New York: Simon & Schuster, 1974); and Robert Gilpin, *U.S. Power and the Multinational Corporation* (New York: Basic Books, 1975).

2. Howard V. Perlmutter, "Towards Research on and Development of Nations," address before the symposium on International Collective Bargaining, sponsored by the International Institute of Labour Studies of the ILO, April 29, 1969, Geneva, Switzerland.

3. For example, see Charles P. Kindleberger, ed., *The International Corporation: A Symposium* (Cambridge, Mass.: M.I.T. Press, 1970).

4. Howard V. Perlmutter, "Attitudinal Patterns in Joint Decision Making in Multinational Firm-Nation State Relationships," in M. F. Tuite, M. Radnor, and R. Chisholm, eds., *International Decision Making* (Chicago: Aldine, 1972), pp. 4–5.

5. Jonathan F. Galloway, "Multinational Enterprises as World-wide Interest Groups," paper delivered at the Annual Meeting of the American Political Science Association, September 1970 (mimeographed).

6. J. N. Behrman, "The Multinational Enterprise: Its Initiatives and Governmental Reactions," March 1971 (mimeographed). See also his *National Interests and the Multinational Enterprise*, op cit., pp. 2–11.

7. Cf. E. J. Kolde, *International Business Enterprise* (Englewood Cliffs, N.J.: Prentice-Hall, 1968), pp. 218–220 and 251–252. See also Raymond Vernon, *Sovereignty at Bay: The Multinational Spread of U.S. Enterprises*, Harvard Multinational Enterprises Series (New York: Basic Books, 1971).

8. Yoshihiro Tsurumi, "The Multinational Spread of Japanese Firms and Asian Neighbors' Reactions," in David E. Apter and Louis W. Goodman, *The Multinational Corporation and Social Change* (New York: Praeger, 1976), pp. 118–146, on p. 125.

9. For example, Charles T. Goodsell, "The Multinational Corporation as Transnational Actor: Observations Based on Peru," remarks at the Annual Meeting of American Political Science Association, September 9, 1971; and Werner Feld, *Transnational Business Collaboration Among Common Market Countries* (New York: Praeger, 1970).

10. For details see OECD, *Development Co-operation* (1976 Review), pp. 216–229; and U.S. Department of Commerce, *Survey of Current Business*, vol. 57, no. 8 (August 1977), pp. 32–64.

11. Richard Barber, *The American Corporation* (New York: Dutton, 1970), p. 252.

12. Cf. Also Stephen Hymer and Robert Rawthorn, "Multinational Corporations and International Oligopoly: The Non-American Challenge," in Kindleberger, ed., *The International Corporation*, op. cit., pp. 74 and 75.

13. Sanford Rose "The Rewarding Strategies of Multinationalism," *Fortune*, September 15, 1968, pp. 100 ff.

14. Peter F. Drucker, *The Age of Discontinuity* (New York: Harper & Row, 1969), p. 48.

15. See John H. Dunning, "Technology, United States Investment, and European Economic Growth," in Kindleberger, *The International Corporation*, op. cit., pp. 141–176, p. 172.

16. For special experiences see Behrman, *National Interests and the Multinational Enterprise*, op. cit., pp. 18, 19.

17. See Feld, *Transnational Business Collaboration*, op. cit., pp. 66–80.

18. Goodsell, "The Multinational Corporation as Transnational Actor," op. cit.

19. See Hearings before the Subcommittee on Multinational Corporations, U.S. Senate, *Multinational Corporations and U.S. Foreign Policy* (Washington, D.C.: U.S. Government Printing Office, 1976).

20. In *The American Corporation*, op. cit., p. 268, Richard Barber refers to the same kind of intracompany divergence of opinion when he discusses the decision making in hypothetical major international corporations regarding the location of new plants in Europe. One group may favor a location in Belgium, while another group prefers a site in France, partly out of a desire to avoid coming into the disfavor of the French government.

21. For greater details see Robert Engler, *The Politics of Oil* (Chicago: University of Chicago Press, 1961), pp. 59–60 and 390–391. For other activities of oil companies see Jack Anderson, "Big Oil Greed Draws Blame," New Orleans *States-Item*, December 22, 1973, p. A-7.

SUGGESTED READINGS

APTER, DAVID E., AND LOUIS WOLF GOODMAN. *The Multinational Corporation and Social Change*. New York: Praeger, 1976.

BALL, GEORGE W., ed. *Global Companies*. Englewood Cliffs, N.J.: Prentice-Hall, 1975.

HELLMAN, RAINER. *The Challenge to U.S. Dominance of the International Corporation*. Translated by Peter Rouf. Port Washington, N.Y.: Dunellen, 1971.

MAGDOFF, HARRY. *The Age of Imperialism: The Economics of U.S. Foreign Policy*. New York: Monthly Review Press, 1969.

ROLFE, SIDNEY E., AND WALTER DAMM, eds. *The Multinational Corporation in the World Economy*. New York: Praeger, 1970.

CHAPTER FOURTEEN
THE IMPACT OF MULTINATIONAL ENTERPRISES ON INTERNATIONAL RELATIONS

The impact of MNEs on international relations stems from

1. the interactions between MNEs on the one hand and parent and host governments on the other, including especially the perceptions of benefits and drawbacks flowing from MNE operation;
2. the responses of international labor federations to the challenges posed by MNEs; and
3. the effects of MNE activities on the international system as a whole.

We will begin our inquiry by examining benefits and drawbacks resulting from MNE operations for host and parent governments and their reactions and possible countermeasures.

BENEFITS OF MNE INITIATIVES

Benefits for Host Countries

Inflows of Capital   Inflows of capital into a country from abroad obviously bring certain primary benefits if the funds are not used simply to acquire existing companies but to establish new facilities. In that event, the construction industry in the host country will profit, employment will rise directly and indirectly, exports may be expanded, imports may be reduced if new products manufactured become substitutes for formerly imported items, the balance of payments may be improved by a more favorable trade balance as well as the inflow of capital, and tax receipts may be increased, although MNEs might be able to manipulate the size of the receipts.[1] In some host countries wage levels may also rise, but such a development might not be an unmixed blessing everywhere because it could lead to or reinforce inflationary pressures.[2]

Transfer of Technology   The contribution of technology and management skills to the operations of MNE affiliates abroad made by the parent organization often spreads beyond the confines of the affiliates in host countries. As Jack N. Behrman points out, commercial activities tend to spread managerial and technical contributions to customers and suppliers of the affiliates. Customers are provided with products of higher quality, perhaps at lower cost and better adapted to local conditions. Technical services include counseling the customer on his product needs and ways of increasing his productivity. At the same time, affiliates of MNEs can assist suppliers in the construction of their plants and advise them concerning equipment layouts, thereby helping in the production of a higher quality of goods for use by the affiliate and other users in a particular foreign country.[3]

Transfer of technology may also help to raise the productivity in host-country industries. For example, mostly as a consequence of American technological contributions, the output of British precision instruments increased tremendously, and the availability of advanced instrumentation also raised the productivity of other British industries.[4]

Reduction of Prices   Another significant benefit for the economy of host countries can be the reduction of prices for goods produced by superior technology. In many instances, however, the prices remain unchanged, resulting in larger returns for the MNE. Then the only benefit for the host government is enlarged tax receipts, which can be important, especially for small countries. Perhaps for this reason, as well as to ensure the continuity of the benefits from technology for their country, host governments are anxious to have research and development institutes established in their own countries. As a consequence, they seek to induce MNEs by a variety of means, including threats, to locate at least some of their research facilities within their boundaries.

Promotion of Regional Development   Finally, benefits from MNE investments and transfers of technology and managerial skills may bolster efforts to promote regional development in host countries. Responding to special inducements and incentives by national governments and their subdivisions, MNEs have located new affiliates in depressed regions more often than have national companies because such action is likely to make them more welcome in a new host country. During the period from 1959 to 1966, foreign-owned companies acceded to Belgian incentive projects for locating plants in the provinces by a ratio of three to one compared with Belgian companies.[5]

Benefits for Parent Company Governments

Benefits not only accrue to host countries of MNE affiliates, but also to the countries where the parent company is located. Foreign investments and transfers of technological and managerial know-how may supplement foreign aid objectives of parent-country governments in developing countries. In the United States a special agency, the Overseas Private Investment Corporation, was established in 1970 to stimulate investments in the Third World and to provide insurance and guarantee programs. In countries such as France and Italy where the state either owns large industrial enterprises or controls them on the basis of being a major shareholder, foreign investments by these enterprises can become potent instruments of foreign policy implementation everywhere. Selective legal or administrative restrictions on the transfer of technology by any kind of MNE to its foreign affiliates also may serve parent company governments as persuasive foreign policy tools.

Benefits for the Third World

The economic and social effects of MNE investments and transfer of technological and managerial knowledge can be most striking when the receiving countries are part of the developing world. As noted earlier, however, a high percentage of total investment by American and other MNEs is devoted to oil and other extractive industries, and only about 22 percent to manufacturing industries, so urgently needed in the developing nations. Nevertheless, even extractive industries often create new social infrastructures of schools, housing, health facilities, and transportation necessary to conduct their business. In addition, local engineers and technicians can learn from exposure to the advanced training and experience of their counterparts brought in by management from the advanced countries.[6] Investments in manufacturing industries are likely to produce more lasting benefits in developing areas because they will provide opportunities for producing goods within a country which otherwise would have had to be imported and paid for with always-scarce foreign currency; in addition, some of the items manufactured might be exported to other countries, thus bringing in foreign earnings. Indeed, all Third World countries aspire to industrialization, and the exports of manufactured goods may lessen the dependence of many developing countries on the often highly fluctuating earnings from agricultural commodities and raw materials. Finally, manufacturing industries offer greater opportunities for employment than extractive industries in areas where high unemployment is chronic, and they introduce technological and managerial skills into developing countries, which are likely to spread as educational levels for the population rise. In some developing countries in Asia, such as India, Pakistan, Sri Lanka, and the Philippines, and in some Latin American countries, such as Argentina and Brazil, there is actually no dearth of persons who already have the general education and a good natural ability to be contemporary effective managers;[7] therefore, new industries can eventually be established and run by citizens of these and other developing countries, causing an overall improvement in social and economic standards which, in turn, may contribute to greater political stability of the new nations.

A few examples illustrate the favorable impact of MNEs on Third World host countries where affiliates are located. Sears pioneered the modern supermarkets of Mexico and established a large number of native manufacturing industries to furnish goods for its retail stores. United Brands, formerly the United Fruit Company, despite its reputation as an "exploiter," expanded the real incomes and welfare of the peoples in Central America where it operated and contributed immeasurably to the control of disease in the area. International Basic Economic Corporation, an organization controlled by the Rockefeller family with affiliates in thirty-three developing countries and concentrating upon agribusiness, promoted innovations in food production and was active in the construction of low-cost housing.[8]

Developing countries with large-scale unemployment and relatively well-educated populations have benefited from the establishment of MNE affiliates which use low-cost labor for the manufacture of parts for electronics and other high-technology products to be sold in established markets, mainly in the advanced countries of the world. Taiwan, South Korea, and Singapore are some of the countries that have benefited from such investments and as a consequence the economic levels of their people as a whole have risen. Other developing countries, such as Mauritius,[9] have geared their current development plans to attracting appropriate MNEs for similar purposes.

While the potential contribution of MNEs to the development of the Third World is large, much depends on the political stability and the attitude of Third World governments toward private investment. If the stability is high and the attitudes favorable, private investment is encouraged and MNEs can fulfill their roles as expanders of economic development. As Neil Jacoby points out, the remarkable evolution of such countries as Mexico, Malaysia, and Taiwan have testified to this truth.[10] Governmental instability and unfavorable attitudes, however, are not the only source of political risks with which MNEs may be faced in developing countries. Others are social unrest and disorder, recent or impending independence, armed conflict, and private vested interests. The extent of these risks depends, to a large degree, on how beneficial or damaging governmental and political elites view the effects of MNE initiatives and activities with respect to their countries and especially their own goals, ambitions, and expectations. This then requires an examination and analysis of actual and perceived drawbacks of MNE initiatives for national governments.

DRAWBACKS AND PROBLEMS FOR GOVERNMENTAL ACTORS

Certain drawbacks caused by MNE activities can affect both developed and developing countries, but the latter may have more difficulty coping with them. Moreover, perception of disadvantages and costs may be more extensive among Third World governmental leaders as problems arising from newly gained independence and "nation-building," as well as from former relations with colonial masters, tend to color their views.

Closing of Plants   Obviously, the closing of plants, either in the country where the parent company is located or in the host countries of affiliates if more favorable production facilities are found elsewhere, will be regarded as a drawback because it reduces employment opportunities and may affect unfavorably the potential for exports. Moreover, the location of new plants desired by MNEs can cause problems. For example, during the past few years many foreign MNEs considered the Rhine River area as the most suitable region to set up production facilities in the European Common Market. For France this location posed problems because only a relatively small piece of her territory is in this area; therefore, she felt less favored than some of the other EEC countries, such as Germany or the Netherlands.[11]

Tapping of Local Capital Markets   Inflationary pressures in host countries may also be fueled by large-scale inflows of capital, but other aspects of investment flows between parent companies and their foreign affiliates may be even more vexing. Once affiliates are established by direct investments, they may seek to obtain additional finances locally. Such tapping of the local capital markets may either be by voluntary decision of the MNE or prompted by mandatory controls imposed by the parent company's government on the outflow of funds, as was done in 1968 by the United States.[12] In any event, the entry of large multinational corporations into a host country's capital market may well dry up the normal sources for financing upon which smaller national companies usually depend.

The mandatory controls devised by the U.S. government also required extensive repatriation of earnings on foreign investments and other short-term financial assets held in foreign countries by parent companies. This provision could not but arouse the displeasure of host governments, which complained that the imposition of capital controls by the American government challenges the sovereignty of the host country by dampening economic growth and altering the investment projections.

Shifting of Resources   The suspicion that the MNE is a tool of the foreign policy of the parent company government is not new and can find much justification in the history of the colonial empires and of American actions in Latin America. Moreover, apprehension regarding the MNE can be aroused simply by its ability to shift important resources, such as capital or knowledge, from one country to another with relative impunity. This places the MNE in a strong bargaining position when it comes to determining the present or future conditions of its operations in a particular country. The combination of powerful resources with worldwide operations affects not only host governments, but also control by the parent company country, inasmuch as it furnishes the MNE with sufficient operational latitude to circumvent such rules as export embargoes by shipment from foreign affiliates.

Transfer Pricing   Host governments may also be apprehensive about the ability of multinational companies to affect tax receipts unfavorably. This can be done through allocation of production to facilities in low-tax countries or through the manipulation of profits on items that can be moved across national boundaries from one subsidiary to another for assembly or sales so that the most profit per item accrues in the countries with the lowest tax rates.[13] The technical term for such activities is *transfer pricing*.

All the above factors are apt to produce fears in the minds of governmental and political leaders that MNE operations can be a liability to their country, inasmuch as they may impose serious constraints on the scope of the national decision-making process by reducing the availability of options and forcing solutions not perceived as in accordance with the national interest. In industrially advanced countries, these fears may stem from three major concerns: foreign domination of industries, technological dependence, and disturbance of national plans.[14]

Foreign Domination of Industries

The concern that the industries of host countries will be dominated by affiliates of foreign MNEs flow, as Jack N. Behrman observes, from three sources: the giant size of MNEs and their affiliates, their concentration on key industrial sectors, and their aggressive behavior. Because the large affiliates of U.S. and other parent companies frequently have a higher rate of profit and reinvest a larger share of these profits than smaller companies—basically a benefit to host countries—they pose a threat to smaller, domestically owned firms. This is viewed as a danger by many Europeans who do not want to be condemned to the fate of Canada, which is regarded as being nearly 50 percent "owned" by U.S. enterprises.[15]

Equally distasteful to the governments and people of many advanced host countries is the thought that certain industrial sectors should fall under the domination of foreign MNEs. This is especially true when technology-oriented and growth sectors, which have strategic significance for a country's national security, are involved. Such control provides these firms with potential means to influence the international behavior of host governments, or at a minimum to restrict their freedom of external action.

Aggressive MNE behavior may range from a very rapid rate of acquisition of national companies, especially when accompanied by extensive publicity, to the displacement of nationals in top executive positions or their rejection for such a post in favor of a citizen of the MNE parent-company country. Other examples of aggressive behavior looked upon as damaging to the host country and its economy are offensive labor recruitment practices, such as the use of loudspeaker trucks placed in front of competitor's factories blaring out attractive offers to the latter's workers,[16] or flamboyant, hard-sell marketing techniques, including severe price-cutting.

Technological Dependence

The benefits that may accrue to host countries from the transfer of technological know-how were stressed above; however, while host country governments may appreciate the benefits they derive from the transfer of technologies, they may also be apprehensive that, in the event of serious needs, such transfers may be withheld either by decision of the headquarters company or by the government of the country in which that company or the parent company is located. The United States, the major "exporter" of technology in the world, has two principal laws on its books, the Trading with the Enemy Act of 1917 and the Export Control Act of 1949, under which the U.S. government can deny another country access to goods or technology generated by affiliates more than 50 percent U.S. owned in that country or a third country. Moreover, multinational corporations pursuing their own self-interests may use the transfer of technology to bargain for more favorable and flexible treatment. Thus, the ability of MNEs to transfer technology to the host countries of its affiliate creates serious dilemmas for the governmental decision makers. Governments fear that, without national sources of technological advance, their economic development will be impeded and their military and political influence reduced. But independent technological advance requires facilities for fundamental research within the national boundaries, which is frequently beyond the financial capabilities of domestic firms and even governments.

Disturbance to Economic Plans

The economically advanced countries of the world have increasingly assumed responsibilities for assuring the social and economic welfare of their citizens despite continued and varying lip service given to the principle of free enterprise. Economic growth and stability and full employment are the major goals of these countries, which they seek to reach through varying degrees of planning and the commitment of public means. France has been in the forefront of economic planning, but most of the other advanced countries have also become involved in some form of governmental planning for their national economies.

Jack N. Behrman argues that the more responsibility for economic growth the government accepts, the greater its control over the economy, and the greater the possibility that the MNE will be viewed as a potential disturber of economic plans.[17] Accordingly, since France has been the most active country in planning the growth and the direction of the economy, it has been least receptive to foreign direct investments, while Germany, Britain, and Italy, less active in economic planning, have been most receptive to these investments.

Although MNEs and their affiliates can make substantial contributions to the economic growth of the host countries, they can also inject uncertainties into the economies of these countries by altering economic factors and reducing the government's ability to predict reactions to its plans because MNEs may be able to ignore governmental persuasions and pursue policies not supportive of the national goals. In particular, they may cause uncertainties and risks by creating economic disequilibriums through concentration of foreign ownership in industries of the highest returns, overinvesting in equipment industries, producing deficits in the balance of payments, and causing disturbances in the labor market.

The Developing Countries

Many of the adverse effects of MNE transnational operations suffered by the economically advanced countries also burden the governments of the Third World; however, since manufacturing facilities of MNEs are mainly located in the advanced countries, some of the problem of control over MNE affiliates examined in the preceding pages and the security concerns flowing from the availability of advanced technologies are much less significant. On the other hand, a different set of issues and problems, many psychological in origin and stemming from the needs of nation-building, from the natural desires of political leaders to retain their power, and from the general Third World conditions of poverty, illiteracy, and traditional political cultures, aggravates some of the drawbacks and generates additional ones.

Without doubt, the governments of all developing countries wish to enhance the standard of living of their people through various means, such as diversification of agricultural commodity exports, industrialization, import substitution, and perhaps exports of manu-factured goods; however, they lack the necessary resources—tech-nology, skills, organization, access to international markets, and foreign exchange. The MNE possesses these resources, but suspicion and distrust on the part of governmental leaders and political elites in the developing countries color their perceptions of possible bene-fits and drawbacks.

What are the major reasons for this coloration of perceptions? All of the present-day Third World leaders have experienced the trauma of colonialism and have had instilled in them a fear of foreign capital as something inherently evil because it was used for the exploitation of resources that, in their view, belonged to the people of their countries. In addition, many of the present-day leaders have been attracted to the socialist model of the economy, either through their educational experiences or by being captivated by the apparent successes of the Soviet and Communist Chinese systems. Other lead-ers had backgrounds in the civil service or the military and therefore had very little comprehension of economic and business issues. In fact, in several developing countries, business activity has not been viewed as an "honorable" profession compared to some forms of public service, being a medical doctor or a lawyer, or joining the armed forces. In many of these countries, businessmen were consid-ered to be too closely associated with the former colonial powers, and some were accused of wanting to maintain the colonial form of government to protect their own economic interests. At the same time, political leaders in the forefront of the independent movements and the postindependence political consolidation period viewed indigenous business groups, especially the large business enterprises, as being too narrow in their outlook and exclusively concerned with the immediate question of profits, which, in turn, made them suspi-cious of all the motives and methods of businessmen.

The attitudes of Third World leadership groups toward MNEs, shaped by their backgrounds and positions held, have been rein-forced by the tasks that need to be performed to retain the position of power assumed after independence had been gained. These tasks include the continuous mobilization of citizens to rally around the nation, highly visible achievements in the enhancement of their economic welfare, and a continuous exaltation of the new nation-hood which must not suffer from any apparent infringement upon the independence and decision-making autonomy of the govern-ment. The priority of these tasks implies that the MNE, with its transnational capabilities and large resources, is likely to be regarded as a potential threat to the leadership groups and to the indepen-dence of their country because it may be difficult to control. Therefore the obvious benefits of an affiliate for a developing country may be outweighed by the problem of control to assure full acceptance by the MNE of the broad objectives of the host government. In practical terms this often means the insistence of the government that ownership of the MNE affiliate be at least 51 percent in its hands, although minority ownership has been accepted at times. Such an arrangement is carried out usually through the country's development corporation, a governmental agency that is the participant in a number of these ventures and supervises compliance with governmental regulations. Of course, these terms are frequently not acceptable to MNEs, and the range of beneficial investments in a given developing country may well be reduced.

Reactions and Counteractions of National Governments

The various benefits that are likely to accrue to parent and host countries from transnational initiatives of MNEs and the drawbacks that might also flow from these initiatives often pose serious dilemmas for political and administrative decision makers in the states affected. While on the one hand these decision makers may feel compelled to compete for these benefits by offering different inducements, such as tax advantages, to MNEs planning new foreign investments or facilities, they are also anxious to control as much as possible the influx of these investments or closely supervise their implementations. A major concern has been the prevention of foreign control of strategically important companies and industries, and for this purpose host governments in the industrially advanced countries as well as the Third World have employed weapons ranging from the stimulation of adverse public opinion to a variety of legal measures. The most extreme of these measures is *expropriation*, which has been carried out in several developing countries. In addition, host governments have attempted to curb and supervise foreign affiliates through various regulations which often have placed constraints on the strategies of maximizing profits through the use of multinational operations.

Governments of countries in which parent companies are located have also interfered with MNEs by regulating the outflow of capital and the transfer of technology. The reactions and counteractions of host and parent governments to MNE initiatives highlight the interaction process, which frequently leads to considerable tension between nongovernmental and governmental actors, as well as among the governments of states involved. The most usual counteractions applied have been: foreign investment controls, countermeasures of host governments to controls by parent governments over the transfer of technology, and operational and ownership restrictions by host governments. Investment controls can be applied by the governments of parent companies or by host governments. Control programs by parent governments tend to arouse the ire and dissatisfaction of host countries of MNE affiliates and lead to attempts to frustrate and counter these regulations, regarded as unwarranted intrusions into the sovereign sphere of the host governments.

Foreign investments and parent company–affiliate relations are also affected by exchange control programs instituted by such countries as Britain and France when balance-of-payments problems cause difficulties for the national economies. Obviously, countries with chronic balance-of-payments problems are undesirable parent countries for MNEs because these problems seriously hamper investments abroad unless such funds happen to be already in the foreign countries concerned.

What can host governments do to counter the possibility that foreign and especially U.S.-owned affiliates of MNEs will become tools for the foreign policy implementation of a third country through restrictions of technology transfers? One preventive step is refusal to authorize the establishment of an MNE affiliate or to insist that majority ownership be in the hands of its own citizens or of a public corporation. Another method is passage of a law compelling MNE affiliates to carry out directives and policies within carefully spelled-out areas regardless of ownership considerations. A final, very drastic measure would be the threat of expropriation, which may however be blunted by the fear of retaliation when industrially advanced countries are involved among which extensive MNE ties exist. While domestic political reasons may be a very persuasive motivation for such a step, the result in terms of economic benefits for the host country may be less than satisfactory. National pride in the new ownership may not be a substitute for proper and profitable management, and the government may be obliged to sign at least a temporary, costly management contract with the former owners, besides paying some kind of compensation.

It is obvious from the examination of parent and host government efforts to control the behavior of MNEs and their affiliates that domestic politics plays an influential role in the shaping of pertinent governmental decisions. Economic egoism and nationalistic forces support strong and extensive regulations and reinforce the suspicion of many governments, especially those in developing countries, that MNEs are acting in partnership with some foreign sovereign or are subservient to them. Certain private economic groups, judging that their vested interests are threatened by MNE activities, are pleased with the imposition of governmental controls and applaud openly or privately the efforts of their governments. One of these groups is organized labor (national and international), which has been strongly irked by the ability of MNEs to "export" jobs from one country to another, despite the advantages that may be offered by the multinational production facilities of these entities to bargain up wages and improve other conditions normally included in cross-national labor contracts. An economist of the AFL-CIO, Elizabeth R. Jager, observed early in 1970 that the fear of working people all over the world is heightened by the operation of the multinational firm.[18] The basic reason for this fear is that the search for cheaper labor is generally accepted as a rational decision for the management of MNEs to make. A similar opinion has been expressed by the former chairman of the German Federation of Trade Unions, Heinz O. Vetter. He declared that "the industrial giants which reach beyond national borders will ruthlessly exploit the international working cost differential for the purpose of increasing their profit."[19]

LABOR'S RESPONSES TO MNE CHALLENGES

The existence of an MNE with headquarters in a country different from where a union represents workers in a production affiliate and where, therefore, management personnel dealing with union officials are subject to pressures or control from a foreign source, is the basic challenge presented by the MNE to organized labor. Aggravating this situation are several additional factors. The headquarters of the MNE may insist that affiliates reflect the broader international or domestic objectives and policies of the parent company, whose industrial relations practices may be at variance with the local conditions. Job security may be more or less dependent on the global operations and performance of the MNE, which means that unprofitable operations in one country may have serious effects on the stability and conditions in another. Finally, nationalist, cultural, and ideological influences may impair a rational approach of union leaders and members in dealing with the affiliate of an MNE.[20]

Strikes

Under the operational conditions enjoyed by MNEs, the ultimate weapon available to unions against a local affiliate, the strike, may not be useful. Measures to reduce production and to apply economic sanctions such as slowdowns may also be ineffective. To the extent that products affected by such measures can be readily imported from facilities in other countries, the union weapons can be blunted. An example is the eight-and-one-half-month-long strike by the United Steel Workers (USW) of America against the U.S. copper, lead, and zinc companies in the 1960s. Because of the multinational nature of the major producers, production was intensified in Chile and other countries where the struck companies had mines, and their products were imported into the United States. Closing down the American mines drove the world price for the metals sky high. Thus, the losses suffered in the United States by the MNEs involved were more than made up by their increased profits from their operations abroad. The result was that the companies could have endured the strike indefinitely.

Two additional factors may be responsible for materially reducing the effectiveness of a strike against a local MNE affiliate. The particular item produced in the affiliate might be only a small part of the MNE's global business and therefore the damage suffered by the entire enterprise may be relatively minor. Moreover, the threat of "exporting" the production facilities themselves is always present and may constitute an alternative option of MNE management to union harassment and unfavorable labor climate. In fact, the governments of third countries and their labor organizations may seek to exploit such situations and induce the MNE through various incentives to shift their production facilities to their own territories.

This problem is highlighted by testimony given during the 1970 Hearings of the Subcommittee on Foreign Economic Policy in the Multinational Corporation and International Investment. Paul Jennings, president of the International Union of Electrical, Radio and Machine Workers, stated:

> About a year ago, General Instrument Corp. transferred TV tuner and other component production to its Taiwan and Portuguese plants, shutting down two New England plants and most of a third. Between 3,000 and 4,000 workers were permanently laid off. General Instrument increased its employment in Taiwan from 7,200 to over 12,000. General Instrument is that nation's largest employer, with more workers employed there than in all its U.S. operations combined.
>
> A few months ago, Motorola shut down its picture plant, selling its machinery and equipment to a General Telephone and Electronics subsidiary in Hong Kong. A second picture tube firm commenced operations in Mexico, taking advantage of item 807 of the Tariff Schedules. Friden, a division of Singer Corp., and Burroughs, both discontinued

production of electronic desk calculators. Their desk calculators are now made for them in Japan by Hitachi and other Japanese firms. The calculators are sold in the United States by their former manufacturers under the latter's label. So, here we have another growth industry that U.S. based multinational firms have abandoned as producers—becoming importers of the products they once made.[21]

The response of the larger labor unions and union associations in the United States and Europe to these problems has been to organize transnational cooperation of unions wherever plants of MNEs are located. David H. Blake observes[22] that this is a rather new phenomenon which has neither deep nor wide-ranging roots. Most of the efforts toward transnational cooperation date from the 1960s, although the International Metalworkers Federation with a membership exceeding 10 million had established world autoworker company councils for Ford and General Motors as early as 1956.

While interunion cooperation is now growing more extensive and intensive, the use of the strike as a weapon on an international basis to force acceptance of union demands remains highly questionable. Only where the technology of an MNE is vertically integrated to a point where interruption would be very costly despite possible alternative technical facilities can a strike directed at the proper plant succeed in checkmating the entire enterprise. MNEs falling into this category are found in the petroleum and aluminum industries, and labor relations in these industries need to be fashioned by management in such a way as to avoid this trouble.

Other Measures

While it is evidently difficult to organize comprehensive strike action against all production affiliates of MNEs, what other measures are available for organized labor to meet the challenges of the multinational corporation? The first task is to ensure having viable cooperative partners in the countries where MNE affiliates are located. This does not present any great difficulty in most advanced countries of the Free World, where unions are recognized as legitimate bargaining partners. Problems, however, exist in many developing countries, in which unions are extremely weak and are subordinated to the national political leadership as instruments of control. R. W. Cox calls these organizations "political front" unions. They may be the downgraded residue of former revolutionary movements or a protective device engineered by a conservative leadership.[23] These unions operate under governmental and political pressures and do not always understand either the advantages or mechanics of collective bargaining, nor do they comprehend the advantages that may flow from increasing productivity and adhering to agreed-upon rules.

Union Strategies

To help these unions grow and develop if governmental policy permits, American and European unions have established training and exchange programs, provided staff and research facilities, offered financial and equipment support, and provided information on comparative wages and fringe benefits of MNE affiliates in advanced countries, as well as on the companies' profits, dividends, executive pay, and the like.[24]

An interesting example of transnational union cooperation in which the success of a local strike was at stake involved the USW, a union of bauxite miners in Jamaica, and the Aluminum Company of America. When the bauxite miners, with the advice of USW officials, went on strike against Alcoa to obtain higher wages and other benefits, the first reaction of Alcoa and the Jamaican government was to throw the American union advisers out of the country; however, USW is an international union representing steelworkers and unions not only in the United States, but also in Canada. Using its office in Toronto, the USW leadership asked to have three experienced Canadian strike leaders sent to Jamaica. Because they held Commonwealth passports, the Jamaican government could not deny their admission. With their help the strike was settled, resulting in substantial benefits to the Jamaican workers.[25]

A second measure of transnational union collaboration consists of the coordination of objectives, policies, and strategies with respect to MNEs. The process of coordination takes place mainly among unions and union federations of specific industries, but at times exceeds these confines. The major vehicle for the automobile industry has been the IMF, whose councils have been expanded to include union representation of Chrysler, Fiat, Simca, Rootes, Volkswagen, Mercedes-Benz, and Japanese firms. Similar coordination attempts have also been made in other industries, such as the production of agricultural implements. In addition, smaller annual meetings between pertinent unions in two countries have also been initiated to coordinate international bargaining. For example, in the summer of 1969, two British unions, the Transport and General Workers Union (membership 1.5 million) and the Amalgamated Union of Engineering and Foundry Workers (membership 1.1 million) met with a delegation from the UAW led by Leonard Woodcock, then vice president of that union. Commenting on the talks, Woodcock said:

> These were but the first of a series, We have much to learn from each other. And we have much accommodating to do to each other. But the rise of internationally-flung corporations operating beyond the reach of any laws dictates that we work out ways to make binding agreements for the protection of all workers with our brother and sister unions all over the world.[26]

Union Objectives

What are the major objectives the transnational union coalition pursues with respect to MNEs? According to Leonard Woodcock, a long-range goal is to "eliminate labor as a competitive factor in the international sphere, just as we have eliminated labor as a competitive factor in the national sphere."[27] This implies transnational bargaining and perhaps negotiating with an MNE giant such as GM on contracts in worldwide terms. It also implies leveling up wage rates in all countries where MNE affiliates are on the basis of a standard rate for a particular job. The European union federations basically support these goals, but because of the regionally limited nature of their activities, demand only that employers be persuaded "to negotiate on the European level."[28]

Some results of the coordinated pursuit of global and regional objectives by unions and union federations have already emerged. Carefully coordinated pressures applied on headquarters and affiliates of MNEs have resulted in wage rises both in advanced countries, such as Australia and Japan, and in many developing countries. Wages in the United States and Canadian automobile factories have been equalized. In one case, Venezuelan union organizers fired by a Ford affiliate in that country were reinstated. And the first EEC-wide collective bargaining agreement was signed in June 1968 between agricultural unions affiliated with the ICFTU and the WCL, on the one hand, and Community farmers organizations on the other.[29]

Appeals to Governments

A final set of measures employed by unions to meet the challenge of MNEs consists of appeals to national governments and IGOs. Some union spokesmen also call for economic and political control of MNEs.[30] Such control could insist on the enforcement of antitrust laws to prevent the giants of the industrial world from abusing their economic power.

The exportation of jobs by MNEs is fought in the United States also by union demands to the government to institute a careful control of the flow of American capital to build foreign plants which would compete unfairly against domestic wages. In addition the union leadership advocates a much higher tax on earnings of foreign affiliates of American MNEs. Some unions also propose import quotas on those items whose production has been shifted to low-cost labor areas such as the manufacture of television sets in Mexico and Taiwan.[31] Finally, the UAW has urged the government to require U.S. foreign affiliates to increase wage standards in their plants as fast as productivity of individual workers rises. All this points up the domestic conflicts that MNEs can cause in various polities which are apt to magnify the drawbacks and may distort or shroud the genuine benefits MNEs can bring to the governments and peoples of the countries in which they operate.

CONSEQUENCES FOR THE INTERNATIONAL SYSTEM

The final point in this discussion of the MNE as a nongovernmental force in world politics is an examination of the consequences for the international system and its subsystems flowing from the effects on national governments that have been and are being caused by transnational MNE initiatives. Are these effects promoting greater collaboration among governments, or are they responsible for a wider range of conflicts? Do they produce greater interdependence between states or are they the cause for greater dependence of particular states on other governmental or nongovernmental actors? Are there indications that the worldwide net of relations created by MNEs is a factor for global political integration and how does it affect schemes for integration of international regions?

A growing number of authors have addressed themselves to these questions,[32] but empirical data are scarce; therefore, it is difficult to come up with anything but highly tentative answers. From the analysis of benefits and drawbacks for parent and host countries, one general impression emerges: while from a rational point of view governmental decision makers of both types of countries are fully aware of the benefits of MNE operations, their inability to control fully the continuity and direction of these benefits is highly frustrating and leads to many conflicts and tensions. For this reason, the motivation for collaboration among these countries is generally low despite the obvious need of MNEs with transnationally integrated production facilities for such collaboration and the clear benefits for governments and people springing from the results. Although the continued association of multinational executives and engineering staffs is likely to lead to the development of a transnationally rather than nationally centered elite, a development accelerated by the formation of transnational professional organizations, its power to bring about greater collaboration among governments is apt to remain small until other, and often more influential, elites shift from their pursuit of mostly narrow national interests and objectives to those of a more global or region-wide nature. Moreover, there is a salient question as to how much intergovernmental collaboration MNEs really want. Raymond Vernon suggests that they tend to support only limited selective intergovernmental agreements, which in their view are particularly helpful. Otherwise, many multinational corporations seem to have elected to present a low silhouette and to tone down previous emphases of the worldwide nature of their activities.[33] While this new shyness may be primarily a tactical move, it may also reflect the recognition of certain domestic and global political realities adverse to many MNE objectives.

Without doubt, the sources for conflict introduced among national governments by MNE activities are substantial. They range from envy because of the uneven distribution of MNE benefits to fears of losing important national prerogatives. This fear is accentuated among the governments of smaller countries because they must reckon not only with the extensive power of larger states but also with that of giant, global enterprises disposing of enormous financial and technological resources.

The conflicts among governments generated by MNE activities are not likely to result in the outbreak of hostilities, but they can be responsible for dangerous suspicions and frictions damaging the climate of international relations. This situation can be aggravated when MNEs try to pit government against government, either by seeking parent government support or by using the threat of moving investments from one country to another. Of course, MNE managers realize that for such actions they may have to pay a price in terms of ill will and retaliation, but nevertheless these are strategies that the particular nature of their operations makes available to them.

If a rising number of conflicts and tensions between governments are generated by MNE activities, one may raise the question of whether these effects are not moderated *per force* by the growing interdependence stemming from the expanding global network of MNE transnational activities, such as investments, integrated production facilities, transfers of technology and managerial skills, and others. This proposition implies that the governments of the states of the world become so mutually dependent on each other because of the transnational interactions caused by MNEs that the high cost of disentanglement compels them to maintain a level of collaboration. However, as Kenneth Waltz has persuasively argued,[34] this proposition is open to question, or at least needs modification, because interdependence is reduced by the immense disparity in the capabilities of states. As a consequence, Waltz asserts that high inequality among states entails lowered interdependence. For example, a powerful country such as the United States can extricate itself from transnational business entanglements with much greater ease and impunity than economically weak countries for whose governments certain MNE activities, including new exports, may be an essential part of economic and perhaps political development and stability. For this reason, governments of smaller countries are strongly constrained to make domestic economic and political decisions with an eye on their external environment and have difficulty in casting off transnational business ties, even if their citizens vehemently object to the relationship of interdependence, as is true of Canada.[35]

Considering that MNEs dispose of tremendous financial resources and are at times willing to use them to mold international regions together while national governments are reluctant to take such action, multinational corporations can sometimes impose interdependence. An example can be found in Latin America, where multinational firms, in order to achieve economies of scale, have obliged two countries to cooperate by specializing production of components in each country.[36] Such instances are rare, however, although from a rational standpoint, a proliferation of similar production arrangements in developing areas could have highly beneficial long-range consequences for the economic development of the Third World.

Waltz argues that the word *interdependence* is pleasing rhetoric, inasmuch as it obscures the inequalities of national capability, points to reciprocal dependence, and suggests that all states are playing the same game.[37] If such perceptions are in fact conjured up in the minds of national decision makers, this would be all to the good. It would induce governments to treat the acts of other governments as though they were events within its borders and this could lead to a feeling of converging interests. However, the realistic recognition of the inequalities of states is more likely to cause or increase perceptions of dependence rather than interdependence and will tend to sharpen suspicion, envy, and tension, thereby contributing to greater conflict rather than collaboration in the international system. The sentiments of frustration harbored by many Canadians vis-à-vis the United States constitute a case in point. As a consequence, governmental leaders may feel called upon to resort to national means and solutions as a countervailing force against the real or imagined threat of dependence on international business and other countries. Such actions harm the prospects for useful collaboration among states and are likely to undermine the fruitful performance of the transnational business network for the transfer of ideas, technology, know-how, and capital.

A special dimension of interdependence and dependence pertains to MNE activities in communist countries. In these countries, the multinational firm can play the role of a *transideological enterprise* where it is involved in a joint venture with a state-operated enterprise and thereby is engaged in an international division of labor across ideological borders. While an increasing number of MNEs, such as Fiat, undoubtedly have played this role, responding to changing attitudes and needs in communist countries and impelled by new opportunities for markets and profits, the number of actual MNEs involved remains small. Nevertheless, certain forces in the capitalist and communist worlds may be instrumental in expanding the transideological experiences of businesses.[38] The agreements reached at the Conference on Security and Cooperation in Europe (Helsinki Accords) in 1975, designed to encourage closer economic and technological cooperation between East and West, are an example. The needs of the Soviet Union for such cooperation motivated an agreement between the Soviet government and General Electric and have led to the establishment of branch offices of American banks in Moscow.

We must also keep in mind that socialism and capitalism are not uniform in all countries where such systems exist, but assume a number of forms, some of which come to resemble each other. Over the years the importance of ideology has receded somewhat, and pragmatic approaches to the solution of problems are preferred. In turn, common ways of looking at problems can produce the feeling that common interests exist.[39] Finally, while competitive coexistence may still be the order of the day, the borrowing of beneficial elements of the respective capitalist or socialist systems has become accepted. For all the above reasons, it is not at all inconceivable that transideological enterprises may contribute to a growing level of interdependence between Communist and Free World countries, but the process of changing the pattern of transnational interaction is likely to be slow and subject to political and military pressures on both sides of the Iron Curtain. As Howard V. Perlmutter suggests, the learning process along the East-West watershed is painful, but in the end it may result in the legitimization of what he calls "transideological zones, mediated through transideological dialogues, and culminating in a greater abundance of already existing transideological licensing, subcontracting and co-production systems."[40]

CONCLUSIONS

In conclusion we may ask what impact the transnational interaction process mobilized by MNEs has now and will have in the future on global and regional integration. While rational thinkers may recognize the existence of true common economic interests, and the need of the world economic system to be a whole, this concept may be accepted by individual national decision makers only in theory and disregarded when it comes to specific decisions for their countries.

Another argument in support of the MNE as contributor to global political integration is essentially functionalist in nature. It states that MNEs satisfy important needs of mankind by raising economic levels, by reducing social disparities in the fields of education and health, by narrowing the gap between the rich and poor countries, and by fostering supporting transnational groups benefiting from the MNE activities (i.e., consumers and workers). Even if we were to accept these results as forthcoming, we would have to remember that functionalist forces are inherently weak and rarely are able to overcome ideologically and emotionally inspired counterforces, such as pervasive nationalism, strong ethnocentric orientation, and powerful political ideologies.

Finally, there is the institutional argument that the proliferation of MNE activities requires international institutions for their regulation.[41] The clamor for such a regime may come from the national governments, powerful labor unions, and the MNEs. The governments may recognize that their interests would be safeguarded better through such a regime which might control transnational movements of capital, profits, and expense allocations. Labor would regard such a regime as a possible protection against a loss of job opportunities in the advanced countries and against the erosion of wages and benefits through competition by low-wage workers in the Third World. The MNEs might find that such a regime would bring greater security, stability, and predictability for the management of their transnational affairs. Such institutions could be incorporated in the United Nations structure, which might give this organization a new important function and needed lift of morale. At the same time, it might instill in the national governments an awareness that the world and mankind are indeed interdependent and that new problems can best be solved on a global basis.

Again, however, a few words of strong caution are in order. Despite a very excellent and balanced U.N. report by "Eminent Persons" regarding a code of conduct for MNEs,[42] the United Nations is making very slow progress with one of the major difficulties lying in the insistence of Third World nations that such a code be mandatory for MNEs, but not apply to governmental actions of parent and host countries. MNEs and developed countries at present are prepared to accept only a voluntary code; but even if mandatory compliance were eventually agreed upon, enforcement would be most difficult. Moreover, a code that would be administered by U.N. civil servants would arouse the ire of national bureaucrats, who may be fearful that a new layer of authority created above them would lower their positions of power and prestige.[43] Similar apprehension may also be aroused in the minds of the national political leadership, which may view the new U.N. administrators as competitors in the exercise of what previously were exclusive national prerogatives.

On balance, then, while the vista of a global industrial estate is appealing, the short-range contribution MNE activities can make to global political integration seems to be limited. Although it is reasonable to assume that, in a shrinking world with a rapidly expanding MNE net, trends toward a global industrial estate should be emerging, little empirical evidence can be offered at present to support this argument.

The situation is somewhat different when it comes to the contribution made by transnational MNE activities toward regional political integration. One reason is that, in a number of regions, such as in Western Europe, a clearly defined institutional framework exists which influences both national governmental agencies and regional organs and provides channels for articulating and presenting coordinated demands of MNEs. If these demands have widespread utilitarian value for the people of the region, favorable responses by the national authorities are not likely to be completely denied no matter how strong the national opposition is. The slow harmonization of fiscal laws and technical standards in the EEC is at least in part the result of the concerted MNE pressures.[44] Under these conditions, the political socialization process among executive elites of the MNEs may also receive a strong impetus. This process is accelerated as MNEs form or participate in functional and general interest group structures within the member states and the regional system.* These transnational groups, operating within a regional context, have the advantage that they can shift their identity and loyalties to a more specific target than is possible on a worldwide basis. Regional ideologies can then be fostered and may become stronger as the number of beneficiaries from these activities increases and the benefits become more visibile. Politically speaking, what is being witnessed is the creation of a penetrative political system in which business elites and bureaucrats of different countries and the regional organization begin to make joint decisions affecting the distribution of resources and values within the region.

All in all, one may conclude that, while the consequences of MNE initiatives and their effects on national governments are clearly visible, it is too early to render definite judgments as to enhanced collaboration or conflict in the global pattern of international interaction. It appears that, from a short-range view, conflict is likely to increase, but that over the long run, collaboration among governmental and nongovernmental actors may win the upper hand as the advantages and disadvantages flowing from growing interdependence are seen in more rational and balancing terms. With respect to global integration, little hard evidence is available to suggest a meaningful contribution by MNE initiatives and activities at the present time; however, the prospects of regional political integration through MNE activities are better but the final outcome depends on many other factors as well. One of these is the continued growth and proliferation of MNEs and their affiliates, and there are some doubts about the continuation of this trend for a number of reasons:

1. The accumulation of private capital in the Western industrialized countries has slowed down and this trend is likely to continue in the foreseeable future. Investment funds may well be rationed, and high-risk investments are likely to have low priorities even for natural resource developments when they are envisioned for less developed countries with hostile investment climates. An example is Exxon's halting exploration in Malaysia in 1975 and cutting out plans for installation of oil production platforms in offshore Malaysian waters. Clearly, the philosophy of "growth at any cost," which used to be espoused by many MNE managements, has given way again to a careful calculation of costs, risks, and profits.

---

* The European Movement, a group strongly promoting West European unification, has 102 corporate members, including a number of American MNEs with affiliates in Britain. These MNEs have given their full support (financially and otherwise) to Britain's entry in the Common Market, which has aroused bitter complaints from British labor unions opposed to British membership in the EEC.

2. The incentive of low wages for American and some European MNEs to set up production facilities in foreign countries is slowly disappearing in the developed world. In mid 1975 average hourly wages in Sweden, Belgium, Germany, and the Netherlands were higher than in the United States and this trend has continued. While in developing countries, such as Mexico or Taiwan, a considerable wage differential vis-à-vis North America and Western Europe continues to exist, the pay for workers has risen there also and is likely to rise further, particularly if unionization makes progress.

3. An important motivation for investments by MNEs in foreign plants has been a variety of trade restrictions making it impossible for goods imported from third countries to compete successfully in national markets. However, tariff and nontariff barriers have been gradually lowered in successive multilateral trade negotiations. The next multinational tariff negotiations to be undertaken under the U.S. Trade Reform Act of 1974 may see the complete elimination of certain tariffs.

4. Some of the home country governments, prodded by domestic political forces, may begin to tax profits generated in host countries even if they are already taxed abroad on the same level as in home countries. The U.S. Congress has begun chipping away at the alleged tax advantage of American MNEs and may go further with the result that the cost of foreign investment will increase. Such "double" taxation could well reduce the appeal of international production and marketing activities. Proper tax harmonization among parent and host countries may be necessary to restore interest in setting up additional MNE subsidiaries in new countries.

Thus, the future of MNE operations throughout the world is somewhat clouded by more careful management considerations, and the frequently expressed assumption that the MNE network will continue to intensify across the globe should perhaps be accepted only with some reservations.

SUMMARY

The impact of MNEs on international relations stems from (1) the interactions between MNEs on the one hand and parent and host governments on the other, (2) the responses of international labor federations to the challenges posed by MNEs, and (3) the effects of MNE activities on the international system as a whole.

MNEs may benefit their host countries through **inflow of capital, transfer of technology, reduction of prices,** and **promotion of regional development.** Industrially advanced countries may view

MNEs as a liability because they fear foreign domination of industries, technological dependence, and disturbance of national plans. In short, they do not want to be condemned to Canada's fate of being 50 percent "owned" by U.S. enterprises.

What can host governments do to counter the threat of MNE control? They can refuse to authorize the establishment of an MNE affiliate, regulate the outflow of funds and the transfer of technology, impose operational and ownership restrictions, or expropriate the facilities.

Under the operational conditions enjoyed by MNEs, the ultimate weapon available to unions against a local affiliate, the **strike**, may not be useful, and measures to reduce production and apply economic sanctions may also be ineffective. The response of the larger labor unions to these problems has been to organize **transnational cooperation of unions** wherever MNE plants are located and to appeal to national governments and IGOs. A long-range goal is to "eliminate labor as a competitive factor in the international sphere."

In communist countries, the multinational firm can play the role of a **transideological enterprise** where it is involved in a joint venture with a state-operated enterprise and thereby is engaged in an international division of labor across ideological borders. In time, transideological enterprises may contribute to increased interdependence between Communist and Free World countries.

In terms of international collaboration and conflict, MNEs are likely to cause more frictions between host and home governments than contribute to greater harmony. Although MNEs have raised the level of interdependence among the countries of the world through the spreading network of subsidiaries, this development has also produced perceptions of dependence, especially in the minds of Third World leaders. Whether U.N. regulation of MNEs through a code of conduct could ameliorate the relationship between MNEs and host countries is far from certain; in fact the controversy about whether the code should or should not be binding on MNEs and governments alike may well prevent agreement on any kind of code.

NOTES

1. See Harry G. Johnson, "The Efficiency and Welfare Implications of the International Corporation," in Charles P. Kindleberger, ed., *The International Corporation: A Symposium* (Cambridge, Mass.: M.I.T. Press, 1970), pp. 35–56.

2. For details see Werner J. Feld, *Nongovernmental Forces and World Politics: A Study of Business, Political and Labor Groups* (New York: Praeger, 1972), pp. 70–82.

3. For other examples see Jack N. Behrman, *National Interests and the Multinational Enterprise: Tensions Among the North Atlantic Countries* (Englewood Cliffs, N.J.: Prentice-Hall, 1970), pp. 23–26.

4. John N. Dunning, *The Role of American Investment in the British Economy* (London: PEP, 1969), pp. 73 and 147–153.

5. Behrman, *National Interests and the Multinational Enterprise*, op. cit., p. 20.

6. Cf. *The Multinational Company and National Development: A Lamp Anthology* (New York: Standard Oil Company of New Jersey, 1970), passim; and Neil H. Jacoby, "The Multinational Corporation," *Center Magazine*, vol. 3, no. 3 (May 1970), pp. 37–55. See also Harry G. Johnson, "The Multinational Corporation as Development Agent," and Paul Streeten, "Obstacles to Private Foreign Investment in the LDCs," *Columbia Journal of World Business*, vol. 5, no. 3 (May–June 1970), pp. 25–30 and 31–39, respectively.

7. For a more detailed discussion of this subject, see Deena R. Khatkhate, "Management in Developing Countries," *Finance and Development*, no. 3 (1971), pp. 8–14. The author argues that, in view of the large unemployment in the Third World, the managerial approach should be qualitatively different from that in developed areas and that high labor intensity should be regarded as a virtue rather than a vice when factories are planned in Third World countries.

8. Cf. Jacoby, "The Multinational Corporation," op. cit., p. 43 for details and sources.

9. Mauritius, *4-Year Plan for Social & Economic Development*, 1971.

10. Jacoby, "The Multinational Corporation," op. cit., p. 44.

11. Gilles Y. Bertin, "Foreign Investment in France," in Litvak and Maule, *Foreign Investment and Host Countries* (New York: Praeger, 1970), p. 116.

12. For details, see Behrman, *National Interests and the Multinational Enterprise*, op. cit., pp. 89–93.

13. See Sanford Rose, "The Rewarding Strategies of Multinationalism," *Fortune*, September 15, 1968, especially p. 104, for details.

14. These categories are borrowed from Behrman, *National Interests and the Multinational Enterprise*, op. cit., chapters 3–5.

15. Ibid., p. 34. Some observers place United States ownership at 67 percent. See *International Herald-Tribune*, Nov. 3, 1971. These figures depend on what is counted and what is meant by being "owned." It is also claimed that companies employing 5,000 workers or more are 90 percent owned or controlled by American firms. The governments in industrialized countries could, of course, insist on 51 percent ownership by their own nationals when new investments are made, but this may invite retaliation when their own companies want to make investments in other developed countries.

16. Roger Blanpain, "American Involvement in Belgium," in Alfred Kamin, ed., *Western European Labor and the American Corporation* (Washington, D.C.: The Bureau of National Affairs, 1970), pp. 455–465.

17. Behrman, *National Interests and the Multinational Enterprise*, op. cit., p. 71.

18. Elizabeth R. Jager, "The Conglomerate Goes Global," *AFL-CIO American Federationist*, January 1970.

19. Heinz O. Vetter, "The Lessons of the ICFTU Congress," *DGB Reports*, vol. 3, no. 4 (1969), p. 38.

20. Cf. David H. Blake, "Multinational Corporations, International Unionism, and Global Integration," paper presented at the Research Conference on the Multinational Corporation in the Global Political System at the University of Pennsylvania, April 22–23, 1971 (mimeographed).

21. See the statement by Paul Jennings in U.S. Congress, Joint Economic Committee, Subcommittee on Foreign Economic Policy, 91st Congress, 2nd Session, July 27–30, 1970, p. 815.

22. "Multinational Corporations, International Unionism, and Integration," op. cit., p. 16.

23. R. W. Cox, "Labor and Transnational Relations," *International Organization*, vol. 25, no. 3 (Summer 1971), p. 573. Cox contrasts this type of union to social reform labor movements and interest group unions in the advanced countries of the Free World. The former are found, for example, in Britain and Scandinavia and can, because of their historical background, subordinate the interests of workers to general objectives of social reform for the benefit of the working class and other low status social groups. The latter are not likely to recognize any conflict between the interests of the workers they represent and broader social objectives and will act without inhibition in their members' particular interests. American unions fall into this category. A final category consists of mobilization unions which, following the Soviet pattern, serve to mobilize, in concert with other groups, the active population in support of revolutionary national goals defined by the political leadership. Each of these types of unions may be found occasionally outside their customary habitat.

24. James P. Gannon, "More U.S. Mining Help Foreign Workers to Pressure American Company Overseas," *The Wall Street Journal*, December 7, 1970, p. 30.

25. USW, Report of Officers, 15th Constitutional Convention (September 28–October 2, 1970), pp. 109–110.

26. *UAW-Solidarity Report*, October 1969.

27. *Journal of Commerce*, May 12, 1971.

28. *Agence Europe Document* no. 528, May 30, 1969, p. 4.

29. *European Community*, June 1969, p. 18.

30. Elizabeth R. Jager, "The Conglomerate Goes Global," op. cit., and *Agence Europe Bulletin*, July 9 and 25, 1969.

31. Cf. the statement by Herbert Maier, ICFTU, in U.S. Congress, Joint Economic Committee, Subcommittee on Foreign Economic Policy, *Foreign Economic Policy for the 1970's*, 91st Cong., 2nd Sess., July 27–30, 1970, Part IV, pp. 821–833.

32. See the various articles of Perlmutter cited earlier; Behrman, *National Interests and the Multinational Enterprise;* Kenneth N. Waltz, "The Myth of Interdependence," and Raymond Vernon, "Future of the Multinational Enterprise," in Charles P. Kindleberger, ed., *The International Cor-*

poration (Cambridge, Mass.: M.I.T. Press, 1970), pp. 205–223 and 373–400, respectively; J. S. Nye, "Multinational Enterprise and Prospects for Global Integration"; and Jonathan F. Galloway, "The Role of Multinational Enterprises in the Integration of Western Europe and the North Atlantic Countries," papers presented for the Research Conference in the Multinational Corporation in the Global Political System, University of Pennsylvania, April 22–23, 1971 (mimeographed).

33. Vernon, "Future of the Multinational Enterprise," op. cit., p. 395.

34. Waltz, "The Myth of Interdependence," op. cit., pp. 207 and 214.

35. See also Litvak and Maule, *Foreign Investment and Host Countries,* op. cit., p. 95.

36. The framework of such cooperation was set by the LAFTA Treaty which advocated the conclusion of complementarity agreements among member countries. See Sidney Dell, *A Latin American Common Market* (London: Oxford University Press, 1966), pp. 125–138 and 174–196.

37. Waltz, "The Myth of Interdependence," op. cit.

38. This term has been coined by Howard V. Perlmutter in "Emerging East-West Ventures: The Transideological Enterprise," *Columbia Journal of World Politics,* September–October 1969, pp. 39–50.

39. Ibid., pp. 44–45.

40. Ibid., p. 50.

41. See, for example, Paul M. Goldberg and C. P. Kindleberger, "Toward a GATT for Investment: A Proposal for Supervision of the International Corporation," *Law and Policy in International Business,* vol. 2, no. 2 (Summer 1970), pp. 295–325.

42. See Werner J. Feld, "UN Supervision over Multinational Corporations: Realistic Expectations or Exercise in Futility," *Orbis,* vol. 19, no. 4 (Winter 1976), pp. 1499–1518.

43. See Werner Feld, "National Bureaucracies of the EEC Member States and Political Integration: A Preliminary Inquiry," in Robert S. Jordan, ed., *International Administration: Its Evolution and Contemporary Applications* (London: Oxford University Press, 1971), pp. 228–244.

44. See Eric Stein, *Harmonization of European Company Laws, National Reform and Transnational Coordination* (Indianapolis: Bobbs Merrill, 1971).

SUGGESTED READINGS

COOPER, R. N. *The Economics of Interdependence: Economic Policy in the Atlantic Community.* New York: McGraw-Hill, 1968.

HAAS, E. G. *The Web of Interdependence.* Englewood Cliffs, N.J.: Prentice-Hall, 1970.

NYE, J. S., AND R. O. KEOHANE. *Power and Interdependence.* Boston: Little, Brown, 1977.

VERNON, R. *Storm over the Multinationals: The Real Issues.* Cambridge, Mass.: Harvard University Press, 1977.

CHAPTER FIFTEEN
THE CHANGING PHYSICAL GLOBAL ENVIRONMENT

In Chapters 1 and 2 we mentioned that changes in the physical environment of the international arena have had and will have significant effects on the pattern of international relations. We pointed especially to the gradual exhaustion of petroleum resources, which already had produced extensive shifts in the power relationship among governmental and nongovernmental actors and was having marked, though differing, impacts on the life-styles and economic welfare of the people of the world.

In this chapter we shall concentrate on additional components of the physical environment of the international system which are likely to bring about changes in the pattern of international interactions. We shall also examine selected advances in technology that might alleviate the problems apt to be caused by the exhaustion of certain critical raw materials, and take a look at other technological innovations that might offer new opportunities as well as dangers for the welfare of mankind. In particular, we shall discuss the peaceful use of nuclear energy for the generation of electric power, the exploitation of hitherto untapped resources of the sea and the sea bed, and the utilization of space-orbiting electronic devices for communications and meteorology. Overarching these activities are ever-present ecological concerns about air and water pollution. The movement toward a "zero-growth population" world is an example of the impact ecological questions can have on international politics; therefore, the problems of the ecology will also be discussed in the following pages.

NUCLEAR ENERGY AND ELECTRIC POWER

Since World War II the consumption of energy worldwide has increased tremendously and has outrun the discovery of new sources, thereby creating an increasingly serious crisis. The politics of oil pursued by the countries in the Middle East have cast the energy problem in stark relief and have suddenly produced a personal awareness of this problem among the peoples of the United States, Western Europe, and other industrially advanced societies.

The worldwide increase in the consumption of energy has been led by the United States. With 6 percent of the world's population, the United States accounts for 35 percent of the world's energy consumption. United States demand for total energy is increasing at a rate of about 4 percent per year; but the demand for electricity has been rising about 7 percent per year in America and thus will double every ten years. The United States is by far the largest producer of electricity, generating more than the next four highest countries combined.

The fuels used for the generation of electricity traditionally have been coal and later, natural gas and oil. With oil and gas having become scarce commodities, American and European utility plants had to look for other kinds of fuel. Coal is still available in large quantities, but much of it contains a high degree of sulfur and therefore its pollution effects are very serious. Despite the fact that up to now nuclear sources have been considerably more costly than the traditional sources, nuclear capacity was explored as a new source for generating electricity because it uses a clean fuel with minimum transportation problems and may, in the long run, be the best economical and environmental choice. As a consequence of improved technology in manufacturing nuclear reactors, it is now estimated that by 1985 about 32 percent of American needs for electricity will be fulfilled by nuclear means. In Western Europe at least 29 percent of electricity production will be fueled by nuclear resources in contrast to 3.6 percent in 1970; and for Australia, Japan, New Zealand, and the Republic of South Africa, the estimates run as high as 23 percent. It is interesting to note that the Soviet Union is also moving toward nuclear reactors for electricity and expects to have 30 percent of its electricity requirements derived from nuclear sources. The figure for Eastern Europe is 10 percent; Latin America, 13 percent; Asia, 14 percent; and Africa, 2.2 percent.[1]

Despite the promising future for nuclear reactors, many international problems are involved in the peaceful use of atomic energy. At the bottom of all of these problems is the fact that nuclear energy remains closely wedded to the production of atomic weapons. As a consequence, the nuclear policy of countries that have developed nuclear weapons, such as the United States, the Soviet Union, Great Britain, and France, has been maximum governmental control over nuclear energy. Although over the years there has been a limited decentralization and a shift of responsibility for atomic development from the government to private corporations, these changes have been accompanied by increased governmental regulation both within nation-states and across national boundaries through the use of special IGOs, such as the International Atomic Energy Agency (IAEA), a specialized unit of the United Nations.

In countries that did not undertake military nuclear activities a somewhat different pattern developed. In such countries, especially the Federal Republic of Germany and Japan, private enterprise played a more important role from the beginning, but in no country has the peaceful use of atomic energy become a purely private affair in terms of research, development, or exploitation.[2]

Developing countries have also placed great value on the acquisition of nuclear technology for both economic reasons and prestige. They recognize that nuclear technology is likely to become a crucial instrument for economic development and for social progress. In view of the extraordinary expenses involved in the development of nuclear technology, however, it is clear that only wealthy, industrially advanced countries can afford to move into the nuclear field, and even in those countries financial support for research and development must be furnished by the governments in order to keep up with the United States and perhaps the Soviet Union.

U.S. Leadership in Peaceful Nuclear Technology

It is because of the large expenditures made by the United States government for nuclear weapons that this country has been clearly the center for the production of reactors for electrical utilities. Since Jersey Central Power and Light Company became the first utility company to sign a contract with General Electric for a major nuclear power plant in 1964, the number of such contracts has increased tremendously. At the same time, American manufacturers of nuclear power plants, such as General Electric and Westinghouse, have been able to capture through direct sales or licensing agreements the lion's share of the world market for reactors with the result that European competitors have had a very difficult time selling their reactors in Europe and other parts of the globe. Even an advanced country such as Sweden, which could have produced its own reactor, has chosen to purchase American products.

An important reason for this near-monopoly of American reactor manufacturers has been another monopoly of the United States, namely the supply of enriched uranium. This type of uranium is produced in three gaseous diffusion plants which have an output 25 times greater than that of the British and French facilities combined. The production of the latter is only enough to meet the requirements for the nuclear weapons of the two countries or alternatively, a very modest commercial program. Hence, the United States has utilized the advantage of its large-scale production of enriched uranium to offer this commodity at very attractive prices and with guaranteed supply of up to five years in advance of actual needs. For this reason, the offers of American manufacturers to furnish nuclear reactors have usually been accepted.

The American near-monopoly on nuclear fuel has raised the salient political question as to whether any industrially advanced country can afford to be dependent on another country for materials needed for electric energy and indirectly for industrial production, expansion, and competitive positions in world affairs. The experience many countries had with Arab oil supply in 1973 has deepened their reluctance to accept such dependence, perceived by many countries to be intolerable. As a consequence, a number of European governments and industries have attempted to work out collaborative arrangements to reduce the dependence for their electric utilities on America and halt penetration by American manufacturers. They have attempted to develop an alternative technology for the enrichment of uranium by experimenting with the gas centrifuge process. In 1969, the United Kingdom, the Netherlands, and West Germany signed a collaboration agreement on joint private and governmental utilization of that process. Another development is in the field of fast breeder reactors. France, Japan, the United Kingdom, and West Germany are now devoting research and scientific attention to this type of reactor, and American firms have become concerned that those countries may capture the bulk of the world market for this promising reactor unless U.S. nuclear authorities speed up their own development program.[3]

Because nuclear fuel can be used not only for running electric power plants, but also for the production of atomic weapons, the United States has continually insisted that sales of this fuel would always be subject to a "peaceful-uses-only" guarantee by the recipient states and acceptance of diversion safeguards. Under American influence similar guarantees were also required by other supplier states of nuclear fuel.

Safeguards

When the Nonproliferation Treaty (NPT) went into effect March 5, 1970, one of its most significant provisions was for the application of international safeguards to the peaceful nuclear programs of all nonnuclear weapons states that ratified the treaty. While up to that time indigenously mined or manufactured nuclear material had remained beyond the supervision of most safeguard systems, the control under the NPT applied to all sources of fissionable material within the countries of NPT signatories regardless of origin. The verification of the adherence of states to their NPT obligation not to divert nuclear materials from peaceful uses to nuclear weapons is now vested in a single IGO, the IAEA.

The value of any international safeguard system depends to a large degree on its capability to satisfy two criteria: acceptability and credibility. Yet it is obvious that the more credible such a system is, the more it will intrude on national sovereignty. Moreover, the more intrusive the system is, the less likely it is to secure the voluntary adherence of the largest possible number of states. The resistance to the safeguards does not stem so much from the desire to seek a nuclear weapons capability through insidious means, but from the concern of governments and private enterprise that they will be discriminated against commercially by states who already possess nuclear weapons. This fear of discrimination has been particularly strong in Japan and West Germany, whose industries and governments charged that the application of NPT safeguards could result in unfair competition and the risk of industrial espionage.

The target of these charges, although not proven, was American industry. In response to these charges, the United States government has offered to place all American nuclear facilities not directly related to national security under the same system of international safeguards that apply to West Germany, Japan, or any other country. As a consequence, the IAEA inspects American peaceful nuclear installations in the same manner as those of other countries and this seems to satisfy the industries and governments of those states which are likely to be in competition with the United States in the manufacture of reactors and the production of enriched uranium. In fact, the acceptance of sageguards plays a valuable role for the governments of the nonnuclear states in communicating their intentions to use nuclear technology and material for peaceful purposes only, and of course also signals their expectations that other states will do likewise.

We can see from our discussion of the development of nuclear electric power plants across the globe that nongovernmental entities (manufacturers of reactors and facilities) play a growing role in the interaction pattern of the international system. Moreover, we have also learned that a universal IGO like the IAEA can assume an important role of constraint on national nuclear policy. There is no doubt that the next two decades will witness the rapid industrialization and commercialization of nuclear power for the production of electricity. New forms of transnational collaboration and conflict may well emerge as the countries of the world compete for new technologies in the manufacture of nuclear reactors and fuels, as well as new markets for these products. But as more and more electric utilities in all countries of the world take advantage of nuclear energy as a source of fuel for the generation of electric power, the danger of diverting fissionable material for the manufacture of nuclear weapons also increases despite the existence of safeguards. That material, in the form of plutonium, is a by-product of the growing number of atomic power plants. By 1982 the world's nuclear power stations are expected to produce about 100,000 kilograms of plutonium a year, enough to manufacture tens of thousands of nuclear explosives. Through this means India became the sixth member of the world's nuclear weapons club in 1974. India had not signed the NPT accord and obtained the plutonium for the atomic device exploded in July of that year from a reactor supplied by Canada in 1956 on the Indian assurance it would be used only for peaceful purposes. No controls were imposed by Canada, and Venezuela, another non-signer of the NPT, is said to have developed and stockpiled several weapons. Argentina and Brazil, which also have refused to sign the NPT, may achieve nuclear weapon status in a few years. Other countries that have signed the NPT accord may also be very close to the production of nuclear weapons. They include Japan, West Germany, Sweden, South Africa, and Taiwan.[4]

New Concerns about Nonproliferation

The dreadful prospect of additional countries obtaining nuclear weapons and the possibility that such weapons may fall into the hands of terrorists, all of which would seriously destabilize the international system in the future, have prompted President Carter to reiterate tougher policies on the nonproliferation of nuclear weapons, policies that had already been basically initiated by former President Ford toward the end of his term. These policies include more effective safeguards, the halt of sales of reprocessing plants for nuclear waste, and the transfer of appropriate technologies to countries not now possessing such facilities.[5] The reason for these measures is the acquisition of plutonium as a by-product when nuclear waste materials are reprocessed. This waste accumulates as a normal consequence of electric energy generation in nuclear facilities.

Countries especially affected by the new U.S. policies were the Federal Republic of Germany and France. Germany had signed a multibillion-dollar contract with Brazil for delivery of nuclear plants, including reprocessing facilities, and France had signed a similar agreement with Pakistan. Despite strong U.S. pressures, Germany declared that she would proceed with the fulfillment of her contractual obligations toward Brazil, regardless of American arm-twisting, because the German government had to be faithful to the contract and, besides, thousands of German jobs were at stake. France, at first more hesitant to defy American policy, later joined Germany in wanting to carry out its commitment toward Pakistan despite the need for delay of deliveries in view of the politically unsettled situation in that country. The potential conflict with the United States has been largely defused, at least for the time being, by an agreement of fifteen countries that have been major exporters of nuclear technology in the past or were on the threshold of joining this group.* Future sales of sensitive nuclear technology would be subject to tough controls, and lax safeguards, as found in the German and French contracts, possibly a means of gaining a competitive advantage, would have to be avoided.

For purposes of ensuring nonproliferation of nuclear weapons, the United States also has indicated the gradual suspension of shipments of highly enriched uranium and has strongly opposed the construction of fast breeder reactors. These positions have also given rise to serious concern in Western Europe. The construction of the fast breeder pilot program there was close to reaching the industrial stage, and these reactors are sixty times more efficient than the light-

---

* United States, Soviet Union, France, Great Britain, Japan, West Germany, and Canada. Newcomers are Poland, East Germany, Czechoslovakia, Belgium, the Netherlands, Italy, Sweden, and Switzerland. See *International Herald Tribune*, September 23, 1977.

water reactors presently used to generate electricity. Moreover, the critical oil supply situation in Western Europe made it imperative to rely in the future on fast breeders.

THE RESOURCES OF THE SEA

While attention of governmental and nongovernmental actors is presently centered on rapid development of nuclear technologies for the generation of electricity, other energy sources have also been considered. Among these sources are the use of wind, solar energy, and temperature differentials in, and the tides of, the high seas. There is now little question that the oceans and the seabed are storehouses for many of the things modern society needs at present, and it is this part of the world's physical environment that we will examine next.

Scientists generally consider the sea to be the area where life on earth originated. The functions of the sea in relation to earthly life are numerous. It acts as a thermostat and heat reservoir, leveling out temperature extremes that would prevail over the earth's surface without its moderating influences. The sea furnishes the water without which the continents would be lifeless deserts. It is a major source for man's food and, unfortunately, a dumping ground for his garbage and wastes. It is a major resource for those minerals that are basic requirements for today's modern industrial society.

The mineral resources of the sea are found in five areas: marine beaches, seawater, the continental shelves, surficial sediments, and the hard rock beneath the surficial sea-floor sediments. A variety of minerals are presently being extracted from the first three parts of the ocean. Very little is known about the fifth part, that of the hard rock underlying the soft ocean-floor sediments. No sample of this rock has yet been obtained for chemical analysis.[6]

It is among the sea-floor sediments that vast mineral resources of great economic promise have recently been discovered. These minerals can be extracted from the marine environment with the proper technology. Although the problem connected with exploiting the mineral resources of the ocean may seem formidable to many, the technology required for this task is less complex than putting men in orbit or on the moon and certainly much less expensive. However, the funds required for the extraction of minerals are still of such dimensions that only financially powerful countries can afford such an enterprise.

While for the time being the reserves of many materials needed for modern industrialized society are extensive, new economic demands and political pressures may require governments and private enterprise to turn their attention to the mineral resources of the sea. Engineering data and cost calculations indicate that the mining from the sea of such elements as phosphate, nickel, copper, cobalt, and manganese can be profitable. Within the next two decades, the sea may also become a major source of molybdenum, vanadium, lead, zinc, titanium, aluminum, zirconium, and perhaps other metals. These metals are all badly needed by modern industry, and some of them have high strategic value as they are being used for the manufacture of sophisticated weapons. The United States imports large quantities of some of these metals, and because shortages may develop by the end of the 1970s as land-based sources are exhausted, the seabed needs to be considered as a new resource. Fortunately, most of the needed minerals are available in abundance in ocean floor sediments. Others are found in ocean floor rocks, and as technology develops further, they may be extracted as well. It has been estimated that, in due time, the sea could furnish all the minerals the world's society would need.[7]

Of course, the minerals listed above are not the only resources found in the oceans. Offshore oil exploration has become a familiar and widespread industry and has benefited from rapidly advancing technology. The best-known areas for offshore oil production are the Gulf of Mexico, California, the Persian Gulf, the North Sea, West Africa, and the East Indian Ocean. Large oil fields are believed to exist along the coasts of Vietnam and Japan.

The seawater itself contains about sixty elements, but only four have been commercially extracted in quantities. They are sodium* and chlorine in the form of common salt, magnesium, and bromide. Attempts have been made to extract other minerals from seawater, but they have not been commercially successful so far. Gold is one of these minerals.

Finally, the sea is the home of another resource: fish. The exploitation of this resource has developed from a plethora of individual romantic fishermen in small, relatively primitive vessels to a highly competitive, mechanized, large-scale business in which governments and private corporations are engaged. While the individual fisherman has not disappeared from the high seas, we find increasingly integrated fishing fleets with modern vessels and highly sophisticated floating canneries in which the catch can be processed immediately into consumer-ready products. The Soviet Union is in the

---

* Sodium compounds can also be extracted from seaweed.

forefront of using large, modern vessels, owning 49 percent of ships of 100 or more tons in size, followed by Japan with 13 percent; however, the largest catch of fish is made by Peru; next in yield are Japan, the People's Republic of China, the Soviet Union, the United States, and Norway.[8]

Legal and Political Problems

One basic attraction of exploiting the resources of the high seas is freedom of political control and of royalties, provided the extraction activities take place outside the territorial sea of riparian states. The traditional three-mile limit of the territorial sea has slowly been replaced by a twelve-mile limit by many states of the world, but even this distance is not sufficient in the eyes of a number of developing countries, who see the oceans as a potential source of significant wealth and therefore would like to exercise control over a body of water much wider than 12 miles. As a consequence, some of these countries, such as Chile, Ecuador, and Peru, proclaimed "sovereignty" over the sea, its bottom and its resources between bottom and surface to a minimum distance of 200 statute miles. Uruguay, Argentina, Brazil, and some African states more recently have followed suit. Most developed states of the world at first refused to accept this extension of control over the "open" sea, and disputes arose when, for example, Ecuador seized American fishing boats within the 200-mile limit. But today an "economic zone" of 200 miles is generally recognized, although the control of the country bordering on the sea is more limited than that exercised over the twelve-mile limit of the "territorial sea" and applies mainly to the renewable and nonrenewable resources of the sea and seabed.

Some developing countries that do not possess the necessary funds and research skills to exploit the seabed have become apprehensive when governmental agencies or private firms of states with very large research capabilities, such as the United States or Japan, have merely undertaken marine research off their coasts. Equating research with exploration for purposes of exploitation, some of the developing coastal states have restricted marine research by foreign firms or governments close to their shores. In view of the large capital investments required for mining sediments in the deep sea, this trend on the part of developing countries is apt to dampen interest in the exploration and exploitation of the mineral resources of the sea by private enterprises unless sufficient profit will compensate these enterprises for the increased risks.

Much of the work leading to the changes in maritime law has

been accomplished within the framework of the Third Law of the Sea Conference, which opened with an organizational session in New York in 1973, followed by substantive sessions in Caracas (1974), Geneva (1975), and New York in 1976 and 1977. Some of the most difficult issues that the various sessions had to deal with were the establishment of a regime for seabed mining and scientific research in the economic zone and of machinery for compulsory settlement of disputes. Also some means had to be found to accommodate the fishing interests of the forty-nine landlocked states of the world. While some of these issues have been solved, agreement on a regime for seabed mining has not been reached. The Third World countries want such mining to be under the strict supervision of the United Nations, but this is strongly opposed by the industrialized countries. Further conference sessions are scheduled to resolve this problem.

An important accepted exception to the twelve-mile limit of the territorial sea and the 200-mile economic zone is the *continental shelf*. In September 1945, President Truman proclaimed that ownership of mineral resources in and on what could be construed as the continental shelf by the contiguous nations was recognized by the United States. Obviously, the United States was an immediate main beneficiary of this principle, but no substantial controversy arose over the new legal pronouncement and the U.S. government urged the United Nations to adopt it as a tenet of international law.

In the codification of the law of the sea, which was accomplished at the 1958 Conference on the Law of the Sea under the auspices of the United Nations, the continental shelf was defined as "the sea bed and subsoil of the submarine areas adjacent to the coast but *outside* the area of the territory to a depth of 200 meters (656 feet) or beyond that limit to where the depth of the superjacent waters admit of the exploitation of the natural resources of the areas."[9] We should understand that continental shelf rights are considerably more restricted than those accruing to a coastal state over its territorial sea or the economic zone. As a consequence, the coastal state must not interfere unduly with other nations' rights in these areas pertaining to the superjacent waters, principally navigation rights, nor can the coastal state impede the laying or maintenance of submarine cables or pipelines in the area or conservation of the sea. Finally, continental shelf rights do not authorize the coastal nation to hinder fundamental oceanographic or scientific research. When coastal states exploit resources of the continental shelf beyond the 200-mile economic zone, they must now share with the international community a specified percentage of the mineral resources obtained. For the benefit of developing and landlocked countries, royalties will have to be paid, based on the value of the production, to an international body, called the International Resource Authority.

In view of the many political questions involved in the exploration of the sea, a number of IGOs have concerned themselves with this matter. These include the International Oceanographic Commission (IOC of UNESCO), Food and Agricultural Organization (FAO), and the International Council for the Exploration of the Sea. The IOC appears to be the central agency for the coordination of plans, programs, and activities for the United Nations in the field of marine science and has established an international committee on which representatives of the United Nations, the FAO, the World Meteorological Organization (WMO), and the Intergovernmental Maritime Consultative Organization (IMCO) have representatives.

On the other side of the fence, international NGOs have also articulated interests regarding the resources of the sea, and the most important of these are the Scientific Committee on Oceanic Research, the International Association for the Physical Sciences of the Ocean, the International Association of Biological Oceanography, and the Commission on Marine Biology. It is surprising that, in an area where potential commercial benefits can be extraordinary, no international NGOs represent the technical aspects of interested parties engaged in fisheries, the exploitation of mineral resources, and underwater structures.[10]

It is clear that the next decades will witness considerable efforts on the part of many states and nongovernmental actors to exploit the resources of the sea on a more intensive and extensive scale. For many countries, the seas may provide resources they do not have now within their territories. As a consequence, we may anticipate various forms of collaborative arrangements and at the same time, severe competition in these undertakings, resulting in changes in the international system and interaction pattern.

POPULATION EXPLOSION AND WORLD HUNGER

The problems of a rapidly increasing world population and world hunger are interrelated, although recurring famines in different parts of the world have other causes as well.

As discussed in Chapter 2, the population in the Third World is growing much faster than in the industrialized countries. In Latin America and Africa the population is likely to more than double from 1970 to the year 2000. In contrast, the population of Europe will grow only by 25 percent and that of North America, not much more.

Although major efforts have been undertaken by U.N. organs and private foundations to solve population growth in the Third World through various birth control means, success has been elusive. Indeed, developing countries have currently twice as much of their population under ten years of age as the industrialized countries. Because this part of the population consumes only and does not produce, it is basically a serious drain on economic growth, although as we have seen, extensive unemployment in the Third World impairs chances for individuals in higher age groups to produce.

To make things worse, malnutrition affects some 400 million people in the developing countries at present. If food resources are not used more effectively, starvation and famine in some areas of the world might occur again and again, inviting economic and political disaster.

In the 1950s and 1960s, global food production was consistently high; per capita output expanded even in food-deficit nations; the world's total output increased by more than half. In the 1970s, however, inclement weather, which affected several subcontinents simultaneously, combined with uncontrolled population growth contributed to widespread food shortages with famine and massive starvation in some areas. As a consequence of the weather, world cereal production fell sharply, from 1.2 billion to less than 900 million tons. At the same time, the rise in oil prices greatly increased the cost of fertilizer (oil is a major ingredient), and made farm operations in general much more expensive.

The U.N. World Food Conference in Rome in 1974 addressed itself to these problems. It urged the production of more grains through expanded acreages and higher investments in agriculture in the developed countries and an increase in agricultural exports to needy areas. It advocated acceleration and more efficiency in the production of foodstuffs, especially grain, in the Third World where postharvest losses to rats, insects, and fungi are excessive. It stressed the need for intensified research and new technologies to increase yields and reduce costs. For this purpose agricultural producers in the Third World are to be linked to research institutions in the developed countries. It advocated improvement in food distribution, which through lack of proper management at times contributed to outbreaks of famines. It urged enhancing food quality through applied nutritional research and the establishment of a global nutrition surveillance system under U.N. auspices. Finally, it recommended strongly the establishment of a grain reserve system to guard against future emergencies.[11]

It is difficult to predict how effective these measures will be to feed properly a world population that may be larger by 4 billion in 2000 than at present. There is no doubt that new technologies have expanded agricultural yields, and some of these technologies are being introduced into the developing countries. Good grain harvests in the second half of the 1970s led to surpluses in North America and Western Europe, prompting the U.S. government to impose again a reduction of wheat acreages. Of course, it is not only the food-growing process itself that is important, a process highly dependent on the weather, but the nutritional content of the food consumed. The greatest challenge to the world community may be to eliminate the widespread diseases in many poor countries stemming from vitamin and protein shortages.

THE USE OF OUTER SPACE FOR COMMUNICATIONS AND METEOROLOGY

Outer space, just as nuclear energy, has become a factor in both national security and nonmilitary use. Although the military exploitation of outer space is confined to a few countries, albeit the most powerful ones, the link to national security has caused many complexities also for states interested only in business and other nonmilitary purposes.

Communications Satellites

The utilization of outer space for communications has produced only one form of commercial profit-oriented exploitation, which is Intelsat. This particular organization combines both governments and business firms as members, and its manager, the Communications Satellite Corporation (COMSAT), is itself a mixed public and private United States firm whose task it is to oversee satellite design, contracting, and operations.

COMSAT and Intelsat The U.S. Congress passed the Communications Satellite Act in 1962. In 1963, COMSAT was organized as the United States's "chosen instrument" to help bring commercial satellite communications to the world. Intelsat was established by international agreement in August 1964, under interim arrangements. From the original eleven countries, it has grown to eighty member countries, with others expecting to join soon. Intelsat was formed to establish and operate a single global commercial communications satellite system. It is the initial and historic cooperative effort for peaceful use of outer space for everyday commercial purposes.

Intelsat has five communication satellites, two above the Atlantic, two over the Pacific, and one in the Indian Ocean basin, from where they can "see" and link the user countries to earth stations. Fifty-six earth station antennas are operating in thirty-five countries, and more will probably be built and installed. Each member country retains full autonomous control over the earth station facilities in its territory. Their cost, at just under $5 million per station, amounts to roughly $250 million.[12]

The communications capability of telecommunications satellites is enormous and will increase with each generation. Intelsat I, the famous Early Bird Satellite, increased transatlantic cable communications capacity by 50 percent, adding 240 telephone circuits, and could carry one TV signal. Intelsat IV has expanded the capacity to approximately 9,000 voice circuits and twelve TV signals. When Intelsat V is launched, it is expected to carry some 20,000 voice circuits. In contrast, the traditional submarine cable can handle only 800 two-way voice circuits and does not have a TV capability.

There **are** also tremendous cost savings through the use of Intelsat. The **cost** of a three-minute, station-to-station, off-hours telephone call from London to New York has been cut nearly in half. The cost of transmitting color TV programs across the Atlantic has fallen by 81 percent. The prospect is for further cost reduction as more efficient equipment goes into operation.

Under the interim arrangements, COMSAT was designated as manager of the Intelsat system; however, new arrangements have changed the management system considerably. Under these new arrangements (agreed upon by the United States and other user countries), COMSAT will be gradually relieved of its management responsibilities, and these will be transferred to an internationally appointed director general. A board of governors is established which will meet at six- to eight-week intervals to discharge its responsibilities for the design, development, construction, establishment, operation, and maintenance of the Intelsat space activities. No single member of the board may cast more than 40 percent of the total vote, regardless of its relative level of use and level of investment in Intelsat. This means that, despite the fact that the United States has the largest investment in Intelsat, the highest ownership quota (53 percent),[13] and manages the organization, it cannot exercise more than a 40 percent vote. This arrangement has been the result of a substantial challenge on the part of West European governments and business companies, who were dissatisfied with U.S. dominance of the organization. Moreover, to meet the demands of West European companies, a larger number of construction contracts has been given to corporations in Western Europe. This, in turn, has aroused the opposition of some of the developing countries because they claim that the cost of goods produced in Europe is higher than that of goods produced in the United States.[14]

There is no question that Intelsat has been a huge success and has largely fulfilled the goal of the Communications Satellite Act of 1962 "to establish in cooperation with other countries a commercial communications satellite system as part of an improved global communications network which will be responsive to public needs and national objectives, which will serve the communications needs of the United States and other countries, and which will contribute to world peace and understanding."

It is noteworthy that at least one communist country, Yugoslavia, is a member of Intelsat. On the other hand, the Soviet Union and its allies have not joined but have instead proceeded to establish their own international space communication system, Intersputnik. Intersputnik is not operational at present, however, and this separate system does not mean that the Russians may not cooperate with Intelsat.[15]

European Launcher Development Organization For some time the European Launcher Development Organization (ELDO) was also interested in launching its own satellites for communications purposes. However, despite many attempts to produce a European rocket for such a purpose, the project ultimately failed, despite an expenditure of $700 million primarily contributed by West Germany, France, and the United Kingdom. As a consequence, financial support for ELDO has dried up and the organization is virtually dead.[16]

Intelsat and Computers The electronic revolution, of which Intelsat is a part, is likely to transform the world in which we live. A particular aspect of this transformation is the linkage to Intelsat of computers, with their vast capacity for storing information. It has been estimated that by the end of the 1970s, perhaps 75 percent of all computers in the United States will be linked via communications facilities which might include Intelsat. This means that just about all the information stored in computers will be retrievable almost anywhere by almost anyone who possesses a computer terminal. Such a development will necessitate the creation of computer information utilities that will serve as brokers between information sources.[17] As a result, information is becoming a central economic resource and as such may contribute to the elimination of differences among societies across the globe in the same way that advances in communications and transportation have reduced rural, urban, and regional differences in the United States.[18]

On the other hand, international tensions may also be aroused by the new communications technologies and the emerging global system of electronic communications. Lester Brown states:

> Not everyone feels comfortable with the new communications technologies and the emerging global system of electronic communications. For many, this global system represents a potential means of political influence and control. . . . Overcoming this concern requires, at a minimum, the internationalization of communications and broadcasting entities operating internationally, as has recently occurred with Intelsat. But even this may not suffice for those countries zealously guarding their sovereignty, whether it be against another country or a supranational institution.[19]

Weather and Navigation Satellites

Two other significant nonmilitary exploitations of space, although not of a commercial nature, are weather and navigation satellites. While navigation satellites are not widely used as yet for either aircraft or ships, weather satellites are being used to an increasing degree.[20]

All of us have seen the satellite cloud cover maps on television. Satellites have improved the accuracy and increased the speed of weather forecasting. A number of economic segments benefit from more accurate and rapid weather forecasting. Farmers are able to plan planting and harvesting operations more effectively. The construction industry can determine with greater efficiency the allocation of workers to construction projects which would suffer from inclement weather. Especially if long-range weather forecasting could be made totally accurate, retail stores could set dates for special sales in such a way as to be reasonably well assured of good weather. This would mean that extensive costs of advertising and additional sales personnel could be arranged with minimum risks of having these special sales fizzle. When solar energy is used to produce electricity, accurate forecasting of cloud cover in different parts of the country will increase its efficiency.

Looking at the benefits of weather forecasting in terms of world politics, countries with efficient systems of weather prediction will be in a better competitive position to meet economic and social welfare demands than countries lacking in such expertise. In addition to the economic and commercial advantages of accurate short-range and long-range forecasting, an effective meteorological prediction service can reduce damage from natural disasters. Accurate prediction of the paths of tornadoes and hurricanes can make it possible for people in affected areas to take necessary precautions to save life and property. Again, in terms of world politics, the prevention of disaster can be seen in competitive terms: countries whose weather forecasting services are not able to warn of natural disasters will be in a disadvantageous position.

The United States launched the first artificial satellite equipped to provide photographs of the earth weather conditions on April 1, 1960. It was known as Tyros I, and its two television cameras transmitted both broad and detailed pictures of the earth's cloud cover. The National Aeronautics and Space Administration (NASA) cooperated with the United States Weather Bureau in launching additional weather satellites and assisted in their utilization. In 1963, the United States and the Soviet Union agreed to exchange weather information obtained from weather satellites.

On the international level, the World Meteorological Organization (WMO), a specialized agency of the United Nations, has coordinated meteorlogical observations and promoted the establishment and maintenance of meteorological services. It has sought to bring about the standardization of meteorological observations and to ensure the uniform publication of observations and statistics in order to make them useful to aviation, shipping, agricultural, and other human activities. In 1963, the WMO approved a plan for mapping the weather around the globe. This plan, known as the World Weather Watch, was initially opposed by a number of countries, as well as by some agencies of the United States government.[21] It was ultimately approved by the General Assembly of the United Nations, and control of the World Weather Watch was vested in the WMO.

One of the intriguing aspects of weather forecasting involves human attempts to modify the weather. Many ancient and primitive societies endeavored to control rainfall and other meteorological phenomena by making offerings or sacrifices to their gods. A modern scientific approach to rainmaking is cloud seeding; however, the technological capability for cloud seeding is still too limited for it to be a reliable instrument in weather modification.

In terms of world politics, the ability to modify weather and climate could have an extraordinary impact on the power of countries involved in such an endeavor. If it were possible to alter the path of the Gulf Stream or to reduce its temperature as little as 1° Centigrade, the effect on European climate would be drastic. If a Russian plan to reverse the direction of four rivers currently flowing northward and emptying into the Arctic Circle were carried out, some climatologists fear that shutting off the flow of the relatively warm water from these four rivers would not only alter the climate in the Arctic, but that of the entire world as well. Another example is accretion of carbon dioxide in the atmosphere that may result from the enlarged scale or intensity of application of chemical technology. This could alter the surface temperature of the world, which could have a deleterious impact on the life of man, animals, and vegetation. A similar effect could be produced by the large-scale consumption of energy, which leads to the discharge of dust particles in the atmosphere and in turn would reduce the inflow of solar energy. Agricultural activity, especially bringing marginal land under the plow, leading to dust bowl conditions, could also cause similar conditions.

It is obvious, then, that the international impact of weather modification could be very grave and far-reaching. Not too much is known about weather modification techniques, but the National Science Foundation (NSF) set up a space panel in 1964 to study its scientific, economic, and social effects. Environmentalists have become increasingly concerned about weather modification that may occur as a result of man's activity on this globe.

ECOLOGICAL CONCERNS
AND WORLD POLITICS

The winds and ocean currents that move ceaselessly across the face of the globe carry with them an immense and growing burden of noxious wastes generated by man's industrial-urban life. Lead from automobile exhausts has been found on the Greenland ice cap. DDT is spread all over the world. Sulfurous smoke from British factories blows with the prevailing winds and pollutes the fields and forests of Scandinavia. Fleets of tankers and cargo ships spill petroleum along the world's sealanes and coastlines. Ever-growing quantities of chemical and animal wastes, produced on land, find their way to the world's final dumping ground, the oceans.

The world's environmental predicament takes other forms, also. Many major nonrenewable minerals and fuels, whose total quantity on earth is unknown but obviously limited, are being consumed at such accelerating rates as to raise serious questions about what will remain for future generations. Many living species have been extinguished for lack of adequate protection, and countless others are in danger of extinction. Topsoil, on which future world food supplies largely depend, washes into the rivers and estuaries of the world at rates equivalent to tens of millions of fertile acres every year.

The pressures of a growing world population and rising economic aspirations on a finite base of resources virtually assure that environmental issues are not transitory but will be important in the decision-making priorities of future generations and that the environmental challenges we now perceive will extend through all foreseeable time.

Since the 1960s, environmental quality has become a major social goal in the United States and, indeed, throughout most of the industrial world. New laws and new agencies have imposed unprecedented controls on air and water pollution, automobile exhausts, municipal dumps, urban sprawl, noise, and every other kind of environmental degradation. Yet while these measures are likely to lead to better and healthier conditions, environmental concerns have also compounded the difficulties of finding substitutes for the declining energy sources of petroleum and natural gas. Some environmentalists have violently opposed the construction of nuclear power plants in the United States and Western Europe because of possible, though very unlikely, accidents that might release radioactive matter harmful to the health of human beings and animals. Another cause for serious apprehension is the difficulty of disposing safely of nuclear waste, the residue from uranium used for the generation of electricity in nuclear power plants. Environmental concerns have also imposed restraints on strip mining of coal, reducing the efficiency and increasing the cost of exploiting this source of energy widely available in the United States. Going much further, some environmentalists have demanded curbing overall economic growth to nearly zero; however, such restraints would result in declining living standards not only for large segments of populations in the industrialized countries, but also in the Third World where they are already very low. At present, such extreme demands are economically and politically unacceptable.

All disturbances of nature, together with the complex global interconnections arising from trade, investment, technology, and travel, affect all countries of the world; but whether these countries will meet the ecological challenge cooperatively is uncertain. Their interests may be neither identical nor converging. Many Third World countries consider ecological restraints a burden on their own development and primarily a responsibility of the industrialized countries and of private business. Yet it seems imperative that all countries join in acquiring and sharing an immense amount of environmental knowledge through scientific research, monitoring, information exchange, education, and training. New international agreements and programs are necessary for the conservation of resources, especially living species, and for the control of pollution of the oceans that lie beyond any nation's jurisdiction.

The Pollution of the Oceans

Petroleum, usually in the form of crude oil, is the most notorious of marine pollutants. Spectacular disasters, like the spilling of 700,000 barrels of oil from the stricken tanker Torrey Canyon off the British coast in 1967, the major oil leaks from drilling operations in the Santa Barbara (California) Channel in 1969, and the series of super-tanker disasters during the past years, have dramatized the pollution menace that grows from year to year.

Estimates vary widely on annual pollution of the world's seas by oil. One informed estimate puts the figure at 5 million metric tons, nearly half from vessels and the rest from runoff of waste crankcase and industrial oil, refineries, and offshore drilling operations. Spectacular tanker accidents actually account for only a minor fraction of the problem. Most spills are deliberate and routine, for example, the discharge of oily water ballast and tank washings from tankers in mid-voyage, which accounts for about 1 million tons of oil pollution a year or 20 percent of total sea pollution.[22]

Another pollution problem arises from the transportation of waste matter out to sea for the express purpose of dumping it. This method of waste disposal is used by many countries and accounts for a significant fraction, perhaps 10 percent, of all man-made pollutants entering the seas. Worse, it includes—in addition to bulky dredge spoils and sewage sludge—some of the most toxic of all wastes: highly radioactive materials, heavy metals such as mercury and cadmium, and an immense variety of chemical compounds whose effects on marine life are not well understood. Moreover, through the 1950s and 1960s, as urban-industrial growth progressed in the world's coastlands and as land dumping sites began to fill, ocean dumping has steadily increased.

In the fall of 1973, seventy-nine seafaring nations reached a historical agreement establishing international machinery for reducing pollution from ships. Under this agreement the washing out of oil tanks is required to be handled entirely aboard ship. All ships of more than 70,000 deadweight tonnage must have segregated ballast tanks to prevent the pollution that occurs when ballast mixes with the oil cargo residue and then is dumped into the sea. Moreover, all oil discharges from ships within fifty miles of land are prohibited. They are banned completely in such heavily polluted waters as the Mediterranean Sea, Black Sea, Baltic Sea, Red Sea, and the Persian Gulf. Lastly, the dumping of ship's sewage and garbage is banned within four miles of land unless fully treated, and within twelve miles unless pulverized and disinfected.

Seabed Pollution

Finally, as new environments are opened up to exploration and use, they are also opened up to pollution. A major case in point is the seabed and ocean floor, where future mining operations of manganese, nickel, copper, and cobalt may add to the pollution of the seas. In view of the energy crisis, remote-controlled drilling for oil and gas under the seabed may be undertaken with further prospects for pollution. This pollution may be fatal for the fisheries of the world and may reduce food resources for many people.

Clean Rivers and Clean Air

Water pollution is, of course, not limited to the oceans. The sad ecological state of some of our Great Lakes, such as Lake Erie and Lake Michigan, is well known. Again, the pollution of lakes is not a problem only in the United States but in other countries as well. The pollution of Lake Baikal in the Soviet Union is another example. As early as 1909, the United States and Canada established an International Joint Commission dealing with waters touching the boundaries of both countries. This body has now become increasingly responsible for major activities affecting the two governments and in particular has recomended measures to improve the quality of the waters in the Great Lakes.

Rivers with several riparian states have also caused pollution problems across national boundaries. An example is the Colorado River flowing from the United States to Mexico whose pollution has been a source of concern to the latter country. Again, a bilateral treaty is being negotiated between the two countries to alleviate injuries as a result of pollution.

One of the outstanding examples of a polluted river touching many countries is the Rhine River, which flows from Switzerland to the Netherlands and is bounded by Germany and France. Severe upstream pollution has caused thousands of fish to die and has produced bad environmental conditions downstream. Attempts are now being made under the auspices of the European Community to improve these conditions.

The problem of air pollution needs little description. Emissions from power plants, aluminum companies, steel plants, and fertilizer industries reduce air quality. "Clean engine" technology has attempted since 1971 to diminish toxic emissions from motor vehicles, but one of the largest sources of all air pollution may come from the fallout of fuel exhaust of jet airplanes.

In the United States stringent laws have been passed to assure cleaner air. On the regional level, NATO has set up the Committee on the Challenges of Modern Society, and the Organization of Economic Cooperation and Development (OECD) has established a special environmental committee. Both committees are attempting to introduce in Western countries standards similar to those existing in the United States.

Environmental Costs and International Trade Compensation

As the public demand for a cleaner environment rises, the effort required to meet this demand becomes a significant item in the cost of manufacturing. This is true whether the demand is for low-pollution products, such as automobiles with clean exhaust, or for low-pollution manufacturing processes. Such industries as steel, paper, electric power, petroleum, and chemicals produce in the course of manufacture a great variety of noxious by-products whose recycling or safe disposal is a serious and expensive problem.

A manufacturer is generally content to pay these environmental costs—and to reflect them in selling prices—*provided his competitors are required to do the same.* But if he has foreign competitors who receive government assistance to help pay for these costs or are subject to less stringent national pollution laws, or to none at all, he may understandably complain of unfair competition. Demands for compensating trade barriers or export subsidies may arise, or manufacturers may find that it pays to build their factories in foreign "pollution havens." Such a competitive trend entails obvious economic and environmental perils. For the sake of fair play as well as of a clean environment, it has become important for the environmental factors affecting international trade and investment to be under international or transnational control.

In 1970 this complex question was tackled initially by the new Environment Committee of the OECD, whose twenty-three members account for two-thirds of world trade. The following year OECD adopted an "early warning" system under which member governments receive notice of each other's environmental laws and regulations governing the use of chemical substances and may consult concerning any economic or trading problems that they cause. Then, in May 1972, OECD adopted a set of "guiding principles" on environment and trade. Most basic is the principle that the "polluter pays": member countries are called upon to require that the polluter—not the government—bear the costs of industrial pollution controls to avoid "significant distortions in international trade and investment." In addition, common standards are to be sought on polluting products that are traded internationally so as to avoid creating new barriers to trade. Finally, the principle was accepted that governments "should seek harmonization of environmental policies" (although allowing for differences in circumstances) and should "strive toward more stringent standards." Observance of these guiding principles should encourage countries to adopt adequate pollution controls without fear of thereby placing their industries at a competitive disadvantage in international markets.[23]

ECONOMIC GROWTH OR ZERO GROWTH?

Not very long ago, every nation of the world was pleased to see smoke belching from factory stacks because it was considered an omen of progress. In many of the developing countries of the world, industrialization continues to receive highest priority as a means to conquer poverty through development.

Yet the gospel of "growth at any cost" has begun to be questioned in many parts of the world. There is a new awareness of the need to plan not only for quantity but also for quality. There is a new concern that social values in housing, health, and education must be maintained and raised. And within this complex of social values, environmental quality has a high priority.

Worldwide concern over these problems led a group of scientists and intellectuals in North and South America and in Europe as well to search for ways to avert the breakdown of society that was felt to be intrinsic in the uncontrolled growth of technology, population, and industrial output. A study was made in 1972 by the Massachusetts Institute of Technology. Entitled "The Limits of Growth" and based on computer simulation it warned that mankind probably faces uncontrollable and disastrous global disequilibrium in which growth of population and industrial output will be halted. The study contends that slowing of growth constitutes the primary task facing humanity and will demand international cooperation on a scale and scope without precedent. Unless the warning is heeded, it is argued that the world's natural resources will be largely exhausted by 2100, and pollution will become intolerable.

Many economists doubt that, given human motivation and diversity, a no-growth world is possible. Moreover, it would lock in the people in the developing countries at roughly their present standards of living, which would be politically indefensible. Opponents of the M.I.T. study also argue that the known resources of nonrenewable raw materials have been underestimated, and the record since World War II indicates that, in many instances, the discovery rate of known reserves has increased faster than the rate of consumption. Moreover, the way in which new technology can increase available reserves—for example, the extraction of manganese from the sea, of sulfur from salt domes, or quantities of metals from previously dumped materials (recycling)—seems to have been ignored. On the issue of pollution, the opponents claim that advanced industrial societies can choose to spend extra money on pollution control and that, while pollution is an acknowledged danger, pollution build-up and world collapse are not necessarily inevitable with continued economic growth.

In view of the worldwide implications of the problems of pollution and economic growth, it should not be surprising that the solution of these problems was submitted to global scrutiny and coordination. To this end the United Nations convened in Stockholm in June of 1972, the first U.N. Conference on Human Environment. The conference was widely acclaimed as an extraordinary success. Attended by 113 governments, including every major power except the Soviet Union, it adopted three important documents:

- A Declaration on Human Environment, containing key principles of international law on the responsibilities of states regarding the environment.
- An "action plan" containing 109 recommendations, addressed to governments and international organizations, for worldwide action on an immense range of environmental subjects, such as controlling marine pollution, monitoring the global atmosphere, saving endangered species, and training environmental experts.
- A recommendation, soon afterward adopted by the U.N. General Assembly, to establish a United Nations Environment Program (UNEP) and an Environment Fund. UNEP and the Environment Fund came into being on January 1, 1973.

Despite the success of the Conference on Human Environment, it should not be assumed that its outcome was foreordained or without suspense. On the contrary, it was marked by a political debate which, though not always of high quality, was about genuine and important global issues: the fixing of responsibility for environmental conservation and the distribution, as well as the preservation, of the planet's limited amenities. Hard, constructive, and imaginative work by several national delegations as well as Secretariat members was necessary to keep the agenda from getting bogged down on extraneous political questions or in the national-ego or personal-ego problems of the delegates.

The absence of the Soviet Union and most of its allies, though ostensibly regretted by all, probably made the work of the Conference easier; it is reasonable to hope, however, that they may not be alienated from future United Nations environmental activities.

Failure of the much-heralded polarization between developed and developing countries to materialize, at least with the sharpness that had been expected, is one manifestation of the governments' gradually converging positions. The developed countries were not disposed to challenge the view that the symptoms of underdevelopment are among the gravest problems of the human environment, although they were reluctant to open their purses to allow the developing countries to pursue both the goals of development and high antipollution standards. The developing countries were somewhat hesitant to acknowledge the full necessity of adopting these standards in their territories. They stressed their fears that antipollution standards adopted by the industrialized countries might restrict their exports, that increased recycling might diminish their sales of raw materials, and that inappropriate pollution control technology might be conveyed to them.

The principle of national sovereignty, the right of a nation to exploit its natural resources as its government sees fit, was obsessively asserted by Brazil, among others. Massive and continuing confrontations between rich and poor countries were avoided, however, because both groups were too divided internally for that danger to materialize: coalitions shifted from issue to issue. Interests—and voting patterns—diverged, for example, between states with long coastlines and those with large merchant marines; between oil producing states and the other developing countries; between producers of oil with low sulfur content and those of oil with high sulfur content.[24]

It is obvious from our discussion that national interests continue to dominate the problems of the availability of natural resources and the environment. Although the steps taken by the United Nations are a good beginning, UNEP and other United Nations agencies have very little power to enforce any of the decisions made during the 1972 conference. Regional IGOs and the specialized agencies must assume many of the responsibilities in the field of resources and environment which can be carried out more successfully on a regional than a global scale. In addition, international NGOs must also be tied in with the efforts of governmental organizations. In fact, this is an important aspect of UNEP's role which requires the securing of effective cooperation of, and contribution from, the relevant scientific and other professional communities and organizations from all parts of the world.[25]

SUMMARY

In this chapter we have examined the impact that the physical environment of our planet can have on international relations and the patterns of interaction among states, IGOs, and nongovernmental actors. Obviously, the various environmental factors discussed are nothing more than selective examples of a large range of fixed and changing circumstances that must be increasingly taken into account by governmental and nongovernmental decision makers when formulating and implementing transnational policies. They will affect both the relations between developed and developing countries and those between the Western and Communist governments. As for the first relationship, the changing factors of the physical environment are likely to increase suspicion and frictions as industrialized and Third World countries jockey for advantageous positions and seek to exploit these factors in pursuit of their own interests. The industrialized states will attempt to secure guaranteed access to scarce raw materials while the Third World will use "commodity power" to obtain special benefits.[26] Only a fruitful North-South dialogue, unfortunately a doubtful prospect, can bring mutually beneficial solutions for raw material problems, environmental concerns, and the use of technological advances.

In the East-West struggle, the competition for scarce raw materials, the successful discovery of appropriate substitutes, and the application of advanced technologies will also play crucial roles in the distribution and balance of global power. All this points up the increasing complexity of international relations and the need for students and practitioners of international politics to take into consideration every element of society and its environment when analyzing the international arena.

NOTES

1. Lawrence Scheinman, "Security and a Transnational System: The Case of Nuclear Energy," *International Organization*, vol. 25, no. 3 (1971), pp. 626–648, on pp. 642–643.

2. The following discussion leans much on the discussion developed by Lawrence Scheinman in the article cited previously and in a paper, "Political Aspects of NPT Safeguards," he offered at Kansas State University Symposium on Implementing Nuclear Safeguards, October 25–27, 1971.

3. Henry R. Nau, "The Practice of Interdependence in the Research and Development Sector: Fast Reactor Cooperation in Western Europe," n.d. (mimeographed).

4. *New York Times*, July 5, 1974.

5. For details of this issue see Andrew J. Pierre with Claudia W. Moyne, *Nuclear Proliferation, A Strategy for Control* (New York: Foreign Policy Association, 1976).

6. John L. Mero, *The Mineral Resources of the Sea* (Amsterdam: Elsevier, 1965).

7. Ibid., p. 275. See also *Mineral Resources of the Deep Seabed*, Hearings before the Subcommittee on Minerals, Materials, and Fuels of the Committee on Interior and Insular Affairs, U.S. Senate, 93rd Congress, First Session (May 17–June 19, 1973). Manganese may be the first one to be mined from the seabed, possibly by 1976.

8. Cf. Edward Miles, "Transnationalism in Space: Inner and Outer," *International Organization*, vol. 25, no 3 (Summer 1971), pp. 602–625, on p. 624.

9. Article I of the Convention on the Continental Shelf, U.N. Document A/conf. 13/L 55.

10. Edward Miles, "Transnationalism in Space: Inner and Outer," op. cit., p. 615.

11. Department of State, *GIST* (December 1974).

12. Abbott Washburn, "The International Telecommunications Satellite Organization," *Public Utilities Fortnightly*, October 28, 1971, pp. 27–33, on p. 28.

13. The United Kingdom has 7 percent; France and West Germany, 5 percent; and Japan, 2 percent.

14. Miles, op. cit., p. 609.

15. Jonathan F. Galloway, "Worldwide Corporations and International Integration: The Case of INTELSAT," *International Organization*, vol. 24, no. 3 (Summer 1970), pp. 503–519, on p. 519.

16. *Facts on File*, May 19, 1973, p. 410.

17. Lester R. Brown, *World Without Borders* (New York: Vintage Books Division of Random House, 1972), p. 263.

18. Ibid., p. 264.

19. Ibid., pp. 264–265; see also Zbigniew Brzezinski, *Between Two Ages* (New York: Viking Press, 1970).

20. Miles, op. cit.

21. For details about disputes in the U.S. government on this matter, see Eugene B. Skolnikoff, *Science, Technology, and American Foreign Policy* (Cambridge, Mass.: M.I.T. Press, 1967), pp. 173–178.

22. Peter J. Bernstein, "New Controls Aim to Curb Ocean Pollution from Ships," *Times-Picayune* (New Orleans), November 17, 1973.

23. For a full discussion of this serious problem see Ralph C. d'Arge and Allen V. Kneese, "Environmental Quality and International Trade," *International Organization*, vol. 26, no. 2 (Spring 1972), pp. 419–465.

24. For details of the conference, see Jon McLin, *Stockholm: The Politics of "Only One Earth"* (JM-4-72), Fieldstaff Reports, West Europe Series, vol. 7, no. 4 (1972).

25. See J. Eric Smith, "The Role of Special Purpose and Nongovernmental Organizations in the Environmental Crisis," *International Organization*, vol. 26, no. 2 (Spring 1972), pp. 302–326.

26. See in this connection Sanford Rose, "Third World 'Commodity Power' Is a Costly Illusion," *Fortune* (November 1976), pp. 147 ff.

SUGGESTED READINGS

FALK, R. A. *This Endangered Planet: Prospects and Proposals for Human Survival.* New York: Random House, 1972.

FRITSCH, B. *Limited Growth and Political Power.* Cambridge, Mass.: Ballinger, 1977.

MESAROVICH, M., AND E. PESTEL. *Mankind at the Turning Point.* New York: Dutton, 1974.

WARD, B., AND R. DUBOS. *Only One Earth.* New York: Norton, 1972.

WILLRICH, M. *Global Politics of Nuclear Energy.* New York: Praeger, 1971.

PART V
Conclusions

CHAPTER SIXTEEN
WORLD WITHOUT WALLS

During the early days of August 1945, an American plane took off from the Marianas in the Pacific, arrived over Japan a few hours later, and delivered a deadly atomic bomb on the city of Hiroshima, spreading incredible death and destruction. A few days later another atomic bomb was dropped on Japan by a U.S. aircraft, but this time the target was Nagasaki.

Although the statesmen of the world agreed quickly after World War II that the military use of nuclear power must ultimately be prohibited and its peaceful use controlled carefully, the stockpile of atomic bombs since then has increased tremendously, their destructive force multiplied fiftyfold since Hiroshima, and their delivery to target speeded up through the introduction of ICBMs. Gradually, however, the superpowers have succeeded in limiting the testing of nuclear weapons, declaring certain parts of the world and space off limits for the installation of these weapons, and finally imposing restrictions on the number of delivery systems deployed. In 1958, a de facto ban on the testing of nuclear weapons emerged, but it was violated in 1961 and 1962. But in 1963 agreement was reached to forego testing in the atmosphere and to limit it to underground sites. The deployment of nuclear weapons was prohibited in the Antarctic, outer space, and under water. As already noted, Phase I of the Strategic Arms Limitation Talks was concluded successfully in 1972, and agreement on Phase II may be reached before 1980. Do these limitations on nuclear arms imply that eventually the prophecies of Isaiah and Micah will come true: "They shall beat their swords into plowshares and their spears into pruning hooks"? Or will the final outcome be Armageddon, proving right the Prophet Joel, who predicted that men "will beat . . . [their] plowshares into swords, and . . . [their] pruning hooks into spears"? Is Thomas Hobbes's 17th century description of man as competitive, diffident, and glory-seeking an accurate characterization of today's international society in which power is more important than justice, survival is often menaced, and the threat of violence is commonplace? Or will it be possible eventually to build a new world where nations will dismantle the walls between them, armaments will lose their significance, collaboration across national boundaries will have the highest priority, and a true world community will emerge? Common sense prescribes such an outcome, but the record so far confirms Joel's prediction and Thomas Hobbes' description.

Despite the new nongovernmental forces that have entered the interaction process of the international system and despite the increasing economic interdependence among the countries of the world brought about by these forces and by the changes in the physical environment of the system, the preceding chapters have demonstrated that progress toward transnational collaboration has been halted again and again by national and international political realities based on narrow considerations of national power. Since the middle 1960s the Western powers and the communist countries of Eastern Europe have attempted to reach a relaxation of tensions, a process and perhaps a state known as "détente"; but East and West seem to have different motivations for and concepts of détente, and only limited progress has been made toward a goal that reason tells us would have benefits for all. Indeed, the term *détente* was viewed by many as odious during the 1976 presidential election campaign in the United States and was officially banned by President Ford. But basically, really nothing changed as far as the relations with East and West were concerned. The Soviet Union uses the term *détente* mainly as a tactic to obtain economic and strategic advantages and perhaps to conceal the substantial increases in its military manpower.* The United States and Western Europe desire genuine relaxation of tensions, but are somewhat baffled about how to com-

---

* From 3.5 million less than a decade ago to 4.6 million in 1977 with a corresponding expansion of its tank forces located mainly in Eastern Europe.

bine this goal with ensuring their national security in the face of expanding Soviet military power. Yet, as the SALT II talks during the second half of 1977 have demonstrated, despite seemingly insurmountable obstacles on both sides, breakthroughs can be achieved and accommodations can be made to improve relations between East and West, and this offers a ray of hope for the future.

We have observed that the chief barrier to a worldwide conflagration is not the United Nations, a task for which it was especially designed, but the continued balance of nuclear terror between the two superpowers. In comparison, the deterrent effect of the nuclear armaments possessed by Britain, France, and China is negligible. Although the cold war physiognomy of the 1950s has, to some degree, given way to the climate of and hope for détente, the path to *permanent* international peace remains rocky. Innovative policies of governmental leaders in the Soviet Union and the United States are frequently attacked by foreign policy hardliners in their own country for reasons of domestic politics, and cold war images of the opponents have a habit of persisting. There are indications that Nikita Khrushchev's efforts to create better relations with the United States in the early 1960s and reduce tension were undermined by hardliners in the Presidium of the Central Committee of the Communist party who were intent on confrontation with the United States with bigger bombs in the 50–100 megaton range and insisted on their testing in the atomosphere in 1961, thereby breaking the de facto test ban of 1958. Khrushchev's attempt to prevent the testing of these large bombs by indirectly mobilizing public and elite opinion in the non-aligned countries against this test[1] failed to change the minds of the Presidium majority, and the views of this majority most likely set the stage for the Cuban missile crisis of 1962.

Leonid Brezhnev may have had similar difficulties with the hardliners and Marxist-Leninist dogmatists in the Presidium during the early 1970s when he sought continuing approval for Soviet-American economic cooperation. The influences of the Soviet hardliners may well have caused the deterioration of conditions for the exchange of information and person-to-person contacts that are part of the 1975 Helsinki agreements between the Western and East European countries on détente and increased European security.[2]

Hardliners have also influenced policy developments in the United States. The spirit of communist containment initiated with President Truman's policy of containment in 1947 has persisted through the administrations of Presidents Eisenhower, Kennedy, and Johnson and colored their policies toward the Soviet Union. Although President Kennedy may well have intended to pursue innovative policies toward the Communist bloc, the Soviet challenges in the Berlin crisis of 1961 and the Cuban missile crisis of 1962 thwarted these intentions. Thus, hardline policies of one superpower appear to have encouraged similar policies by the other. This tendency has been bolstered by the participation of foreign service and other bureaucracies in the foreign policy making process and their normal inclination to maintain the status quo and to oppose innovation. Even when President Nixon announced during the early 1970s the new era of negotiation with the Communist World instead of periodic confrontations, he felt that these negotiations could be successful only if the United States dealt from military strength. The Soviet Union, perhaps motivated by apprehension about our greater technological sophistication, has expanded its military power even further. Nevertheless, as we have seen, U.S.-Soviet negotiations have succeeded in limiting somewhat the nuclear arms competition.[3] The spiraling cost of this competition, as well as perceptions of future economic benefits from possible American-Soviet cooperation, may have been largely responsible for this development. Perhaps reason may indeed prevail in the future.

The hope that regional integration would lead gradually to a world without walls has been dimmed: regional integration has not even resulted in a "region without walls." True, in Western Europe the economic borders have been largely dismantled, but the political boundaries still stand. As we have observed, in other regions of the world, even economic integration has been mostly a failure. Power-oriented politicians and ego-oriented national bureaucracies, intent on maintaining or perhaps promoting their goals and the continuity of national institutions, have been the major obstacles in the forward movement of regional integration. Despite the economic and political benefits that may accrue to the peoples of the region from political integration, the prospects are bleak that the "region-state" is in the offing in Western Europe or anywhere else in the world.

We have noted earlier that some observers have seen the rise of multinational business enterprises as challenging the future of the nation-state. The argument has been made that the political boundaries of most countries are too narrow and constricted for the scope and sweep of modern international business, whose market is the entire world. Hence there has been a movement toward economic one-worldism in which businessmen often act as diplomats and may be more influential than statesmen in many parts of the globe. In many instances, MNEs are acting and planning in global terms and these are clearly incompatible with the political concepts of the nation-state.[4]

Samuel Huntington counters these assertions by stating that the predictions of the death of the nation-state are premature. He says:

These predictions of the death of the nation-state are premature. They overlook the ability of human beings and human institutions to respond to challenges and to adapt themselves to changed environments. They seem to be based on a zero-sum assumption about power and sovereignty: that a growth in the power of transnational organizations must be accompanied by a decrease in the power of nation-states. This, however, need not be the case. Indeed . . . an increase in the number, functions, and scope of transnational organizations will increase the demand for access to national territories and hence also increase the value of the one resource almost exclusively under the control of national governments. The current situation is, in this respect, quite different from that which prevailed with respect to state governments and national corporations within the United States in the nineteenth century. There, the Supreme Court held that except in rare circumstances, state governments could not deny or restrict access to their territory by businesses based in other states. The interstate commerce clause left such regulatory power to Congress. In the absence of any comparable global political authority able to limit the exclusionary powers of national governments, transnational organizations must come to terms with those governments.[5]

An important factor to keep in mind when considering the possible overthrow of the nation-state by the MNE is the purposes the two entities serve. These purposes are different and so are the needs these entities are to meet. In fact each has an interest in the survival of the other, and whatever conflict exists between them is mainly jurisdictional in nature.

It is a conflict not between likes but between unlikes, each of which has its own primary set of functions to perform. It is . . . conflict which . . . involves the structuring of relations and the distribution of benefits to entities which need each other even as they conflict with each other. The balance of influence may shift back and forth from one to the other, but neither can displace the other.[6]

Because of the differences in the very nature of the MNE and the nation-state, the former cannot replace the latter. Multinational business activities may cause trouble for national governments, but they are not capable of eliminating the state as a unit in the international system regardless of how powerful an MNE might be. This would not change if parent companies of MNEs were attempting to divest themselves from attachment and loyalty to a particular nation-state. An "anational" MNE with headquarters in several states and subsidiaries in many countries and with a completely international management staff would still be subject to the national laws and power of the states where the headquarters and subsidiaries are located. Nor would it make much difference if control over MNEs were vested in an agency of the United Nations or an institution of a regional IGO. Given the political realities under which IGOs operate at present and probably will in the foreseeable future, the implementation of IGO control is unlikely. Even if MNEs and the IGOs (universal or regional) were to ally themselves on the basis of perceived converging interests to bring about a genuine world community unhampered by national boundaries and by concerns for parochial power, they would probably not prevail so long as the authority of IGOs is closely circumscribed and supervised by the national governments.

If the financially powerful MNEs are not able to create a world without walls, what prospects have the rapidly growing number of international NGOs to achieve this goal? Might they be the Lilliputians who could tie down the Gulliver of nation-states by a spreading net of cross-national activities and functions that meet the needs of people, promote economic and social welfare in unspectacular ways, and at the same time, pre-empt governmental functions and make them unnecessary? No conclusive evidence is available to support such a hypothesis. In view of the limited resources and influence most international NGOs possess, it would be sheer fantasy to attribute to these organizations the kind of power necessary to transform the world of the nation-state into a true world community, although much of what is being accomplished by NGOs makes this planet a better place to live.

What is the impact of the growing economic interdependence of the people and countries of the world on the possibility of creating a global community, a world without walls? We see this interdependence most clearly when we worry about gaining access to or preserving the world's natural resources, or preventing the pollution of the oceans and atmosphere. And the awareness of this interdependence has been spreading not only among the people and governments of the industrially advanced countries, but also in the Third World. Nothing has brought this interdependence more to the attention of the people of the world than the petroleum shortage of 1973, although the making of this crisis should have been visible to all of us.

But even in the years that followed 1973, the world—and this includes the United States—has not learned to understand the very serious consequences of the petroleum shortage. It took a spate of extremely cold weather in the United States during the winter of 1977 to make the American people realize that their life-styles must be changed in the future. While initially the shortage of gasoline prompted many prospective buyers of new automobiles in the United States to opt for smaller cars to save fuel, a few years later it was again "business as usual," and the small cars were spurned in favor of the big fuel guzzlers. While the gasoline shortage may have only inconvenienced many Americans, the shortage of various energy sources, especially natural gas, has brought on the realization that people's lives become endangered.

On the other hand, the worldwide increases in the crude oil prices had the beneficial effect of making exploitation of marginal oil wells profitable, thereby increasing domestic sources of petroleum. These price increases also enhanced the commercial attractiveness of other energy sources, such as coal, oil shale, and nuclear power, whose use required enormous investments for research and development, especially if protection of the environment is taken into account. In short, the oil actions taken by the Arabs have compounded an already precarious situation, have produced economic dislocation and high social cost, but have also created opportunities for the development of substitute sources of energy. Indeed, a number of the Arab oil producing countries have invested their expanded incomes in North America, Western Europe, and Japan and therefore have helped the recovery of the economies of these countries. Moreover, in one way or another, some of the industrialized countries have found ways to adapt themselves to the new international economic conditions and have been able to reduce somewhat the high inflation rates caused by the increase in petroleum prices.

The actions of the Arab oil producing countries have not only harmed the economies of the industrially advanced countries, but also adversely affected much of the Third World. The rising cost of oil is hurting the balance-of-payments of the developing countries and adds to their debt burden. These countries also depend heavily for their exports on the markets of the developed countries; and as the economies of the latter suffer, these exports are likely to diminish. At the same time, the goods Third World countries must import from the industrialized states have also risen in cost as the result of the higher fuel prices. It has been theorized that the Arab states may divert funds to their hard-presseed friends in the Third World while the energy crunch is going on, but even such aid will not make much difference because the Third World economies are inextricably tied to the Western World's financial status. On the other hand, the developing countries that possess quantities of scarce natural resources may follow the example of the Arab oil producing countries and ask higher prices for such raw materials as copper, zinc, and bauxite and thereby improve their own economic conditions. Considering that, according to estimates of the U.S. Department of the Interior, the United States will have to depend on imports for more than half of its iron, lead, and tungsten by 1985, and for more than half of its copper, potassium, and sulfur by the year 2000, some of the Third World countries may move from the "have not" category to the "have" group of states and are likely to demand greater slices of the economic and political pies.

The growing muscle that some of the Third World countries have acquired as a result of their control over important raw material resources may well have encouraged them to demand a new international economic order. The forums for this demand are the United Nations and its specialized agencies, particularly UNCTAD. Although, as we have seen, the UNCTAD conferences of 1964, 1968, and 1972 did not meet the expectations and aspirations of the Third World, the 1976 conference in Nairobi was somewhat more successful. The advanced industrialized countries of the West began to recognize the justification for global commodity agreements which would alleviate the external fluctuations to which some of the raw materials exported by developing countries has been traditionally subjected. At the same time, the Western countries recognized that new rules should be evolved for the transfer of technology to Third World countries to help them with their industrialization. Finally, the near bankruptcy of many Third World countries not able to overcome their extreme poverty made it imperative for private and public lending institutions to rearrange repayment debt schedules and to declare a moratorium regarding the interest payments.

The extensive dependence of the industrialized economies on a number of raw materials, including of course petroleum, and the need for the Third World countries to find relief from export price fluctuations and heavy indebtedness gave rise to the North-South dialogue, initiated in Paris in 1975. In recognition of the extreme importance of the North-South relationship for international economics and the welfare of all the people of the world, efforts were made to find mutually beneficial solutions for the many problems arising from the existing asymmetry of natural resource distribution in the world; however, progress in the North-South dialogue has been extremely slow. The negotiations in Paris constituted a hard-fought bargaining game whose outcome cannot be predicted at this time in spite of the obvious need for a solution.

Is there a chance that the spreading awareness of global interdependence stemming from the rapid exhaustion of energy sources coupled with the danger of greater air and water pollution could convince the governments of the world to move to a zero-growth economy as discussed earlier? It is very doubtful because such a move would encounter the massive economic, social, and political forces that sustain the present system and are based on the values of continuing expansion and improvement. Nevertheless, the interdependence of the world will continue to grow and become more complex as interactions between governmental and nongovernmental actors becomes more frequent and more complex as well. Many issues now dealt with in a purely domestic context will acquire a transnational character, and more parties will have a specific interest in these issues. Politicians and diplomats will be forced to accept the increasingly important role of such functional specialists as economists, engineers, investment counselors, and meteorologists.

Looking into the future, it is probable that the growing awareness of the complexities of interdependence will have a moderating influence on the international behavior of all countries, although individual responses by governments will vary. Countries with fundamentally autarchic inclinations, such as the Soviet Union and China, and with strongly controlled domestic systems may tend to oppose the force of interdependence as they perceive it as threatening their autonomy. Some of the newly independent countries may feel the same way. However, in the long run, the fragmentation of the communist world and its increasing pragmatic approach to solving international problems may lead to the acceptance of the realities of an interdependent world and the need for concomitant procedures to assure long-term benefits for all, rather than to win at the expense of others. And this may be a first step toward a world without walls.

What does all this mean to you as a student of international relations? It is evident that international relations is not a clear-cut academic discipline based on well-thought-out principles from which solutions for all problems can be smoothly deduced. Rather, we are faced with a very complex world in which the dividing line between international and domestic policies has become increasingly blurred and in which the notion of national sovereignty may become outmoded in due time. But despite the fact that this notion may be obsolete, the power of nongovernmental actors who control enormous economic and financial resources has not been able so far to replace that of the nation-state. Yet it is also clear that the economic dimension in international relations has become increasingly significant because of the increasing power of MNEs and of the enormous economic problems inherent in the North-South relationship. Moreover, one must recognize that regardless of the crucial nature of national security issues, the two superpowers find themselves in a virtual stalemate as far as nuclear weapons are concerned, despite jockeying for improved positions by both sides. This makes the economic manager all the more important, be he the leader of a government or the chief executive of an MNE.

What does this shift in emphasis to the economic factor in international relations mean to you as a young citizen? It seems to be a very hopeful development because, in general, the management of economic affairs responds more easily to reason than do the emotion-laden issues of national security. Of course, powerful economic forces operating in the international arena, for example OPEC, are able to put constraints on people that can hurt their individual welfare, but they can also furnish substantial benefits when properly guided. The advancement of agricultural technologies through research financed by business and foundations is an example. If we want to help create a "world without walls," the economic route based on governmental and nongovernmental cooperation undoubtedly offers the best prospects.

NOTES

1. During a speech to the 22nd Congress of the Communist party, Khrushchev bragged about the planned test of 50 megaton bombs by stating this was also a test for the trigger of the 100 megaton "monster bomb" in the Soviet arsenal. Nehru and other leaders of nonaligned countries promptly protested the planned tests. For details see R. M. Slusser, *The Berlin Crisis of 1961* (Baltimore: Johns Hopkins University Press, 1973), pp. 313–314.

2. See also *Die Zeit*, August 31, 1973, p. 5, and Walter Laqueur, "A New Era or Mostly Bubbles," *New York Times Magazine*, June 17, 1973.

3. See also Albert Wohlstetter, "Is There a Strategic Arms Race?" *Foreign Policy*, no. 15 (Summer 1974), pp. 3–20; and "Rivals, but no 'Race,'" *Foreign Policy*, no. 16 (Fall 1976), pp. 41–81.

4. See Samuel P. Huntington, "Transnational Organizations in World Politics," *World Politics*, vol. 25, no. 3 (1973), pp. 334–368, on p. 363, and the citation there.

5. Ibid., pp. 363–364.

6. Ibid., p. 366.

7. *The States Item* (New Orleans), January 1, 1974, p. A-8.

SUGGESTED READING

KAHN, HERMAN AND ANTHONY J. WIENER. *The Year 2000.* New York: Macmillan, 1967.

GLOSSARY

Adjudication In international law, adjudication refers to a decision made in a dispute between two or more parties by a permanent court of law such as the International Court of Justice located in the Hague in the Netherlands.

Alliance for Progress A program conceived by the U.S. government to assist Latin America in its economic and social development from 1962 to 1972. Although $20 billion of public and private funds were to be spent for this purpose, the preconditions set by the United States for the implementation of the program were not fulfilled by most Latin American countries and the program did not achieve its objectives.

Andean Common Market An economic cooperative arrangement based on a customs union which currently consists of Venezuela, Colombia, Ecuador, Peru, and Bolivia. Chile was a charter member, but for political reasons formally withdrew from participation in 1977.

Arbitration A process by which parties to a dispute agree to submit the issue in question to one or more umpires or judges for a decision which is binding. Basically, the selection of the umpires or judges is up to the parties to the dispute and they are not necessarily persons with judicial training.

Assured destructive capability The ability to destroy without question the society of an enemy with nuclear weapons *after* receiving an all out nuclear attack by that enemy.

Balance-of-power A situation in which two or more states are in a rough equivalence of power. It is also a prescription for international action to checkmate the increased power aspirations of other states and thereby prevent wars.

Balance-of-terror Refers to mutual deterrence from nuclear attack by both the Soviet Union and the United States against the other. Because both countries possess such powerful nuclear weapons neither would emerge a victor.

Bureaucratic politics model The notion that foreign policy making is the result of overlapping bargaining activities among officials in various governmental ministries and agencies.

Collective security The notion that all member states of a security organization would assist any member attacked by either another member state or several other member states or by states outside the organization.

Colombo Plan Designed for the co-operative development of its member states in Southeast Asia. Formed in 1950, its headquarters is in Colombo, Sri Lanka. The economically advanced members aid the developing member countries through bilateral agreements for the provision of capital, technical experts and training, and equipment.

COMECON The Council for Mutual Economic Assistance. Formed in 1949, its members are Bulgaria, Cuba, Czechoslovakia, East Germany, Hungary, Mongolia, Poland, Romania, and the Soviet Union; an associate member is Yugoslavia. Headquarters is in Moscow. Its purpose is to coordinate and integrate member's economies, under USSR leadership.

Cominform The communist information bureau established in 1947. Its aim is to coordinate contacts among the communist parties in different countries of the world and serve as an instrument of Soviet control over these parties to assure their persistent opposition to Western policies.

Comintern The Communist International founded in 1919. It is the predecessor of Cominform and served mainly as a vehicle to promote Soviet interests on a worldwide basis.

Customs union Refers to an economic cooperative arrangement between two or more states which culminates in the elimination of tariff barriers between the member states and the establishment of a common external tariff imposed on imports from nonmember countries.

Deténte Refers to efforts by the communist and noncommunist countries of Europe and North America to reduce tensions and to bring about greater economic intercourse, cultural exchanges, and human contacts.

East African Community An economic cooperative arrangement consisting of Kenya, Tanzania, and Uganda based on a customs union and common transportation and communications services.

Economic union Refers to full harmonization of economic policies among the member states of a regional economic cooperative arrangment such as the European Community.

Economies of scale May also be called economies of mass production, which means that if a large enough number of units is produced, specialization of labor and of manufacturing functions will result in considerably lower cost per item than if only a small number of units is produced.

European Community A collective term for three European communities, the European Coal and Steel Community, the European Economic Community, and the European Atomic Energy Community.

Formulation of policy The process, sometimes long and complicated, during which transnational or foreign policies are shaped. Many levels of public officials and private groups or individuals may participate in forming these policies.

Free trade area An economic cooperation arrangement in which two or more states participate and which culminates in the elimination of all tariff barriers between the participating countries.

Functionalism The process by which the economic and social needs of peoples are successfully met through border-crossing collaboration arranged by intergovernmental organizations. The result may be a shift of loyalty from nation states to these organizations and shaving off successive layers of sovereignty from these states.

Image The perceptions policy making officials have regarding the external environment of their country and of its strengths and weaknesses. These images shape the input into the policy making process.

Implementation of policy The various measures necessary to carry out the transnational and foreign policies formulated by governmental authorities. These measures may be the use of diplomacy, economic actions, psychological and political warfare, or military action.

International relations The traditional interactions and relations *between* the governments of states and IGOs.

Intranational relations The interactions and relations *within* a particular nation state among nongovernmental groups or individuals and between these actors and governmental authorities.

Joint equity venture A cooperative arrangement between business firms without legal corporate ties to pursue jointly particular economic activities.

Licensing agreements Vehicles to transfer patents and technological expertise from one business firm (the holder of the patent) to another firm within or outside national bounderies. A fee is paid for the transfer which can often be quite high.

Lomé Convention An economic cooperative arrangement between the European Community and about 50 African, Caribbean, and Western Pacific developing countries. It provides preferential access of imports of these countries into the community member states as well as financial aid and technical assistance.

Monetary union The complete harmonization of monetary policies among the countries of a regional economic cooperative arrangement such as the European Community, and the eventual emergence of a uniform currency.

Natural law A law considered as flowing from morality, natural justice, and the rational nature of man as opposed to a law made by legislatures or international treaties.

Neo-functionalism A concept which asserts that the forces of functionalism must receive a special impetus to be effective. For this purpose a number of strategies are used such as the creation of regional institutions especially designed to further regional integration and promoting decisions made by governmental authorities that upgrade transnational common interests.

North-South dialogue Talks and negotiations between the economically advanced countries of the world, mostly located in the Northern Hemisphere, and the developing countries, mostly located in the Southern Hemisphere, about the improvement of the economic welfare of the latter and the supply of raw materials to the former.

Optional clause The acceptance by national governments of the compulsory jurisdiction of the International Court of Justice. Many governments including the United States accept this jurisdiction only with considerable reservations.

Organizational process model The concept that foreign policy is the output stemming from the interplay among major governmental organizations participating in the formulation and implementation of foreign policy goals and actions.

Rational policy model The notion that the making of foreign policy is done through a rational intellectual process.

Roman law As a source for international law, this concept stems from laws of the Roman Empire, which were seen as the sum of principles that control human conduct.

Socialization The learning process through which persons acquire political orientations and patterns of behavior.

Spillover A desirable process to promote regional integration. It refers to a situation created when the attainment of an original goal within the regional integration context can be assured only by taking further actions. These actions in turn may create additional situations needing further actions to attain regional goals. Spillover may take place from one sector of the economy to another, or from one economic sector to a political sector, or through the expansion of authority in one of the regional institutions, or by creating additional institutions.

Supranational power The authority of IGO institutions to exercise certain powers transferred to them by sovereign states and normally only exercised by the latter. An example is the power of the Commission and Council of Ministers of the European Community to issue regulations having the force of law and therefore binding on all residents in the member states.

Transfer pricing The ability of multinational companies to affect tax receipts unfavorably. This can be done through allocation of production to facilities in low tax countries or through the manipulation of profits on items moved across national boundaries from one subsidary to another for assembly or sales so the most profit per item occurs in the countries with the lowest tax rates.

Transideological enterprise A joint venture of a multinational corporation with a communist state-operated enterprise thereby engaging in an international division of labor across ideological borders. The number of actual MNEs involved remains small. Nevertheless, certain forces in the capitalist and communist worlds, such as the pursuit of deténte, may be instrumental in expanding the transideological experiences of businesses.

Transnational relations Interactions and relations between nongovernmental groups and individuals of different countries as well as between these actors, governments, and IGOs across national boundaries.

Yaoundé Convention Formed in 1963, this agreement is an economic cooperation arrangement between the European Economic Community and eighteen former colonies of the EEC member states in Africa. It is the predecessor of the Convention of Lomé.

INDEX

Adjudication, in international law, 207, 208–209, 212

Administrative and bureaucratic elites, 100–101

Afro-Asian group, in United Nations, 234

AGITPROP (The Department of Propaganda and Agitation), 110, 149

Algeria, and OAU intervention in dispute with Morocco, 250

Alliance for progress, 175, 249

Alliances, 166–71, 210
  in balance of power situation, 183–84, 185
  commitment of partners of, 168–69
  conflict of interests among signatories of, 166–68

Allies
  in balance of power situations, 187–88
  for MNEs, 332–33

Allison, Graham T.
  on civil servants, 86–87
  foreign policy models of, 82–87

Almond, Gabriel, categories of elites of, 99–110, 124

American People and Foreign Policy, The (Almond), 99

American Petroleum Institute (API), 332

American Selling Price Clause, and the chemical industry, 102

Amin, Idi, 47, 80, 306

ANCUS Mutual Security Treaty, 170

Andean Common Market, 139, 173, 300

Antiballistic Missiles (ABMs), 158–59, 193

Arbitration, in international law, 207, 209–210, 212

Argentina, and LAFTA, 298

Armaments, increased, in

balance of power situations, 187
Armed demonstrations, as political warfare measure, 152
Asian and Pacific Arrangement (ASPAC), 176
Association of Atomic Scientists, and influence on foreign policy, 104
Assured destruction capability, in use of nuclear weapons, 191–92, 211
Atlantic Alliance, 83, 84
Atomic energy. *See* Nuclear energy.
Attitudinal integration, as category of political integration, 273

Balance of power, 181–97, 210
  concepts and patterns, 182–84
  Kaplan's essential rules for, 186–87
Balance of terror, 191, 211, 398
Balancer, 210
  function of, described by Morgenthau, 184
  Great Britain as, 184–86
Barber, Richard J., 327
BBC, propaganda and, 147, 148, 149
Behrman, Jack N., on MNEs, 316, 343, 345
Belgium, overseas possessions of, in 1957, 287
Best and the Brightest, The (Halberstam), 89
Bilateral foreign aid, 145
Black propaganda, 146. *See also* Propaganda.
Blake, David H., 351

Blockade, as political warfare measure, 152
Bolivia, and LAFTA, 298
Boycott, 142–43
  of France within EEC, 286
Brademas, John, 5
Brazil, and LAFTA, 298
Brezhnev, Leonid, 398
  détente under, 114
  and SALT agreement, 194
Brierly, J.L., on international law, 204
British Confederation of Industry, as example of interest elite, 101
Brown, Lester, on new communications technologies, 382
Buffer zones, in balance of power situations, 187
Bulletin of Atomic Scientists, The, 104
Bundesnachrichtendienst (BND). *See* Federal Information Service of West Germany.
Bundy, McGeorge, 88
Bureaucratic elites. *See* Administrative and bureaucratic elites.
Bureaucratic politics model, in foreign policy making, 83, 85–87
Bureaucratic-pragmatic leadership, 116
Bureau of Intelligence and Research of the Department of State, 91
Buy-American Act, 140

Cambodia, war in, 121
Canada, growth of U.S. MNEs in, 317
Carter, James, 115

and nonproliferation of nuclear weapons, 371–72
and SALT, 194, 196
Castle, Barbara, on civil servants, 85–86
Causes of war, 197–202
Central African Customs and Economic Union (UDEAC), 303, 307
Central American Common Market (CACM), 139, 173, 302–303
Central Intelligence Agency. See CIA.
Charismatic-revolutionary leadership, 117–18
Chile
    CIA actions against, 119
    effect on U.S. mining strike of, 350
    and LAFTA, 298
    political activities of ITT in, 330
China,
    and balance of power, 190
    relations with U.S. of, 183
Churchill, Winston, on national interest, 79
CIA, 91
    and overthrow of Allende, 151
    and political warfare, 152–53
Civil servants
    as administrative and bureaucratic elites, 100–101
    Barbara Castle on, 85
    and EEC, 286
    input into foreign policy of, 85–87
Civil service(s), 70, 85–87
    Barbara Castle on, 85–86
    Graham Allison on, 86–87
    Henry Kissinger on, 86

Claude, Inis, 235, 253
Climate, as element determining power, 34–35, 58
Closed images, 88
Coal, as alternative energy source to oil, 37–39, 367
Collaboration, in international relations, 165–79
Collective security, 189, 211, 221
Colombo Plan, 176
COMECON, 172–73
    differences from E.C., 311(N)
Cominform, 153
Comintern, 153
Commission(s), of EEC and EURATOM, 282
    functions of, 283
    merger, 285–86
Committee of Permanent Representatives, 286
Committee on the Challenges of Modern Society, 388
Common Agricultural Policy (CAP), 284–85
Common market, as level of economic integration, 272
Common Schedule, 298, 300, 301
Communications elites, 100, 107–110
Communications failure, as cause of war, 198–99
Communications Satellite Corporation (COMSAT), 379–80
Communist countries
    and GATT, 138
    government expenditures in, 54
    ideological leadership in, 117
    and interdependence with Free World, 357
    See also Dictatorships

Community of the Six. *See*
  European Economic
  Community.
Compatible foreign policy
  goals, 78, 95
Composition, of population, as
  element determining
  power, 47–48
Conference of Contracting
  Parties, of LAFTA, 299
Conference on Human Envi-
  ronment, 390
Conference on International
  Economic Cooperation
  (CIEC), 177
Conference on Security and
  Cooperation in Europe,
  357
Conference on the Law of the
  Sea, 135, 376
Conflict, in international rela-
  tions, 165, 181–212
Congo
  OAU involvement in internal
    conflict in, 250
  Security Council and crisis
    in, 232
Congress of Vienna, 130
  as first IGO, 218
Constraints, in foreign policy
  making, 79
Consultations, between alliance
  partners, 169
Continental Shelf, 376
  definition of, at Conference
    on the Law of the Sea, 376
Conventional war, 154–56
  armed forces in, 154
  weaponry in, 155
Coplin, William D., 87, 110
  and O'Leary, Michael K., 27
Council of Ministers, for EEC
  and EURATOM, 282, 286
  functions of, 283

Court of Justice of the Euro-
  pean Communities, 208,
  209
Covenant of the League (of
  Nations), 221–23
  four major organs of, 222
Cox, R.W., 351
Crotonville Conference, 134
Cuba, OAS and, 248
Currency regulations and
  restrictions, as economic
  tool for policy implementation, 140
Customary international law,
  205
Customs duties, effect of, 137
Customs unions, 172–73
  as level of economic integra-
    tion, 272
Cyprus, and Security Council's
  prevention of war, 232
Czechoslovakia
  communist coup d'etat in,
    151
  invasion by Soviet Union of,
    118, 167, 230

Decision-making approach, to
  study of international rela-
  tions, 10–12
Declaration of Intention, of
  EEC Treaty, 287
Declaration of Presidents of
  America, 301
Defense Intelligence Agency
  (DIA), 91
de Gaulle, Charles
  armed forces under, 72
  boycott in EEC and, 286
  Britain's entry into EEC and,
    284, 285
  influence of political parties
    under, 106
  NATO and, 170

Democracies
  domestic structure in, 111
  and peace, 118–19
Denmark, and entry into EEC, 294
Department of Commerce, 91
Department of Energy, 91
d'Estaing, Valéry Giscard,
  influence of political
  parties under, 106
Détente, 90, 397
Deuxième Bureau, of France, 93
Developing countries
  growth rate in, 43–46
  raw materials of, 39
  See also Third World
Dictatorships
  domestic structure in, 111
  interest groups in, 105, 107
  and peace, 118–19
  public opinion in, 110
Diplomacy
  depreciation of, 136–37
  functions of, 131
  as instrument for policy im-
    plementation, 129, 130–37, 161
Directives, as type of order in
  EEC, 283
Domestic intelligence, 90
Domestic investment, in analy-
  sis of GNP, 53
Domestic politics
  influence of foreign policy
    on, 119–25
  influence on foreign policy
    of, 99–119
Drucker, Peter, 328
Dumbarton Oaks Conference, 224–25
Dye, Thomas, 14

Early Bird Satellite, 380

East African Community
  (EAC), 139, 173, 303–307
  background of, 303–305
  countries of, 303
  organization of, 305–306
  results of, 306–307
East European Soviet Bloc, in
  United Nations, 234
Economic advantages or
  desperation, as cause of
  war, 200–202
Economic and Social Council
  of United Nations, 228–29
Economic Commission of
  Latin American (ECLA), 297
Economic Community of West
  Africa (ECWA), 303, 307
Economic cooperation
  arrangements, 171–78, 179, 210
Economic determinism, as approach to study of international relations, 7–8
Economic development, as a
  determinant of power, 48–56, 59
  effect on foreign policy of, 81
Economic integration, 272, 307
  and the European Commu-
    nity, 296
Economic measures, as instru-
  ments for policy imple-
  mentation, 129, 137–45, 161
Economic union, as level of
  economic integration, 272
Economies of scale, 275
Ecopolitics, 48
Eden, Sir Anthony, and Suez
  crisis, 122
Education
  of military, 72
  of population, as element de-
    termining power, 46

EEC. *See* European Economic Community.
Effects of war, 202–203
Egypt, and Suez crisis, 121–22
Eisenhower, Dwight D., and Suez crisis, 123
Electric energy
  as element determining power, 51
  from nuclear reactors, 367–73
El Salvador
  and OAS Council, 248
  and war with Honduras, 200–201
Embargoes, as economic warfare tool, 141–42
Embassies
  classification of rank in, 130
  establishment of, 130
Equilibrium, 9, 182, 188, 210
Essential rules, for balance of power situations (Kaplan), 186–87
Ethnic diversity
  as cause of war, 199
  as element determining power, 47–48
  use of, in subversion, 150, 151
Europe, growth of U.S. MNEs in, 317
European Agricultural Guidance and Guarantee Fund (EAGGF), 285
European Atomic Energy Community (EURATOM), 282
European Coal and Steel Community (ECSC), 172–73, 177, 178, 278, 280–81
  countries in, 278
  establishment of, 280

objectives of, 280
organization and structure of, 280–81
European Common Market
  as example of customs unions, 139
  as example of IGOs, 21
  as example of regional system, 9
  food production and, 40
  and interest elites, 101
  preferential trade agreements and, 139
  See also European Economic Community
European Community. *See* European Coal and Steel Community, European Economic Community, European Common Market, European Atomic Energy Community.
European Community of Nine, 190.
  See Also European Common Market.
European Court of Justice of Human Rights, 208
European Development Fund (EDF), 288
European Economic Community (EEC), 172–74, 281–83
  assessment of, after 12-year transition period, 284–286
  basis of, 281
  future prospects of, 295–96
  Great Britain and, 283–84
  in 1970s, 289–95
  organization of, 282–83
  and relations with Third World, 286–89
  weakness of British pound in, 295

See also European Common
Market.
European Free Trade Associa-
tion, 139, 172–73
European Launcher Develop-
ment Organization
(ELDO), 381
European Parliament, 282, 295
European Security Conference
Soviet Union and, 114
Export controls, 141–42
Expropriation, 347
Extinction, as effect of war,
202–203

Famine, 377–78
FBI, 91
Federal Bureau of Investiga-
tion. *See* FBI.
Federal Information Service
(BND), of West Germany, 92
Federation of German In-
dustry, as example of
interest elite, 101
Flexible response strategy, 158,
162
Food and Agricultural Organization (FAO), 377
Ford, Gerald
and détente, 90
and SALT agreement, 194
Foreign aid, as economic tool
for policy implementation,
144, 161
bilateral versus multilateral,
145
types of, 144–45
Foreign intelligence, 90
Foreign investments
in analysis of GNP, 54–55
benefit for host country of,
337–38
control of, 349
effects of, 323–24

and exports, 327
as indicators of change, 324
profitability and, 328
Foreign Ministry, 84
Foreign policies
domestic politics and, 99–125
formulation of, 13–16, 78–96
image of country in making,
87–90
instruments for implementation of, 129–63
intelligence and, 90–95
perspectives of, 82–87
of the U.S., 17
Formulation of policy, 13–17,
78–96
France
economic planning of, 345
influence of political parties
in, 106
instability of government in,
67
intelligence collection by, 93
nuclear energy and, 368, 372
overseas possession of, in
1957, 286, 287
Suez crisis and, 121–22
withdrawal from NATO, 189
Free trade areas, 172–73
as lowest level of economic
integration, 272
Fulbright, J. William, 5
Functionalism, 276–77, 307

Galloway, Jonathan, F., on
MNEs, 316
Game theory approach, to
study of international rela-
tions, 11–12
GATT (General Agreement on
Tariffs and Trade), 133,
138–39, 161
Gehlen, General, agency of,
92–93

General Agreement on Tariffs
and Trade. *See* GATT.
General Assembly, of United
Nations, 135, 227
General Motors, as the largest
MNE, 22
General principles of law,
207–210
Geneva Conference, 238
Geography, as a determinant
of power, 32–40, 58
effect on foreign policy, 81
Geopolitics, as element determining power, 32–33
German-American Bund, 150
Germany, West,
food production and, 40
foreign investments of, 327
intelligence collection by,
92–93
MNEs of, 322
nuclear energy and, 368, 372
population structure in, 42–43
significance of role of parties
in, 106
U.S. policy and, 17
Goods and services, production
of, as element determining
power, 52
Goodsell, Charles T., 330
Government, 19
and administration, as variable determinant of power,
66–70, 75–76
administrative efficiency of,
68–70
attitude of the people
toward, 67–68
instability of, 67
rapidity of decision making
in, 66–67
Government expenditures, in
analysis of GNP, 53–54

Government loans, as type of
foreign aid, 144–45
Gray, Justice, 206–207
Gray propaganda, 146. *See also*
Propaganda.
Great Britain
as balancer, 184–86
coal and iron in, 35
economic cooperation
arrangements in, 177–78
and the EEC, 283–84, 293,
294
food production in, 40
intelligence collection by, 92
MNEs of, 322
national interest of, 80
nuclear energy in, 368
population structure in,
42–43
propaganda and, 148, 149
racial differences, 47
Suez crisis and, 121–22
Greece, application for EC
membership of, 295
Gross National Product (GNP)
domestic investment in analysis of, 53
foreign investment in analysis of, 54–55
government expenditures in
analysis of, 53–54
per capita, 50
per capita income, 50
personal consumption in
analysis of, 52
Grotius, Hugo, 207
Growth rate, 43–46
Guerrilla groups
Arab, 22
Baader-Meinhof, 152
definition of, 153 (fn)
and foreign policy goals,
152–53

Palestinian, 152
sales of weapons to, 202
Gulf of Tonkin Resolution, 120

Halberstam, David, 88–89
Halperin, Morton H. and
Kanter, Arnold, on presidential use of foreign policy, 123–24
Hammarskjöld, Dag, 231
Hardliners, influence on U.S. policy of, 398–99
Haushofer, General Karl, 33
Health, of population, as element determining power, 46–47
Heath, Edward, and British entry into EEC, 294
Helsinki agreement, 167
Hilsman, Roger, on functions of the press, 108
Historical-descriptive approach, to study of international relations, 6
Hitler, Adolph, 190, 201
attack on Poland, 198
violation of international law of, 204
Hobbes, Thomas, 188, 200, 397
Ho Chi Minh, 119
Honduras, and war with El Salvador, 200–201
Host countries, of MNEs
benefits for, 337–39
disturbance of economic plans in, 344–45
drawbacks for, 341–49
foreign domination in, 343–44
measures preventing foreign control by, 347–49
technological dependence in, 344

Huntington, Samuel, on nation-states, 399–400

Ideological cohesion, 65–66, 75
Ideological leadership, 117
IGOs. See Intergovernmental organizations.
Images, of country, in making foreign policies, 87–90
conservative, 88–90
open versus closed, 88
public versus private, 89–90
Imperialism, 8
Incompatible foreign policy goals, 78, 95
India
interest groups in, 102–103
nuclear explosion of, 371
Industrialization, 50–51, 59
Inputs, in analysis of transnational policy, 14–15
Institutional integration, as category of political integration, 273
Integration
categories of (Nye), 271, 272–74
definition of, 271
in East Africa, 303, 306–307
in the European Community, 278, 296
incentives for, 274–75
in Latin America, 297–98, 301
Intelligence
collection of, 90–93
foreign policy making and, 90–95, 96
information, 93–95
Intelsat, 379–81
and computers, 381–82
Intercontinental ballistic missiles (ICBMs), 73, 193
Interdependence, 27, 29, 356

Interest elites, 100, 101–105
Intergovernmental Council of
    Copper Exporting Coun-
    tries (CIPEC), 142
Intergovernmental organi-
    zations (IGOs),
    categories of, 217–18
    characteristics of, 216–17
    diplomatic behavior in,
    134–36
    as economic cooperation
    arrangements, 172, 216
    effects of NGOs on, 265–66
    in implementing policies, 130
    regional, 240–51, 279
International Atomic Energy
    Agency (IAEA), 368
International Basic Economic
    Corporation, 340
International Chamber of
    Commerce, as example of
    NGO, 255, 261
International Communication
    Agency (ICA), 148
International Convention of
    Constantinople, and Suez
    crisis, 121
International Council for the
    Exploration of the Sea, 377
International Court of Justice,
    of the United Nations, 208,
    209, 229
International firm, definition
    of, 315
International law, 203–210
    sources for, 205, 211
International Oceanographic
    Commission (IOC of
    UNESCO), 377
International Petroleum Com-
    pany (IPC), in Peru, 332
International Red Cross, 161
International relations, 25, 29

collaboration in, 165–79
    impact of MNEs on, 337–62
International Resource Author-
    ity, 377
International trade patterns
    and job markets, 4
International treaties and
    agreements, 205–206
Intersputnik, 381
Intranational relations, 25, 29
Ireland, and entry into EEC,
    294
Irredentism, 151
    as cause of war, 199–200
Israel
    foreign policy of, 81
    size of military in, 70
    and Suez crisis, 121–22
Italy, overseas relations of, in
    1957, 287
ITT
    political activities of, in
    Chile, 330
    political activities of, in Peru,
    330–31

Jackson, Henry "Scoop," 5
Jacoby, Neil, 341
Jager, Elizabeth R., 349
Jamaica
    bauxite miners of, and USW,
    352
    and effort to form bauxite
    cartel, 142
Japan
    economic dependence of, 81
    MNEs of, 322
    nuclear energy in, 368
Jennings, Paul, 350
Job Markets, changing interna-
    tional trade patterns and, 4
Johnson, Lyndon, and Vietnam
    war, 120

Joint Defense and Economic
Cooperation Treaty, The,
168
Joint equity venture, in
transfer of knowledge, 329
Joint Intelligence Committee,
of Great Britain, 92
Journal of Conflict Resolution,
198

Kampala-Mbale Agreement,
305
Kanter, Arnold. *See* Halperin,
Morton H. and Kanter,
Arnold.
Kaunda, Kenneth, on NGOs,
265-66
Kennedy, John F.,
and Bay of Pigs, 123
and fight with Congress, 123
foreign policies and, 88-89
and NATO's dependence on
nuclear weapons, 157
Kennedy Round negotiations,
102, 133-34
Kenya, and EAC, 303
KGB, and political warfare, 153
Khrushchev, Nikita, 114, 398
Kissinger, Henry, 68, 124, 137
on civil service, 86
on nuclear weapons, 156-57
on types of leadership
groups, 115-18, 124-25
Kommunist, 149. *See also*
AGITPROP.
Korean conflict, 3, 118-19, 230
Korea, South, MNEs and, 341

Labor unions, responses to
MNEs, 349-54
strikes, 349-51
strategies, 352-53
objectives, 353

appeals to governments by,
353-54
Latin America, growth of U.S.
MNEs in, 317
Latin American Free Trade
Association, (LAFTA) 139,
172-73, 178, 297-303
countries of, 298
prospects of, 301-303
results of, 300-301
treaty provisions of, 298-99
Law of Nations (Brierly), 204
League of Nations, 189, 220-24,
252
as example of IGO, 21
failure of, 223-24
*League of Nations—A Practical
Suggestion* (Smuts), 221
League of Women Voters
(LWV), and influence on
foreign policy, 104-105
Lenin, V. I., 112-14
Levi, Werner, on Third World
problems, 239
Liberation wars, 199
Licensing agreements, in
transfer of knowledge, 329
Lincoln Laboratories, of MIT, 91
Lobbying, 329-33
Lomé, Convention of, 174-75,
289, 293
Long-range foreign policy
goals, 78, 95

McCarthy, Eugene, as opposer
to Vietnam war, 120
Mackinder, Sir Halford, 32-33
McNamara, Robert, and
NATO's dependence on
nuclear weapons, 157
Malaysia, MNEs and, 341, 360
Management, organization of,
316

Marshall, George C., 95

Marx, Karl, 7

Marxist-Leninist ideology,
  as approach to international
    relations, 8
  influence of, on Soviet
    foreign policies, 112–15

Marxist Popular Movement for
  the Liberation of Angola
  (MPLA), 250

Massachusetts Institute of
  Technology (MIT), 91
  on economic and population
    growth, 389

Mauritius, 341

Media, power of, in foreign
  policy affairs, 107–110

Meir, Golda, 22

Meynaud, Jean, on interest
  groups, 102

Mexico
  and LAFTA, 298
  MNEs and, 341

Middle East
  oil reserves of, 36–38
  Security Council's efforts to
    maintain peace in, 233

Militärische Abschirmdienst
  (MAD), of West Germany,
  92

Military
  education and training of, 72
  as element determining
    power, 56–57, 70–75
  organization of, 70–75, 76
  reserves, 73
  size of, 70
  spirit and commitment of, 72
  weapons and materiel of,
    73–75

Military action. See War.

Military-industrial complex,
  103

role of, in causing war,
  201–202

Military intelligence organization (MI), of Great Britain, 92

Ministry of Defense, 84

Ministry of Finance, 84

Mitrany, David, on functionalism, 276

MNEs. See Multinational enterprises.

Modelski, George, on national
  parties, 106

Monetary union, as highest
  level of economic integration, 272

Monroe Doctrine, 80, 184

Morgenthau, Hans J., 6, 28
  on function of the balancer,
    184
  on nuclear weapons, 74

Morocco, and OAU intervention in dispute with Algeria, 250

Most-favored-nation Clause, 67,
  138

MPLA. See Marxist Popular
  Movement for the Liberation of Angola.

Multilateral foreign aid, 145

Multinational enterprises
  (MNEs), 22–25, 314–34,
  337–62
  definitions of, 315–16
  difference from nation-states
    of, 400
  as disturber of economic
    plans, 344–45
  economic warfare and, 143
  foreign domination of,
    343–44
  impact of, on international
    relations, 337–62

labor unions and, 349–54
location of parent companies of, 317
pattern of growth of, 316–23
and policy implementation, 137
transnational initiatives by, 323–33
Multinational firms, definition of, 315
Multiple independently targeted reentry vehicles (MIRVs), 73, 191

Nasser, Gamal Abdel, and Suez crisis, 121–22
National Aeronautics and Space Administration (NASA), 383
National and international court decisions, 206
National character, 62, 75
National Council of Churches, and influence on foreign policy, 104
National Intelligence Estimates (NIEs), 94
National interests, 79–82, 96
definition of, 79–80
Nationalism, 20, 29, 62–65, 75
National Schedules, 298, 300, 301
National Science Foundation (NSF), and weather modification techniques, 384
National Security Agency (NSA), 91
National stereotypes, 62
Nation-states, 19, 28, 399–400
difference from MNEs, 400
NATO. See North American Treaty Organization.
Natural law, 207

Natural resources, as element determining power, 35–40, 58
See also Raw materials
Negotiation, as function of diplomats, 131, 132–34
Neofunctionalism, 277–78, 307
Netherlands, overseas possessions of, in 1957, 287
New York Times, and Bay of Pigs, 108
NGOs. See Nongovernmental organizations.
Nixon, Richard
economic policies of, 17
international politics and, 4–5, 399
Vietnamization program and, 120–21
visits to China and Soviet Union of, 123
Non-aggression Pact, 168
Nongovernmental organizations (NGOs), 23, 29, 255–68
coalitions of, 264–65
consequences of, 267–68
criteria for international, 255
effects on IGOs, 265–66
financing of, 262–63
functional types of, 256–57
organizational effectiveness of, 259–62
Non-proliferation Treaty, 82, 370
Nontariff barriers, as economic tool for policy implementation, 140
Normative approach, to study of international relations, 12–13
Normative view of national interest, 79

North Atlantic Council, of
    NATO, 241
North Atlantic Treaty Organi-
    zation (NATO), 21, 82,
    166–71
    commitments of, 241
    nuclear war and, 157–58
    organization of, 241–44
    problems in, 244–45
    as regional IGO, 240–41
    Warsaw Pact and, 114–15
North-South arrangements, of
    economic cooperation,
    174–78, 179
North-South dialogue, 177, 392,
    403
Nuclear energy, 367–73
Nuclear Nonproliferation
    Treaty, 196–97
Nuclear Test Ban Treaty, 196
Nuclear war, 156–59
Nuclear weapons, 73–74,
    156–59
    Nonproliferation Treaty and,
    82
    problems of use of, 191–97
Nuclear weapons and Foreign
    Policy (Kissinger), 156–57
Nye, Joseph, distinctions of in-
    tegration of, 271
Nyerere, Julius, on power in
    OAU, 251

Observation, as function of
    diplomats, 131, 132
Office of War Information, 147,
    148
Offshore oil production, 374
    pollution from, 386
Oil crisis of 1970s, 3, 21, 369
Oil embargo (Arab)
    as economic warfare tool,
    141, 201

and effect on American life-
    style, 3
multinational oil companies
    and, 21
Oil producing countries
    effects of price increases by,
    402
    flow of liquid funds to,
    143–44
Oil resources
    as element determining
    power, 36–39
    nuclear and solar energy as
    substitutes for, 25–27
    of the seas, 374
O'Leary, Michael K. See
    Coplin, William D. and
    O'Leary, Michael K.
OPEC. See Organization of
    Petroleum Exporting
    Countries.
Open images, 88
Open sea, 375
Optional clause, 208, 212
Organizational process model,
    in foreign policy making,
    83, 84–85
Organization of African Unity,
    168
    as regional IGO, 240, 249–51
Organization of American
    States (OAS), 21, 175
    as regional IGO, 240, 245–49
Organization of Petroleum Ex-
    porting Countries (OPEC),
    176
    effect on American life-style
    of, 3
    as price cartel, 142
Outcome, in analysis of trans-
    national policy, 14–15
Outer space, and link to na-
    tional security, 379

Output, in analysis of transnational policy, 14–15
Outright grants, as types of foreign aid, 144
Overkill, in use of nuclear weapons, 191–92, 211
Overseas Private Investment Corporation, 399

Pact of Bogotá, 246
Pact of Steel, 167, 168, 170
Paraguay, and LAFTA, 298
Parent companies, of MNEs, benefits for governments of, 339
   drawbacks for, 341–49
   growth of, 317–22
Parks, Richard L., on interest groups in India, 102–103
Payment of reparations, as effect of war, 202–203
Peaceful-uses-only guarantee, on sales of nuclear fuel, 369–70
People's Democracies, 112
"Perfidious Albion," 185
Perlmutter, Howard, 357
   definition of MNEs of, 315–16
Permanent Court of Arbitration, 209
Permanent Court of International Justice, 208
Personal consumption, in analysis of GNP, 52
Peru
   fishing in, 375
   IPC in, 332
   and LAFTA, 298
   political activities of ITT in, 330–31
   U.S. mining companies and, 330

Petroleum. See oil.
Physical features, man-made, as element determining power, 40, 58
Platig, E. Raymond, 23, 24
Poland, as buffer state, 187
Policy integration, as category of political integration, 273
Political elites, 100, 105–107
Political front unions, 351
Political Intelligence Service, of Soviet Union, 91
Political integration, 273–74
   in the European Community, 296
Political warfare, as instrument for policy implementation, 129, 150–53
Politics of Policy Making in Defense and Foreign Affairs, The, 108
Pollution, 384–89
   havens, 388
   of inland waters, 387–88
   international trade control of costs of, 388, 389
   of the oceans, 386
   of the seabed, 387
Pompidou, Georges, and British entry into EEC, 293
Popular Front for the Liberation of Palestine (PFLP), 152
Population
   as a determinant of power, 41–48, 58
   world hunger and increase in, 377
   zero-growth, 366–67
Portugal
   General Instrument Corp. in, 350
   possible EC membership of, 295

Power
   disparity of, as cause of war, 198
   elements determining, in international relations, 31, 58
   miscalculations of, as cause of war, 198
   See also Balance of power.
Pravda, 149. *See also* AGIT-PROP.
Prebisch, Dr. Raul, 297
Preferential trade agreements, 139–40
Press, the. *See* Media.
Price and marketing cartels, as form of economic warfare, 142
Price reduction, as benefit to host country of MNE initiatives, 338
Profitability, 328
Propaganda
   definitions of, 146
   evolution of, 148–49
   types of, 146
Prussia, as leader of Zollverein, 220
Psychological warfare, as instrument for policy implementation, 129, 145–49, 161–62
Public international unions, as type of IGO, 220

Quality of population, as element determing power, 46–48

Racial differences
   effect on foreign policy, 81
   as element determining power, 47
Radio Free Europe, 149

Radio Liberty, 149
Rand Corporation, 91
Rational policy model, in foreign policy making, 83–84
Raw materials
   effect on life-style and jobs of, 3–4
   as element determining power, 35–40
   stockpiling of, 36
Reagan, Ronald, 90
Realist approach, to study of international relations, 6
Regional development, following MNE initiatives, 339
Regional security units to overcome military deficiencies, 275
   See also IGOs.
Regulations, as type of order in EEC, 283
Religious differences
   as cause of war, 199
   as element determining power, 48
Representation, as function of diplomats, 131
Research and development, as element determining power, 57–58
Research Department of Foreign Office, of Great Britain, 92
Rhine Commission, 219–220
RIAS (Radio Information in the American Sector of Berlin), 149
Rio Pact, 246
River Commissions, as type of IGO, 219–20
Roman law, 207
Runaway technology, 57

SALT I. *See* Strategic Arms Limitation Talks (SALT).
SALT II. *See* Strategic Arms Limitation Talks (SALT).
San Francisco Conference, 225
Satellites
communications, 379–81
weather and navigation, 382–84
Schumann, Robert, and merger of French-German coal and steel industries, 280
Science and technology, as determinant of power, 55–58, 59
Sears, impact of, in Mexico, 340
Sea(s)
pollution of, 386–87
as source of fish, 374–75
as source of minerals, 373–74
as source of oil, 374
SEATO. *See* Southeast Asia Treaty Organization.
Secretariat, of United Nations, 229
on NGOs, 265
Security Council, of United Nations, 135, 227–28
Security integration, as category of political integration, 273
Seizure of property owned by foreign nationals, as political warfare measure, 152
Separation-of-powers principle, 66
Separatism, as cause of war, 199
Sharp, Walter R., 266
Short-range foreign policy objectives, 78, 95

Singer, J. David and Small, Melvin, on war, 154
Size, of military forces, 70
Size, of population, as element determining power, 41
Size, of state, as element determining power, 32, 58
Skjelsbaek, Kjell, 267
Small, Melvin. *See* Singer, J. David and Small, Melvin.
Smoot-Hawley Tariff, 138
Smuts, Jan C., on League of Nations, 221
Snake arrangement, 292
Social integration, 272–73
Socialization, 274, 307
Social superiority syndromes, as cause of war, 200
Societal cleavages, 65, 75
Southeast Asia Treaty Organization (SEATO), 10, 166
Sovereign states, 20, 29, 211–12
Soviet News Agency, TASS, 149
Soviet Union
ethnic diversity in, 47–48
fishing fleets of, 374–75
influence of Marxist-Leninist ideology in, 112–15
intelligence collection by, 91–92
invasion of Czechoslovakia by, 118
military weapons of, 73
minerals in, 35
nuclear energy in, 368
political warfare in, 153
politics of, in U.N., 235–36
population structure of, 42–43
propaganda and, 149
relationship with U.S. of, 183
and SALT, 193–96
space communication

system of, 381
subversion and, 150–51
vetoes in U.N. by, 229–30,
   232–33
Spaak, Paul-Henri, 281
Spain, possible EC member-
   ship of, 295
Spillover
   definition of, 277
   in EEC, 292
"Spirit of The Hague," 290, 295
Stalin, Joseph, 95, 112–14
Standard operating procedures
   (SOP), 84
Standing Executive Committee,
   of LAFTA, 299
State, 19. *See also* Nation-
   states.
State Security Committee
   (KGB), of Soviet Union, 91
Stockpiling, of raw materials,
   36, 141
Strategic Arms Limitation
   Talks (SALT), 85, 133,
   193–196, 211
Strikes, 349–51
Structure, of population, as
   element determining
   power, 41–46
Subsidies, as economic tool for
   policy implementation, 141
Subversion, as political warfare
   measure, 150–51
   use of ethnic ties in, 150, 151
Subversive war. *See* Unconven-
   tional war.
Suez crisis
   as example of foreign policy
   affecting domestic politics,
   121–22
   United Nations Emergency
   Force and, 231
Sukarno, overthrow of, 151
Summit Conference of the

Heads of State and
   Government, 289–92
issues of, 290
results of, 291–92
Supranational firm, definition
   of, 316
Supranational IGO, definition
   of, 218
Switzerland, GNP of, 22, 50
System, definition of, 8
System theory, 9
Systems approach, to study of
   international relations,
   8–10

Taiwan
   General Instrument Corp. in,
   350
   labor costs in, 4
   MNEs and, 341
Tanzania, and EAC, 303
Tariffs, as economic tool for
   policy implementation,
   137–40
Technical assistance, as type of
   foreign aid, 145
Technology. *See* Science and
   Technology.
Tenth Department, of Soviet
   Union, 92
Territorial sea, 375
Third Law of the Sea Conference, 376
Third World
   attitudes of, toward MNEs,
   345–47
   benefits from MNE initiatives in, 339–41
   CIEC and, 177
   difficulty of economic cooperation in, 173
   ecological restraints and, 385
   foreign aid and, 144, 145
   growth rate in, 43–46, 378

health of population in, 47
investments in, 324
preferential trade agree-
    ments and, 139
relations with EEC of, 286–89
seizure of property owned
    by foreign nationals in, 152
socializations in, 272–73
U.N. and, 238–40
Topography, as element deter-
    mining power, 34, 58
Trade Agreement Act, 138
Trade unions. *See* Labor
    unions.
Tradition and social psychol-
    ogy, as variable determin-
    ant of power, 61–66
Transactional flows, 27, 29
Transfer of knowledge, 328–29,
    334
  benefit to host country of,
    338
  control of, by host country,
    349
Transfer pricing, 343
Transideological enterprise,
    357
Transnational cooperation of
    unions, 352
Transnational policy(ies), 14–17
  foreign policies and, 78
  instruments for implementa-
    tion of, 129–63
Transnational relations, 25, 29
Transportation and communi-
    cation, as element deter-
    mining power, 40, 56
Treaties of Rome, 282
Treaty of Brussels, 168
Treaty of Montevideo, 298
Treaty of Paris, 280
Treaty of Versailles, 221
Treaty of Westphalia, 20
Tripartite Pact, 166, 168, 169

Triple Alliance, 185
Truman, Harry S
  and defense of Taiwan, 124
  on mineral resources on the
    continental shelf, 376
Trusteeship Council, of United
    Nations, 229
Turkey, possible EC member-
    ship of, 295

Uganda, and EAC, 303
Unconventional war, 159–61
UNCTAD. *See* United Nations
    Conference on Trade and
    Development.
Union of Central African States
    (UEAC), 303, 307
United Brands, in Central
    America, 340
United Nations, 21, 134–35,
    224–40, 252
  associated agencies and in-
    stitutes of, 237
  Charter of, 226–29
  economic and social pro-
    gress of, 236–40
  membership of, 233–34
  NGOs and, 265–66
  political process of, 234–36
  problem areas of, 229–40
  purposes of, 226–27
  role of diplomat in, 135
  structure of, 227–29
  and World Court, 208
United Nations Conference on
    Trade and Development
    (UNCTAD), 238–39, 253, 403
United Nations Emergency
    Force (UNEF), 231
United States
  acceptance of World Court
    of, 208
  consumption of energy of,
    367

ethnic diversity in, 47–48
foreign investments of, 55, 327
intelligence collection by, 91
military weapons of, 73
minerals in, 35
MNEs of, 317
national interest of, 80
nuclear energy in, 368–70
policy on nuclear war, 192
political warfare in, 152–53
politics of, in U.N., 235–36
population structure in, 42–43
propaganda and, 148
relationship with China of, 183
relationship with Soviet Union of, 183
and SALT, 193–96
subversion and, 151
veto in U.N. of, 233
violation of international law of, 204
United States Information Agency (USIA), 148
United States policy
diplomatic negotiation and, 133
influence of hardliners on, 398–99
on nuclear war, 192
toward Germany, 17
United States Weather Bureau, 383
United Steel Workers (USW), 350
Uniting for Peace Resolution, 230, 252
Uruguay, and LAFTA, 298

Venezuela, and LAFTA, 298
Vernon, Raymond, on MNEs, 316–17, 355

Veto power, in United Nations, 229–33
Vetter, Heinz O., 349
Vienna Convention on Diplomatic Relations, 130
Viet Cong, 160
Vietnam War, 3, 89
as example of foreign policy affecting domestic politics, 119–21
unconventional warfare in, 160
von Clausewitz, Karl, on war, 153
Voice of America, 147, 149

Waltz, Kenneth, 356
War(s)
categories of, 154
causes of, 197–202, 211
conventional, 154–56
definition of international, 154
effects of, 202–203, 211
as instrument for policy implementation, 129, 153–61, 162
and military draft, 3
nuclear, 156–59
since 1967, 197
unconventional, 159–61
Warsaw Pact, and NATO, 114–15
Watergate
effect on attitude toward government, 68
intelligence estimate on impact of, 94
Weapons and materiel, of military forces, 73–75
Weber, Max, 85
Weimar Republic, attitude of people under, 68
West African Customs Union (UDEAO), 303, 307

Westmoreland, William C., and Vietnam war, 120
White, Eric Wyndham, 134
White propaganda, 146. *See also* Propaganda.
Wilson, Woodrow, and League of Nations, 221
Wolfers, Arnold, 23
Woodcock, Leonard, 353
Working Peace System, A. (Mitrany), 276
World Affairs Councils, and influence on foreign policy, 104
World Court. *See* International Court of Justice.

World Food Conference, 378
World Meteorological Organization (WMO), 383
World's Evangelical Alliance, as first NGO, 257
World Wars I and II, 3
science and technology in, 56–57
World Weather Watch, 383
Writings of legal authorities and specialists, 206–207

Yalta Conference, 95, 225
Yaoundé, Convention of, 288

Zollverein, 220